The Idea of the State

For a half-century or more, political theory has been characterized by a pronounced distrust of metaphysical or ontological speculation. Such a disposition has been sharply at odds with influential currents in post-war philosophy – both analytic and continental – where metaphysical issues have become a central preoccupation. *The Idea of the State* seeks to reaffirm the importance of systematic philosophical inquiry into the foundations of political life, and to show how such an approach can cast a new and highly instructive light on a variety of controversial, seemingly intractable problems of tolerance, civil disobedience, democracy and consent. The author considers the problem of the state in light of recent developments in philosophy and social thought, and seeks to provide an account of what the state really is. In doing so he pursues a range of fundamental issues pertaining to the office, the authority and the internal organization of political society.

PETER J. STEINBERGER is Robert H. and Blanche Day Ellis Professor of Political Science and Humanities and Dean of the Faculty, Reed College. His published books include *Logic and Politics: Hegel's Philosophy of Right* (1988) and *The Concept of Political Judgment* (1993).

T0370689

Contemporary Political Theory

Series Editor
Ian Shapiro

As the twenty-first century begins, major new political challenges have arisen at the same time as some of the most enduring dilemmas of political association remain unresolved. The collapse of communism and the end of the Cold War reflect a victory for democratic and liberal values, yet in many of the Western countries that nurtured those values there are severe problems of urban decay, class and racial conflict, and failing political legitimacy. Enduring global injustice and inequality seem compounded by environmental problems, disease, the oppression of women, racial, ethnic and religious minorities, and the relentless growth of the world's population. In such circumstances, the need for creative thinking about the fundamentals of human political association is manifest. This new series in contemporary political theory is needed to foster such systematic normative reflection.

The series proceeds in the belief that the time is ripe for a reassertion of the importance of problem-driven political theory. It is concerned, that is, with works that are motivated by the impulse to understand, think critically about, and address the problems in the world, rather than issues that are thrown up primarily in academic debate. Books in the series may be interdisciplinary in character, ranging over issues conventionally dealt with in philosophy, law, history and the human sciences. The range of materials and the methods of proceeding should be dictated by the problem at hand, not the conventional debates or disciplinary divisions of academia.

Other books in the series

Ian Shapiro and Casiano Hacker-Cordón (eds.)
Democracy's Value

Ian Shapiro and Casiano Hacker-Cordón (eds.)
Democracy's Edges

Brooke A. Ackerly
Political Theory and Feminist Social Criticism

Clarissa Rile Hayward
De-Facing Power

John Kane
The Politics of Moral Capital

Ayelet Shachar
Multicultural Jurisdictions

John Keane
Global Civil Society?

Rogers M. Smith
Stories of Peoplehood

Gerry Mackie
Democracy Defended

John Keane
Violence and Democracy

The Idea of the State

Peter J. Steinberger

CAMBRIDGE
UNIVERSITY PRESS

CAMBRIDGE UNIVERSITY PRESS
Cambridge, New York, Melbourne, Madrid, Cape Town, Singapore, São Paulo, Delhi

Cambridge University Press
The Edinburgh Building, Cambridge CB2 8RU, UK

Published in the United States of America by Cambridge University Press, New York

www.cambridge.org
Information on this title: www.cambridge.org/9780521119061

First published 2004
Reprinted 2006
This digitally printed version 2009

A catalogue record for this publication is available from the British Library

Library of Congress Cataloguing in Publication data

Steinberger, Peter J., 1948–
The Idea of the State / Peter J. Steinberger.
   p.   cm. – (Contemporary political theory)
Includes bibliographical references and index.
ISBN 0 521 84214 X
1. State, The.   I. Title.   II. Series.
JC11.S78   2004
320.1–dc22   2004051949

ISBN 978-0-521-84214-3 hardback
ISBN 978-0-521-11906-1 paperback

For my Mo

Table of Contents

Preface

Historically, political philosophy has functioned largely – and also quite self-consciously – as a branch of philosophy *per se*, its propositions deeply embedded in and systematically underwritten by broader philosophical arguments and presumptions about how things in the world really are. This was certainly true of Plato and Aristotle, Cicero and Augustine, Aquinas, Hobbes and Hegel. In each such case, claims about politics and society reflected and were justified explicitly in terms of more fundamental claims of an ontological or metaphysical nature.

This kind of close connection seems no longer to exist. Political thought now purports to operate typically as a more or less independent enterprise, relatively unconnected to and unconstrained by larger traditions of systematic philosophical inquiry and reflecting, thereby, the sharp division of labor characteristic of contemporary academic life. Emblematic here is the well-known proposition that political speculation should indeed be "political, not metaphysical." Such a proposition is embraced, explicitly or otherwise, not only by those engaged in the detailed analysis of liberal principles but also by those who operate within various traditions of what might be called literary prudence, as exemplified by the writings of, among others, Hannah Arendt and Michael Oakeshott.

Remarkably enough, this rejection of systematic metaphysical speculation in political theory has occurred precisely during an era in which philosophers – "analytic" and "continental" alike – have been deeply and increasingly preoccupied with metaphysical questions. Quine's account of ontological commitment, Strawson's conception of descriptive metaphysics, Putnam's development of an internal realism – these and related notions have become common currency in contemporary Anglo-American philosophical discourse; while from a seemingly quite different perspective, the pursuit of ontological questions by students of Heidegger, most notably Gadamer and Levinas, has become a central focus of present-day hermeneutical and phenomenological inquiry. It is at least somewhat surprising that the fruits of such speculation have only rarely and fitfully found their way into serious writing about politics.

To be sure, many will regard the putative separation of philosophy and political thought as a good thing, evidence of a new-found appreciation for the distinctiveness of the political enterprise and for the peculiar nobility that it confers upon those so engaged. But it seems to me that the costs of such a separation far outweigh the benefits. Indeed, a political philosophy, and a political practice as well, that is substantially uninformed by and that seeks to distance itself from systematic inquiry into our thoughts about the larger truth of things runs the risk of irrelevance, anachronism and error – including and especially the error of self-delusion. The present work may be thought of as an effort, however modest, to help reestablish at least some of the relevant connections by examining certain fundamental issues of political thought explicitly in the light of broader philosophical themes. It proposes, specifically, a meta-physical or ontological theory of the state. As such, it seeks to address important questions of toleration, limited government, obligation and democracy directly in the context of influential philosophical and social/theoretical arguments – post-Kantian arguments – about the nature of things.[1]

It is true, of course, that in a work of conceptual analysis governed, to the degree possible, by principles of objective and dispassionate inquiry, expressions of partisan political sentiment ordinarily have no place. In the present case, however, the risk of serious misinterpretation – in particular, the risk that certain kinds of philosophical arguments will be thought to entail or reflect certain specific partisan political commitments – suggests the need for an exception, if only as a prefatory matter. For what it's worth, then, I myself happen to believe in a sharply progressive income tax. I prefer a broader rather than a narrower interpretation of the first ten amendments to the United States Constitution. I'm a supporter of affirmative action. For both aesthetic and economic reasons, I think we must be willing to accept a great deal of short-term inconvenience in order to protect the natural environment. I believe that men and women are much more alike than different, and that public policy should reflect this fact. Perhaps above all, I am convinced that the natural and social lotteries are inherently unjust and that we should use government, as an instrument of human reason, to reduce or eliminate undeserved inequalities. I am, in

---

[1] It may be that a new-found interest in metaphysical or ontological questions is already brewing among political theorists, though the evidence for this seems to me slim at best. See, for example, Stephen K. White, *Sustaining Affirmation: The Strengths of Weak Ontology in Political Theory* (Princeton: Princeton University Press, 2000); and David Mayhew, "Political Science and Political Philosophy: Ontological Not Normative," *PS: Political Science and Politics* 33 (June 2000). To the degree that there is indeed movement along these lines, I am happy to be part of the trend.

short, a liberal, through and through. How, then, to explain my having written a book that defends the absolute authority of the state, insists on an essentially unlimited area of legitimate state activity, urges an organicist, hence non-individualistic, view of the state itself, and purports to raise serious doubts about the possibility and/or desirability of liberal toleration, civil disobedience and democratic government? Positions such as these would suggest, at least to some people, a sharp anti-liberalism. More seriously, they might seem to resonate with the very darkest impulses of some very dark times. As such, and in the present climate of political and scholarly opinion, they run the risk of appearing, at best, peculiar, unserious, even parodic. Insofar as they are intended to be taken seriously – and I assure the reader that they are – do they not utterly contradict their author's own political inclinations?

In fact, there is no contradiction. The exploration of the idea of the state is neither more nor less than an inquiry into the meaning of an idea, a work of conceptual analysis, hence an attempt to get clear about how we conceive of – how we understand the nature of – a particular part of the world. It is, as such, quite distinct from any and all claims about which kinds of political policies are apt to work best in which kinds of circumstances. Philosophical questions are different from, and not reducible to, pragmatic or prudential ones; and this suggests, as I shall argue, that an examination of the idea of the state should not be confused with an examination of government and policy. Indeed, it seems plain to me that the idea of the state is, in fact, quite consistent with an entire range of political forms and practices. Hobbes argues that a legitimate commonwealth might be monarchically, aristocratically or democratically organized. In saying this, he suggests, in effect, that the notion of the state itself does not entail and does not depend on any specific answers to questions about the best form of government, the proper scope and direction of governmental activity, the true nature and range of civil liberties, and so on. Such a view is shared, *mutatis mutandis*, by a variety of authors – Aristotle, Locke and Rousseau especially come to mind – and it seems to me absolutely correct.

The argument should not be misunderstood, however. If the state is what it is independent of particular public policies, the reverse is not true. For everything that government does is hostage to, and must be reflective of, the idea of the state. In this context, Hobbes's point can be expressed somewhat differently. The state is in fact quite generous regarding government and governmental activity; it can embrace many different kinds. But government – however formulated – is always underwritten by, and must always serve the interests and goals of, the state. To get clear about the idea of the state is to say little if anything about which particular

governmental forms, procedures and policies should be adopted in any
particular circumstance; but it is to provide, nonetheless, at least one indispensable basis for their justification and, at the same time, for ruling out
practices that cannot be so justified. Political preferences, whether of the left
or right, make sense and can be coherently defended only if they reflect the
political state as it really, essentially is; and as I shall argue, this means that
they should reflect the fact that the state is, among other things, omnicompetent in scope, absolute in authority and organic in composition.

Some readers may think of my account as "rationalistic," and this is a
label that I would not disavow. We are often told that everything is
"political" in the sense of being ideological, that the laws of logic are
not only optional but somehow biased, that political philosophy is primarily an aesthetic endeavor. Indeed, claims such as these seem to
compose something of a present-day orthodoxy, but I myself find them
largely untenable. I do agree that every kind of discourse – even the most
severely technical, the most austerely logical – has a rhetorical dimension.
But I don't think it follows from this that all discourse is merely, or even
mainly, rhetoric. My analysis of the state presupposes a strong and
extremely important difference between sound argument and gaudy
assertion, and I am convinced that most of us are at least implicitly
committed to such a difference most of the time.

Parts of this book have previously appeared, in a somewhat different
form, as articles in learned journals, including the *American Political
Science Review*, *American Journal of Political Science*, *Journal of Politics*
and *Kant-Studien*. These sections deal largely with exegetical issues pertaining to, among others, Plato, Hobbes, Kant and Rawls. While each of
them seems to have functioned well enough as a self-standing piece, they
were all originally conceived and written as integral parts of the present
work. I wish to thank the editors in question for permission to republish
here the relevant material.

I am profoundly grateful to Jens Bartelson, Casiano Hacker-Cordon,
Richard Dagger, Bob Jessop, Jeff Johnson, Michael Parkhurst, Susan
Shell, Joseph Tobin and Elizabeth Wingrove, each of whom read all or
much of this work in draft and provided, without exception, stimulating,
edifying and enormously helpful comments. I am very much indebted, as
well, to Cambridge University Press – in particular, to John Haslam and
Ian Shapiro – for being willing to publish a book that is in many ways
orthogonal, one might say, to much of what is published today in political
theory. Finally, and as always, I am enormously grateful to Reed College –
students, colleagues, staff, friends – for providing an environment that is
most unusual in the degree to which it inspires, sustains and celebrates
the activity of being an intellectual.

Part 1

The Basic Idea

1   The State as a Structure of Intelligibility

This work presents and defends an ontological theory of the state. Its basic strategy is to consider the problem of the state in the light of recent and influential developments in social thought and philosophy, and to provide thereby an account of what the state really is – a description of its essential nature.

The very idea of pursuing an account of this kind will undoubtedly strike some readers – perhaps suspicious of ontological or metaphysical inquiry *per se*, or else doubtful that the state could ever be the legitimate object of such inquiry – as eccentric, anachronistic, even perverse. In fact, my project is intended to be none of these. To the contrary: it purports to uncover and explicate an understanding of the state that is implicit in and that helps to underwrite our own ordinary ways of thinking about politics. It seeks, in other words, to reconstruct a theory to which most of us are already (tacitly and unselfconsciously) committed, and that informs and directs our own engagement in the world of affairs. It thus aims to derive the idea of the state from certain fundamental, though typically unstated, presuppositions of contemporary political life.

The account of the state itself is developed and defended in the three chapters that compose Part III pertaining, respectively, to the activity, the authority, and the internal constitution of the state. But those chapters are dependent on, and are fully intelligible only in the light of, certain premises of a speculative or theoretical nature. In particular, the idea of the state presupposes: (1) a sharp methodological distinction between philosophical and prudential ways of thinking about politics, along with an account of their unavoidable mutual connections; (2) a corresponding conceptual distinction between the state, on the one hand, and the government of a state, on the other; (3) an understanding of what it might mean to pursue an ontological or metaphysical theory, based on important and widely shared principles of post-Kantian philosophy, broadly construed; and (4) an approach to institutions and social action derived from emergent and important trends in nineteenth- and twentieth-century social thought. These formulations are developed at length in Part II, the first and second of them primarily in Chapter 2, the third and fourth primarily in Chapter 3. Each of them constitutes, in a sense, an independent and self-standing argument, something to be explored and analyzed on its own account. Seen from the perspective of the idea of the state, however, they are also deeply intertwined and interdependent, the one with the other. Thus, the theory of the state is an ontological or metaphysical theory, but also, at the same time, the theory of an institution. Institutions, in turn, are understood not simply as objects of ontological analysis but as embodiments and reflections – systematic, organized distillations – of ontological claims. Every institution is, at base, an incarnation, a concrete reiteration, of cultural and intellectual judgments about how things in the world really are; and this suggests an ontological theory of the state according to which the state, qua institution, is itself a kind of ontological theory – a structure of metaphysical presupposition, of propositions about the nature of things, propositions that are rendered, through the state, authoritative and suitable for practice.

Before exploring these premises and the account of the state derived from them, however, I begin by offering, in Part I, a brief sketch of the basic idea. This is best read as a first approximation, designed to introduce certain central claims and to orient the reader to the overall structure of the theory. It is important to note, of course, that a first approximation is very different from a condensed version. Indeed, the argument of this book is not easily summarized; it can be understood and evaluated only on the basis of propositions elaborated in detail and defended at length. Nonetheless, Part I provides what I hope to be a useful glimpse of the theory as whole – an overview, perhaps, that can help the reader make better sense of the main arguments to be found in Parts II and III.

1. Two ways of thinking about politics

Political theory has, broadly speaking, two kinds of subject matter. On the one hand, it is concerned with the various particular activities that compose the political life of a state, activities undertaken by the instrumentalities – primarily governmental – of political society. On the other, it seeks to investigate the idea of the state itself. This difference of subject matter gives rise, in turn, to two kinds of political theory – two different ways of thinking about the political world, sharply distinct from one another both methodologically and substantively. Anyone who would attempt to pursue either of them in a serious way would do well to get clear about their profound differences and, equally, their unavoidable mutual connections.

1. To say of one kind of political theory that it is concerned with the various particular activities that compose the political life of a state is to

say that it studies activities that actually take place, or might take place, in the world, and that help determine, whether by design or not, the development and distribution of social goods, material and moral alike. Again, our inclination is to associate such activities with government, and we are usually right to do so. But what best distinguishes them as *political* activities is not so much their official character as the degree to which they represent efforts – governmental or otherwise – to address serious social problems by invoking in a more or less comprehensive and authoritative manner the collective resources of a community.

Pursuing political theory with respect to this kind of subject matter means, in the first instance, asking about decisions, actual or prospective. The political theorist examines the nature or meaning of particular decisions, considers their efficacy and suitability, and perhaps suggests alternative decisions that might be more appropriate. Inquiries of this sort, however, naturally give rise to any number of broader questions about government itself or, correlatively, about non-governmental or quasi-governmental entities exercising political power. Such questions might pertain, for example, to the proper scope of governmental activity or to the ways in which that activity is organized. But these larger questions often stimulate, in turn, even more general questions concerning the *character* of political endeavor. For example, the theorist might ask about a government's particular manner of acting – whether its behavior seems to reflect, say, the economic, religious or aesthetic practices of society – and this might result, finally, in a comprehensive theory of political activity *per se*.

Of course, investigations of these various kinds often explicitly rely on or are otherwise influenced by causal analyses of decisions and decision-making. But they are not themselves examples of such analysis. They are not primarily scientific. Rather, they treat the political world essentially as an on-going and open-ended series of loosely connected exercises in practicality and judgment, informed, to be sure, by an understanding of what nature itself permits, but guided as well by a more-or-less systematic and self-critical account of aims to be achieved.[1] To speak of "politics" is

---

[1] As such, they depend upon but are different from all varieties of "political science," wherein theories and methods derived from other social science disciplines – primarily sociology, psychology and economics – are utilized in order to account for political behavior. In my view, the distinction between political theory or philosophy and political science has nothing to do with the difference between "empirical" and "normative" thought, or between "descriptive" and "prescriptive" theory. In some sense, any systematic analysis will be both empirical and normative, descriptive and prescriptive. The crucial question is whether or not a particular inquiry seeks primarily to discover and describe a world of causes and effects. Political science does, and this is largely what makes it a science.

to speak of a world not only of causes and effects but of alternatives, of choices freely chosen, a world composed of things that "could have been otherwise" (*Nicomachaean Ethics* 1141b.10–11). The individuals and organizations that inhabit such a world are thought to be engaged, singly or collectively, in a process of deliberation about goals and strategies. This process is understood to be influenced by, but not reducible to, the causal nexus of social facts; for it involves, as well, the activity of identifying moral intuitions – a sense of right and wrong, of value and purpose – and applying those intuitions to particular circumstances. In this sense, political endeavor is a species of prudential endeavor; and it is precisely with some such conception in mind that the political theorist examines the decision-making process, evaluates its outcomes, and seeks to make a contribution by bringing to bear upon it a perhaps more thoughtful and considered kind of prudence.

To contemplate in this way particular decisions or groups of decisions, or the institutions that make those decisions, or the character of the activities that those institutions undertake is, I would suggest, to adopt a family of subject matters all of which focus directly on problems of a practical nature, problems of policy. I construe "policy" here in a broad sense to include not only decisions about the exercise of public authority but also decisions about how those decisions should be made. Thus, we have policies for dealing with the distribution of particular benefits and obligations in society, and we also have policies about the design of social institutions and institutional procedures. A political theory that adopts one or more subject matters of this general kind is, we may say, a *theory of policy and government*, where the word "government" is understood in the broadest sense to refer not only to official policy-making entities but, when appropriate, to unofficial ones as well. The goal of any such theory is to describe just what it is that we are doing when we make social or political choices, and to consider, in the light of our moral intuitions, the possibility that it might be prudent for us to do things otherwise.

2. Very different from this is a kind of political theory that focuses on the nature of the state itself. Here the goal is to offer an analysis not of policy

It is sometimes argued that political science cannot truly be a science, but it is hard to see why this should be so. Political events are real events – things in the world that are caused and that have effects. As such, they are as suited to scientific study as any other set of phenomena. Political science may not be able to achieve the degree of precision and certainty characteristic of other sciences, but this doesn't prevent it from being itself a science. Moreover, the fact that political phenomena must be conceptualized and interpreted before they can be analyzed scientifically is a feature shared by all phenomena, natural and social alike, and again casts not the slightest doubt on the possibility of a science of politics.

and government but of a concept, a philosophical theory rather than a prudential one. Such a theory – a *theory of the idea of the state* – seeks to contemplate the state as it actually is, rather than as it appears to be. It purports to describe, among other things, those features of particular states that are common to all and that determine the fundamental nature of each. It seeks to indicate what we mean when we refer to something as a state, when we talk of the activities or reasons of state, when we speculate about the authority of the state, and so on. As such, it pursues an ontological or metaphysical theory.[2] In so doing, it attempts to uncover and identify the conceptual foundations upon which much of our political thinking is based, foundations that reflect, in turn, emergent, influential and extremely powerful notions about the very nature of human thought and action.

Systematic and self-conscious political philosophy of this kind is no longer widely practiced. Indeed, it is often explicitly rejected as unsuitable. The appropriate task of political theory is thought to be distinctively "political" and, as such, decidedly and pointedly non-metaphysical; and it is a fact that a great many political theorists today devote themselves almost exclusively to the pragmatic or prudential study of policy and government, focusing in particular on issues internal to the political life of modern liberal societies and avoiding, or attempting to avoid, larger questions about the idea of the state itself. This seems to me both peculiar and unfortunate. It is peculiar because it runs directly counter to extremely important and influential currents in the larger world of philosophy, both analytic and continental, where metaphysical or ontological questions have become a central preoccupation. It is unfortunate, because I believe that many of the most important controversies of contemporary political theory – controversies about policy and government – are deeply bound up with questions of a conceptual or ontological nature; and I believe, further, that the seeming intractability of such controversies often reflects what might fairly be called a culture of philosophical uncertainty, born of indifference and inattention and nourished by a well-developed and widespread mood of skepticism.

Under the influence of such a mood, many political theorists have come to ignore – or have dismissed as uninteresting or unintelligible – precisely the kinds of fundamental questions that inform and authorize,

---

[2] Here and throughout, I follow Strawson in presupposing that the words "metaphysical" and "ontological" can be used more or less interchangeably, at least for some purposes. See P. F. Strawson, *Metaphysics and Analysis: An Introduction to Philosophy* (Oxford: Oxford University Press, 1992), p. 30. For a standard and representative textbook view of this matter, see Stephen Laurence and Cynthia Macdonald, *Contemporary Readings in the Foundations of Metaphysics* (Oxford: Blackwell, 1998), pp. 3–4.

however tacitly, our own various theories of politics. As a result, we have all too often lost sight of what is really at stake when we disagree about policy and government. Relatively trivial political differences have become, in our eyes, ironclad oppositions; fundamental agreements remain unacknowledged or unappreciated. To get clear about the idea of the state, on the other hand, is precisely to clarify, perhaps even to resolve, many of our deepest political differences. For the fact is that all of our beliefs about public life – including our beliefs about policy and government – inevitably reflect deep-seated assumptions regarding the very nature of the state: its essence and purpose, its justification, its internal constitution. We need to examine those assumptions in detail, hence to make them available for intelligent criticism, if we wish to see our disagreements for what they really are.

2. State and government

The word "state," as it operates in contemporary political discourse, is used characteristically in two quite different and fundamentally incompatible ways, the one corresponding roughly to prudential, the other to philosophical, modes of theorizing. Of course, what is true of theories is also true of words: observing and attending carefully to (in this case terminological) differences is a minimal requirement – too often unmet – for thinking clearly and perspicuously about politics and the state.

1. On the one hand, we commonly talk about the "separation of church and state," or about "state-sponsored terrorism," or about the "regulation of the economy by the state," and when we do so we think of the "state" as more or less synonymous with "government" and as sharply distinguished from "civil society." Certainly, this latter distinction – state versus civil society – has become an absolutely central preoccupation of contemporary political thought. The state has thus increasingly "come to be seen by many as merely an apparatus of rule, an apparatus distinguished preeminently by the fact that it involves a monopoly of coercion."[3]

It should be noted that the state/civil society distinction has its origins not so much in Hegel's *Rechtsphilosophie* as in Marx's astonishing, perhaps intentional, misreading of it. I say misreading, because Hegel, despite what Marx said,[4] never understood *Staat* and *bürgerliche Gesellschaft* to

---

[3] Murray Forsyth, "State," in *The Blackwell Encyclopedia of Political Thought*, ed. David Miller (Oxford: Basil Blackwell, 1987), p. 505.
[4] Karl Marx, *Critique of Hegel's 'Philosophy of Right'* (Cambridge: Cambridge University Press, 1970 [1843]), pp. 5–11, 73–83.

denote independent and opposed realms of human activity, the one exercising power or authority over and against the other. Rather, he viewed them – and all the other "moments" of right, including systems of property, abstract law, morality and the family – as constitutive elements of a single, all-encompassing, organic entity. Hegel's work thus reflects a quite different and quite venerable tradition of discourse in which the word "state" is used much more broadly, as for example when we talk about the "city-states" of ancient Greece or renaissance Italy, or of the "modern nation-state," or of the "newly independent states of the post-colonial world," or of "the Organization of American States." Here "state" is not synonymous with but, to the contrary, sharply distinguished from "government" as the whole is distinguished from the part. The state itself is a larger notion that refers, essentially, to the entirety of political society, i.e., to "the body politic or political community as such, something that has existed throughout history in a wide variety of differing forms."[5] According to this usage, the term "state," far from being distinguished from, is in fact roughly synonymous

---

[5] Forsyth, "State," pp. 503–4. The dual uses of the term "state" are widely remarked upon in early twentieth-century writings. Sidgwick indicates that "I must begin by distinguishing between (1) the narrow use of the word 'State' to denote the community considered exclusively in its corporate capacity, as the subject of public as distinct from private rights and obligations; and (2) the wider use to denote the community however considered" (Henry Sidgwick, *The Elements of Politics* [London: Macmillan, 1908], p. 220). Anson says much the same: "[W]hen we talk of the State we often use the term with some uncertainty as to its meaning. Sometimes the expression is used as equivalent to a whole community, or independent political society. Sometimes it is limited to the central force, or sovereign, in that society" (William R. Anson, *The Law and Custom of the Constitution, vol. 1: Parliament* [Oxford: Oxford University Press, 1911], p. 15).
   For a related contemporary discussion, see Stuart Hall, "The State in Question," in George McLennan, David Held and Stuart Hall, eds., *The Idea of the Modern State* (London: Open University Press, 1984). In many ways, the essays in this latter volume reflect the ambivalences and inconsistencies that I have described. Thus, Hall indicates that "there has been a long-standing debate as to whether the terms 'government' and 'state' are interchangeable" (p. 19). He denies that they are. But only a few pages later, David Held's article, "Central Perspectives on the Modern State," begins with the flat assertion that the state is nothing other than "an apparatus of 'government'" (p. 29). See also David Copp, "The Idea of a Legitimate State," *Philosophy and Public Affairs* 28 (Winter 1999), according to which (p. 7) "the state is the system of animated institutions that govern the territory and its residents, and administer and enforce the legal system and carry out the programs of government."
   Along these lines, it is revealing, I think, that the Greek word *polis*, as it appears in, say, Plato's work, is often translated by scholars as "state." Compare, for example, various English language renditions of *Crito* 50a–c and 52a–b. Grube (1975) tends to translate *polis* as "city," but he also uses "state" (50a). Church (1948) generally uses "state," but also uses "city" (52b) and "commonwealth" (50a). Gallop (1997) prefers "city" but also uses "state" (50a), whereas Tredennick (1954) prefers "state" but also uses both "city" (50b) and "government" (50a). Doherty (1923) usually uses "state" but also uses "government" (50a). Jowett (1937) sometimes prefers "state" (50b–c, 52c), sometimes "city" (52b–c), and at least once uses "government" (50a). Much the same is true of Fowler (1914), who likes

with "civil society," and with a host of other terms including "common-wealth," "commonweal," "political community," "political society," "body politic," "republic" or "res publica," "civitas," and the like. Thus, state and civil society are opposed not to one another – they are the same – but to a particular kind of human circumstance, what is sometimes referred to as the "natural condition" of humankind or any other circumstance that arises when the agreements and understandings about law and authority that make political society possible collapse. Such agreements and understand-ings compose, in some larger sense, the idea of the state or civil society, and their absence is what is often called "anarchy."

2. The fact that a single term can be used in two quite different ways is hardly unusual. Nor is it especially problematic, provided that we are careful. When, however, we are not careful – when we fail to keep the relevant distinctions clearly in mind – the result can be all manner of miscommunication and theoretical error.

Consider, in this regard, the very end of Skinner's important two-volume study of the *Foundations of Modern Political Thought*. Skinner argues per-suasively that the sixteenth century saw a fundamental change in the use of the term "state." Whereas earlier writers employed the term largely to describe either "the state or condition in which the ruler finds himself" or else the "'general state of the nation,'" sixteenth-century writers gave it a "modern and more abstract meaning."[6] The trouble, however, is that Skinner's account of this latter meaning is often highly problematic. His central claim is that "state" was used to refer to an independent or distinct "apparatus" of politics or policy-making, suggesting thereby that it was essentially synonymous with government itself as distinct both from the particular individual(s) in whom governmental power resided and from the body of citizens.[7] But several of the key passages that he cites, even as he glosses them, do not seem to support such a reading, at least not unambiguously. For example, he attributes to Bodin the notion that the "state" is "a locus of power which can be institutionalised in a variety of

both "state" (50a–c and 52c) and "city" (52b–c), and who also uses "commonwealth" (50b). And similarly for Livingstone (1938), who uses "city" (52b–c), "state" (50b–c, 52c) and "government" (50a, 52c). The point is not to criticize translations but merely to note the varied and often inconsistent usage of the word "state." What seems clear is that *polis* denotes not simply the apparatus of decision-making, not simply government, but the entire community understood as a political or civil society; and virtually every translator at least on some occasions renders this as "state."
[6] Quentin Skinner, *The Foundations of Modern Political Thought*, vol. 2 (Cambridge: Cambridge University Press, 1978), p. 353. For a rather different and extremely helpful account, see Kenneth H. F. Dyson, *The State Tradition in Europe: A Study of an Idea and Institution* (New York: Oxford University Press, 1980), especially chs. 1 and 2.
[7] Skinner, *The Foundations of Modern Political Thought*, vol. 2, pp. 353–55.

ways," implying that the state is indeed a policy-making apparatus. But he also quotes Bodin to the effect that while "the government of a common-weale may be more or less popular, aristocratic or royal ... the state in itself receives no comparisons of more or less."[8] Here, government is explicitly distinguished from the commonweal; if the commonweal *has* a government – the government *of* a commonweal – then it cannot *be* a government. It is also explicitly differentiated from the state, which in this passage seems to be the same thing as the commonweal. Moreover, the larger contexts in which passages such as this occur show Bodin's usage, as translated (in 1606) by Knolles, to be in fact uneven throughout and often rather differ-ent from what Skinner suggests. For example, Bodin sometimes uses the word "state" (Knolles's translation of *etat*) interchangeably with "com-monweale" (Knolles's translation of *république*), though the latter appears with greater frequency. And while he occasionally thinks of "common-weale" and "government" as synonyms ("a commonweale is a lawfull government"[9]), he also says, among other things, that a power may try "to invade the State of other princes," clearly implying that a state is more than its government; and he adds that a commonweal – hence a state? – is composed not just of a common government but of "markets, churches ... lawes, decrees, judgements, voyces, customs, theaters, wals, publick build-ings, common pastures, lands, and treasure."[10]

Elsewhere, Skinner quotes Raleigh to the effect that the identity of a state may continue essentially unchanged even if the particular form of government – not simply the identity of the ruler(s) but the structure itself – were to change substantially. The passages in question are entirely apposite, but it is hard to see how they support Skinner's claim that Raleigh thinks of the state as merely a political or policy-making apparatus. Indeed, Raleigh's usage is, like Bodin's, highly equivocal and inconsistent. He writes, for example, that "a monarchy is the government of a state by one head or chief ... an aristocracy is the government of a commonwealth by some competent number of the better sort ... a popular state is the government of a state by the choicer sort of people."[11] It is a peculiar passage, and characteristically so. In the first two clauses, "state" seems to be interchangeable with "commonwealth" and differ-entiated from "government," but in the third clause it seems to be differentiated from, dare I say, itself. Soon thereafter Raleigh gives

[8] *Ibid.*, p. 356.
[9] Jean Bodin, *The Six Bookes of the Commonweale*, tr. Richard Knolles (Cambridge: Cambridge University Press, 1962), pp. 1 and 12.
[10] *Ibid.*, p. 11.
[11] Walter Raleigh, *Works*, vol. 8 (Oxford: Oxford University Press, 1829), pp. 2–3.

a very special, technical meaning to the term "commonwealth," indicating that it denotes a corrupt form of popular rule.[12] Only a few pages later, however, he describes two kinds of principles for preserving political society: "I. General, that serve for all commonwealths. II. Particular, that serve for every several state,"[13] plainly identifying "commonwealth" and "state."

None of this is to deny that these various usages do indeed depart from the practice of the late Middle Ages, as Skinner claims. But it is doubtful that in the early modern period the term "state" is simply or even primarily synonymous with "government" or that it merely denotes the apparatus of politics. Perhaps most revealing here is Hobbes, to whom Skinner attributes the first "systematic and unapologetic" account of the modern idea of the state.[14] On the very first page of the introduction to *Leviathan*, Hobbes clearly indicates that "state," "commonwealth," and "civitas" are to be regarded as virtual synonyms and that none of them is reducible to the mere apparatus of government and policy.[15]

In themselves, terminological differences or ambiguities are of little philosophical interest. But when they lead to internal terminological inconsistencies – when the very different senses of a single word are used interchangeably – the results can be disastrous. In the instant case, I believe that an on-going and recurrent failure on the part of political theorists to be clear about what they mean when they use the word "state" has led to an entire range of important theoretical confusions. To pick a characteristic example: debates about the proper scope of governmental activity – the question of limited government – are often misconstrued as debates about the structure and function of political society itself, with the result that important pragmatic or prudential questions are often misidentified as conceptual or philosophical ones, hence never addressed on their own terms. Similarly, contemporary theorists of deliberative democracy emphasize, plausibly enough, the virtue of a democratic society "that accords equal respect to the moral claims of each citizen,"[16] but then uncritically transmogrify this into a very different set of

---

[12] *Ibid.*, p. 4.
[13] *Ibid.*, p. 9.
[14] Quentin Skinner, "The State," in *Political Innovation and Conceptual Change*, ed. Terence Ball, James Farr and Russell L. Hanson (Cambridge: Cambridge University Press, 1989), p. 126. This article is a more elaborate restatement of the position presented in *Foundations*.
[15] It is, I should note, only with the greatest trepidation that I criticize, even in this very limited sense, Skinner's magnificent work.
[16] Amy Gutmann and Dennis Thompson, *Democracy and Disagreement* (Cambridge, Mass.: Harvard University Press, 1996), p. 26.

propositions – highly controversial propositions – about the need for democratic institutions of government. To the extent that claims about the state as government are used to justify claims about the state as a commonwealth or a body politic, and vice versa, we are all talking past one another.

The present work is devoted to an exploration of the state understood in the larger, more traditional, pre-Marxian sense. The goal is to provide an account of the underlying nature of political society itself, formulated in the light of recent, influential developments in philosophy and social theory. From the perspective of such an analysis, government is but an instrumentality of the state, albeit a necessary one. It is part of a whole, not the whole itself – a privileged and special part, to be sure, but a mere part nonetheless. It is true that any plausible theory of government, and of policy-making in general, must be informed by (among other things) a philosophy of the state. But such a philosophy remains, as such, a distinct and independent enterprise.

3. Institutions and intelligibility

The state is best understood as a *structure of intelligibility*. By this I mean that it is reducible, at one level, to a series of propositions. The propositions of which the state is composed are those that collectively embody the various judgments that the citizens of the state have made about how things really are. As such, they reflect a complex and comprehensive intellectual world – an immense world of concepts and beliefs. The state is the orderly and authoritative arrangement of this intellectual world, formulated so as to reflect and promote the social good.[17] It is a world of concepts rendered suitable for practice.

I intend this to be a claim about our own implicit notion of what the state really is. As such, it is meant to be taken quite literally. In my view, the state is not primarily a geographically defined piece of the earth; nor is it a collection of people, past, present or future; nor yet again, a set of civil and military capabilities or a pattern of on-going social interactions. It is, rather, a structure of judgments about what is true and what is not.

---

[17] Obviously a great deal is packed into this small passage. The notion that the state is a structure of intelligibility is defended both in the present chapter and in Chapter 3. The idea that the authoritative purview of the state is very wide and covers an entire world of concepts and beliefs – an entire way of life – is discussed in Chapter 4. The nature of the state's authority itself is treated in Chapter 5. The sense in which the state is concerned with the social good is outlined in Chapter 6.

Put somewhat differently, the idea of the state is precisely that the state *is* an idea or, perhaps more accurately, a composite of ideas.

To some readers, such a formulation might seem to resonate with themes found in certain ancient, roughly Platonic traditions of political thought. I think this would be misleading, however. For Plato, the *kallipolis* is, indeed, an idea. But it is not the idea of an idea; rather, it is the idea of a supposedly material thing, just as the idea of, say, chair is the idea of material chairs. The idea of the state, on the other hand, is such that particular states – particular instantiations of the idea – themselves subsist primarily as ideas, i.e., as structures of metaphysical commitment. We would be somewhat closer to the mark, therefore, if we looked for provenance in a variety of Hegelian and other post-Kantian formulations; and indeed, to the best of my knowledge the most explicit statement of the kind of position I have in mind is to be found in Coleridge's extraordinary (and quite Kantian) essay *On the Constitution of the Church and State*, which explicitly distinguishes the narrower sense of "state" as government from its larger sense as "Body Politic," "Realm," "Commonwealth" or "Nation," and which repeatedly insists that the latter is, indeed, an "Idea."[18] My account agrees broadly with Coleridge when he distinguishes "conceptions" and "ideas" – a distinction between the explicit description of things, on the one hand, and the underlying, implicit knowledge that we have of them, on the other. It agrees, as well, that ideas are in some sense prior to the particular things that are thought to be their embodiments. It agrees, further, that an idea may well "powerfully influence a man's thoughts and actions, without his being distinctly conscious of the same, much more without his being competent to express it in definite words."[19] And most importantly, it agrees that the state not only "is" an idea but actually "exists" or functions as an idea, i.e., our idea of the state is the idea of an idea.[20] To be sure, my understanding of exactly what constitutes the idea of the state – its specific content – is sharply different from Coleridge's, as is my notion of the underlying social theory that underwrites such a formulation. But the overall intellectual strategy, and the

---

[18] "On the Constitution of the Church and State," in *The Collected Works of Samuel Taylor Coleridge*, vol. 10, ed. John Colmer (Princeton: Princeton University Press, 1976), for example at pp. 19, 101, 107–8.

[19] *Ibid.*, p. 12.

[20] *Ibid.*, p. 19. For a useful introduction to Coleridge's views on these questions, see David P. Calleo, *Coleridge and the Idea of the Modern State* (New Haven: Yale University Press, 1966), pp. 76–79, 105–24. It would be not quite accurate to say that my ideas directly reflect the influence of Coleridge; they were rather well formed before I encountered his writings on the state. My original path to Coleridge was through Rothblatt's criticism of Newman. See n. 27, below.

underlying sense of what *kind* of thing the state might be, is strongly similar.

1. The claim that the idea of the state is that the state is an idea may seem bizarre, evidence of philosophical mentalism run amok. In fact, though, it is no more peculiar than to say that a university is constituted, in some substantial measure, by a set of educational principles, or that a religion essentially represents a structure of belief. A little bit of reflection will suggest, I think, that social institutions of whatever kind exist primarily in this way. As such, they stand as paradigmatic and unusually persuasive examples of the rather larger claim that reality itself is a world of ideas.[21]

Now one might want to argue that while institutions may certainly be *animated* or *governed* by concepts, judgments and beliefs, they are hardly *reducible* to them. Particular institutions seem to be composed of more tangible things: people and spaces for people, money and power, artifacts, activities, rules. Such things establish an elaborate framework within which human behavior occurs and on the basis of which it becomes organized or patterned. The sheer physical setting of an institution – the layout of buildings, the size and configuration of individual workplaces, even their decor – may conduce to certain kinds of activity and discourage others; and so too with the distribution of material resources, the arrangement of operational hierarchies, and the like. Such factors are crucial to the integrity and efficiency of an institution. This is to say that they are "functional." They permit, or compel, an institution to do what it is supposed to do. Of course, sociologists have long recognized that among these functional, patterning factors are beliefs or "norms," i.e., certain kinds of ideas. They have understood that such ideas are invariably an important feature of any institution, serving to authorize, justify and reinforce activities that are, from an institutional point of view, desirable. Indeed, some social theorists would go so far as to assign a certain causal priority to organizational norms. But even the majority of these would agree that such norms, however important, are merely one of a number of factors that establish an institution as a more-or-less fixed structure of human interaction.[22]

Without denying the details of any such analysis, the approach that I have in mind differs in at least three ways. First, it sees institutions as

---

[21] Michael Oakeshott, *Experience and its Modes* (Cambridge: Cambridge University Press, 1933), pp. 48–81.

[22] For a standard sociological account of institutions, see Talcott Parsons and Neil J. Smelser, *Economy and Society: A Study in the Integration of Economic and Social Theory* (New York: Free Press, 1956), pp. 101–3.

essentially constituted, and not simply regulated, by ideas.[23] Concepts, judgments and beliefs are not mere instruments that institutions find useful; they are fundamentally constitutive of institutions, such that any particular institution essentially *is* its ideas. Second, ideas of this kind are understood not solely or even primarily as describing moral rules governing the conduct of individuals or groups of individuals. Rather, they are complex propositions about the truth of the world that reflect (usually) tacit but reconstructable arguments about how things really are. An institution is, at base, an intellectual structure, a structure of claims and theories that tell us not simply what to do but what the world itself, or at least some portion of it, is. Finally, all of this implies that the other features of an institution are in some sense secondary. They are accidents attached to an underlying substrate. The various physical, social-structural and normative properties of an institution acquire meaning and identity only in virtue of their relationship to the institution's intelligible core. The intelligible core has, so to speak, a certain ontological priority. It composes the essence of the institution.

In adopting such an approach, I have been influenced by the so-called "new institutionalism" of sociology, according to which, to pick one very typical claim, "institutions are descriptions of reality, explanations of what is and is not, what can be and what cannot."[24] The work of Mary Douglas is, I think, especially compelling. According to Douglas, "the entrenching of an institution is essentially an intellectual process as much as an economic and political one ... [E]very kind of institution needs a formula that founds its rightness in reason and in nature."[25] This is to say that each institution is underwritten – perhaps constituted – not primarily by natural or even utilitarian considerations but by a shared structure of thought, value and information. Douglas suggests, moreover, that such a structure must be fundamentally composed and reflective of claims about reality itself. Institutions are the entities that determine how the various things that we encounter in the world are to be divided up into intelligible categories: "sameness is conferred and fixed by institutions."[26]

[23] One might say that I give priority here to what Scott calls the "cognitive pillar" as opposed to the "normative pillar." W. Richard Scott, *Institutions and Organizations* (Thousand Oaks, California: Sage, 1995), pp. 37–45. For Scott's general definition of institutions, see his p. 33.

[24] John W. Meyer, John Boli and George M. Thomas, "Ontology and Rationalization in the Western Cultural Account," in W. Richard Scott and John W. Meyer, *Institutional Environments and Organizations: Structural Complexity and Individuals* (Thousand Oaks, California: Sage, 1994), p. 24.

[25] Mary Douglas, *How Institutions Think* (Syracuse, New York: Syracuse University Press, 1986), p. 45.

[26] *Ibid.*, p. 53; also p. 63.

The implications of such a perspective are immense. Since our understanding of the world is in large part an understanding of similarity and
difference, it follows that institutions are both embodiments and deter-
minants of the most fundamental claims that we make about how things
really are. Consider, for example, an institution of higher education.[27]
We know that any such institution will be composed of many different
kinds of things – students and professors, buildings and grounds, collections of documents, laboratory equipment, and the like. But the role that
each of these plays is not simply self-apparent. Walking along the Charles
river, we say in casual conversation that Harvard is "over there," and by
this we generally refer to a collection of buildings sitting on a piece of land
beyond MIT in the city of Cambridge. But if the entire faculty, staff and
student body of Harvard were to vacate those buildings and take up
residence elsewhere, one would hardly want to say that Harvard no longer
existed. We would say, rather, that it had moved, and this suggests that
the particular buildings themselves and the particular piece of land on
which they sit cannot be essential. So we might decide that if Harvard is
not primarily a collection of buildings, then it must be primarily a collection of people. But of course, the people themselves change all the time –
students graduate, faculty retire or die or are terminated – while the
institution itself persists. Certainly Harvard must have at least some set
of suitable physical arrangements – perhaps a discrete and self-contained
campus of bricks and mortar; or a collection of buildings scattered
throughout a city as is the case with many European universities; or,
more controversially, a location in cyberspace – on the basis of which
individuals can be connected with one another in appropriate ways; and it
must have certain special kinds of individuals, students, faculty, staff; and
by the same token, it must have a set of governing documents, including a
charter, that describe decision-making processes, budgetary practices,
legal status, and the like. But while Harvard needs to have all such things,
I doubt that any of them, either singly or even in combination, is sufficient

---

[27] The notion that an institution of higher education is primarily an idea is, of course,
broadly consistent with Newman's approach. See John Henry Newman, *The Idea of a
University* (New Haven: Yale University Press, 1996). For an excellent discussion that
shows the connection between Newman's account and the kind of account that I am
offering, see Sheldon Rothblatt, *The Modern University and its Discontents: The Fate of
Newman's Legacies in Britain and America* (Cambridge: Cambridge University Press,
1997), ch. 1. While Rothblatt says that Newman "employed" Coleridge's method
(p. 12), the implication that Newman was directly influenced by Coleridge does not
seem clearly to be supported by the evidence. See also, Sheldon Rothblatt, *The
Revolution of the Dons: Cambridge and Society in Victorian England* (New York: Basic
Books, 1968), pp. 113–14.

to make Harvard what it is. Indeed, one is tempted to say rather the reverse. Harvard is what makes *them* what *they* are.

Each of the various elements of which an institution is composed derives its identity from an interpretation of the whole, i.e., from our sense of the meaning of the institution qua institution. Thus, for example, a university building – say, a dormitory – is what it is only because it has been *conceived* of in a certain way, and any such conception will itself be embedded in a system of ideas that determine what a university is, how it will function, and what kinds of hardware (including dormitory buildings) would best serve its needs. Absent such determinations, the dormitory simply would not be a dormitory; for no such building could possibly be built unless there were a judgment to the effect that it should be built; and such a judgment could not but reflect a prior idea of what it means for a university to be a university, an idea that somewhere contemplates the notion of "students" being "in residence." This is to say that a building could not function as a dormitory unless that function had been considered, evaluated and deemed appropriate and necessary in light of some notion as to what the building, and the entity of which it would be a part, is all about. Thus, a building filled with bedrooms and beds would not be a university dormitory, a place where *students* live, unless it had been so conceptualized. After all, such a physical structure might as easily be a barracks, or a condominium, or a clinic, or a homeless shelter – and these would be very different kinds of buildings, even if, from the outside, they seemed indistinguishable. Moreover, what is true about the creation of a new building would be equally true of its perpetuation. The *continued* existence of a dormitory as a dormitory would depend equally on the at least tacit and on-going *reaffirmation* of those judgments that made it what it was in the first place. Buildings can be razed or remodeled, or simply used in different ways. When such changes do not occur, then this generally reflects a continued commitment, however inexplicit, to the idea that made the building what it was in the first place.

If, then, we are often inclined to speak of a university as a collection of buildings located in a particular place, we must nonetheless concede that it is a collection of buildings *understood* in a certain way and that this understanding is somehow decisive. In the end, it seems to me that any university is finally and ultimately constituted by one or another idea of higher education itself. Such an idea describes what the university basically is. It seems to me, further, that the particular way in which the idea manifests itself in buildings, curricula, organizational hierarchies, rules of conduct, and the like is something that can be authoritatively determined only as an intellectual matter, by the theoreticians and practitioners of educational policy. Their job is precisely to discover or formulate a concept of higher

education, identify the various propositions of which that concept is composed, and put those propositions into practice. No university, therefore,
could be thought of as a mere spontaneous event. Each is a particular
configuration of diverse elements, the arrangement of which inevitably
reflects, however tacitly and imperfectly, a prior notion of what a university
is. It is, and can only be, understood as a more-or-less conscious and
systematic effort – a pragmatic or prudential effort – to incorporate an
idea, and this confers upon that idea a certain ontological priority.

   History shows, of course, that such efforts are themselves rarely unproblematic. People often disagree about the most effective way of embodying
the idea of higher education. But they may also disagree vociferously about
the idea of higher education itself; they may conceive of higher education
differently. As a result, particular universities often differ from each other in
very substantial ways, and all of them, to one degree or another, experience
serious internal disagreements. But what is important to note is that such
differences and disagreements are often, literally, academic. By this I mean
that fundamental controversies in college or university politics (though
certainly not all controversies among people who happen to be
academics) are, in the end, controversies over the proper interpretation
of the concept of a university, hence are – like all conceptual disputes –
essentially philosophical in nature.[28]

2. What is true of universities is, I believe, true of institutions in general.
To pick another example, consider an organized religion – a "church."

---

[28] Rothblatt criticizes Newman (and, by extension, Coleridge's approach to institutions in
general) by denying that the modern American university embodies a single idea: "In
place of an idea, there was in time a multiversity containing many ideas and very little
unity . . . In historical perspective it is certain that Americans abandoned or failed to adopt
the Coleridge–Newman premise that institutions embodied an essential idea"
(Rothblatt, *The Modern University and its Discontents*, p. 30). It is doubtful, however,
that Rothblatt's empirical claim, which seems to me quite correct, has much force
against the philosophical premise in question. On the one hand, the idea of a university –
or of higher education – need not be Newman's, nor need it be in any way a simple,
monochromatic idea. The fact that modern universities embody a variety of ideas is
certainly consistent with the possibility that those ideas are, at the same time, unified by
and manifestations of some larger, more encompassing notion. On the other hand, to the
degree that there is in fact no such larger notion that animates and informs the operations of
a university, one might well say that the university itself is seriously defective as a university
and an institution, that it is very possibly in danger of coming apart at the seams or,
alternatively, that its continued existence might reflect the fact that it has simply become
a quite different kind of institution animated by a different overarching idea. Indeed, I think
it plausible to argue that at least some contemporary multiversities are universities in name
only, and that they really function as little more than convenient administrative and
financial (usually non-profit) corporations whose functions are not much affected by the
particular product that they happen to be selling.

Such an institution might choose to build or abandon cathedrals, cherish or abhor relics, embrace or expel members, ordain or defrock clergy, canonize or marginalize texts, all presumably guided and justified by some set of doctrinal determinations. The meaning of each individual object connected to the church is always hostage to a set of ideas that compose a more-or-less coherent theory. In this sense, a church is constituted fundamentally by its dogma, its religious beliefs; and these, in turn, determine how the religion will manifest itself, how it will appear to the outside world.

Thus, when Abbot Suger, in the twelfth century, rebuilt the cathedral of St. Denis, he did so under the influence of sixth-century philosophical writings attributed to the so-called Pseudo-Dionysus, whose neo-platonic theories had proclaimed God as the "light divine" and the "first radiance." Those theories provided a rationale for Suger to construct his church with brilliant stained-glass windows and to decorate it with lavish ornaments fabricated of gold and silver and encrusted with precious and colorful gemstones.[29] The results were momentous and hardly confined to St. Denis. The outward face of Christianity itself would never be the same. Notions of what a place of worship should look like, and of the role that the arts should play in the Christian pageant, were changed forever, and the revolution manifested itself in the most tangible ways – in bricks, mortar and human behavior. But the important point is that the change was, at base, philosophical. It involved an original and complex interpretation of the Bible's seemingly ironclad injunction against the worship of graven images. As such, it reflected a new understanding of the nature of Christianity itself, and of Christianity's relationship to the physical world; and this, in turn, led to a new idea of the function of a place of worship.

As with universities, religious developments of this kind are apt to be controversial in the extreme. Suger himself had his troubles with St. Bernard, among others; and we know only too well how the world is routinely turned upside down by conflicts about the way in which a church should be embodied, not simply in buildings but in rituals, rules, governance structures, and the like. In the last analysis, however, such disputes are almost always doctrinal. They speak to questions of substance, foundational questions, and we make a serious error if we confuse the outward appearance for the inner reality. Ideas constitute the essence of an institution. The rest – the furniture – is, to one degree or another, incidental.

---

[29] Abbot Suger, *On the Abbey Church of St.-Denis and its Art Treasures* (Princeton: Princeton University Press, 1979). Panofsky's introduction to this edition is especially helpful. But see also pp. 43, 47–49, 63–65, 73–77, and 107–11.

Understood in this way, institutions provide the theoretical foundation upon which humans coordinate and focus their otherwise unconnected and disorderly interactions with the world of things. We deal with physical objects – including our own bodies – only and exclusively in the light of our understanding of how things really are. We make sense of the world by thinking about it, by formulating ideas and theories, and on that basis we actively shape the world in ways that we deem appropriate. The conceptual apparatus that we bring to the physical realm imposes upon it a set of discriminations. These discriminations, taken together, transform what might otherwise be chaos into something approaching order. Institutions – universities, churches, states – at once reflect and empower such discriminations, making it possible for them to function as the foundations of organized social existence.

The physical order includes both objects over which we have comparatively direct and immediate control, our bodies, and objects that are typically less tractable, external things. But in each case, our relationship to the physical object is inevitably mediated by an idea. We control one group of things, our own physical capabilities, directly in terms of a conceptual apparatus; and this apparatus dictates, in turn, how those capabilities will be used to deal with the second group of things, the less immediately tractable ones. We utilize our bodies to move the earth, level trees, channel rivers, cultivate the soil and tame animals; we also use them to construct machines, synthesize chemicals, fabricate weapons. With these tools at our disposal, we refashion the world about us, something that is always done under the aegis of, and is always directed by, the structure of concepts, judgments and beliefs of which our intellectual life is composed. Human institutions are, in effect, one means by which we organize our tools – mechanisms for coordinating and implementing our collective capacities. As such, they are themselves created, guided, and ultimately constituted by an understanding of how things in the world really are.

The state is nothing other than, and nothing less than, a systematic structure of ideas on the basis of which the individuals of a society seek jointly to control the physical objects that surround them. The organs of the state – primarily the instruments of government, military as well as civil – are complex tools with which the state attempts to implement its judgments. These tools are integral parts of the state and yet, at the same time, secondary and derivative. At the core of the state, one finds not tools but a conceptual apparatus; and this is what makes it, in essence, a structure of intelligibility.

Understood in this way, the state is much like any other social institution. To be sure, it does play a unique role; it is a different kind of institution. But its distinctiveness should not be overestimated.

Paraphrasing Aristotle,[30] we may suggest, provisionally, that it functions primarily as the institution of institutions. It is the institution that directs all of the lesser institutions of society – universities and churches and all the rest. Its distinctiveness is, thus, largely a matter of scope and authority. Indeed, the state is nothing other than the authoritative manifestation of an entire way of life, reflecting, as such, the full gamut of judgments about how things in the world – all things in the world – really are. It articulates and codifies a structure of truth about the nature of reality, i.e., the shared, typically tacit assumptions, presuppositions, theories, commitments and understandings on the basis of which individual members of a society are able to communicate intelligibly and to interact coherently. Indeed, the propositions that constitute the idea of the state pertain not to this or that sector of society but to the full range of social enterprises; it is composed of notions about how institutional conflicts within society are to be resolved for the good of society; it is a comprehensive structure of ideas that functions as a kind of rule-book of last resort, a final court of appeal on the basis of which all social disputes are evaluated; it is distinctive, then, in being made up of judgments on the basis of which the order and security of society as a whole is to be achieved. In these respects, the activity of the state is quite special; and as we shall see, this will turn out to have important implications for our understanding of its internal constitution. But as a structure of intelligibility – a systematic order of concepts, judgments and beliefs – the state is of a piece with all social institutions.

3. The approach that I have sketched thus far resonates in various ways with the influential view that social life itself is primarily "composed of representations," that such representations are social facts reflecting shared or common judgments of reality and of value, that institutions are best understood as representational patterns or structures, and that the state itself is a kind of *représentation collective*.

Now it is true that Durkheim often adopts a post-Marxian terminology in distinguishing "state" from "political society." For him, "political society" designates a particular form of social organization that is distinctive in at least two respects. First, it is complex or "polycellular," i.e., composed of "secondary" groups the existence of which makes politics both possible and necessary.[31] Second, it is, or includes, a structure of sovereign authority on the basis of which the various parts of society are

---

[30] *Nicomachean Ethics*, 1094a 27–30.
[31] Emile Durkheim, *Leçons de Sociologie: Physique des Moeurs et du Droit* (Paris: Presses Universitaires de France, 1950), p. 57.

arranged and controlled.[32] The "state," on the other hand, designates merely an organ of political society, albeit an extremely important one. This is the organ of ultimate decision. It is composed of "the agents of sovereign authority," i.e., those individuals to whom the authoritative power of society has been specifically entrusted; and thus, when we speak of the state we are primarily speaking of "a particular group of officials."

But Durkheim, like Coleridge, also recognizes the fact that "very often what one calls the State is not the governmental organ but the political society in its entirety."[33] And if the terminology I have adopted is not always consistent with his, this should not obscure the fact that certain features of his account point very much in the direction that I am proposing. To begin with, he insists on separating the state as an idea from any kind of territorial or demographic structure, a view that differs sharply from Weber's. Even more importantly, he denies against Weber that the state itself is ever engaged in "action, execution or external achievement . . . The State does not execute anything."[34] In this respect, Durkheim's words are worth emphasizing: "[the state's] essential function is to think."[35] Or again: "the State is above all an organ of reflection . . . It is intelligence substituted for an obscure instinct."[36] In passages such as these, Durkheim assigns action, execution and external achievement to the government, understood not as the state but as an instrument for putting into practice the results of the state's thinking. At the same time, he provides a powerful intimation of political society as something intellectual or mental, as a structure of intelligibility, as an idea. The state depends upon the "entire mental life [*vie psychique*] that is diffused throughout the society," i.e., the collective intelligence.[37] Its role is to interpret, articulate and explicate that intelligence in an authoritative manner, to "work out certain representations." Such representations constitute society's understanding of the general truth of things; hence, the state is deeply connected to and defined in terms of broad conceptions of how the world really is.

If Durkheim seems to think of the "state" as an "organ" of intelligibility whereas I prefer to think of it as the intelligible structure itself – a structure that includes, by the way, an account of the nature and status of any and all organs of intelligibility – the disagreement is, in the end, internal to a broadly and essentially intellectualistic view of political society. Such

---

[32] *Ibid.*, p. 59.
[33] *Ibid.*
[34] *Ibid.*, p. 62.
[35] *Ibid.*, p. 63.
[36] Emile Durkheim, *Durkheim on Politics and the State* (Stanford: Stanford University Press, 1986), pp. 46–47.
[37] Durkheim, *Leçons de Sociologie*, p. 60.

a view, in turn, gives rise to a further proposition that I believe to be true and for which I intend to argue primarily in Chapter 6, namely, that the idea of the state is the idea of an organism – a view that resonates, once again, with Durkheim's, and decidedly not with Weber's, account of things.

Having said all this, it needs also to be said that my specific approach owes less to Durkheim (and, indeed, Coleridge) than to a host of loosely related but otherwise quite different perspectives in nineteenth- and twentieth-century philosophy and social thought. I would include here the long and complex tradition of *Geist* philosophy, of which Hegel is only the most famous proponent; the historical-hermeneutical theory of "horizons" associated with Heidegger and Gadamer; the idea of a "universe of discourse" pursued by Mead and others in the pragmatic and symbolic-interactionist tradition; the literary-analytic conception of an "interpretive community," as formulated by Fish; Bourdieu's primarily anthropological notion of the "habitus"; and – in a seemingly unrelated vein – philosophical theories of internal realism and transcendental argument developed variously by Putnam, Searle, Strawson and others. Without denying obvious and immense differences among such formulations, I believe that each of them is deeply involved in, is part and parcel of, a central and defining current of modern intellectual life, what might be called a post-Kantian convergence. Each demonstrates, rather more clearly than Durkheim, the sense in which the distinctly moral imperatives of the *conscience collective* are bound up with and dependent upon much broader presuppositions about how things really are, presuppositions of an ontological nature rooted in an underlying, largely unstated conceptual apparatus – an implicit structure of truth, of metaphysical and moral presupposition. And each understands, as well, the sense in which a great deal of social and political life involves an on-going and unending struggle to reveal and explicate that structure.

4. The priority of ideas in a world of cause and effect

It may seem that I am proposing here the complete independence of the mental over and against the physical. But any such claim would be ludicrous. Ideas obviously reflect, as well as influence, the external world. Who can deny that basic physical states give rise to thoughts? And who can deny that actions, including political ones, sometimes take on a life of their own, become detached from the ideas upon which they were originally based and begin independently to generate new kinds of arguments and justifications?

1. All of this must be conceded, indeed embraced, yet none of it has any force against the view of things that I have been presenting. For that view tells us, and purports to tell us, nothing whatever about the sources or origins of concepts and propositions, hence is entirely compatible with many varieties of determinism and materialism. The question of whether or not our ideas arise from, say, the exigencies of economic life, or from the influence of spatial and moral density, or from biological or psychological imperatives is a question about cause and effect, a scientific question, not a philosophical one. Any philosophy must, I think, be consistent with a range of accepted scientific possibilities, but doing philosophy is not the same as doing science. To say, then, that a university is in essence a structure of propositions is not at all to deny that the first universities may have arisen in the late Middle Ages as a result of material factors: economic, geographical, military, or what have you. Similarly, our understanding of St. Denis would not necessarily change even if we discovered that Suger had built his church because of an idiosyncratic psychological predisposition, or because of unconscious class prejudices, or because of scientific and technological discoveries that made it possible to construct a pointed arch, a flying buttress and a ribbed vault. And we are certainly free to believe that the modern nation-state emerged primarily as the tool of an emergent commercial class that sought to break the bonds of an obsolete but tenacious system of feudal privilege. But none of this would contradict the claims that I have made about the ontological priority of ideas. For, to use a somewhat different terminology, the question of material and/or efficient cause is quite distinct from that of final cause. My account insists that institutions are essentially structures of concepts, judgments and beliefs and that, from an ontological point of view, things in the world are rendered meaningful and important only and entirely in terms of ideas. But it certainly does not claim that the actual physical existence of things is caused by concepts in the way that a punch causes a bloody nose.

The philosophy of the state privileges ideas without at all denying the force of material nature. But there is yet more to be said here. For while I do believe that institutions are fundamentally structures of concepts, judgments and beliefs, it is also clearly true that the existence of any particular institution presupposes *some* kind of embodiment. Ideas are constitutive, fundamental and determinative, but they must also manifest themselves in objects – in people and actions and inanimate things. Without this they could not function as the essence of institutions but, rather, would exist only as mere abstractions. Stated otherwise, the various propositions that compose the core of any institution are necessary but insufficient conditions for the institution actually to exist in the world.

This is perhaps another way of saying that "mind has for its *presuppos-ition* nature."[38] The material world is the indispensable medium through which thought comes to know itself and manifest itself as something substantial. As one commentator puts it, ideas are governed by a "prin-ciple of necessary embodiment."[39] A university, for example, *is* a set of propositions about the meaning of higher education, but as such it also must incorporate itself in a curriculum, a faculty, a physical space; and so too with a church and with all other social institutions, including the state. But again, while material things are required in order for ideas to become embodied, the particular nature of those material things – their function and status, their very existence as one *kind* of thing as opposed to another – is determined by the intellectual structure that they instantiate. That structure has, then, a special role to play: "nature is posited by mind, and the latter is, therefore, the absolute *prius*."[40] It would be quite correct to believe that the existence of Harvard very much depends on the availability of physical spaces suitable for its activities, but it would still be wrong to claim that those spaces *are* Harvard.

2. The relationship of the state as an idea to the paraphernalia of the state is a complicated affair. Paraphernalia are suffused with thought, so to speak; objects are what they are only insofar as they have been interpreted as such. But at the same time, interpretations need something to interpret, some-thing material. There is no state – there are no institutions – without embodiments. The ideal and the physical, thought and object, are mutually dependent, sharply distinct and yet utterly inseparable; and this creates serious theoretical difficulties, for when things are inseparable, they can be hard to differentiate in practice. Although the idea is the essence and the embodiment the accident, their utter organic interconnectedness means that it is not always easy to distinguish with confidence that which is primary from that which is secondary, the core from the periphery.

As we have seen, an idea of higher education must be fundamental to the identity of any university, whereas the specific embodiments of such an idea – curricular practices, organizational structures, physical arrange-ments, and the like – are secondary. The latter compose, in effect, an interpretation, and an attempted embodiment, of the former. The cur-riculum is what it is because of – it has been formulated and continues to be evaluated on the basis of – the relevant idea of higher education. Yet

[38] G. W. F. Hegel, *Encyklopädie der Philosophischen Wissenschaften im Grundrisse* (Frankfurt: Suhrkamp, 1970), § 381.
[39] Charles Taylor, *Hegel* (Cambridge: Cambridge University Press, 1975), pp. 82–83.
[40] Hegel, *Encyklopädie*, § 381 *Zusatz*. Also, § 126–30.

our analysis of that idea may itself be influenced by curricular experience; the logic of practice often has strong implications for philosophy. Thus, in the process of implementing our curriculum, of actually teaching our courses, we may discover hitherto unrecognized but nonetheless enlightening and important connections between subject matters; and from this we might conclude that the elucidation of such connections should be central to our idea of higher education, hence that the curriculum should be revised accordingly. Indeed, if actual curricular practice becomes deeply inscribed in the philosophy of the university, then it may not always be so easy to say what is fundamental and what is secondary. At some point, I may have difficulty even articulating the idea except by pointing precisely to the curriculum itself.

Institutions of whatever kind are apt to be characterized by such an interpenetration – an on-going dialectic – of the material and the ideal. This is certainly not to deny the priority of ideas. We simply cannot make sense of a university curriculum that sustains itself apart from an independent concept of higher education; nor can we conceive of church practice uninformed by a definite structure of religious dogma; nor again can we understand political activity except in the context of the structure of metaphysical presupposition upon which a particular state is based. But the identity and character of concepts, dogmas and metaphysical presuppositions rarely presents itself as something rigid, fixed, immutable and self-evident in all respects. The interpenetration of the ideal and the material – the primary and the secondary – means that our understanding of the essence is apt to be, beyond a certain point, fluid, unstable and imprecise. It is, as such, almost certain to be a source of contestation.

Any attempt to understand the nature of the state will be, largely for this reason, an on-going effort to maintain distinctions that often appear impermanent and elusive. It is almost certainly an endless task – an effort to maintain a stable distinction between core and periphery that is likely to resist any kind of determinate and final accounting. The uncertainties inherent in such an endeavor are apt to be numerous and persistent. The orderly structure of ideas of which a state is composed is always only prospectively that. Any society's conceptual apparatus will change constantly as experiences and perspectives change. Its coherence – its intelligibility – will be perpetually in question, and this will inevitably give rise to debate and disagreement. To be sure, we cannot passively accept the dynamic, dialectical, elusive nature of the state. We are driven constantly to seek a fixed and coherent resolution. But we must also recognize with a clear head that such a resolution may be impossible, that the solution to one conundrum may itself bring to light another, and so on ad infinitum.

It is here, moreover, that we may get an intimation, however fleeting, of what it might mean to talk about "politics" itself. The politics of a state is, in some measure, precisely a matter of trying to manage intellectual uncertainties and tensions of the sort that I have just described, to maintain the integrity or wholeness of a conceptual apparatus in the face of its inherent messiness and fluidity, to distinguish clearly the essential from the secondary and to establish that distinction authoritatively. In the last analysis, the primary modes of everyday political endeavor – the exercise of power and influence, the attempt to control the political agenda, the effort to reshape the "mobilization of bias," the rough-and-tumble of negotiation and extortion, payoff and coercion – are the tools we use to resolve, however temporarily, contested questions of meaning, i.e., to effect a redefinition or reconceptualization of one or another feature of the world (or, alternatively, to perpetuate an existing definition or conceptualization), hence to establish an authoritative account of the state as a structure of propositions about how things in the world really are. Understood in this way, political questions are ontological ones, political activity a species of ontological inquiry.

The conceptual materials of any society are invariably multiple and complex, far beyond possible human imagining. The notion that any single mind, or even any coordinated group of minds, could be in complete and confident command of those materials is untenable. If political philosophy is, in part, the effort to keep our conceptual materials in order – so that ordinary political activity can enjoy a coherent and persuasive justification – then pursuing such a philosophy is almost certainly a permanent and on-going feature of social existence.

5. The several senses of the ontological state

The notion of a philosophical approach to the state – a theory of the idea of the state as an idea – in fact describes a single but very complex project composed of more-or-less distinct yet deeply interrelated strands.

1. On the one hand, it suggests an effort to describe the essence of the state itself and to adduce, thereby, standards or criteria by which all particular existing political societies can be judged. Like a Platonic form or a Weberian ideal-type, the idea of the state is something to be instantiated by actual states existing in space and time. It defines the underlying nature of all such instantiations, which is to say that individual states essentially *are* attempts to implement the idea of the state. And to the degree that such states fail completely and perfectly to reflect the idea, as presumably they always will, it provides a basis for their intelligent criticism.

On the other hand, the idea of the state tells us that any particular existing (or formerly existing) state is itself an embodiment and reflection of the particular, perhaps culturally or temporally specific, ontological claims and commitments of its citizens. The state is both the subject of metaphysical theory and a metaphysical theory in its own right – an institutionalized and authoritative account of how things in the world really are. The notion of an "ontological theory of the state" thus has a double connotation. To identify and analyze the particular metaphysical theory, or family of metaphysical propositions, that is embodied in a particular existing state is to provide an account – a philosophical interpretation – of *a* state; but that is not quite the same as providing a philosophy of *the* state, i.e., an analysis of what makes a state a state. *That* a state is composed of particular propositions about how things in the world really are is a metaphysical claim about states *per se*, an argument about the idea of the state; and so too are associated claims about the scope, authority and organic constitution of the state, i.e., the kinds of claims that will be developed and defended in Part III below and that compose, or so I argue, the substantive core of the theory of the state. But all of this is, as such, distinguishable from an analysis of the particular metaphysical propositions upon which a particular existing state is based.

The relationship between a philosophical theory of the idea of the state and a philosophical analysis of a particular state is, however, intricate and multi-layered. For the fact that the state is fundamentally a structure of propositions about how things in the world are is itself a fact about the world, hence, like other facts, something to be institutionally and authoritatively reflected in the (usually implicit) self-understanding of any particular existing state. The structure of moral and metaphysical presupposition that is embodied in a particular state will include a virtually infinite array of claims about reality, but among those will be claims about the nature of states *per se*. The theory of *the* state is necessarily reflected (however tacitly) in the structure of intelligibility of which a *particular* state is composed. Stated otherwise, the idea of the state *per se* is internal to – is a small though extremely important part of – the vast structure of metaphysical truth, the idea or set of ideas, that constitutes the essence of a particular state.

In effect, the state has itself for a subject matter. But what this means is that any attempt to examine the nature of the state *per se* – including, presumably the present book – will be a profoundly *political* endeavor, a matter of a particular state, in one form or another, seeking to understand itself, to discover, and to achieve in practice, its own coherence. As I argue in Chapter 3, metaphysical or ontological inquiry is always, in a sense, immanent. Through metaphysical inquiry, an intelligible structure seeks to make sense of itself, to make implicit claims explicit, to correct its own inconsistencies, to evaluate the degree to which discrete propositions comport with the overall system and to revise those that do not. Insofar as any particular state is essentially just such a structure, all metaphysical inquiry, including inquiry into the nature of the state itself, will have the character of an immanent political critique.

Of course, if the idea of the state, as part of our idea of reality, is always necessarily internal to and subsumed by any particular state as an idea of how things in the world really are, then it is also true that the latter is, in a sense, governed by the former. This is to say that the theory of the state tells us what kind of thing a particular state must be. It is legislative. In effect, a particular state encompasses its own constitutive principle of existence. The theory of the state is the underlying idea of the particular idea, that which makes the particular idea what it is in the first place.

If, however, the theory of the state is internal to and subsumed by the particular state as an idea, then does this suggest a kind of relativism? Does the theory of the state in fact vary from particular state to particular state? But certainly that can't be the case, since the fact that the theory of the state is internal to the particular state is, as such, determined by – is true in virtue of – the theory of the state itself. One might thus be inclined to take a sharply anti-relativist approach, i.e., to ask if the idea of the state and the state as an idea do not both reflect a meta-theory of some kind – a universal system of metaphysical and moral presupposition external to any and all states and inquiries, on the basis of which any and all particular claims and formulations can and should be assessed. This question is addressed from a historical perspective in Chapter 3, section 3, subsection 4 (henceforth 3.3.4). But there is a sense in which, from a purely theoretical perspective, it misses the point. For it seems to me that such a question can itself be asked and answered only internal to a particular structure of intelligibility. As I argue elsewhere in Chapter 3, there is no Archimedean standpoint, no independent point of view utterly free of moral and metaphysical presupposition. Indeed, in assessing philosophical claims – both claims *about* the state and claims *by* the state, including claims that the particular state makes about the idea of the state – the proof of the pudding can only be in the eating, namely, in the actual discovery of coherence and the actual achievement of rational agreement. To be specific: the discovery of coherence and the achievement of agreement is all that is possible and, at the same time, all that is required; and the question of whether or not such agreement represents or reflects some kind of ultimate, independent and transcendent reality is both unanswerable and, in the end, unimportant. This may seem an unsatisfying conclusion, but it is in fact perfectly consistent (see 3.2.2) with extremely powerful and highly compelling notions – post-Kantian notions– of objectivity and truth.

2. A great deal of contemporary political theory is devoted to the analysis of particular existing states. Rarely, though, is such analysis understood explicitly as ontological or metaphysical. Instead, political theorists see themselves as "interpreting" political practices and forms, much as one might interpret an historical event or, perhaps, an aesthetic object; or they see themselves engaged in a kind of *kultur kritik*; or again, as seeking to unmask ideologies, conceived as proxies for underlying material interests. Such accounts, moreover, are endemic to, are generally part and parcel of, theories of government and policy – motivating, informing and justifying prudential or pragmatic claims about how the political apparatus should be organized and what it should do. But the notion that all of this is rooted in fundamental presuppositions of a metaphysical nature is rarely understood or acknowledged – in part because of the widespread failure to distinguish state from government, in part because of the widespread discomfort with anything metaphysical. As a result, a great deal of political theory fails, I believe, to come to grips with its own implicit philosophical or theoretical foundations.

My point is not at all to deny the legitimacy of pragmatic or policy-oriented ways of thinking about politics, but merely to emphasize their particular and limited character. Whereas the theory of the state is a philosophical theory aimed at discovering what makes sense, theories of government are prudential theories aimed at discovering what works. Whereas the philosophy of the state is an inquiry into ontological commitment informed by linguistic and conceptual interpretation, theories of government are pragmatic exercises informed by experience (including scientific experience), interpretation and historical insight. Whereas the philosophy of the state tells us what we must believe if we are to be coherent, theories of government tell us what actions we should perform in order to achieve our goals. It is hard to imagine two more different kinds of intellectual endeavor, and the distinction between them informs virtually every feature of the various arguments that follow. But the larger point should, by now, be clear: a distinction is not the same as a separation. For every prudential analysis of governmental decisions and decision-making is inevitably underwritten by and reflective of some notion, however inchoate, of the nature of the state itself. One might say that the state is to government and policy as musical harmony is to melody. Any particular harmonic structure can sustain an immense variety of melodic choices; but all such choices must be consonant with or otherwise "justified" in terms of their harmonic setting.[41] And so too for politics. To get clear about the idea of the state is to say little if anything about which particular governmental processes and policies should be adopted in any particular circumstance; but it is to provide, nonetheless, at least one indispensable basis for their justification and, at the same time, for ruling out policies that cannot be so justified. Political preferences, whether of the left or right, make sense and can be coherently defended only if they reflect the political state as it really, essentially is.

It is a fundamental premise of this book that the effort to formulate a theory of the state, if pursued with care, promises to uncover a structure of theoretical insight and understanding on the basis of which we can begin to consider in an entirely new light a range of important and seemingly irresolvable controversies concerning government and policy. Indeed, I propose to show that many of the most stubborn oppositions of contemporary political thought – involving liberals and communitarians, individualists and holists, elitists and democrats – turn out to be far more tractable than we have thought, and may even dissolve altogether in the face of a serious and sustained conceptual or ontological analysis of the state.

3. If, in pursuing such an analysis, we are stepping somewhat outside the current mainstream of political inquiry, it is also true that we will not be entirely on our own, for the problem of the state, as an ontological problem, has only quite recently lapsed into obscurity. The Western tradition of political theory long preoccupied itself precisely with the task of adducing and analyzing those features of political society that might be deemed essential; and we certainly have much to learn by reconsidering some of the ways in which this tradition addressed, in particular, the relationship between political prudence and political philosophy.

One might be tempted to think of such a reconsideration as little more than an exercise in moral archeology, an effort to deal with contemporary problems by appropriating the wisdom of another place and time. But this cannot be quite right. For despite recurrent and insistent protests to the contrary, the simple fact is that traditional practices of theoretical speculation, ontological as well as prudential, continue to hold sway over us today. Such practices are deeply inscribed in each and every one of our beliefs

---

[41] Dissonant sounds, crucial elements in most musical vocabularies, are dissonant only in the context of particular harmonies. Thus, the characteristic function of dissonance – the creation of "tension" to be released through "resolution" – is entirely dependent on a harmonic substrate.

about how things really are; and those beliefs cannot but reflect an elaborate conceptual and theoretical apparatus, a complex structure of thought
on the basis of which we seek to make sense of the world. It is true that
making sense of the world now involves us, more than ever, in the protocols
of the natural sciences. But even these reflect, however unselfconsciously,
an underlying structure of truth – a set of metaphysical presuppositions
about the nature of things.

Stated otherwise, the most scientific and technical of enterprises entail
and presuppose, like any others, profound ontological commitments,
hence implicate the scientist in one or another theory about what the
world itself is really made of. It is difficult to imagine, moreover, that any
such theory could have emerged spontaneously, out of thin air, fully
formed and ready-at-hand. We would be much closer to the mark if we
thought of ontological commitment as a kind of inheritance, the product
of a long-standing and still vigorous culture of systematic inquiry into the
nature of things, political and otherwise. That culture has bequeathed to
us a rich universe of discourse composed of concepts and interpretations,
premises and presuppositions, all of which determine, in large part, what
we think and how we think it. To the extent that we are creatures of mind,
this inheritance has made us who we are. As such, it establishes, admittedly, the conditions of our unfreedom; it determines what it is possible
for us to think. But it explains, as well, the precise sense in which we are in
fact quite free, for it defines not only the horizons but also, at the same
time, the as-yet-unimagined possibilities of our intellectual life. It is, in
effect, a prison-house of ideas without which, however, we could not even
begin to think for ourselves.

6. Political practice and the theory of the state

To pursue the idea of the state, or alternatively to examine and evaluate
the underlying presuppositions of any particular existing state, is to be
doing philosophy and politics at the same time. Such a suggestion, briefly
introduced in 1.4.2 above, calls for some elaboration.

Since any particular existing state is a reflection and embodiment of a
society's understanding of how things in the world really are, and since
the idea of the state is necessarily a part of that world, any effort to get
clear about the world, hence about the idea of the state, necessarily has
important political implications. Again, inquiry into the nature of things,
including the nature of the state, produces fundamental claims of an
ontological or metaphysical nature. Those claims become institutionalized and embodied in a particular state. As a result, they cannot but
have a profound effect on what that particular state does and how it is to

be understood. In an important sense, then, all philosophical activity is necessarily civic, civic activity necessarily philosophical; and if that is so, then all philosophers of the idea of the state must be, as such, citizens, and all citizens philosophers of the state.

1. This may seem an odd conclusion. But the universality of philosophy, i.e., the fact that nearly everyone is a philosopher of the state and of many other things besides, is no more peculiar than, say, the universality of science. It is, I think, a simple fact that virtually all of us seek to understand in scientific terms – in terms of cause and effect – how at least some significant portions of the world work. We try to figure just what it is that makes our boss happy, makes this apple pie taste better than that, makes a golf ball go straight, makes an investment profitable, makes one movie more popular than another, makes for a happy marriage, makes this crop grow better than that one, and so on ad infinitum. Each of us develops hypotheses and theories about such things, and in doing so each of us constructs a scientific conception of the world as an immense and complex nexus of causality. Of course, some of us do this systematically and rigorously, with an unusual degree of talent, training, professional commitment and self-reflection. The vast majority of us do not. But this only means that some of us – the ones officially called "scientists" – are simply better at science than the rest. The enterprise itself, the attempt to understand causes and effects, is universal.

And so too with the activity of trying to figure out what the world is composed of, what particular things really are. We have ideas not only about the nature of the state but about the nature of virtually everything that we encounter: bosses, apple pies, golf balls, investments, movies, marriages, crops, etc. We cannot but be aware that our ideas about such things are often problematic and controversial. Is it a golf ball if it has no dimples? or if it is larger or smaller than the regulations prescribe? or if it is composed of a new kind of material that makes it behave in new ways? Is a happy marriage necessarily monogamous? necessarily heterosexual? necessarily sexual at all? Our ordinary lives are deeply preoccupied with such questions. We think and talk about them all the time, and in doing so we are trying to get clear about how things in the world really are, about how they should be conceptualized. We are, in short, doing philosophy. Again, some of us do it rigorously, systematically and with unusual perspicacity; most of us do not. But this simply means that, as with science, some of us are better at it than others. The activity itself is universal.

Each of us is a theorist of the state. Each of us considers and arrives at conclusions about those things that compose, and that are summarized and ratified by, the state as a structure of intelligibility, and this includes conclusions about the nature of the state itself. Hence, each of us – whether in the ivory tower or on the street corner, on the editorial page or over the backyard fence – is engaged in an enterprise at once philosophical and political, an enterprise that speaks to the most fundamental and constitutive aspects of human social existence. The present project is simply an effort to pursue this enterprise rigorously, to uncover and reconstruct our shared understanding of the state – in Coleridge's terms, to eliminate particular "conceptions" that fail to comport with the underlying "idea" and to affirm, instead, a fully coherent theory.

2. To say that the idea of the state is that the state is an idea – a structure of metaphysical presupposition about how things in the world really are – is, at the same time, to say something about the *activity*, the *legitimacy* and the *internal constitution* of the state. While particular states may differ insofar as they reflect different metaphysical theories, each state cannot but be a reflection of some such theory; and from this basic fact, it follows – as I hope to show in Part III – that all states are essentially similar with respect to their proper scope of action, the nature of their authority, and their basic principle of organization. To demonstrate that this is in fact true, and to show what it actually says about a state's activity, authority and internal constitution, is largely what it means to pursue an ontological theory of the state.

In a contemporary context, these three features of the state – its activity (or purview), its authority and its internal constitution – manifest themselves perhaps most prominently in terms of three specific problems: the problem of toleration, the problem of consent and the problem of democracy. Where and when should the state act to enforce, rather than tolerate, individual and social behavior? What legitimizes – that is, renders authoritative – the activity of the state? Does the legitimacy of the state somehow depend on the degree to which its internal decision-making apparatus is democratic? These are complex problems, deeply contentious. They have given rise to enormous literatures of a prudential nature – theories of government and policy – and to energetic, persistent debate. At times, they seem to us hopelessly intractable. When seen in the light of the ontological state, however, they may well begin to take on a rather different character, and may even reveal themselves to be, in the end, rather less troubling. For while they are, in the first instance, problems of policy and government, they are also connected with and reflective of a number of deeper and more fundamental questions about the idea of the state itself: what should a state do, why is it justified in doing it, how should it be done? To pursue such questions, hence to specify in philosophical terms the idea of the state, is, in my view, to establish at the same time an indispensable foundation for addressing at least some of the most pressing and difficult issues of contemporary political life.

The approach is radical – in the sense of fundamental or elementary – and the results are apt to be radical as well. If we conceive of institutions as ideas or structures of intelligibility, and if we conceive of the state as the institution of institutions, hence nothing less than the orderly and authoritative arrangement of our intellectual world formulated so as to reflect and promote the social good, then I think that several conclusions necessarily follow:

First, the range of activity that falls within the purview of the state is, in principle, unlimited. There is nothing that we do, no part of our existence, that is by definition independent of, protected from, or external to the state's authority. As an embodiment of a society's understanding of how things in the world really are, the state necessarily captures the complete range of judgments and discriminations, beliefs and discoveries, conceptions and theories that compose, collectively, a particular way of life. Historically, it is hard to identify any feature of human existence that some state somewhere has not sought to control: producing, consuming, buying, selling, killing, inflicting pain, procreating, educating, speaking, thinking, worshipping, loving, and so on. But these historical facts merely reflect the conceptual fact that every state everywhere necessarily has within its plausible scope of authority virtually every aspect of our lives. This doesn't mean that the state must *actively* and *directly* regulate everything we do. No state has ever done that, in part for technical, in part for doctrinal, reasons. But what it does mean is that when the state decides not to regulate some activity, it arrives at that decision not by avoiding but, to the contrary, by making a judgment about the activity itself. It is hard to see how it could be otherwise. An activity is left alone not because it is by definition a non-political matter, but because the state has determined, explicitly through analysis or implicitly through default, that, given the nature of the activity and the contexts in which it occurs, leaving it alone is what is called for. The activity is, for whatever reason, categorized and classified by the state as one of those things *not* to be actively and directly controlled. In the light of such a determination, the state might choose to adopt a short-term expedient, e.g., for now the state will let the value of its currency be determined by the market rather than by centralized decision-makers. Alternatively, it might develop a longer-term governmental principle, e.g., the state will establish for its citizens freedoms of religion, speech, press, assembly and petition. But in either case, the decision will be a prudential one, a matter of policy and

government; and if the state's understanding of the activity changes –
always a possibility – then the policy might have to change as well.

Second, the authority of the state, whatever its scope, is and can only be
absolute. As the embodiment of society's understanding of how things in
the world really are, hence as the institution of institutions – the institution
of last resort – the state can accept no rival, no higher or even co-equal
power. This doesn't mean that the decisions of the state cannot be
questioned; it doesn't rule out dissent, debate, discussion or the most
vigorous kind of political conflict; and it certainly doesn't presuppose that
the state is infallible. To paraphrase Rousseau, the decisions of the state
are always authoritative in a moral sense, but not always correct in a
practical or pragmatic sense. What it does mean, however, is that social
disagreements can be resolved only with reference to the society's broader
view of the nature of things, i.e., the underlying structure of concepts,
theories and claims – moral, metaphysical, empirical – that define the
society itself and that make it possible for its citizens to interact with one
another in a coherent, intelligible and productive fashion. Insofar as the
state represents that underlying structure, it is sovereign, and absolutely so.

Finally, political society, understood along these lines, is an organic
structure in which individual citizens play essentially functional roles.
So-called atomistic or methodologically individualistic conceptions, as
usually formulated, are not consistent with the idea of the state. For the
larger structure of metaphysical and moral presupposition embodied in the
state constitutes, at the same time, the mental life of individual citizens.
Their thoughts, hence their actions, cannot but reflect deep-seated notions
of how the world really is, notions that are inscribed in the conceptual and
linguistic infrastructure of society itself. By describing the nature of things,
that infrastructure necessarily prescribes, *inter alia*, the kinds of activities
that society itself requires for its survival and health, the kinds of individuals
suited to those activities, and the kinds of abilities, dispositions and skills
characteristic of each particular person. In this context, the individual
citizen cannot but be understood, and can only thrive, as a part of a larger
entity. At the same time, of course, the larger entity's existence is entirely
hostage to the healthy activity of its citizens. There is no state – no
conceptual infrastructure – apart from the individual human beings in
whose thoughts and actions that infrastructure is reflected and embodied.
The whole is, thus, utterly dependent on the parts, the parts on the whole;
and this is essentially what we mean when we refer to something as an
organism.

To some readers, at least, these claims will surely seem peculiar, perhaps
even disturbing. In fact, together they constitute the substantive core of my
account of the state and will, as such, be defended at length in Part III

below. But what must always be remembered is that they are claims about the state, not about the government of a state. The distinction makes all the difference. For as I propose to show in Part III, the unlimited authority of the state is in fact fully and completely compatible with the doctrine of limited government, the absolutism of the state fully and completely compatible with the most extensive right of resistance and revolution, the organic nature of the state fully and completely compatible with deep and robust notions of democracy and freedom. Indeed, the arguments that I will be making are motivated in large part by the belief that fundamental features of liberal doctrine can be properly understood, evaluated and, in at least some cases, best defended only when viewed clearly and explicitly in light of the idea of the state; and this reflects, once again, my conviction that many of the most important and troubling political controversies of our time – controversies of prudence – can be resolved not primarily through prudence itself but through the philosophical analysis of a concept, the concept of the state.

Part 2

Philosophical Foundations of the State

2   Politics, Prudence and Philosophy

The idea of the state presupposes a strong distinction between prudential and philosophical ways of thinking about politics. The distinction is, to begin with, one of subject matter. Prudential theories of politics pursue questions about policy and government and, where appropriate, non-governmental or quasi-governmental entities, understood as instrumentalities of the state. Philosophical theories of politics, on the other hand, pursue, directly or indirectly, the nature of the state itself, understood as a political or civic community encompassing virtually all facets of organized social life. This difference in subject matter, however, is deeply bound up with larger intellectual differences. For we are in fact talking about two quite distinct manners of thinking, sharply different from one another in terms of goals, methods and standards of judgment. Getting clear about their differences – and also about the ways in which they are closely and inexorably connected to one another, despite those differences – is absolutely crucial in a double sense. It is crucial in thinking about what it might mean to pursue a philosophical theory of the state. And it is crucial in thinking about the state itself, understood as a structure of intelligibility composed of propositions and claims – metaphysical or ontological claims – about how things in the world really are.

This chapter is broadly divided into two parts. Sections 1–3 explore the prudence/philosophy distinction in detail by focusing on the work of Hobbes (though I also look briefly at Plato, Aristotle and Rousseau by way of comparison). Section 3 is perhaps especially important. It argues that Hobbes's political writings provide an ontological or metaphysical account of political society, a theory of the "essence" of the state. In doing so, it considers in a preliminary way what it might mean to pursue such a theory, hence functions as a kind of introduction to the more extended discussion of ontological or metaphysical inquiry that one finds in Chapter 3.

Before moving on to Chapter 3, however, sections 4–6 of the present chapter explore the claim of contemporary liberalism to have produced a political philosophy fundamentally innocent of important ontological or metaphysical premises. My account of the state presupposes that any political

41

theory must be rooted in larger conceptions of how things in the world really are, hence must be, so to speak, "metaphysical as well as political." But such a presupposition flies in the face of much current thinking about politics. The contemporary prejudice against metaphysical or ontological approaches to politics needs to be confronted head-on, in particular by demonstrating what I believe to be the impossibility of a purely "political" conception.

Insofar as sections 1–3 lead directly to the broader metaphysical arguments of the next chapter, sections 4–6 may be considered a kind of digression. Given the centrality of Rawlsian liberalism for contemporary political thought, however, the digression seems to me a necessary one.

1. Theories of government and the philosophy of the state

The modern theory of the state, in its canonical version, holds that a commonwealth is created when a group of individuals "confer all their power and strength upon one man, or upon one assembly of men, that may reduce all their wills, by plurality of voices, unto one will."[1] This one man or one assembly of men is, of course, the sovereign, and a commonwealth is defined precisely as a social organization that has, at its apex, some such entity. To have a sovereign – an instrument of government that possesses an unchallenged right of final decision – is what makes a commonwealth a commonwealth. It is what distinguishes commonwealths from all other kinds of social institutions.

The important point for our purposes is that the modern theory of the state is entirely indifferent as to whether the sovereign is in fact "one man" or "one assembly of men." This may seem a surprising claim. For while it is no secret that Hobbes does indeed allow for a variety of regimes, his preference for monarchy, as opposed to democracy and aristocracy, is well documented as an historical and biographical fact,[2] and is announced unambiguously and at length in each of his principal political

---

[1] Thomas Hobbes, *Leviathan*, in *The English Works of Thomas Hobbes of Malmesbury* [hereafter *EW*], ed. Sir William Molesworth (London: John Bohn, 1839), vol. 3, p. 157.

[2] See, for example, Robert P. Kraynak, *History and Modernity in the Thought of Thomas Hobbes* (Ithaca: Cornell University Press, 1990), especially chapter 2. Also, Quentin Skinner, "Conquest and Consent: Thomas Hobbes and the Engagement Controversy," in *The Interregnum: The Quest for Settlement 1646–1660* (London: Archon Books, 1972), pp. 79–98, where the emphasis is on Hobbes's defense of *de facto* powers. In Mintz's view, the argument of *Leviathan*, though clearly absolutist, "expressed no particular bias in favour of monarchy." Samuel I. Mintz, *The Hunting of Leviathan: Seventeenth- Century Reactions to the Materialism and Moral Philosophy of Thomas Hobbes* (Cambridge: Cambridge University Press, 1962), p. 13.

writings.[3] Sabine offers what has long been the standard view, namely, that those writings were intended "to exert influence upon the side of the king. They were designed to support absolute government and in Hobbes's intention this meant absolute monarchy; all his personal interests attached him to the royalist part."[4] There are reasons to be careful about such a view, however. The Hobbesian corpus is not small. It treats a wide range of topics and presents a diversity of arguments, each of which needs to be approached with due regard for the context in which it appears. Thus it is true, to be sure, that whenever questions of regime-types arise, Hobbes always prefers monarchy. But when the discussion turns to the *concept* of a commonwealth *per se*, things seem to be quite different, for then we discover that the distinguishing features of political society properly understood – absolute sovereignty and all that it entails – may be every bit as characteristic of aristocratic and democratic regimes as of monarchical ones. As far as I can tell, moreover, Hobbes never wavers from either position. He never seriously questions the superiority of monarchy, but also never gives us any reason to doubt that aristocracies and democracies can embody, in an eminently satisfying way, the basic principles of Hobbesian political science.

How best to reconcile such apparently divergent views? I believe that the answer is to be found precisely in the distinction between philosophical and prudential theory and in the related distinction between the state, understood as a political community, and the government of a state, understood as an instrumentality. Hobbes's preference for monarchy is a governmental preference rooted in considerations of prudence and good judgment; his account of sovereignty is, to the contrary, a philosophical matter pertaining to the nature of the state involving necessary truths about concepts. There is no contradiction or even tension between them, since they deal with

---

[3] Thomas Hobbes, *The Elements of Law*, *EW*, vol. 4, pp. 166–69; *De Cive*, *EW*, vol. 2, pp. 129–42; *Leviathan*, *EW*, vol. 3, pp. 173–77. For discussions of this point, see Howard Warrender, *The Political Philosophy of Thomas Hobbes* (Oxford: Oxford University Press, 1957), p. 304; David P. Gauthier, *The Logic of Leviathan: The Moral and Political Theory of Thomas Hobbes* (Oxford: Oxford University Press, 1969), pp. 108–10; D. D. Raphael, *Hobbes: Morals and Politics* (London: George Allen & Unwin, 1977), p. 57; Jean Hampton, *Hobbes and the Social Contract Tradition* (Cambridge: Cambridge University Press, 1986), pp. 105–7; Deborah Baumgold, *Hobbes's Political Theory* (Cambridge: Cambridge University Press, 1988), pp. 75–79; Kraynak, *History and Modernity in the Thought of Thomas Hobbes*, pp. 172–86; S. A. Lloyd, *Ideals as Interests in Hobbes's Leviathan: The Power of Mind over Matter* (Cambridge: Cambridge University Press, 1992), pp. 290–99; Richard E. Flathman, *Thomas Hobbes: Skepticism, Individuality and Chastened Politics* (Newbury Park, California: Sage, 1993), pp. 134–40.

[4] George Sabine, *A History of Political Theory* (Hinsdale, Illinois: Dryden Press, 1973), pp. 422–23. Sabine quickly offers a series of apt qualifications, distinguishing Hobbes's monarchism from the larger influence of his work.

completely different kinds of questions and do so in substantially different ways.[5]

1. When defending monarchical government, Hobbes provides what might best be described as a set of empirical propositions purporting to show why, all things being equal, the rule of one man is usually "less inconvenient" than that of an aristocratic or democratic assembly. He claims, for example, that the private interest of the sovereign and the public interest of the body politic are more apt to coincide in monarchies than in other regimes, in part because order and peace – fundamental to the public interest – provide the sovereign with benefits that are likely to be felt more keenly if the sovereign is but a single person; and one result of this, according to Hobbes, is that sedition and popular rebellion are apt to be comparatively rare in monarchical regimes. Monarchs are also more inclined to solicit and heed the advice of prudent, experienced counselors; and where one person rules, government is less likely to suffer from the types of conflict that commonly plague the internal workings of sovereign assemblies, large or small.[6] Each of these claims is presented as a kind of educated guess about what sorts of political arrangements produce what sorts of outcomes. Each is plainly based on Hobbes's own study of history – both ancient, as with the Peloponnesian War, and modern, as with the English Civil War. And each is informed by a more-or-less careful and systematic examination of human psychology. Together they may well constitute a formidable argument on behalf of monarchical government. But they do not speak at all to the idea of the state, either singly or collectively, hence make no contribution whatsoever to the project of uncovering and articulating the nature of political society itself.

That project is, for Hobbes, philosophical rather than prudential. It aims to describe not what is likely to happen in the world but what we must believe about the world if our thinking is to be at all coherent. As such, it is a matter not of educated guesses, not of mere probability and prediction, but of proof or demonstration.

Thus, in the Preface to *De Cive*, Hobbes says that he very much wants

not to seem of the opinion, that there is a less proportion of obedience due to an aristocracy or democracy than a monarchy. For though I have endeavoured, by arguments in my tenth chapter, to gain a belief in men, that monarchy is the most commodious government; which one thing alone I confess in this whole book not to

---

[5] Of all recent commentaries on Hobbes, that of S. A. Lloyd, *Ideals as Interests in Hobbes's Leviathan*, for example at pp. 290–95, is perhaps closest to the account that I am proposing.
[6] See n. 3, above.

be demonstrated, but only probably stated; yet every where I expressly say, that in all kind of government whatsoever there ought to be a supreme and equal power.[7]

Evidently he believes that he *has* demonstrated, as a conceptual matter, "what civil government, and the supreme power in it, and divers kinds of it, are." He has proven, specifically, that the existence of a commonwealth – whether democratically, aristocratically or monarchically governed – depends on the transfer of rights from subject to sovereign. He also believes, however, that he has *not* proven, but "only probably stated," the superiority of monarchical government. He thus acknowledges that while some of his claims present demonstrable philosophical truths, others reflect, at best, a cultivated sense of what works and what doesn't.

Some commentators have insisted that there is in fact no such distinction in Hobbes's writing and, in particular, that the "defense of monarchy runs along the same lines as the defense of unified sovereignty."[8] Specifically, Hobbes is thought to have believed that government by assembly and divided sovereignty share a common defect: each tends towards disunity, hence civil war. And if this is so, then his grounds for rejecting them – the former in favor of monarchy, the latter in favor of a unified sovereign – must presumably be the same and essentially pragmatic in nature. According to such an interpretation, the Hobbesian theory of sovereignty and the state might *appear* to be a philosophical or conceptual theory; but it is really just another prudential one, no different from the gamut of practical claims that we find in *Leviathan* and the other major political texts.

I think that this reading cannot be sustained. For Hobbes indicates quite clearly that, in his view, divided sovereignty is problematic not because it leads to disunity but, rather, because there is simply no such thing. A "sovereign" that is divided among, say, the monarch, the aristocracy and the people is not a sovereign at all: "it is not one independent commonwealth but three independent factions."[9] If the sovereign is understood to be that entity which reigns supreme over all others in a state, then to say of two or more distinct entities in a single state that each is sovereign is to say something that is plainly incoherent: "the speech is absurd."[10] When confronted with multiple claims to sovereignty, then, only two possibilities could really make any sense at all: either (a) one of the putatively sovereign entities actually *is* the sovereign, or (b) none of

[7] *De Cive, EW*, vol. 2, pp. xxii–xxiii.
[8] Baumgold, *Hobbes's Political Theory*, p. 76; see also, Hampton, *Hobbes and the Social Contract Tradition*, pp. 105–7.
[9] *Leviathan, EW*, vol. 3, p. 318.
[10] *Ibid.*, p. 169.

them is. Of course, (b) would mean that the commonwealth does not have a sovereign; but this cannot be, since a commonwealth that has no sovereign is, according to Hobbes, no commonwealth. Thus, to speak of a commonwealth is necessarily to presuppose (a), and this means that we have no choice but to accept the principle of unified sovereignty. It is literally impossible for us coherently to conceive of a commonwealth in any other way. In light of this, of course, considerations of probability, predictability or prudence are clearly irrelevant. The defense of unified sovereignty, unlike the argument for monarchy, is simply and solely a matter of conceptual or philosophical necessity. As such, it culminates in a proposition – a philosophical claim – about what it means for a state to be a state.[11]

2. The distinction between prudential and philosophical or scientific modes of thought is an explicit methodological premise of *Leviathan*. According to Hobbes, "prudence is a *presumption* of the *future*, contracted from the *experience* of time *past*." He provides an apt illustration: "[H]e that hath seen by what courses and degrees a flourishing state hath first come into civil war, and then to ruin; upon the sight of the ruins of any other state, will guess, the like war, and the like courses have been there also."[12] In contradistinction to prudence, we have science: "As much experience, is *prudence*; so, is much science *sapience*." Again, he illustrates:

[L]et us suppose one man endued with an excellent natural use and dexterity in handling his arms; and another to have added to that dexterity, an acquired

---

[11] Baumgold explicitly distinguishes "prescriptive" from "analytic" approaches to these issues, a distinction that seems similar to the one I have offered here between a theory of policy and a philosophy of the idea of the state. She insists that Hobbes's defense of unified sovereignty is fundamentally prescriptive rather than analytic, but her argument is unpersuasive. She says that "the strong analytic thesis that sovereignty is necessarily indivisible renders superfluous an enumeration of the essential powers (versus marks) of sovereignty" (p. 66). It is simply hard to see why this should be so. One can well imagine any number of reasons why Hobbes, having analytically established the truth of unified sovereignty, would then wish to enumerate essential powers understood, for example, as elaborations and entailments of the basic idea. But even if Baumgold's point regarding superfluity is conceded, in and of itself it has no force against the analytic thesis.
  I would say much the same about Hampton's reconstruction of a Hobbesian argument against democracy. She claims that Hobbes's rejection of divided sovereignty is based on a concern about inevitable "power grabs" or "jurisdictional fights" (Hampton, *Hobbes and the Social Contract Tradition*, p. 105). This concern can then be applied to governmental institutions, with the result that absolute monarchy is proved to be the "sole legitimate [Hobbesian] form of government" (p. 106). But again, Hobbes's rejection of divided sovereignty is quite different from this, as at *Leviathan*, *EW*, vol. 3, p. 318. The problem is not a matter of power grabs and jurisdictional fights; the problem is that such a theory is incoherent.
[12] *Leviathan*, *EW*, vol. 3, p. 16.

science, of where he can offend, or be offended by his adversary, in every possible posture or guard: the ability of the former, would be to the ability of the latter, as prudence to sapience; both useful; but the latter infallible.[13]

It is true that Hobbes does not always apply the distinction between prudential and philosophical analysis with the greatest clarity. But this only points to a second and equally crucial feature of the argument. For while prudential and philosophical theories generally address different kinds of questions and do so in substantially different ways, they are also certain to be deeply and inextricably interconnected. Specifically, every prudential account of government is inevitably underwritten by one or another philosophy of the idea of the state, however tacit and inchoate it may be; and this suggests that any theory of policy or government can only be as good as the account of the state upon which it is based.

Thus, while Hobbes's defense of monarchy is to be sharply distinguished from his analysis of the idea of a commonwealth, it is also entirely dependent upon it. Specifically, monarchy is preferable precisely because it is, in Hobbes's view, unusually well-suited to achieving the desideratum of a commonwealth, namely, unity. This, and this alone, is what makes monarchy desirable. To be sure, one might choose monarchy for any number of other reasons, e.g., monarchy is aesthetically more pleasing, or is just more fun, or best serves my interests if I am in line to become monarch. But insofar as we wish to pursue a serious *political* defense of monarchical rule, one that views government primarily as a functional attribute of political society, then our argument for such rule must be connected to and underwritten by a particular philosophy of the state; and in Hobbes's case, it was.

The point is worth emphasizing: in Hobbesian thought, *the superiority of monarchical government is to be understood on the basis of criteria established not by independent considerations of policy or government but by the idea of a commonwealth itself.* Absent that idea – absent the fundamental notion of a commonwealth or state characterized by a unified sovereign whose function is to provide peace and security – Hobbes would lose the main foundation upon which his institutional prescriptions are based.[14]

Such an intermingling of different arguments operating at different levels – the prudential and the philosophical – sometimes raises interpretive problems; disentangling the one from the other is not always easy. But

---

[13] *Ibid.*, p. 37.
[14] It is worth noting in this connection that Hobbes's philosophy of the state focuses not just on the notion of sovereignty but also deals with questions of political obligation, the nature of law, and the function of ecclesiastical office; and some of these discussions are, in turn, bound up with considerations of policy involving questions of government structure, the role of ministers and magistrates, etc.

the effort to do so can be crucial in helping clarify doctrinal matters that might otherwise remain obscure. For example, at several points Hobbes seems to suggest that the kinds of inconveniences associated with mixed government (e.g., internal conflict) would also result from divided sovereignty.[15] But if there is literally no such thing as divided sovereignty, then how can this be? How could divided sovereignty cause problems if it cannot even exist? This seems a vexing exegetical problem indeed, but the line of analysis that I have pursued suggests, I think, a clear solution: the inconveniences in question must result not from the fact of divided sovereignty, which fact is impossible, but from the mistaken *belief* in the possibility of divided sovereignty, and the misguided attempt to put that belief into practice. The culprit, in other words, is an untenable view of sovereignty reflecting, however unselfconsciously, a fallacious theory of the state. To correct the theory is to eliminate the problem.

The point is generalizable: philosophical inquiry is, for Hobbes, a fundamental and necessary feature of any effort to think prudently about politics in the real world. By failing to understand the concept of sovereignty, we are apt to pursue policies and institutional strategies – e.g., mixed government – that are doomed to fail; and so too with all manner of conceptual error. Hobbes argues, in effect, that incoherence resulting in mistaken belief is not simply an intellectual problem. It can have the most serious practical consequences as well. For him and, as I hope to show, for us as well, sound policy absolutely presupposes sound philosophy.

Hobbes's defense of monarchy thus needs to be evaluated precisely in terms of the degree to which it shows monarchical government to serve best the purposes inherent in the idea of political society. If we wish to reject Hobbesian monarchy – and I suppose that most of us do – then *those* are the grounds upon which to base our objections. And whatever the conclusion might be, our purchase on the question of monarchy, and of institutional policy in general, is necessarily hostage to a prior understanding about the very idea of the state.

3. Sovereignty is plainly central to the Hobbesian philosophy of the state, but it is not alone in being so. Hobbes believes that our idea of the state includes, adverts to, or is in some way closely connected with a host of related notions: natural laws that describe the foundations of the state, natural rights that describe the powers of citizens and sovereigns, a conceptual account of the relationship between temporal and ecclesiastical authority, and so on. Perhaps most important of all is a description of the

---

[15] *Leviathan, EW*, vol. 3, pp. 172–73.

ultimate aim or purpose of the state, namely, the pursuit of order, peace
and unity. Such a purpose is fundamental to and at least partly constitutive of the essence of political society. The idea of a state that sacrifices or
even compromises this purpose in the interest of some other goal is, for
Hobbes, not an idea of the state at all. It is an incoherence.

In giving pride of place to order or unity, Hobbes is often thought to be
making (perhaps in company with Machiavelli) a substantial and distinctively "modern" departure from earlier traditions. But this seems to me
overstated. For Hobbes, order is a constitutive end of political society
precisely because it is (an important part of) what makes political society
useful in promoting human flourishing. The principal achievement of the
state is to permit individuals to thrive, to enjoy the kind of secure,
productive, commodious, pleasant and rewarding existence that cannot
reliably be enjoyed in the natural condition where life is literally brutish or
sub-human. But the views of, say, Plato are really quite similar, *mutatis
mutandis*. The *kallipolis* is essentially a structure of the highest order or
unity and is, as such, useful and valuable in promoting the various kinds
of flourishing appropriate to the different types of individuals. And so too
for Aristotle, where the harmonious city – peaceful and self-sufficient –
makes it possible for humans to fulfill their potential as humans, rather
than to live as mere "beasts" or "savages";[16] and again for St. Augustine,
where the "peace of the [temporal] city is an ordered concord" that
facilitates and underwrites the peace of the heavenly city in which individuals can discover a "fellowship perfectly ordered and harmonious,
enjoying God and each other in God."[17] Of course, such writers have
very different views of what human flourishing means, very different
views about how to conceptualize political order itself, and very different
views about how the state actually works to improve the lives of individuals. But in each case, the achievement of stability and security – of
domestic tranquillity – is a *sine qua non* of political society.

Understood along these lines, Hobbes's philosophical theory of the state
is an ontological or metaphysical theory embracing and subsuming a broad
range of ontological claims. It involves an account of what it means to be a
human being, including and especially a psychological theory that purports
to describe the underlying reality of human action; and this theory, by
specifying what is distinctive about human beings, implies in turn an
understanding – however tacit – of the nature of other things in the world
including animals and inanimate objects. The centrality of such an

[16] Aristotle, *Politics* 1253a28 and 1253a36.
[17] Augustine, *The City of God*, Book XIX, ch. 13.

understanding is amply demonstrated in Book 1 of *Leviathan*; and indeed, it is hard to see how it could be any other way. To describe the idea of political society is to presuppose an understanding of how things in the world really are. It is to presuppose an intellectual and conceptual structure, a structure of metaphysical presupposition or truth, of which the idea of the state is itself an important part; and this suggests, in turn, that a philosophical theory of the state must itself be an ontological or metaphysical theory.

This fact – which is, in the first instance, a formal fact about theories – will have large substantive implications for our conception of the state itself; and it would not be wrong to say that all of the arguments that I have presented thus far, and all that I will present in the remainder of this book, are devoted precisely to the elucidation and elaboration of at least some of those implications.

2. Prudential and philosophical argument

The distinction between prudential and philosophical modes of thought is hardly peculiar to Hobbes. To the contrary, it is a fundamental feature of political thought in general. As such, it can help us better understand the arguments of a wide range of political theorists, including many whose work could hardly be more different from Hobbes's.

It is also true, however, that the distinction manifests itself in a variety of ways. Hobbes's approach is but one of many, and an often idiosyncratic one at that. To understand the distinction truly – to see more clearly its larger import – thus requires, I think, at least some brief consideration of how it is treated at the hands of certain other, decidedly non-Hobbesian authors.

1. The idea of a philosopher-king, presumably central to any comprehensive account of ancient political thought, makes a most curious debut. Specifically, it does not appear in the *Republic* until 472b–473d, virtually half-way through the dialogue, and emerges only in the context of a very particular kind of question, namely, how can empirical cities be reformed so as to approximate most faithfully the idea of the *kallipolis*, as outlined in Books 2–5?[18] Socrates himself formulates the issue as follows:

We must try to find out and demonstrate what is badly [*kakos*] done in cities today, and thereby prevents them from being governed in this way, and with what

---

[18] The argument that follows originally appeared in Peter J. Steinberger, "Ruling: Guardians and Philosopher-Kings," *American Political Science Review* 83 (December 1989), pp. 1207–25.

smallest change [*smikrotatou metabalaontos*] – preferably one, if not, two and, if not, the fewest in number and the smallest in impact [*smikrotatōn tēn dynamin*] – a city would come to be this kind of polity... With one – not, however, a small or an easy one, but possible – we can, in my opinion, show that it would be transformed. (473b–c)

The one change he has in mind is, of course, for philosophers to become kings and kings philosophers. But again, this is the very first time in the *Republic* that we encounter such a notion. The analysis of the *kallipolis* itself makes no mention of it at all, at least until the middle of Book 5; and as Socrates clearly indicates (472b–e), by that point the description of the *kallipolis* is quite complete. He must be correct in this latter respect, moreover, since how could we possibly know that establishing philosopher-kings in empirical cities would be a good way to instantiate the idea of the *kallipolis* unless we already had that idea well in hand? The implication seems clear: if the account of the *kallipolis* has been completed prior to any mention of the idea of philosopher-kings, and if that idea arises only in connection with the quite different project of reforming empirical cities, then we must conclude that there are, in the *kallipolis*, no philosopher-kings.

It is true, of course, that the guardians who govern the *kallipolis* are often described as having a natural capacity for philosophy. But this certainly does not mean that they actually are or have ever been philosophers.[19] Indeed, to my knowledge, an explicit connection between the guardians of the *kallipolis* and the idea of the philosopher-king is made at only one point rather late in the *Republic* (502d–503b); and that connection itself is, arguably, undermined by a host of rhetorical and theoretical problems that serve strongly to suggest that guardians and philosopher-kings must in fact be quite different kinds of beings.[20]

It should be understood, of course, that the *kallipolis* is nothing other than the idea or model (*paradeigmatos*) of the city. It is discovered by engaging in a philosophical argument aimed at describing the essential features of political society. Those features include a well-ordered structure of classes based on a rational division of labor according to which each class performs only those functions to which it is uniquely suited; and just as Hobbes's account of the idea of the state invokes a more comprehensive understanding of the truth of things, so too does Plato's rest upon an account of the world as it really is, politically and otherwise.

---

[19] Plato tells us, for example, that many sophists have precisely the same kind of capacity, yet are, in most respects, the polar opposites of philosophers (491d–e).

[20] For example, the guardians are depicted in the context of educational, economic and sexual practices that would be both unnecessary and inimical to a class of true philosophers.

His metaphysics of the state is merely part of his larger metaphysics. But again, Plato's account of the *kallipolis* makes no mention of philosopher-kings; the elaborate hierarchical structure that he proposes plainly does not include, and may well have no place for, a class of philosophers. From this we are forced to conclude, I think, that the idea of the philosopher-king plays no role whatsoever in Plato's account of the idea or model of the city, and that his preference for government by philosopher-kings has, therefore, nothing directly to do with his philosophy of the state. This is certainly not to deny that he provides an elaborate philosophical account of the idea of a philosopher-king. Such an account is to be found in much of Books 6 and 7, where he describes precisely what it is to be a philosopher. But to have analyzed philosophically the idea of the philosopher is not, in and of itself, to have demonstrated philosophically that empirical cities should be ruled by philosopher-kings. To my knowledge, no such demonstration appears in the *Republic*. Plato's defense of government by philosopher-kings is prudential rather than philosophical.

There seems to be an obvious objection. For central to the idea of the *kallipolis* is the notion that the rational element of any city should be the ruling element; and since philosophers will, by definition, be the most rational element in any city in which they are found, it would appear to follow as a matter not of mere prudence but of rational necessity that philosophers should rule. This is, indeed, a standard view of what Plato has in mind, but I doubt that it can be sustained. For as numerous commentators have shown, Plato's idea of the philosopher is such that, by definition, individual philosophers would be unenthusiastic and perhaps unwilling candidates for kingship; and by the same token, his account of non-philosophical people (primarily pleasure lovers and honor lovers) makes it unlikely that the ordinary citizens of empirical cities would be inclined to accept, much less encourage, the prospect of a philosopher-king. Thus, government by philosopher-kings can occur, and perhaps is advisable, only when the circumstances are propitious. *If* one or more philosophers were willing to get involved in the administration of a city, and *if* somehow the non-philosophers of that city could be persuaded to accept and encourage such involvement, then it follows from the idea of the *kallipolis*, with its emphasis on rule-by-rationality, that philosophers should be kings. But all of this is very different from the philosophical analysis of the *kallipolis* itself, which is an account not of what should happen if certain circumstances obtain but of what a particular kind of thing – the city – essentially is.

In light of all this, I think we can see that for Plato, as for Hobbes, the distinction between philosophical and prudential claims reflects a difference of argumentation, of logic. The argument for the *kallipolis* is, in a manner of speaking, categorical, that for philosopher-kings, hypothetical. This is to say that our commitment to the idea of the *kallipolis* is, or ought to be, absolute; the *kallipolis* simply *is* the idea of the state. Our commitment to government by philosopher-kings, on the other hand, can only be contingent, for in certain situations such a commitment cannot sensibly be sustained. Indeed, it seems that Plato explicitly contemplates such situations. Sometimes a city should be ruled not by a philosopher-king but by a "statesman" or, elsewhere, by the "laws," depending on the circumstances. It is true, of course, that the connection between Plato's principal political dialogues is a matter of much debate. But it is at least plausible to suggest that the author of the *Republic* wrote the *Laws* not because he had changed his mind but because a world in which, for whatever reason, philosophers could not become kings nor kings philosophers would still be a world in need of good government.

Plato's writings also illustrate rather more clearly than Hobbes's, I think, the precise sense in which the logic of argumentation is connected to questions of evidence, a fact that turns out to have important implications for the problem of truth. Hypothetical claims are hypothetical precisely because they depend upon empirical circumstances. We say that if certain circumstances obtain, then certain conclusions follow. This is surely a natural and common way of speaking; and at first blush, it does not appear to imply any denigration of prudential theory, since hypothetical claims could be every bit as accurate as categorical ones. The empirical proposition that X generally leads to Y is, in principle, neither more nor less true of the world than the conceptual or philosophical proposition that X necessarily entails Y. But if we combine the hypothetical-categorical distinction with Plato's well-known distrust of empirical evidence, we can see that for him the fruits of prudential speculation are likely to be profoundly unreliable. Insofar as hypothetical claims depend on empirical premises, and insofar as those kinds of premises reflect, for Plato, the insubstantial and often illusory appearance of things rather than their underlying reality, then such claims can be, at best, guesses or approximations. They cannot provide us with knowledge but only with something much inferior, namely, informed and educated but invariably undemonstrated opinion (which may, however, be indispensable for certain purposes).

On the one hand, then, the *kallipolis* is an idea, something that has been discovered through a philosophical or conceptual analysis. Like the Hobbesian commonwealth, it is based not primarily on the evidence of practical experience but on reason itself, and it expresses a categorical truth, i.e., a truth that is necessary and irrefutable. The theory of the philosopher-king, on the other hand, is more a matter of good counsel, much like Hobbes's preference for monarchy, involving a plausible but nonetheless tentative account of how the world works. As such, it expresses a truth that is neither necessary nor irrefutable but only contingent and probable.

But it is also clear that Plato's hypothetical argument, like Hobbes's, absolutely presupposes the categorical one. For the reform of empirical cities is informed and authorized precisely by the philosophical analysis of the city. To the degree that we do prefer government by philosopher-kings, this must be because such a government allows empirical cities to approximate most closely the paradigm of the *kallipolis*; and while, in certain circumstances, the rule of a statesman or of the laws may well be the best that can be expected, any city governed in that way will necessarily be inferior to a city of philosopher-kings, precisely because it will be further from the ideal. The *kallipolis* thus provides the standard against which any particular city must be judged and on the basis of which all policies have to be evaluated. For Plato, as for Hobbes, prudence is distinct from but nonetheless dependent upon conceptual truth.

2. What holds for Plato and Hobbes holds for others as well, both ancient and modern. Consider Aristotle. In the first book of the *Politics*, we encounter a reconstruction of the idea of the *polis* that establishes parameters on the basis of which particular kinds of regimes are to be assessed. Those parameters emerge from an analysis of the logic of human association itself, involving notions of self-sufficiency, harmony, and the principle of ruling and being ruled in turn. Through such an analysis, Aristotle purports to have demonstrated categorically the nature or essence of the *polis*. His is an ontological theory of the state. As such, it must be sharply distinguished from the explicit and lengthy discussions of governmental forms that we find elsewhere in the *Politics*. It is revealing that Aristotle, perhaps even more than Plato and Hobbes, is deeply equivocal on the question of the best regime. In conceptual or philosophical terms, monarchies, aristocracies and polities are all "right" regimes; they are all compatible with criteria inherent in the idea of the *polis*. That idea establishes the fundamental goals and principles of political society *per se*, but it does not prescribe any particular form of government. If, then, Aristotle finally does prefer a kind of mixed aristocracy – or, in other circumstances, a monarchy of the one outstandingly best man – this can only be the result of prudential or strategic rather than conceptual factors.

And similarly for Rousseau. Just as we think of Hobbes as a monarchist, so we are apt to regard Rousseau as a democrat. But again we have to be careful. For Rousseau says explicitly and unambiguously that "there is not a single unique and absolute form of government" (*du Contrat Social*,

III, 1), that democracy, aristocracy and monarchy each have their advantages and disadvantages, and that the choice among them depends largely on contingent circumstances of population, custom, climate, and the like. Indeed, he saves perhaps his harshest criticisms for democratic rule (III, 4). In doing so, he indicates precisely what I have been arguing, that claims about forms of government are likely be prudential in nature. Such claims are very different from the kinds of claims designed to show, say, that the concept of the general will is an essential feature of the idea of political society. The treatment of government to be found in Book III of *du Contrat Social* is purely hypothetical and based on contingent empirical circumstances, whereas the analysis of political society, confined largely to Books I and II, is categorical and based on the logic of human action and freedom. That analysis provides, in effect, an account of the idea of the state, an ontological account that, though apparently "democratic" in certain ways, is also functionally similar to Plato's description of the *kallipolis*, Aristotle's analysis of the self-sufficient community (*koinonia telos*), and Hobbes's deduction of sovereignty and the modern nation-state.[21]

In all of these cases, the philosophy of the state reflects and embodies an entire range of claims about the truth of things. Just as Hobbes's political thought reflects an account of what it means to be a human being, emphasizing a psychological theory that purports to describe the essential nature of human action, and just as Plato's theory of the *kallipolis* is virtually unintelligible without the theory of ideas and everything that it implies, so does Aristotle's politics involve a metaphysics that tells us, among other things, that man is by nature a social animal, and so is Rousseau's theory of the social contract hostage to a conception of what it means to say that humans are free, whether naturally or morally. In each case, prudential arguments presuppose an ontological account of the state, which, in turn, involves a range of explicit or implicit understandings about how things in the world really are.

3. Surely to lump together in this way such a diversity of authors – ancient and modern – is to risk the most elementary kind of error, an error of anachronism in which basic facts of history are blithely ignored in favor

---

[21] It is true, of course, that for Rousseau the sovereign, not government, is primarily responsible for "legislation." But by legislation, Rousseau generally means the kind of activity – guided by the "Legislator" – that establishes fundamental constitutional principles and procedures and that "determine[s] the form of the government" (*du Contrat Social*, II, 12). What Rousseau calls the executive power of government almost certainly includes most of we today think of as regular legislative activity, i.e., the making of particular laws to deal with particular problems.

of an artificial and abstract interpretive scheme that pays no attention to the actual production of texts in the real world. Such a scheme is, it will be argued, bound to make a shambles of its subject matter. To view Hobbes's political philosophy as a disengaged meditation on conceptual truth is to miss what is really important, namely, that it is the expression of a concrete political ideology, something to be understood in the context not of Plato, Aristotle and Rousseau but of Charles I, Cromwell and the New Model Army. *Leviathan* reflects, above all, a set of immediate practical concerns formulated in terms of a distinctive vocabulary more or less unique to its age; and so too with the political writings of Plato, Aristotle, Rousseau and others, *mutatis mutandis*.

Of course, I am raising here a very old issue, and it may be that I have nothing new to say about it. But it is an issue that bears an unusually close relationship to the larger themes of the present book, and does so in ways that may not be immediately apparent. For criticisms of the kind that I have described represent, albeit in a rather distinctive form, the idea of political theory as "political, not metaphysical." They presume that all political thought is about prudence and policy, and that so-called philosophies of the idea of the state should really be understood as mere reflections of practical, ideological concerns. In effect, the relationship that I have proposed above, whereby prudence is based on and justified in terms of underlying philosophical considerations, is reversed, but with the additional difference that philosophies of politics are perhaps not to be taken very seriously on their own terms.

Such claims strike me as invariably underargued. Surely, it is important to have demonstrated what seems plainly true, that the prudential concerns of political authors invariably reflect some kind of engagement with real political controversies. Plato's account of philosopher-kings must be understood in the light of fifth- and fourth-century struggles between oligarchs and democrats, Hobbes's preference for monarchy in the context of the Civil War. But from this alone it certainly does not follow that larger, transhistorical considerations are absent from their work. The fact that political authors are interested in policy or government says nothing about whether or not they are also interested in questions of ontology; and by the same token, the fact that historical analysis does indeed shed light on theories of prudence says nothing about whether or not it is possible to formulate theories of the state that in some sense transcend historical circumstances. To claim otherwise is to commit a fallacy.

The critic will persist. Even if political theorists do pursue ontological questions, their efforts will inevitably reflect some set of presuppositions about human thought and action; and such presuppositions, in turn, will always be traceable to the vagaries and vicissitudes of a particular time and place. History is inescapable; and insofar as historical reality is always bound up with one or another set of practical political controversies, it is inevitable that political thought, however intended, will always be fundamentally ideological.

To this there are, I think, three things to be said. First, the impulse to reduce everything to history is a dangerous one. Surely it would be most peculiar to claim, for example, that understanding the Pythagorean theorem requires a special understanding of the world of southern Italy in the sixth century BC; and if Pythagoras's concept of a triangle does in fact speak to a kind of larger rationality, then why not Plato's concept of a city or Hobbes's account of a commonwealth? Is there anything about mathematical – or scientific or historical – reasoning that allows for a non-historicist interpretation in a way that reasoning about the foundations of political society does not? I doubt that there is; and I am certain that most of the authors in question would quite agree. Hobbes and Rousseau understood themselves to be engaged in an on-going conversation not only with their contemporaries but with their forebears, ancient as well as modern. They understood their own views about the idea of the state to be based on claims about the essences of things, claims that were indeed shaped by, but hardly reducible to, the peculiarities of a particular day and age.

But second, even if we were to concede the historical nature of all philosophical arguments, it is hard to see why this would matter. For what is history itself but a structure of implication in which what happens at one point in time has an intelligible connection with what has gone on before? The world of Hobbes is profoundly different from that of Aristotle. Yet the two are also deeply connected insofar as the mind-set of seventeenth-century England emerged out of tendencies already implicit in the Renaissance, which were shaped by the perplexities of a medieval world that had arisen from the disruptions of late antique civilization, itself characterized by struggles between classical and Christian culture that reflected, in any number of quite tangible ways, the intellectual achievements of the so-called Greek revolution. Certainly the process is hardly ever smooth or strictly linear; nor do I presuppose that it is free from the kinds of paradigm shifts or epistemological ruptures that have preoccupied intellectual historians in recent years. But it also seems to me a plain fact that Hobbes can converse with and sharply criticize Aristotle, and that this is no accident. The need for interpretation – for hermeneutical engagement across time – seems clear enough. But the notion of a radical incommensurability, often implicit in ideological accounts of political thought, defies our common sense of how cultures and conceptual schemes actually evolve.

But finally, and most generally, to acknowledge the force of social and historical factors in shaping the kinds of questions we ask and the kinds of answers we propose is not to imply that all political thought is merely a matter of *political* ideology. It may well be that every ontological theory is ultimately rooted in some set of unargued presuppositions about the world. Indeed, I will soon be strenuously urging just such a view. But presuppositions of this kind often reflect features of cognition that seem to transcend merely partisan considerations. We might advert, for example, to the so-called "laws of thought," as well as to fundamental categories or concepts (space, time, cause) that are, or appear to be, characteristic of rationality *per se*, independent of any particular cultural milieu. But we might also include certain culturally specific features of cognitive activity that describe, in effect, the particular practice of thinking – the conceptual apparatus or universe of discourse – upon which a particular way of life is based. Such features must certainly involve presuppositions of a metaphysical nature, tacit assumptions about how the world really is; and there is no prima facie reason to believe that assumptions of this kind could not, and do not regularly, accommodate an enormous range of partisan views. To observe that human thought reflects the particularities of space and time is a far cry from showing that all thinking about politics is merely sectarian.

It may be that our understanding of the extreme diversity among authors such as Plato and Aristotle, Hobbes and Rousseau, is precisely what has kept us from seeing the degree to which their theories actually do share certain formal or logical properties of the kind that I have described. But as my own argument unfolds, I propose eventually to show that even this sense of diversity is perhaps overblown, and that what such authors share is much more than merely formal. The idea of the state may manifest in a variety of ways; its trappings are motley indeed. But it is, at base, a single thing.

3. **Hobbesian metaphysics**

I have argued that a philosophical theory of the state, as distinguished from a prudential theory of policy and government, must be an ontological or metaphysical theory of some kind. Such a claim, however, would seem to raise serious exegetical problems. To attribute to Plato or Aristotle an explicit and critically self-conscious ontological theory of the state is hardly surprising, but to think of Hobbes and Rousseau along these lines seems to be another matter altogether. The case of Rousseau is particularly difficult, in part because he has so little to say about the traditional questions of philosophy; and it is precisely for this reason that Hobbes is likely to be the more instructive. Here is a thinker, after all, whose entire career was formulated in vigorous and determined opposition to the "vain philosophy" of dogmatic metaphysics and scholastic realism. Indeed, if anyone would appear to have abjured – in principle and in practice – the very idea of a political metaphysics, it would be the author of *De Cive* and *Leviathan*; and we can hardly be surprised when he vigorously and vehemently rejects the very idea of *essence per se*.[22] But despite this, the fact is that Hobbes's political philosophy is, like any other, deeply metaphysical.

1. One cannot begin to understand Hobbes's thought without coming to grips with the fact that he explicitly and pointedly claims to have described the *essential* feature of political society. In the sovereign, he says, "consisteth the essence of the common-wealth."[23] What can he mean by such a proposition, and any number of similar ones,[24] if he truly believes that there are no such things as essences – if, as he insists, essences are but "empty names" and metaphysics but an illusion?

Of course, we might choose to believe that when he makes positive use of the word "essence" he is doing so only casually, and that we really should not take him too literally. But this seems hardly likely since, as we shall see, Hobbes is quite self-conscious in talking about the essences of things. Still, the exact role that the idea of essence plays in his system is not immediately apparent; and as far as I can tell, even his most perspicuous readers have generally failed to address the problem directly. This is curious since its solution resides, I believe, in a reconsideration of some of the most basic features of Hobbesian philosophy, features that no commentator could afford to overlook.

For Hobbes, human thought is profoundly linguistic. To think rationally is necessarily to have, and to employ, a semantical and syntactical system of some kind.[25] As to language itself, he understands it to be composed in large part of "names" that we regularly and routinely use to "mark" the ideas that we have about the various things that we find in the world. Some names are particular names that pick out this or that

---

[22] *Leviathan, EW*, vol. 3, pp. 672–76.

[23] *Ibid.*

[24] For example, *De Corpore, EW*, vol. 1, p. 117. In the political writings alone, Hobbes explicitly discusses the "essence" of many things including commonwealth, sovereignty, government, law, the body politic, mankind, covenant, the Christian religion, charity, oath, and marriage. See *Leviathan, EW*, vol. 3, pp. 158, 167, 206, 272, 313, 442, 462 and 622; *De Cive, EW*, vol. 2, pp. ix, 27, 86, 154, 191 and 235; *Elements of Law, EW*, vol. 4, pp. 91, 93, 114, 136 and 223.

[25] *De Corpore, EW*, vol. 1, pp. 15–16, 50.

individual item, but others are "universal names" that denote "the conceptions we have of infinite singular things."[26] Hobbes elaborates this
latter point by suggesting that universal names refer specifically to our
conceptions of the "properties" or "accidents" that we attribute to individual objects. As such, they play a particularly important role in any
analysis that purports to be systematic or scientific.

Now Hobbes believes that our use of names, hence our decision to
predicate a specific universal name of a particular thing, is based on observations or sense perceptions. Observations, that is, "cause" us to say certain
things, hence – given the close connection between language and ideas – to
think certain thoughts.[27] This means, *inter alia*, that our conceptions of
things are in some sense reducible to the properties that we observe those
things to have. Hobbes knows what we all know, that our perceptual apparatus is imperfect and that its imperfections can result in serious errors.[28] But
this doesn't pose any real problems for his theory. Misperceiving is simply an
unfortunate, albeit sometimes unavoidable, fact of life.

It is true that commentators have disagreed about whether or not the
connection between universal names and conceptions of things is, for
Hobbes, merely arbitrary or conventional; and so too with the question of
whether or not his theory of language makes any sense at all.[29] But two
things are clear. First, he believes that we humans do somehow arrive at
more or less agreed- upon names and that, as a result, we are normally
able to enjoy with one another a coherent intellectual life. Second, he
believes that the truth of our discourse about the world is based in part on
the degree to which our observations of it are accurate.

This is not the whole story, however. For he also believes that the
question of truth and error is a matter of right reasoning as well, hence
at least to some degree independent of or not fully reducible to mere
observation.[30] He says that the fact that we have certain ideas often
implies that we should have other ideas; the tracing out of such implications is, roughly, what he calls "ratiocination."[31] Thus, if I know that

---

[26] *Ibid.*, p. 80.
[27] *Ibid.*, pp. 72–73, 80, 389. See Tom Sorrell, *Hobbes* (London: Routledge & Kegan Paul,
1986), p. 69.
[28] *De Corpore, EW*, vol. 1, pp. 55–56.
[29] See, for example, Richard Peters, *Hobbes* (Hamondsworth: Penguin, 1956), pp. 121–23;
John (J. W. N.) Watkins, *Hobbes's System of Ideas* (London: Gower, 1989 [1964]), pp. 104–9,
and Sorrell, *Hobbes*, pp. 45–50.
[30] I believe that my account is similar to, or at least consistent with, the historical arguments
offered by Steven Shapin and Simon Schaffer, *Leviathan and the Air Pump: Hobbes, Boyle
and the Experimental Life* (Princeton: Princeton University Press, 1985), for example at
pp. 146–51.
[31] Sorrell, *Hobbes*, pp. 39–41.

object *a* is characterized by property *G*, and if I also know from other experience that the presence of *G* seems always to be associated with the presence of property *H*, then I can conclude through ratiocination that *a* is characterized by *H* as well as by *G*, even if I don't immediately observe it so. I should accept this conclusion simply because it would be imprudent for me not to; and to that extent, the conclusion certainly amplifies my understanding of *a*, at least as I conceive it. Of course, the faculty of ratiocination is not flawless. But again, this presents no serious theoretical problem. Just as our perceptual apparatus is hardly flawless, so is thinking like perceiving in being a source of error when done poorly, a source of truth when done well.

I wish to say three things about this picture:

(1) While our concepts are in some sense "caused" by observations, *the process of science and philosophy itself is, for Hobbes, wholly abstract.* Failure to understand this fundamental feature of Hobbesian philosophy can lead to any number of interpretive errors. In Hobbes's view, all truly systematic thinking is thinking about names – their similarities and differences, their mutual implications. Indeed, he understands reason itself to be nothing other than "*reckoning* – that is, adding and subtracting – of the consequences of general names"; and he says that the result of such reckoning is precisely what we call "science" or philosophy.[32] But such a science, focusing in this way on the analysis of names, could have, at best, only an indirect relationship to the external world. For again, names are used solely and exclusively to mark or signify our thoughts, and this means that they "are signs of our conceptions... not signs of the things themselves."[33] The importance of this latter claim can hardly be overstated. If names attach not to objects in the world but merely to our ideas about those objects, and if science is nothing but the systematic analysis of such names and their implications, then it follows that science or philosophy is directly concerned not with things or even with the names of things but, rather, with the names of ideas of things. This suggests, in turn, that arguments involving, say, *a*, *G* and *H* are not in fact what they might seem to be. Again, if empirical experience tells me that object *a* is characterized by property *G* and that property *G* is associated with property *H*, then I am likely to conclude that *a* is characterized by *H* even if I don't immediately observe it so. This would be a plausible conjecture on the basis of which I could derive a recommendation of prudence; but it would *not* be a conclusion of science or philosophy. For such a conclusion could

---

[32] *Leviathan, EW,* vol. 3, pp. 30 and 35.
[33] *Leviathan, EW,* vol. 3, p. 30; and *De Corpore, EW,* vol. 1, p. 17.

only emerge from an analysis of the words – "a," "G" and "H" – that we use to signify our conceptions of those things and on the basis of which we could say that *a* is necessarily characterized by *H*.

Thus, if I observe that a particular political society *a* has a monarch *G*; and if I also observe that monarchies tend to be orderly societies, i.e., they tend to be *H*'s; then it would be plausible to conclude that the society in question is apt to be an orderly one, even if I don't have any direct evidence on that score. Indeed, it would be imprudent to conclude otherwise, though such a conclusion would describe a probable rather than necessary state of affairs. On the other hand, if the meaning of the idea that is denoted by the word "commonwealth" ("a") includes the notion that a commonwealth has a sovereign of some kind ("G"); and if the definition of "sovereign" is such that for any particular society the sovereign is an entity that actually establishes order ("H");[34] then it follows not probably but necessarily that any commonwealth will be orderly.

What would be the connection between these two kinds of arguments, the experiential/prudential and the philosophical? This is a complicated question and one that, as we shall see, Hobbes does not address very adequately. But what we can say, at a minimum, is that the analysis of the names "a," "G" and "H" provides a set of principles for understanding and evaluating particular societies and conditions such that we can decide whether and to what extent *a*, *G* and *H* are in fact instances of "a," "G" and "H" or, what is the same thing, to what extent our ideas about them have been correctly named. Thus, if society *a* is in fact disorderly (not-*H*), then this means that *G* is not truly a sovereign (though he or she or it might appear to be) and *a* is not a commonwealth, properly so conceived.

Of course, most of the judgments that we actually make are likely to be matters of degree, i.e., a particular society embodies the idea of a commonwealth more or less satisfactorily. In the instant case, we might want to continue to call *a* a "commonwealth" and *G* a monarchical "sovereign," but our analysis of the concepts would help us to decide exactly to what extent we are right to do so. The point is precisely that philosophical arguments provide the criteria upon which we base our claims about the world. The degree to which *a* really is a commonwealth is determined by the meaning of "a." Without an understanding of "a," no such claim would be possible; and so too for all empirical propositions.

---

[34] As will be shown in chapter 5 below, for Hobbes a "sovereign" that fails to provide order is not a sovereign at all.

Am I thus suggesting that Hobbes, of all people, is an idealist? In fact, I am not, at least not in the usual sense. As we have seen, Hobbes clearly believes that our having the ideas we have is caused, in part, by the observations we have of material things and that, as a result, science and philosophy must be connected in important ways to a real world composed of bodies. But it is crucial to understand that, for him, the procedures of science and philosophy, the "adding" and "subtracting," begin where empirical observation leaves off, hence are directly concerned not with things in the real world but with the names of ideas of things in the real world. It is only and exclusively from such names that one derives "assertions," and then "syllogisms," and then, finally, "knowledge" itself;[35] and this means, in turn, that systematic human thought aiming towards truth is always, as it were, one or even two steps removed from empirical reality. Hobbesian science is, indeed, "logic-book" science[36] – even if the logic-book is based on a structure of premises composed either exclusively or largely of sense perceptions.

(2) Among our conceptions of things, the notion of *essence* plays a crucial role, indispensable for any account that purports to be scientific. According to Hobbes, the essence of a thing is nothing other than our conception of the single property (or, presumably, set of properties) that indicates most clearly and directly just what the thing is. It is "the accident which denominates its subject."[37] Thus, for example, "rationality is the essence of a man" and "extension is the essence of a body" – by which Hobbes means that to be rational just is what it means to be a man and to be extended just is what it means to be a body, at least according to our way of thinking.[38] In this sense, then, *the concept of the essence of a thing and the concept of the thing are virtually identical; and the names that mark these two concepts are, Hobbes explicitly tells us, synonyms.*[39]

(3) Points (1) and (2), taken together, mean that when we speak of the essence of a thing we are naming a conception of the thing, or a conception of a property of the thing, rather than the property or the thing itself. Again, the difference is crucial, for it alone allows us to understand both why Hobbes is so critical of dogmatic metaphysics and why we should view him, nonetheless, as a metaphysician in his own right. In an important and revealing passage, Hobbes writes as follows: "when it is said the

---

[35] *Leviathan, EW*, vol. 3, p. 35.
[36] Sorrell, *Hobbes*, pp. 41–42.
[37] *De Corpore, EW*, vol. 1, p. 117.
[38] *Ibid.*
[39] Which is to say that they have the same "reference" (a concept), though certainly not the same "sense."

essence of a thing is the cause thereof, *as to be rational is the cause of man*, it is not intelligible; for it is all one, as if it were said, *to be a man is the cause of man*."[40] He is saying here that there is no possibility of conceiving a separation between essence and thing. The essence must be thought of as part and parcel of the thing itself. But it is also true that causes and effects are always conceived of as separate things; nothing can be thought to be its own cause. Together with the first point, then, this suggests that, for Hobbes, we can make no sense of the fundamentally Aristotelian idea that essence is the cause of the thing. Indeed, it is largely on these grounds, I think, that Hobbes rejects notions of formal or final causation upon which much "vain philosophy" is based. The dogmatic metaphysical realist insists that the essence of a thing is nothing other than its formal or final cause. As such, it must be something independent of and external to the thing itself. But if, as we have seen, the essence of a thing cannot be conceived of as a cause of the thing, and since it seems that the formal or final cause could be nothing other than the essence of a thing, we are forced to conclude that there can be no intelligible concept of formal or final cause. All causation, therefore, is "efficient."

Why then do we need the idea of essence at all? Hobbes is quite clear. While the essence of a thing cannot operate as a cause, our *conception* of the essence of a thing can, albeit in a rather special way. Specifically, "the knowledge of the *essence* of anything is the cause of the knowledge of the thing itself; for, if I first know that a thing is *rational*, I know from thence, that the same is *man*."[41] What can this mean, other than that an account of the essence of a thing can function as an *efficient* cause *not of the thing itself but of our understanding of the thing*? Such an account can force us to think about the thing more intelligently by giving rise to – efficiently causing us to hold – a new and clearer notion of it, one that presumably makes more sense to us in the light of our other ideas and that constitutes, in effect, our best conception of what the thing really is.

Any such conception is plainly the product of two factors, or two causes. On the one hand, it must be consistent with our observations of the material world, hence is in part caused by those observations. Again, we have the ideas that we have because, in part, of our experience of the world. But any conception of the essence of the thing is also produced – caused – by an analysis of the meanings of the names that denote those ideas; and it is only through such an analysis that we can attain the kind of insight and clarity that is the hallmark of serious scientific inquiry.

---

[40] *De Corpore, EW*, vol. 1, p. 131. The point is restated in *Leviathan, EW*, vol. 3, p. 674.
[41] *De Corpore, EW*, vol. 1, p. 132.

Thus, Hobbes does indeed reject the doctrine of "separated essences."[42] He denies that essences exist independent of bodies. Peters is correct, as far as he goes: "there are [for Hobbes] no essences behind the appearances of our universal names to fit."[43] But to leave it at that is to miss the point. For essence remains, in Hobbes, an absolutely crucial scientific and philosophical category. To name the essence of a thing is, in effect, to name our idea of the thing in a particularly perspicuous and enlightening way, hence to say what the thing really is, at least according to our lights.

2. For Hobbes, this kind of systematic or scientific thinking manifests itself not only in "natural philosophy" but in "civil philosophy" as well – the type of philosophy that one finds in *The Elements of Law*, *De Cive* and *Leviathan*.[44] Civil philosophy is concerned, in large part, with what a commonwealth really is, just as natural philosophy is concerned with what natural objects really are; and this means that Hobbes, in his political works, understands himself to be engaged primarily in the project of deducing the definition of a commonwealth, of describing its essence. When he tells us, then, that the sovereign is the essence of a commonwealth, he is saying nothing other than that, as an ontological matter, a commonwealth *is* a kind of social organization characterized by the presence of a sovereign entity. The presence of such an entity constitutes, in effect, the uniquely necessary and sufficient condition for something to be a commonwealth.[45]

As we have seen, civil philosophy of this kind is to be distinguished sharply from the study of history, "as well natural as political," in which knowledge "is but experience, or authority, and not ratiocination."[46] Again, such knowledge is prudential knowledge. It is based not an analysis of names like "a," "G" and "H," but on the observation of things like *a*, *G* and *H*. As such, it is by no means to be disparaged. Hobbes's own *Behemoth* is, in large part, an extended exercise in historical prudence; and considerations of experience and good judgment are to be found cheek by jowl with the most abstract passages of his political writings. But however important prudential knowledge might be, it is not to be confused with philosophical knowledge. Thus, again, whereas Hobbes's defense of monarchy is best understood as a conclusion of prudence

---

[42] *Leviathan, EW*, vol. 3, p. 675.
[43] Peters, *Hobbes*, p. 121.
[44] *De Corpore, EW*, vol. 1, pp. 73–75.
[45] *Ibid.*, pp. 65–66.
[46] *Ibid.*, pp. 10–11.

based on considerations of an historical nature, his account of the state is an exercise in philosophical analysis, an analysis of language and concepts resulting in an ontological theory of political society itself.

I do not think that it is possible to make sense of Hobbes's writings unless we see that his empiricism and his rejection of so-called dogmatic metaphysics in no way undermines, and is in fact integral to, his insistence on taking seriously claims that can only be called ontological or metaphysical. But to see Hobbes in this way is also to find in his work the glimmer of an idea that is, at once, astonishing in its simplicity and astounding in its reach. It is the idea that the truth of our propositions about the world around us is not entirely determined by the world but is also, in some sense, a function of the peculiar character of intellectual activity itself. In the end, thinking has standards of its own, and this means that the external world out there – at least insofar as *we* know it – must in part be accommodated to thought, and not simply vice versa. The distinction, elaborated by Locke, between propositions that are true by definition and those that are empirically true, is not quite apt, at least as usually understood. For Hobbes, ratiocination is far from being an airy, irrelevant exercise in pedantry. To the contrary, our understanding of *the world itself* is hostage to and shaped by our own form of thinking.

As we have seen, Hobbes believes that propositions are directly about names of ideas or conceptions, hence only indirectly about the world itself. But even more strongly, he believes as well that the truth of a proposition is determined in large part by the logical properties of names, hence is not simply reducible to its correspondence with observations. It is in this sense, for example, that certain "theorems of reason" can be regarded as true even though they cannot plausibly be thought of as simple reflections of empirical perceptions. Consider Hobbes's famous "laws of nature." Experience causes us to have certain ideas – regarding, say, human psychology – to which we have attached a variety of names. Those names, in turn, cause us to have other ideas, which is to say that they have implications on the basis of which we can arrive at deductions about how we should organize ourselves and that we can refer to as, among other things, natural laws. Such laws purport to describe a part of the world itself. They are natural indeed, and surely they are true, if they are true, in part because they are consistent with our experience of the world, especially our experience of human behavior and motivation. But this is hardly sufficient for us either to discover those laws or to accept them as valid. Principles of inference and deduction – ratiocination – must also come into play, and this means that the truth of natural law is, in part, a function not of the world but of reason itself.

3. Hobbes is, thus, far from being a crude or simple-minded empiricist. By viewing philosophy or science as one or two crucial steps removed from experience – by insisting that systematic thought is about names of things rather than things themselves – he sees that truth must be, at least to some extent, mind-dependent.

It is also the case, however, that he sees this only dimly, imperfectly. Indeed, his approach to truth, insofar as it can be inferred from what he says, begs as many questions as it answers. Among other things, if each of our ideas is, in the end, a reflection of sense perceptions, as Hobbes suggests, then it would appear that the truth of our deductions, which are nothing but complex ideas, must be simply and solely a matter of their correspondence with external reality. If an analysis of the names "a," "G" and "H" leads me to conclude that object a is characterized not only by property G but by property H as well, even if I don't immediately see it so, then it would seem that I am forced to believe that my conclusion corresponds to the facts of the real world and that, given sufficient instrumentation, I should be able to observe that a is indeed characterized by H. In other words, the truth of my proposition will appear not to be independent of but, to the contrary, precisely reducible to its correspondence with reality. It is hard to reconcile this conclusion with the notion that the truth of propositions, being about names of things rather than things themselves, is to some degree based on criteria inherent not in the world but in thought itself; and indeed, one wonders how the truth of, say, Hobbesian laws of nature could ever be empirically tested.

It is, I think, this kind of difficulty that led to the development of what might be called "strong empiricism." According to the strong empiricist, the content of human thinking is provided entirely by sense perception. Every one of our thoughts, without exception, is reducible to experience, hence no propositions about the world are true a priori. On the one hand, humans have "simple ideas" that are originally "deriv'd from simple impressions, which are correspondent to them, and which they exactly represent."[47] On the other hand, humans also have "complex ideas"; but these are nothing but "combination[s] of other ideas, themselves copies of simple impressions, where the method of combination is recorded in a conjunctive definition listing intrinsic features of the thing whose idea is being analyzed."[48] Such a formulation rejects altogether the claim that the truth of any proposition about the world could involve concepts whose origins are somehow independent of empirical experience, since

---

[47] David Hume, *A Treatise of Human Nature* (Oxford: Clarendon Press, 1989), p. 4.
[48] David Pears, *Hume's System: An Examination of the First Book of his "Treatise"* (Oxford: Oxford University Press, 1990), pp. 24–25.

there are literally no such concepts: "what we call a *mind*, is nothing but a heap or collection of different perceptions, united together by certain relations, and suppos'd, tho' falsely, to be endow'd with a perfect simplicity and identity."[49] This presumably entails the further claim that no analysis, theory or explanation purporting to account for experience (usually by relying, at least in part, on propositions about the world itself) can ever be rationally justified.

The argument in support of this latter claim is straightforward. Theories that purport to explain our experiences must involve at least some ideas that are themselves irreducible to those experiences, for otherwise the so-called explanations would not really be explanations at all; but since there are no such ideas, there can in fact be no explanations. It is true, of course, that we *seem* to have many theories that purport to explain experience, but the strong empiricist advises us not to take them too seriously. Exactly what this advice amounts to is, to be sure, not always clear. Strong empiricism might be a truly radical form of skepticism, one that denies the very possibility that theories about experience and the world could even be comprehended, much less proven. Alternatively, the empiricist might really be saying that such theories, though utterly lacking in any kind of rational or inferential justification, are nonetheless produced by "natural, primitive dispositions of the mind," and that these dispositions require us to believe in, among other things, the existence of material bodies and causal powers. Or again, the empiricist teaching might be two-fold, requiring a kind of epistemological skepticism – we cannot *know* anything about cause and effect – while nonetheless permitting a type of ontological naturalism according to which we can continue to maintain our ordinary *beliefs* about the external world.[50]

But no matter how we interpret it, the strong empiricist purports to solve the problems we have encountered in Hobbes by claiming that processes of rational inference and judgment independent of and supplementary to sense experience are just not features of human cognition. Unfortunately, such a claim seems to create more problems than it solves.

---

[49] Hume, *A Treatise of Human Nature*, p. 207.

[50] The skepticist interpretation, famously associated with Thomas Reid, is vigorously restated by Wayne Waxman, *Hume's Theory of Consciousness* (Cambridge: Cambridge University Press, 1994). The "naturalistic," as opposed to "skeptical," reading is attributable, of course, to the pathbreaking work of Norman Kemp Smith, *The Philosophy of David Hume* (London: Macmillan, 1941), for example at pp. 84ff.; this account is also strongly endorsed by Barry Stroud, *Hume* (London: Routledge and Kegan Paul, 1977), for example at pp. 68ff. For the epistemological–ontological distinction, see Galen Strawson, *The Secret Connexion: Causation, Realism, and David Hume* (Oxford: Oxford University Press, 1989).

From an empiricist perspective, for example, Hobbesian laws of nature could have no inferential justification whatsoever; and since it seems unlikely that such laws are the kinds of things that could be empirically experienced, it follows that they cannot be known to be true. If we are to believe in such laws, it can only be because we are naturally disposed to do so, i.e., our innate inclinations, in conjunction with empirical experience, establish "habits of association" on the basis of which we are likely to endorse, without possibility of rational justification, the kinds of conduct that natural law prescribes.[51] But this does not seem nearly sufficient to account for a great deal of human intellectual activity. For example, we certainly want to retain the distinction between acknowledging the laws of nature blindly and doing so because we have good reasons; and indeed, it seems easy enough to imagine ordinary circumstances in which we understand and accept the reality and authority of those laws – we know them to be true – *despite* a natural disposition to deny their validity.[52]

The empiricist position is problematic in other ways as well. For example, if all of our ideas are reducible to sense experience, then what could it mean even to discuss, much less criticize, ideas that are not so reducible? Consider the touchstone question of cause. The strong empiricist says that we can have no empirical experience, hence no knowledge, of causal power in the world. For us, cause can only be a matter of observing "constant conjunction" and, thus, the theory of causal power must necessarily be without foundation. One wonders, though, how we could communicate this claim unless we can somehow grasp, hence have, the concept of causal power itself. In other words, to argue that we can have no empirical experience of causal power in the world seems precisely to presuppose an understanding of that concept, for otherwise the argument would not be intelligible; and from this it follows that we must be able to possess and utilize an idea that is not reducible to sense perceptions – exactly what the empiricist appears to deny.

---

[51] On the question of the association of ideas, see Robert Paul Wolff, "Hume's Theory of Mental Activity," *Philosophical Review* 69 (July 1960), pp. 289–310. Wolff's account is a "naturalistic" one, explicitly in the tradition of Kemp Smith.

[52] It may appear that I am illicitly mixing questions of nature and questions of ethics. But in fact, the "naturalistic" reading of Hume explicitly denies any kind of sharp distinction between such questions. Hume is thought to have adopted a theory of aesthetic and moral judgment derived largely from Hutcheson, and to have generalized it by applying it, *mutatis mutandis*, to all empirical claims about the world, including scientific ones. See Norman Kemp Smith, "The Naturalism of Hume," *Mind* 14 (1905), pp. 151–52. It seems to me, further, that the particular type of case I have in mind here – rationally accepting the validity of natural law despite a natural disposition to do otherwise – is precisely that kind of thing that Kant sought to account for in his moral philosophy.

It is worth noting that such a case is sharply different from what might be called "squared circle" cases. There is no doubt that we can formulate intelligible sentences denying the possibility of squaring a circle. But what accounts for our ability to do so, given the fact that we have literally no concept of a "squared circle"? The answer might be something like this: because the idea of a "squared circle" is really no idea at all, when we purport to talk about the impossibility of squaring a circle we are not actually using any such concept but are rather saying, in effect, that "we cannot conceive of that which we cannot conceive." We do have the concept of a circle and the concept of squaring, and this enables us to utter the phrase "squared circle." But combining the two intelligible concepts in a particular way does not necessarily produce a new intelligible concept; and indeed, in the present case it produces gibberish. The question of causal power seems not to be like this at all. It would be bizarre to think that we don't have a notion of causal power, for we plainly do; and again, it seems that we can sensibly and justifiably acknowledge this fact even if we concede that cause is something of which we can have no direct empirical experience.

The more general point is that when empiricism denies the possibility of proving or even conceptualizing theories that purport to explain ordinary experience, the result seems to be a self-contradiction. The empiricist claims, typically, that ideas are nothing other than "faint reflections" of impressions that appear on the blank paper of the mind. But what could this be other than an attempt to account for ordinary experience? To talk of impressions and faint reflections is to offer an explanatory theory about the world and its relationship to human thought, a theory of cause and effect; and to offer such a theory is inevitably to presuppose an entire range of ideas and assumptions about how the world really is, including assumptions about "causal power," that would seem to defy direct empirical inspection. Indeed, the theory in question invokes a range of ideas – mind and reflection, to pick but two – the existence of which would directly violate its own strictures. In what sense could the notion of mind be best understood as the "reflection of an impression"? How could the idea of reflection itself be a faint copy of anything?

4. Such difficulties helped pave the way for a massive and decisive revolution in European thought during the latter part of the eighteenth century. That revolution emphasized precisely what empiricism had denied: we cannot account for experience, properly so conceived, unless we understand that some of our thoughts must have a foundation in something other than sense experience. If such experience were all there was to it, if our minds were indeed nothing but "a heap or collection of

different impressions," then humans would be little different from what we might imagine, say, amoebae or other lower orders to be – creatures of pure sensation, each undergoing a continuous regimen of raw feels, unconnected, unorganized and random. The feel of a pin prick *simpliciter* is nothing but a single, isolated event. It suggests, on its own account, no connection of sequence or location – indeed, no connection whatsoever – to any other such event in and of itself, it implies nothing about space and time, cause and effect, or any other relational category; and an infinite number of pin pricks would, in and of themselves, be nothing more than an infinite number of discrete individual occurrences. A raw feel, in its purity, provides no information whatsoever beyond itself; and presumably, this suggests why it is that the lowest orders, at least as we imagine them to be, have no sense of space, time or cause, but only a chaotic and literally mindless existence. If we are to take the idea of mind seriously, on the other hand, we must presuppose, in addition to immediate perceptions, a faculty of cognition that imposes upon those perceptions a kind of structure such that they cease to be mere raw feels and become, instead, *experiences* properly so-called. Individual pin pricks can emerge as a *sequence* of pin pricks only if the mind itself has the capacity to order and arrange them according to some kind of intelligible scheme.

From such a perspective, truth is deeply dependent on features not only of the world but of intellectual activity itself: mind makes an independent and indispensable contribution. This general proposition has had, of course, a complex and difficult career. In its original formulation, it involved an effort to describe universal features of human cognition – faculties of discrimination and analysis shared by all rational creatures and absolutely required in order to account for even the most rudimentary experience of the world. Subsequent formulations, however, insisted that cognition must itself have a history. Our intellectual faculties, although in some important sense independent of the external world, are not static and unchanging. Rather, they develop and mature on their own account and according to a kind of internal logic; and as a result, the nature of human thought may vary quite dramatically, depending upon its level of development and maturity. Still other formulations have agreed that modes of cognition may differ substantially from one to another, but have denied that such differences reflect any kind of underlying developmental process. Distinct modes or manners of thought are merely manifestations of deep-seated cultural differences, themselves of uncertain origin; and such cultural differences, although quite common-place, are also thought to present fundamental and vexing problems of interpretation and understanding.

These various positions are deeply at odds with one another. And yet they are also profoundly similar in at least this respect, that they share a broad view of human cognition – a view that accords a certain priority to subject rather than object, mind rather than matter, thought rather than thing. They compose what might be called a post-Kantian convergence of otherwise widely disparate philosophical perspectives. Such a convergence situates the individual human being firmly within communities of interpretation reflecting a range of factors: cultural, social-psychological and linguistic. In doing so, it gives rise to a particular conception of human agency, wherein the very capacity for systematic thinking – thinking about how things in the world really are – is in some sense constitutive of action itself. This is, in effect, a species of holism; and from such a perspective, metaphysical speculation is not simply possible but, in fact, an unavoidable and fundamental feature of intelligent and intelligible activity.

The idea of a post-Kantian convergence is taken up systematically in Chapter 3, which examines, respectively, the idea of ontological or metaphysical analysis *per se* and the implications of that idea for our understanding of social action and social institutions. Before moving on to such matters, however, we need to consider in some detail a potentially powerful challenge to my earlier foundational claim that prudential theories must always be profoundly dependent on philosophical ones.

4. The impossibility of a "political" conception

To propose a philosophy of the state is to propose an ontological theory about what the state really is, one which itself reflects a broader view of the truth of things; and to propose a prudential theory about what states should do or how they should do it, a theory of policy or government, is necessarily to presuppose, if only tacitly, just such an ontological foundation. These propositions, absolutely central to my account of the state, would seem to be directly and massively refuted by the most influential political theory of the day – liberal theory – which claims to be "political, not metaphysical," hence to be substantially free of ontological commitments. If the claims of liberal theory are correct, then plainly my account of the state will be seriously compromised.

1. According to its principal theoretician, contemporary liberalism is based on a "freestanding" conception of justice. Some such conception is required if we are to formulate principles suited to the peculiar realities of contemporary politics. Modern societies are composed of groups and individuals holding diverse philosophical or moral views representing a

plurality of more or less explicit and mutually inconsistent "comprehensive doctrines." Because differences among such doctrines are apt to be quite serious, any conception of justice presented in terms of one doctrine will likely be regarded with deep suspicion by individuals committed to another. As a practical matter, then, comprehensive doctrines "no longer can, if they ever could, serve as the professed basis of society."[53]

Justice as fairness is understood to be freestanding in that it is to be presented apart from any specific comprehensive doctrine. It is a conception of justice that may be shared on the basis of "a reasoned, informed, and willing political agreement ... independent of the opposing and conflicting philosophical and religious doctrines that citizens affirm."[54] This is what Rawls means when he says that justice as fairness is "political not metaphysical." The serious moral and philosophical differences that divide the citizens of a complex modern society are held in abeyance while those same citizens accomplish the practical task of agreeing to a framework of institutions and principles for a well-ordered society. This practical task, however, aims not to establish a mere modus vivendi based on a balance of particular interests. It seeks to formulate, rather, a shared understanding about right and wrong, an understanding that in some sense claims to be objective.

Rawls has been criticized largely on the grounds that a freestanding, non-metaphysical conception is unable to provide an adequate justification for political principles. Something more is required if such principles are to be recognized as valid.[55] Such a criticism does reflect, I think, a very serious problem in Rawls's theory. But as stated, it misses the point. For the real problem is not so much the inadequacy of a freestanding conception as its literal impossibility. Rawls fails – and cannot help but fail – to construct a "political" theory along the lines that he proposes. To ask, then, if political philosophy should be done without metaphysics is to overlook the sense in which political claims *unavoidably* presuppose serious ontological or metaphysical commitments of one kind or another.

[53] John Rawls, *Political Liberalism* (New York: Columbia University Press, 1993), p. 10.
[54] *Ibid.*, p. 9.
[55] For example, Jean Hampton, "Should Political Philosophy Be Done Without Metaphysics?" *Ethics* 99 (1989), pp. 791–814; Joseph Raz, "Facing Diversity: The Case of Epistemic Abstinence," *Philosophy and Public Affairs* 19 (Winter 1990); Jean Hampton, "The Common Faith of Liberalism," *Pacific Philosophical Quarterly* 75 (September/ December 1994); Bruce W. Brower, "The Limits of Public Reason," *Journal of Philosophy* 91 (January 1994), pp. 5–26; and Jürgen Habermas, "Reconciliation through the Public Use of Reason: Remarks on John Rawls's Political Liberalism," *Journal of Philosophy* 92 (March 1995), pp. 109–31.

According to Rawls, "there is no accepted understanding of what a metaphysical doctrine is."[56] He appears rather little troubled by this, since he himself offers no explicit account of the meaning of metaphysics. It does seem, though, that he believes at least this, that a metaphysical claim, whatever else it may be, is in the end a claim about how things really are, a claim about what is true of the world. Such a view is plainly consistent with everything that I have said thus far, as far as it goes; but Rawls offers what seems to me a useful, if only implicit, elaboration. Specifically, he often speaks of metaphysical *and moral* claims in the same breath – especially when referring to the kinds of claims of which comprehensive doctrines are composed and which, as such, are different from political claims. This seems confusing at first, since he certainly understands political claims as well to be, in some sense, moral claims. Evidently, then, he wants to distinguish two kinds of moral claims: those that are political, of the sort that he proposes in *Political Liberalism*, and those that purport to describe some true (moral) fact about the world out there, perhaps in the way that Aristotle or Augustine or Hegel thought such facts to exist. Stated otherwise, political claims are not truth claims about the world, moral or otherwise, hence are different from all metaphysical theories, including metaphysical theories that purport to describe true moral facts.

Rawls insists that a political conception is, by definition, not only different from but *independent of* metaphysical doctrine. This raises some additional and rather more difficult problems, however. For he acknowledges more than once that a political conception will be independent of metaphysical doctrine only "so far as possible,"[57] thereby explicitly leaving open the possibility that any such conception will have at least *some* connection with claims about how things really are; and as we shall see shortly, Rawls's treatment of those kinds of connections is deeply ambivalent, sometimes giving them pride of place, other times denying them altogether. He suggests, further, that "if metaphysical presuppositions are involved, perhaps they are so general that they would not distinguish among the metaphysical views – Cartesian, Leibnizian, or Kantian; realist, idealist, or materialist – with which philosophy has traditionally been concerned."[58] But this is a red-herring, for while it is certainly true that metaphysical philosophy standardly focuses on questions involving the most basic categories of being (e.g., substance and

---

[56] Rawls, *Political Liberalism*, p. 29. See Hampton, "Should Political Philosophy Be Done Without Metaphysics?" p. 794.
[57] *Ibid.*, pp. 9, 13, 144.
[58] *Ibid.*, p. 29 n.

accident, quality and concept, freedom and determinism), to show that a particular theory of politics is indifferent to such questions is a far cry from claiming that it is, or could ever be, a purely practical notion based on a set of working agreements that do not speak at all to issues of an ontological or metaphysical nature. Perhaps a political conception need not deal directly with arguments in *metaphysica generalis*; but this is not to say that it could ever be truly freestanding with respect to one or another kind of *metaphysica specialis*.[59] And even if we were to agree that a political conception should be non-metaphysical "so far as possible," the crucial task is to determine just how far that is.

It seems that Rawls wants to say something like this: a political conception is non-metaphysical insofar as it is the result not of some generalized theoretical conclusion regarding the underlying nature of justice and politics but of a practical accommodation.[60] Again, such an accommodation should be understood as describing not a mere modus vivendi among self-interested parties. It is a moral conception of some kind. Nonetheless, its criterion of validity is agreement rather than truth.[61] It is justified to the degree that all citizens might "reasonably be expected" to endorse it without thereby endorsing any particular moral or metaphysical truth claim, of the sort that we typically find in comprehensive doctrines.[62]

All of this may seem clear enough, but in fact it is consistent with at least two contradictory positions, both of which Rawls appears at different times to defend:

(a) On the one hand, he says that a political conception is "the focus of an overlapping consensus of reasonable comprehensive doctrines,"[63] and this implies that it describes an area of theoretical truth that otherwise discrepant doctrines share. Thus, for example, an atheistic/hedonistic materialist and a Christian/ascetic mystic, however violently opposed they might be to one another, may nonetheless agree on a political conception involving principles that are consistent with each of their larger world-views. Both the materialist and the mystic would endorse that

---

[59] D.W. Hamlyn, *Metaphysics* (Cambridge: Cambridge University Press, 1984), p. 2.

[60] Rawls describes a political conception in terms of three features: it concerns only the basic structure, it is presented independently of comprehensive doctrines, and it reflects the particular ideas of a democratic political culture (*Political Liberalism*, p. 223). I think that the first and third of these are ultimately reducible to the second. For a discussion, see Stephen Mulhall and Adam Swift, *Liberals and Communitarians* (Oxford: Blackwell, 1996), pp. 171–75. The important issue of how a political conception is "presented," as opposed to what it really is, will be discussed below.

[61] Rawls, *Political Liberalism*, pp. 94–97, 126–29.

[62] *Ibid.*, p. 137.

[63] *Ibid.*, p. 44.

conception; but they would do so for different reasons, reflecting their different and incompatible comprehensive doctrines. Rawls is quite specific about this:

All those who affirm the political conception start from within their own comprehensive view and draw on the religious, philosophical, and moral grounds it provides. The fact that people affirm the same political conception on those grounds does not make their affirming it any less religious, philosophical, or moral, as the case may be, since the grounds sincerely held determine the nature of their affirmation.[64]

He thus seems to be defending what we might call *justificatory liberalism*. Such a liberalism would be similar to all non-liberal systems in that political outcomes are to be fully justified with reference to comprehensive doctrines. Specifically, all citizens "affirm a comprehensive doctrine to which the political conception they accept is in some way related."[65] But because of the complex and pluralistic nature of modern societies, *justificatory liberalism* would allow, indeed would require, that justifications themselves vary dramatically from citizen to citizen, depending upon the particular doctrine to which each is committed. Obviously, the resulting political arrangement could not be said to represent any one comprehensive doctrine; and this, presumably, is an important part of what makes *justificatory liberalism* liberal.

(b) Rawls appears to undermine this, however, when he says that "we do not look to the comprehensive doctrines that in fact exist and then draw up a political conception that strikes some kind of balance of forces between them.... We leave aside comprehensive doctrines that now exist, or that have existed, or that might exist."[66] Here he seems to be saying that a political conception should be separate from comprehensive doctrines altogether, hence should involve no truth claims whatsoever. In doing so, he is thus proposing what might be called *pure liberalism*, according to which political outcomes are to be justified independently of any and all moral or metaphysical theories.

Surely Rawls cannot have it both ways. Either a political conception functions as a kind of least-common-denominator embodying some set of theoretical claims common to all relevant (i.e., reasonable) doctrines; or else it is utterly unconnected in any important way with any such claim.

[64] *Ibid.*, pp. 147–48.
[65] *Ibid.*, p. 12; the point is reiterated at p. 126.
[66] *Ibid.*, pp. 39–40.

2. It will be useful, I think, to reformulate these distinctions in schematic terms. For Rawls, all varieties of *non-liberalism* (*NL*) look something like the following:

$$(1) \quad P_1 \quad > \quad P_2 \quad > \quad P_3 \quad > \quad CP$$

NL

$$(2) \quad P_1 \quad > \quad P_2 \quad > \quad P_3 \quad > \quad CP$$

where (1) and (2) are individual citizens; P1, P2 and P3 are metaphysical principles that compose a comprehensive doctrine; CP is a conception about politics (e.g., justice as fairness), though not necessarily a "political" conception in Rawls's sense; and > describes an inferential or theoretical connection of some kind. In *NL*, then, CP is justified on the basis of P1, P2 and P3, hence is not at all freestanding; and this means that (1) and (2) are in political agreement because they hold the same comprehensive doctrine.

Against this we have, on the one hand, *justificatory liberalism* (*JL*):

$$(1) \quad P_1 \quad > \quad P_2 \quad > \quad P_3 \quad > \quad CP$$

JL

$$(2) \quad P_4 \quad > \quad P_5 \quad > \quad P_6 \quad > \quad CP$$

Here, (1) and (2) are committed to very different principles (P1, P2 and P3 in the one case, P4, P5 and P6 in the other), and this means that they accept CP for very different reasons. In other words, they agree about CP not because of any agreement in comprehensive doctrines but because CP represents an overlapping consensus, something that is consistent with their otherwise discrepant views. Thus, while CP is justified for both (1) and (2) on the basis of metaphysical principles, it is not tied to, hence cannot be said to represent, any *particular* comprehensive doctrine.

We also have *pure liberalism* (*PL*):

$$(1) \quad P_1 \quad > \quad P_2 \quad > \quad P_3 \quad \mathbf{V} \quad CP$$

PL

$$(2) \quad P_4 \quad > \quad P_5 \quad > \quad P_6 \quad \mathbf{V} \quad CP$$

where **V** denotes the *absence* of any inferential connection at all. In this model, comprehensive doctrines are entirely irrelevant. (1) and (2) each endorses CP for reasons that have nothing to do with metaphysical principles, and this means that their agreement is purely political.

Again, I believe that Rawls's text is unclear as to whether he is advocating *JL* or *PL*. But perhaps he could advocate both without contradiction. For he does place great emphasis on the idea that political conceptions are only to be "presented" or "expounded" or "professed" independently of comprehensive doctrines;[67] and this might suggest a difference between the actual justification of such conceptions and the ways in which they are advertised. In effect, *JL* perhaps reflects the underlying reality, *PL* the outward face, of liberalism. This would seem to save Rawls's larger project of finding the basis for a freestanding conception; for even if individual decisions are rooted in doctrinal considerations, political outcomes nonetheless reflect no such considerations since they have been packaged – and presumably discussed – in purely "political" terms.

But such an argument, while focusing the issue considerably, fails to clear it up. Exegetically, I doubt that Rawls says nearly enough to indicate that this is what he really has in mind; the apparent inconsistencies that I have outlined above largely remain unacknowledged, hence unaddressed. Theoretically, and more importantly, the argument itself depends upon the claim that *JL* and *PL* are functionally equivalent, at least to the extent that the former can honestly be "presented" in terms of the latter. If *PL* is not to be a lie, then we must be able to show how a political conception could be truly "political" despite the fact that it reflects, in various ways, the moral and metaphysical commitments of individual decision-makers. More generally: is it possible, in either *JL* or *PL*, to conceive of a political arrangement the justification of which is sufficiently "political" that we might plausibly think of it as, indeed, freestanding? I believe that it is not.

3. Most characteristically, Rawls refers to his own political conception – justice as fairness – as a kind of "module," i.e., something that "fits into and can be supported by" the various reasonable comprehensive doctrines of which a political culture is composed, doctrines that may well have nothing else in common.[68] Such a module "can be presented without saying, or knowing, or hazarding a conjecture about, what [comprehensive] doctrines it may belong to, or be supported by."[69]

---

[67] *Ibid.*, p. 12.
[68] *Ibid.*
[69] *Ibid.*, pp. 12–13.

This is a crucial claim upon which a great deal of Rawlsian theory rests, but for a variety of reasons it strikes me as insupportable.

It is easy enough to make sense of the idea of a module that could be shared by various and otherwise incompatible comprehensive doctrines. Think of a jigsaw piece that happens to fit into a variety of puzzles. We can imagine, say, a blue shape of some description that could function equally well as part of the sea in one puzzle depicting a nautical scene, the sky in another depicting a landscape, a soldier's uniform in a third depicting a battle scene from the Civil War, and so on. A political conception could function in roughly this way with respect to diverse doctrines, such that an atheistic/hedonistic materialist and a Christian/ascetic mystic could accept the same conception, hence share membership in the same political community, despite the fact that their reasons for doing so might be sharply different. Moreover, just as knowing only that the puzzle piece is blue and of a certain size and shape is not necessarily to know what the different puzzles themselves depict, so too understanding the details of a political conception is not necessarily to understand everything important about the various comprehensive doctrines into which it fits.

But, *pace* Rawls, it is to know at least some very important things about those doctrines. To begin with, it is to know that each of them will necessarily be so constituted as to accommodate the particular module in question. In other words, there will be no contradiction between the module and any of the other values or principles of which the doctrine is composed, at least not to such an extent as to make it unacceptable. This may seem to be a minimal criterion, but it is not easily met and its implications are substantial. For as indicated above, the module doesn't simply fit into but is "supported by" the relevant doctrine. Indeed, Rawls concedes that "we want a political conception to have a justification by reference to one or more comprehensive doctrines."[70] He acknowledges, then, that the relationship between module and doctrine is theoretical, as in *JL* above. The doctrine's larger claims, such as they may be, provide the intellectual underpinnings of the module, at least as it functions within the particular doctrine; and since some of those larger claims will inevitably be moral or metaphysical in nature, anyone who holds a political conception necessarily does so for moral or metaphysical reasons. In this sense, no political conception could be entirely innocent of metaphysical theory.

Again, Rawls argues that since the very same conception can be justified from many different comprehensive perspectives, hence for many

[70] *Ibid.*, p. 12.

different moral and metaphysical reasons, its status as the object of society's overlapping consensus makes it independent of any one such perspective. This seems plausible enough. But it also seems to ignore or underestimate the sense in which these various comprehensive doctrines must share a great deal. Specifically, each must be so constituted as to justify the political conception in question. However different they might be in other respects, they must be alike in being composed of principles – metaphysical principles – that are consistent with and that entail the module. Schematically, in

$$(1) \quad P_1 \quad > \quad P_2 \quad > \quad P_3 \quad > \quad CP$$

JL

$$(2) \quad P_4 \quad > \quad P_5 \quad > \quad P_6 \quad > \quad CP$$

P3 and P6 may be importantly different from one another, but they must also be similar at least to the extent that each is inferentially connected to, or actually entails, CP; and this, in turn, has implications for P1 and P4 and for P2 and P5. In other words, (1) and (2) hold doctrines that, however different, must nonetheless be thought to compose, in effect, a family of doctrines sharing a range of basic theoretical commitments, commitments sufficiently similar as to imply justice as fairness.

But just how closely knit is such a family likely to be? Consider the instant case, Rawls's political conception of justice. Justice as fairness is, of course, composed mainly of two principles, the principle of equal liberty and the difference principle. Together they constitute a proposal for the basic structure of society, one that is to be agreed to by an over-lapping consensus of individuals holding a potentially wide variety of comprehensive doctrines. Presumably, different people would endorse justice as fairness for different reasons, depending on the doctrines that they hold. Like any module, it could fit into a range of schemes involving a range of specific metaphysical theories.

It is nonetheless hard to imagine that anyone could endorse such a conception without at least holding to a particular *kind* of metaphysical theory. The difference principle, in particular, is clearly designed to controvert and override any distribution of material and cultural assets that arises more or less spontaneously, i.e., prior to the establishment of justice as fairness. But why would anyone wish to override such a distribution unless one believes it to be, in and of itself, inappropriate as a foundation for social justice? And why would anyone believe that, unless one had a theory about how the world really is, a moral or metaphysical account about the origins and/or nature of material and cultural assets that would account for such a belief?

In Rawls's own case, the argument for the difference principle involves what might be called a theory of metaphysical luck. This theory holds that many if not most of our personal and social characteristics are products of a "natural and social lottery." Our physical attributes, intellectual abilities and even character traits such as perseverance and diligence, are best understood as "contingent" or "accidental" factors for which we deserve neither praise nor blame.[71] To this claim about the nature of human beings Rawls adds a moral one: no theory of justice can be derived from, or unduly influenced by, contingent or accidental factors. Mere luck is insufficient to provide moral legitimacy. From this he concludes that the natural and social lottery can be neither just nor unjust. It is outside the realm of justice. And this means that if we wish to develop principles of justice, we must do so in a way that is "removed from and not distorted by the particular features and circumstances of the all-encompassing background framework."[72] We must bracket out the effects of the lottery and decide on some other basis. Of course, such bracketing is accomplished by the veil of ignorance, with the result that principles generated from behind the veil will be, *ceteris paribus*, fair and just.

Now it may be that theories other than the theory of metaphysical luck could justify equally well the difference principle. But any such theory would have to explain, as the theory of metaphysical luck explains, exactly why the natural and social lottery is not an appropriate foundation for justice. And any theory that did so would share with Rawls's theory a fundamentally similar understanding of the nature of our various inherited traits.

This fact becomes clear, I think, if we consider what seems to me undeniable, namely, that a great many comprehensive doctrines could *not* embrace a theory of this kind. For example, orthodox Calvinism attributes our various personal traits and dispositions not to blind luck, nor to anything like it, but to a divine source – itself associated with a principle of "election" – such that social and political institutions should not merely acknowledge but be fundamentally based upon the

[71] *Ibid.* On the connection between Rawls's account of human nature and the veil of ignorance, see Peter J. Steinberger, "Desert and Justice in Rawls," *Journal of Politics* 44 (November 1982), pp. 983–95, and Peter J. Steinberger, "A Fallacy in Rawls's Theory of Justice," *Review of Politics* 51 (Winter 1989), pp. 55–69.

[72] *Political Liberalism*, p. 23; reiterated at p. 79. Cf. John Rawls, *A Theory of Justice* (Cambridge: Harvard University Press, 1971), pp. 101–7.

82   The Idea of the State

distribution of those traits and dispositions.[73] In view of this, a strict Calvinist would have great difficulty appreciating the virtue of the veil of ignorance or of any functionally equivalent scheme, hence would have great difficulty accepting the justice of the difference principle; and this means, I think, that justice as fairness could not function very well as a modular part of Calvinist doctrine. Much the same could be said for a host of other comprehensive doctrines, including many if not most of the world's great religions, strictly interpreted. Such doctrines would fail to see the moral and political irrelevance of the natural and social lottery – often by denying that it is a lottery at all – hence could not accept the underpinnings of justice as fairness; and this in itself suggests that justice as fairness can hardly be freestanding.

4. But couldn't a Calvinist decide that justice as fairness, though perhaps incompatible with fundamental Calvinist ideas, is nonetheless a useful basis for political agreement, hence something that could be adopted on other than religious grounds? Perhaps Rawls has something like this in mind – a complex, pluralistic society composed of Calvinists, Muslims, atheistic/hedonistic materialists, Christian/ascetic mystics, and the like, all of whom have either (a) reinterpreted or adjusted their strictly doc-trinal views or else (b) have placed those views in partial abeyance so as to establish reasonable foundations upon which to build a well-ordered society. In this way, a diversity of citizens could adopt justice as fairness without giving up their sharply divergent views about the world.

Things are not so simple, however. If, for example, a pragmatic Calvinist were to adjust (his or her view of) Calvinist doctrine so as to accommodate justice as fairness, then such a doctrine would in some sense no longer be the doctrine that it was. It would have become some-thing quite different: *a different view of the world*. Instead of holding simply to the principle of election, our Calvinist would now hold to that principle only with respect to certain issues or circumstances and not others. Formerly it was thought that wealthy people were entitled to their wealth,

---

[73] It is doubtful that this was Calvin's own view. He certainly held that salvation is predestined. But the notion that all or most of our traits, including and especially our material and social conditions, reflect more-or-less directly the will of God is probably best attributed to a number of Calvin's most influential followers, some of whom attained prominence in seventeenth-century England and America. See William J. Bouwsma, *John Calvin: A Sixteenth-Century Portrait* (Oxford: Oxford University Press, 1988), pp. 171–74, 196. For an excellent discussion of the sociological and theological functions of the doctrine of predestination in "orthodox" Calvinism, see Alister E. McGrath, *A Life of John Calvin: A Study in the Shaping of Western Culture* (Oxford: Basil Blackwell, 1990), pp. 208–18, 237–45.

since it is God-given. But now the view is that wealthy people are entitled to their wealth *unless* and *until* civil authorities, under the influence of the difference principle and with a view towards establishing a stable and orderly society, decide otherwise. This would in fact constitute a deep and fundamental change involving, among other things, a moral decision to give a certain priority to political as opposed to religious consider-ations.[74] Such a decision clearly would be doctrinal in nature and would, indeed, speak to very basic questions of Calvinist moral theory. It would establish a new ethical rule for Calvinists: where the theory of election and the difference principle come into conflict, considerations of stability and order require that the latter trump the former. Such a change should not be underestimated. For the result might be to elevate human will above God's, placing earthly comforts before divine rewards, the secular before the sacred, thereby turning Calvinist cosmology on its head and creating, in effect, a radically new doctrine, one that Calvin himself would not have recognized as his own. Instead of Calvinism we would have modified Calvinism; and presumably such a Calvinism, unlike the original, would share a fundamental moral and metaphysical point of view with any religious doctrine that emphasized the value of political stability over other doctrinal considerations.

I think the implication is that the "reasonable" comprehensive doc-trines of which a Rawlsian state is composed, however different they may be, will necessarily be fundamentally alike *as doctrines*. Each will be composed, in part, of metaphysical and moral principles that either (a) are functionally equivalent to the Rawlsian theory of metaphysical and moral luck or (b) deny any such theory but nonetheless permit, *as a doctrinal matter*, the value of reciprocity and political stability to outweigh other important values. Comprehensive doctrines that do not share one or another of these principles would presumably be ruled out as "unreasonable."

5. The reasonable and the rational

A Rawlsian might respond by seeking to formulate the issue in rather different terms. Perhaps modified Calvinism would indeed be different from orthodox Calvinism, and perhaps the latter would not comport very well with justice as fairness. But modified Calvinism would remain an identifiable form of Calvinism nonetheless. Its compromises would be minimal and, in the end, not really doctrinal. They would not require any

---

[74] Rawls, *Political Liberalism*, pp. 139–40.

disavowal of Jesus Christ, the authority of scripture, the principle of election, and so on. They would merely append to basic Calvinist principles an inclination to get along with people of other faiths. Modified Calvinism would indeed be a "reasonable" comprehensive doctrine. This means, specifically, that its followers would tend to be cooperative people, willing and eager to engage in peaceful, reciprocal relations with individuals whose religious, moral and metaphysical views might be very different from their own.[75] As a political matter, such people would be strongly inclined to accept principles pertaining to the basic structure of society that would allow for precisely this kind of cooperation to occur, for example, Rawlsian principles of justice. The result would be that Calvinists *qua* Calvinists could pursue Calvinist life-plans in peace and prosperity; and so too with Muslims, atheistic/hedonistic materialists, Christian/ascetic mystics, and the like.

To the degree that justice as fairness, or any political conception, speaks to this kind of cooperative inclination, it is freestanding. For while it reflects the *reasonableness* of political arrangements, it does not represent in any appreciable way the *rationality* of truth claims. Rawls is quite explicit about this. A political conception

specifies an idea of the reasonable and applies this idea to various subjects: conceptions and principles, judgments and grounds, persons and institutions. In each case, it must, of course, also specify criteria to judge whether the subject in question is reasonable. It does not, however, as rational intuitionism does, use (or deny) the concept of truth; nor does it question that concept, nor could it say that the concept of truth and its idea of the reasonable are the same. Rather, within itself the political conception does without the concept of truth.[76]

In other words, a political conception does not presuppose or entail any kind of systematic, theoretical understanding about the nature of things themselves, of the sort that is characteristic of comprehensive doctrines. Its justification is a matter not of rational truth but of reasonable consensus.

Now it should already be clear that, in my view, such an argument necessarily minimizes the sense in which a decision to adjust basic

---

[75] *Ibid.*, pp. 50–51. Wenar has demonstrated the multiple and, often, inconsistent ways in which Rawls uses the term "reasonable." He concludes, accurately I think, that "'reasonable person'...is to be the concept that grounds the meanings of all of Rawls's other 'reasonable' terms." Leif Wenar, *"Political Liberalism*: An Internal Critique," *Ethics* 106 (October 1995), p. 36. As to the concept of a reasonable person, Wenar notes that it involves several factors beyond a simple willingness to be cooperative. But it seems to me that all of those factors – including the "reasonable moral psychology" outlined on pp. 81–86 of *Political Liberalism* – either underwrite or are derived from such a willingness.
[76] *Political Liberalism*, p. 94.

principles, or to place them in partial abeyance, constitutes a doctrinal change. The difference between modified Calvinism and orthodox Calvinism is quite fundamental, and this means that any political conception that presupposes the former rather than the latter cannot be simply freestanding. But I think that the specific argument about the reasonable and the rational is also mistaken, and that its errors show even more clearly the degree to which any theory of justice or the state must ultimately be a theory about truth, a metaphysical theory.

1. Following Sibley, Rawls insists that the distinction between the reasonable and the rational is amply reflected in our ordinary language. Sibley claims that while in nonmoral situations "reasonable" generally means the same thing as "rational," in moral situations this is not so.[77] If *A* cheats *B* out of some money by violating an agreement that they had made, our inclination is to say that *A*'s action was "unreasonable." But assuming that *A* correctly understood that he could get away with it, we would not generally say that it was an "irrational" thing to do, certainly not in the sense of being "foolish, absurd or unintelligent." Although *A* acted selfishly, he did so rationally, with sufficient care and accuracy to ensure that his desires would be satisfied.

Sibley concludes that "rationality" refers to (a) the intelligent selection of ends, (b) the intelligent selection of means to achieve those ends, and (c) the capacity to act in accordance with those selections. "Reasonableness" is quite different. It involves primarily an inclination or willingness "to see the matter – as we commonly put it – from the other person's point of view, to discover how each will be affected by the possible alternative actions; and, moreover, not merely to 'see' this ... but also to be prepared to be disinterestedly *influenced*, in reaching a decision, by the estimate of these possible results."[78] Rawls endorses this analysis, and concludes that the reasonable and the rational, though "complementary," are nonetheless sharply distinct from one another.[79]

But the analysis, understood to begin with as an argument about ordinary language, strikes me as wrong. It is true that when we say someone acted unreasonably, we are often implying that this involved a failure to take into account the other person. In doing so, however, we are

---

[77] W. M. Sibley, "The Rational versus the Reasonable," *Philosophical Review* 62 (October 1963), pp. 554–60. See also, V. Held, "Rationality and Reasonable Cooperation," *Social Research* 44 (1977), pp. 708–44. My own argument is consistent with, but nonetheless very different from, that of Alan Gewirth, "The Rationality of Reasonableness," *Synthese* 57 (1983), pp. 225–47.

[78] Sibley, "The Rational versus the Reasonable," p. 557.

[79] Rawls, *Political Liberalism*, p. 49 n.

really saying, I think, that such a failure can be best formulated as a failure to act on the basis of reasons. In this case, literal meaning strongly informs "implicated" meaning. A's iniquitous act in cheating B was "unreasonable" because it was undertaken *without reasons* or, more accurately, because it was insufficiently informed by *certain kinds* of reasons. Of course, it was informed by *some* reasons pertaining, presumably, to A's own selfish interests; and indeed, if someone were to ask "In the context of his *selfish* interests, did he act reasonably in cheating B?" we would surely say that he did.[80] Thus, the claim that his act was unreasonable really means that it was lacking in the kinds of reasons appropriate to the moral nature of the situation; and this means, further, that its unreasonableness reflects not primarily A's failure to take into account B's interests but, rather, his failure to act on the basis of a plausible moral theory.

The difference may seem trivial, since moral reasons generally involve a willingness to take into account the other person's interests; but I think that it is not trivial at all. For by recognizing the centrality of reasons, we can see that reasonableness is bound up with a way of thinking that involves analysis, argument, justification and, ultimately, rationality. The connection is not difficult to trace. In moral situations, a reasonable person acts, at least in part, on the basis of moral reasons. But not just anything will count as such a reason. For a reason to be truly a reason, it must *make sense*; it must be explicable in such a way that the actions that it underwrites can be *shown* to be justified, at least hypothetically.[81] This doesn't mean that everyone who acts reasonably necessarily acts on the basis of a correct and proven moral theory; for while we believe that at least some people are reasonable at least some of the time, we might also consistently believe that there is no such thing as a correct and proven moral theory. But it does mean that reasonable actions are based on what could plausibly be thought of as such a theory – which is another way of saying that the action is explicitly or implicitly informed by reasons that are intelligible, at least when viewed in the light of some general conception of right and wrong. And to say this, I would suggest, is to say that the action is rational; for what could it mean to claim that a reason is intelligible or makes sense other than that one can somehow see – and, in principle, argue for the proposition – that it is logically connected to a moral theory that has, at the least, some plausibility and currency?

---

[80] Sibley would agree; for again, in non-moral contexts he sees no distinction between the reasonable and the rational.

[81] Understanding "reason" here not in the sense of material cause ("the reason he did that is that he was psychotic") but in the sense of justification ("let me explain my reasons for doing what I did").

Thus, when we say that someone in a moral situation acted in a reasonable manner, we are suggesting that there is, potentially, a line of argumentation involving logical connections between the action itself, a set of reasons, and a moral theory of some kind that claims to be true, connections that could be rationally reconstructed and that have in some way underwritten the action itself. Of course, the actor need not be explicitly aware of those connections; but presumably they could be rendered explicit if one so desired and if the circumstances were right. Conversely, when we say that A acted unreasonably in cheating B, we are indicating that somewhere along the line this chain of rational connectedness has been broken. The reasons do not make sense, or the theory upon which they are based is incoherent. Understood in this way, the reasonable and the rational are inseparable and perhaps indistinguishable.

2. But even if reasonable does imply rational, isn't Sibley nonetheless correct in saying that rational does not always imply reasonable? Again, A's selfish action certainly doesn't appear to be irrational in the sense of being foolish, absurd or unintelligent. Here, however, it seems that Sibley has simply chosen to focus on only one sense of rationality. As indicated above, he claims that the rational refers to (a) the intelligent selection of ends, (b) the intelligent selection of means and (c) the capacity to act in accordance with those selections. But all of these construe rationality *per se* as being equivalent to instrumental rationality, i.e., simply and solely a matter of means-to-end reasoning. While this is clearly true of (b) and (c), it is in fact equally true of (a). Sibley denies this. He understands the rational selection of ends to be a matter of picking "that end which I really prefer."[82] Further, he conceives of all such preferences as utterly beyond, or beneath, rhyme or reason. He says, for example, that in selecting ends it would be rational for me to discover whether or not my preferences are "egoistic" or "altruistic" and to choose my ends accordingly; but he also insists that those preferences themselves could be "neither rational nor irrational." To choose an "end," therefore, is simply to choose something that will be useful in serving a non-rational disposition of some sort; and to do this effectively is to be rational, no matter how bizarre the disposition is. He claims that "[i]t is not in the least irrational of me to thrust my arm into the fire – if my aim is to cripple or destroy myself."[83]

---

[82] Sibley, "The Rational versus the Reasonable," p. 555.
[83] *Ibid.*, p. 556.

Now this hardly seems plausible. Our natural inclination would be to call irrational someone whose aim is to cripple or destroy him- or herself, unless and until we had heard some elaborate story as to why, despite appearances, pursuing such a goal might actually make sense. But the more important point for our purposes is that Rawls implicitly accepts Sibley's reduction of "rationality" to mere instrumental rationality. In so doing, he commits a certain error of substitution upon which much of his argument about the freestanding nature of political conceptions seems to be based. Once the substitution is revealed, I believe, the argument is seriously compromised.

It is true that Rawls explicitly denies that rationality *per se* is the same as instrumental rationality: "rational agents are not limited to means-ends reasoning."[84] In attempting to clarify this claim, however, he actually undermines it. Rational agents, he says, "may balance final ends by their significance for their plan of life as a whole, and by how well these ends cohere with and complement one another."[85] But the idea of "coherence" is presumably part and parcel of any conception of rationality, instrumental or otherwise. We cannot pursue ends intelligently unless we understand how the achievement of one end might affect the achievement of others. As to "balancing final ends" by their significance for our plan of life, what can this mean other than to say that such ends are really the means with which we achieve some larger goal? The real end is the life-plan. What Rawls calls "final ends" are not ends at all, but mere instrumentalities.

With this in mind, it seems that Rawls's philosophical – as opposed to simply linguistic – argument regarding the freestanding nature of political conceptions rests on two propositions:

(a) *The reasonable cannot be derived from the rational, understanding the rational here to be essentially a matter of instrumental rationality.* Note that in criticizing those who would deny this proposition, Rawls mentions only one author, David Gauthier, whose conception of rationality is narrowly and avowedly instrumentalist.[86] The argument against Gauthier is not presented in any detail, but presumably it is based on Sibley and can be reconstructed easily enough. We can certainly imagine a political conception that provides a reasonable basis for reciprocal cooperation among

---

[84] Rawls, *Political Liberalism*, p. 50.
[85] *Ibid.*, p. 51.
[86] *Ibid.*, pp. 52 n, 53. See David Gauthier, *Morals by Agreement* (Oxford: Oxford University Press, 1986), pp. 4–8, 25–26. Gauthier adopts a "maximizing" rather than "universalizing" conception of rationality. See also, David Gauthier, *Moral Dealing: Contract, Ethics and Reason* (Ithaca, New York: Cornell University Press, 1990), pp. 209–33.

different kinds of people in a well-ordered society but that does not necessarily serve to maximize and, more importantly, is not justified as maximizing the interests of such people. Whether or not stability achieves the greatest good for the greatest number, or passes some other test of utility, is separate from the question of whether or not it is agreeable. Similarly, we can equally well imagine individuals who are rational in the sense of being able effectively to pursue ends and interests peculiarly their own (whether selfish or otherwise), but who lack the "particular form of moral sensibility that underlies the desire to engage in fair cooperation as such, and to do so on terms that others as equals might reasonably be expected to endorse."[87] Thus, to be a reasonable person is not necessarily to be a maximizer.

(b) *Since the reasonable is "distinct and independent of" the rational, and since the rational is fundamentally a matter of truth rather than mere agreement, the reasonable is not reducible to, nor derivable from, truth claims about the world,* including and especially truth claims of the sort that we encounter in "rational intuitionism" and, more generally, in comprehensive doctrines.[88] Thus, a reasonable political conception can, and indeed must, be largely freestanding with respect to any and all metaphysical theories about how things really are.

Clearly, (a) provides the premise for (b). But whereas (a) refers only to *instrumental* rationality, (b) concludes that the reasonable must be sharply differentiated from rational thought *per se* – including the kind of thought that typically provides a basis for comprehensive claims about reality. The argument is fallacious; for to show that reasonableness is not the same as maximization is plainly very different from showing that it is or could ever be free of important and potentially controversial metaphysical commitments. To have established that reasonableness cannot be derived from David Gauthier's rationality is a far cry from demonstrating that it is or could ever be independent of, say, Platonic or Thomist or Kantian rationality.

By failing to provide such a demonstration, Rawls offers, in effect, no direct argument for the freestanding nature of political conceptions: the distinction between reasonableness and instrumental rationality fails to justify the sharp distinction between reasonable agreement and rational truth. The implications of this failure are substantial. For if it turns out, as I believe it will, that any political conception must indeed be a metaphysical one, then this will help us to see exactly why so many questions of

---

[87] Rawls, *Political Liberalism*, pp. 50–51.
[88] *Ibid.*, p. 94.

policy or government turn upon, and are resolvable in the light of, a conception of political society that is not at all freestanding but that in fact presupposes an ontological theory of the state.

6. Reasons

When discussing the "objectivity" of political conceptions, Rawls does explicitly invoke the language of reasons. In doing so, he seems to have anticipated some of the criticisms that I have proposed above. Specifically, he defines the objectivity of political conceptions to be a matter of "political constructivism," according to which the citizens of a pluralist society, interested in stability and cooperation, formulate principles of social organization based on an "objective order of reasons." Such an order of reasons justifies and legitimizes the basic structure of society, but does so without invoking considerations of truth. Justification of this kind will be very different, therefore, from anything that might emerge from either rational intuitionism or Kantian moral constructivism, both of which involve metaphysical or moral claims about how the world really is. By avoiding any such claims, political constructivism produces a conception of politics that is independent of theoretical commitments, hence is freestanding.

1. Rawls appears, then, to have worked the idea of having reasons back into the concept of the reasonable. But the result, I fear, is a hopeless tangle. The following passage is both central and symptomatic:

> Political convictions (which are also, of course, moral convictions) are objective – actually founded on an order of reasons – if reasonable and rational persons, who are sufficiently intelligent and conscientious in exercising their powers of practical reason, and whose reasoning exhibits none of the familiar defects of reasoning, would eventually endorse those convictions, or significantly narrow their differences about them, provided that these persons know the relevant facts and have sufficiently surveyed the grounds that bear on the matter under conditions favorable to due reflection .... To say that a political conviction is objective is to say that there are reasons, specified by a reasonable and mutually recognizable political conception ... sufficient to convince all reasonable persons that it is reasonable.[89]

The argument seems to be as follows: a political conception is objective insofar as it is reasonable; it is reasonable insofar as it is founded on a suitable order of reasons; an order of reasons is suitable insofar as *it* is

---

[89] *Ibid.*, p. 119.

reasonable; and *it* is reasonable insofar as it is endorsed by all reasonable persons. Rawls believes, in other words, that the reasonableness of a political conception is indeed a matter of its being based on reasons that are themselves reasonable. But he also believes that the reasonableness of such reasons has little if anything to do with their intrinsic merits. It is reducible, rather, to the fact that they are agreed to by reasonable persons; and, of course, he understands the reasonableness of persons to be essentially a matter of cooperation and reciprocity. Admittedly, such persons are also understood to be at least minimally "rational," and that they will have "surveyed the grounds that bear on the matter" in an intelligent fashion. But this means only that they agree about the most rudimentary kinds of facts, which are, in and of themselves, hardly sufficient to justify political principles. Thus, the reasonableness of reasons is not to be thought of in terms of their quality as reasons. The question of whether or not they make sense does not seem to arise. Agreement among cooperative persons is all that appears to matter; and this means that when Rawls says that a political conception depends upon reasons, he is really not saying much of anything.

Rawls is both explicit about this and, I think, painfully equivocal. On the one hand, he denies that "an objective order of political reasons consists in various activities of sound reasoning."[90] Such an order is warranted or justified simply if it succeeds in eliciting the support of citizens; mere agreement, rather than objective reasoning, secures legitimacy. But in the very next breath he insists that legitimacy also presupposes our ability to "use and apply the concepts of judgment and inference, and ground and evidence, as well as the principles and standards that single out the kind of facts to count as reasons." A political conception thus involves "reasoning in the light of mutually recognized criteria."[91] Indeed, time and again Rawls talks about reasons and reasonableness in terms that strongly imply something much more than mere cooperation and consensus. For example:

- In selecting political principles, citizens are to "reason in common."[92] What could this mean other than that they are to exchange and evaluate arguments according to some kind of rational criterion?
- The appropriate outcome of any political discussion is that which is supported by "the preponderance of reasons."[93] How is such a preponderance to be determined other than through a more-or-less

---

[90] *Ibid.*, pp. 119–20.
[91] *Ibid.*, p. 120.
[92] *Ibid.*, p. 49 n.
[93] *Ibid.*, p. 115.

systematic process whereby various reasons are weighed and evaluated *as reasons*, i.e., with a view toward their intellectual merits?

- Reasons are only good if they reflect "none of the familiar defects of reasoning."[94] As such, they will be based on established "principles of inference" and "rules of evidence."[95] Does this not suggest that good reasons will be judged according to "standards of correctness and criteria of justification"[96] that would be familiar to any rationalist?

None of these propositions can be accounted for by reasonableness understood simply and solely as a social or psychological disposition to engage in cooperative and reciprocal arrangements. Yet, to my knowledge, Rawls provides no other independent account of the reasonable. The language of rationality continually intrudes into his discussions of reasonableness in ways that undermine his claim that the two are conceptually distinct; and in the absence of a clearer argument to the contrary, his insistence that justice as fairness is freestanding – or that any political conception could be freestanding – is unpersuasive.

Rawls fails, then, to see that reasonableness and rationality cannot be merely complementary. To propose that an action is reasonable because it is justified on the basis of reasons is necessarily to propose an *argument* of some kind; and to propose an argument is, in and of itself, to offer a truth claim, something that other individuals should accept precisely because it is true. Of course, to *propose* such a claim is not necessarily to *prove* it; nor is it a requirement that such claims be offered with certainty or even conviction. We can present our reasons for believing something to be true without denying that even the most rational kind of discourse may be governed by the "burdens of judgment."[97] But none of this is sufficient to distinguish and separate the reasonable from the rational. Again, any reasonable claim is, in effect, a claim about reasons; and any claim about reasons – including reasons that purport to justify a political conception of some kind – is something to be argued about, something to be analyzed and evaluated in terms of the degree to which it is true, at least as far as anyone can tell.[98]

---

[94] *Ibid.*, p. 119.
[95] *Ibid.*, p. 220.
[96] *Ibid.* Also, p. 225.
[97] Rawls himself acknowledges this: the sources of reasonable disagreement "are not peculiar to the reasonable and the rational in their moral and practical use" (*ibid.*, p. 56). But what can this mean other than to say either that there is no particular connection between the burdens of judgment and reasonableness or that reasonable discourse about politics – public reason – is not to be distinguished from scientific, metaphysical or moral discourse, properly conceived?
[98] The arguments against Rawls that I have made in the last several sections may seem similar to views recently expressed by Stanley Fish in *The Trouble with Principle* (Cambridge, Mass.: Harvard University Press, 1999). The similarities, however, are

2. We have seen with Hobbes, perhaps the least ostensibly "metaphysical" of political theorists, the sense in which the modern philosophy of the idea of the state is an ontological philosophy, an effort to describe the essence of political society. Hobbes's work thus helps perpetuate a venerable tradition of political/ontological speculation, rooted in fifth- and fourth-century Greece; and it inspires, as well, a host of subsequent efforts, themselves culminating in the attempt to describe a "rational state," wherein the apparent opposition between the particular and the substantial is annulled yet preserved in a higher conception of community.

Recent political speculation has explicitly disavowed such larger philosophical pretensions; and this disavowal has now acquired a new and impressive justification, rooted not so much in doubts about the possibility of metaphysics as in concerns about the realities and vicissitudes of contemporary politics. But any such effort to be free of ontological commitment is destined both to fail and to mislead. Political thought necessarily rests upon a foundation of metaphysical presupposition, a structure of concepts and theories that renders the world meaningful and comprehensible, and without which intelligible thought and action would not be possible. To understand truly our own theory of the state, and our own sense of prudence, of policy and government, thus requires that we attend precisely to that foundation. We need to examine our own presuppositions with care, and attempt to determine exactly what kind of political theory they entail, if we are to make sense of the social and political problems that confront us. And I hope to show that, in the crucible of such an examination, many of our most vexing and contentious difficulties will take on an entirely new character, presenting the political theorist with a host of new challenges and, at the same time, an array of unforeseen opportunities.

Before dealing with these issues, however, we need first to get some clarity on just what it might mean to pursue a metaphysical theory *per se*. How is it possible to do metaphysics in what continues to be, after all, a decidedly scientific age? It is to this question that we now turn.

---

superficial at best. Like me, Fish rejects the idea of a purely political conception – a conception uncontaminated by or truly neutral toward presuppositions of a metaphysical or moral nature. But his reasons for doing so, and his understanding of what the issue is all about, couldn't be more different. In brief, Fish argues against relying on "principles." Yet his own arguments are themselves shot through with principles, and would make no sense without them. For a detailed discussion, see Peter J. Steinberger, "The Trouble with Fish," unpublished manuscript (July 2003).

3   The Post-Kantian Convergence

I have proposed a sharp distinction between prudential and philosophical argument – between theories of policy or government and the ontological or metaphysical theory of the state. But I have also observed what is, I think, undeniable, that a distinction does not necessarily imply a separation, and that, in the instant case, prudential or "political" claims unavoidably presuppose serious commitments of a philosophical or metaphysical nature. This fact will turn out to have decisive consequences for our understanding of the state as a structure of intelligibility. Before we can begin to think seriously about those consequences, however, we need to consider in more detail just what it might mean to pursue an ontological or metaphysical theory *per se*.

I have already briefly described (in 2.2 above) the sense in which certain canonical authors based their political recommendations on explicit or implicit metaphysical claims. I have also considered Hobbes's approach to metaphysical questions, have identified certain difficulties with his view, and have briefly sketched an alternative approach – an approach of the greatest importance that began to emerge in the latter part of the eighteenth century and that continues to be immensely influential today. It is, I think, a fact that older theories about how one actually does metaphysics – whether Platonic, Aristotelian or Hobbesian – have fallen into disrepute. But while many writers have concluded from this that metaphysical speculation *per se* is untenable, others have sought rather to place such speculation on an entirely new footing. Specifically, they have sought to show how older arguments might be recast in new and powerful ways, and have tried to explain thereby the means by which we can and do formulate intelligible claims about reality. I propose now to investigate some of these latter developments more closely, for they provide plausible answers – perhaps our best answers – to what is, for us, a fundamental problem: in an age at once skeptical about all manner of abstract inquiry and, at the same time, deeply invested in the achievements of physical science, how is it that ontological or metaphysical questions can be intelligently asked and answered? As should by now be apparent, the question is especially pertinent to the idea of the state. For insofar as any state is itself primarily a structure of intelligibility composed of propositions about how things in the world really are – hence an embodiment and authoritative institutionalization of metaphysical or ontological claims – to explore the nature of metaphysical theory is at the same time to explore the nature of the state.

In section 1, I consider an ancient piece of philosophical writing – a Platonic dialogue – understood both as an exemplar of the elenchic method and as a case study in metaphysical or ontological inquiry. The second section builds on this case study from a post-Kantian perspective, and proposes a strong connection between coherence and objectivity. In section 3, I suggest that such a perspective resonates – vertically and horizontally – in a wide variety of philosophical traditions, analytic and continental alike. Sections 4 and 5 outline some of the implications of this post-Kantian convergence for our understanding of social action and social institutions.

1. Coherence and ontology

To ask after the idea of the state is to pose the simplest kind of question: how are we to think about a particular feature of the world? To pursue such a question is to investigate the meaning of a concept or group of concepts with a view toward understanding the nature of the individual things to which those concepts might be applied. Of course, philosophers have long been devoted to questions of this kind. But it is also the case that the impulse to wrestle constructively with them, with conceptual problems, is hardly limited to the community of professional thinkers. In fact, the impulse is universal. For each and every one of us, in living out our lives, cannot help but try to come to terms with the world in which we find ourselves; and such a coming to terms cannot but involve some effort, however undisciplined and unfocused, to make rational sense of how things really are. To be a human being is, in no small measure, to use one's intellectual powers to characterize things, to arrange or classify them in terms of ideas and theories, hence to render them meaningful and intelligible; and insofar as I am right about this, it suggests that each and every one of us is, to one degree or another, involved in the enterprise called ontology.

Our engagement in such an enterprise actually involves us in two distinct activities or, if one wishes, a single activity having two distinct aspects. On the one hand, we are trying to discover what certain individual things really are, at least according to our lights; and we do this, in part, by getting clear about the meaning of the concepts that we predicate of those things. On the other hand, we are also seeking to establish a map of the world that will guide our behavior, a set of discriminations or judgments on the basis of which we can intelligently decide what to do and how to do it. All of us are unavoidably involved in both kinds of activities. For to live a human life is to confront practical problems, to encounter and attempt to deal prudently with an endless flow of choices and decisions, some quite trivial, some not, but each of which requires of us a more-or-less reasoned response; and what could it mean to make any such decision, no matter how inconsequential, without relying on at least some claims about the actual state of things? It is true, of course, that some people arrive at their judgments about the world in a systematic and self-conscious manner, and some do not. Some display considerable perspicacity and insight, others rather less. But such differences in no way undermine this basic fact, that the effort to formulate a set of ideas about how things are – ideas on the basis of which we are to find our way in the world – is a common and constitutive aspect of human thinking *per se*.

When we begin, then, by examining briefly one of our earliest and most influential philosophical traditions, we are seeking not simply to describe some facts of intellectual history but to discover the rudiments of an ontological or metaphysical manner of thinking that is common to all of us alike – ancient and modern, philosopher and politician, intellectual and citizen.

1. The Socratic dialogue, as a philosophical genre, presents a particular kind of puzzle. Consider the *Euthyphro*, in many ways a paradigmatic case. Two interlocutors, Euthyphro and Socrates, decide jointly to find out whether or not the former is being pious in seeking to prosecute his father for the alleged murder of a worker. We see right away that such a question is apt to be an extremely difficult one, involving daunting, perhaps even impenetrable issues of right and wrong. Despite this, however, the interlocutors seem intent on pursuing the inquiry by themselves, without help from anyone else. Theirs is not a research project in the usual sense. They will not be consulting outside authorities. They will not be scouring the empirical world for new information. They will employ no new observational techniques, no experimental designs, no surveys or focus groups. In seeking to answer their question, they are evidently determined to rely exclusively on their own independent, unenlarged resources.

What is perplexing, in part, is that those resources appear so meager. Specifically, neither Euthyphro nor Socrates seems to know what piety actually is. It is true that Euthyphro claims to know. But the claim is implausible, in part because of the unsatisfactory answers that he actually gives, in part because his estimate of his own intellectual powers is so dubious. He says, specifically, that he has "never foretold anything which has not come true" (3b); but when he assures Socrates, in virtually the next breath, that certain imminent and soon-to-be notorious legal proceedings will come to nothing, his credibility certainly dissolves. As for Socrates, the fact is that he does not even pretend to know what piety is – a stance perfectly consistent with his own famous claim not to know much of anything. Of course, the precise meaning of this latter claim is an old and difficult question. But in the present circumstance, the claim itself is not easily dismissed. For we can say, at a minimum, that if Socrates is not as ignorant as he sometimes insists – if, in the instant case, he really *does* know what piety is – then it is at least curious that he chooses not to share his knowledge. At the end of the *Euthyphro*, after all, poor Euthyphro himself remains in what might charitably be described as a state of unclarity.

One could argue, I suppose, that Socrates knows very well what piety is but decides to withhold the information for pedagogical reasons. Perhaps he feels that he will better teach about piety if, feigning ignorance, he can force Euthyphro to engage in a certain kind of intellectual exercise wherein various definitions are tested and rejected. Perhaps he believes that only in the light of such an exercise can Euthyphro come truly to appreciate the nature of piety, to understand it in a way that would be unavailable to him if he were simply spoon-fed the correct answer. But even if this could account for Socratic reticence, it would raise a host of further and even more troubling questions about both Socrates the inter-locutor and Plato the scribe. For again, if Socrates wishes to teach Euthyphro about piety, he certainly seems to have failed miserably, since the conversation ends long before a satisfactory conclusion is even in sight; and to the degree that Plato wishes to teach us, his readers, about the same subject, he too seems to have failed, since the *Euthyphro* is an archetypically aporetic dialogue.

We might well be inclined, then, to take things at face value: neither Euthyphro nor Socrates knows what piety is, hence, of course, neither knows for sure whether or not Euthyphro is being pious in seeking the prosecution of his father. But this only makes things more perplexing. For how is it possible that two individuals, each of whom is truly ignorant of some thing, could discover that thing by themselves? Imagine, for example, that you and I are completely unschooled in calculus, that we are jointly instructed to solve a complex calculus problem, and that we are required to solve it while locked in a room lacking any and all access to external sources of information or expertise about calculus – no textbooks, no telephone with which to call a professor of mathematics, no e-mail. It certainly seems doubtful that in such a circumstance we could possibly be successful. Being ignorant of calculus, we would not know where to begin. Indeed, it is unlikely that we could even recognize the calculus problem for what it is, or that we could understand what is problematic about it. If we saw some numbers and letters and things that looked like equations written on a page, we might guess that it was a problem in mathematics, though that in itself would presuppose at least some knowledge of mathematical notation. But there are many kinds of mathematical problems; and unless the problem in question were clearly identified as a problem in calculus, it is hard to see how we would be able to understand it as such. Moreover, even if the problem had been so labeled, we would still be in trouble; for such a label would be comprehensible to us only if we had at least *some* knowledge of calculus, e.g., the knowledge that calculus is a part of higher mathematics. And even if we possessed this kind of knowledge, surely it would be insufficient to permit us to solve the problem. Solving the problem would require not just some knowledge of calculus but a certain kind of knowledge, a working knowledge.

Euthyphro and Socrates seem to be in a roughly analogous situation. If, in fact, they really do not know what piety is, then we have to wonder how they would even be able to recognize it if, in the course of their inquiry, they should happen to stumble upon it. On what basis could they identify piety as piety without knowing at the outset the characteristics of piety that distinguish it from other kinds of things, characteristics that, in large part, make it what it is? And if they are unable to recognize piety, how could they possibly decide whether or not Euthyphro is being pious in seeking to prosecute his father?

I think that these are substantial questions, but the puzzle only deepens when we consider the fact that the *Euthyphro*, though aporetic, is hardly vacuous. For it turns out that Euthyphro and Socrates are able to carry on a perfectly intelligible and apparently constructive, albeit rather brief and inconclusive, conversation that certainly seems to be very much on topic. They consider a variety of theories about the nature of piety. They evaluate those theories and reject them, evidently for good reasons. Having rejected one such theory, they plausibly move on to another, and then to yet another; the discussion seems to unfold naturally, rationally. These facts need to be explained. We need to determine how it is possible for them to talk intelligently about something of which they are ignorant; and we need to understand how it is possible for *us* to know that their conversation really is about piety if we too are more-or-less equally ignorant.

In another dialogue, the *Meno*, Plato describes this kind of problem with particular clarity:

How will you look for something when you don't in the least know what it is? How on earth are you going to set up something you don't know as the object of your search? To put it another way, even if you come right up against it, how will you know that what you have found is the thing you didn't know? (*Meno* 80d–e)

And in an important and famous passage from the same work, he suggests a solution:

The soul, since it is immortal and has been born many times, and has seen all things both here and in the other world, has learned everything that is. So we need not be surprised if it can recall the knowledge of virtue or anything else which, as we see, it once possessed. All nature is akin, and the soul has learned everything, so that when a man has recalled a single piece of knowledge – learned it, in ordinary language – there is no reason why he should not find out all the rest, if he keeps a stout heart and does not grow weary of the search; for seeking and learning are in fact nothing but recollection. (*Meno* 81c–e)

There are, it seems, two types of knowledge. We might simply call them "explicit" and "implicit." When we say that Euthyphro and Socrates do not know what piety is, we are really saying that they lack explicit knowledge. They are unable to bring clearly to mind, hence unable to express precisely in words, the nature of piety; and this means that, as a practical matter, they have problems identifying it confidently and accurately. But again, they are able to discuss it intelligently, to pose and respond to any number of questions about it, and Plato suggests that this cannot be explained unless we presuppose that they really do know what piety is. They know it implicitly. When they discuss piety, that is, they must be relying in some way on a storehouse of information and understanding, a preestablished structure of insight and truth that each of them already possesses, that licenses the various particular things that they actually say, and that underwrites the ways in which they apply the concept of piety to particular things in the world. This is the doctrine of *anamnesis*, and for Plato there is simply no other way to account for their behavior.

Implicit knowledge is, it seems, never wholly that. It is partly but not entirely hidden. Or, perhaps more accurately, some aspects of our knowledge are completely obscure, others only partially so, and still others not at all; and the three parts are somehow connected such that by consulting those that are crystal clear, or that are only partially obscure, we can come gradually to uncover the rest. For Plato, I think, this is an important part of what philosophical inquiry is all about. The primary purpose of the Socratic elenchus is to permit individuals to know explicitly that which they know implicitly, and to do so by extrapolating from – unearthing the implications of – that which they already explicitly know. Understood along these lines, philosophy is a matter not of invention but of disclosure; and it is in such terms, I believe, that we can best approach the argument and action of virtually any Socratic dialogue, even the most aporetic of them.

Thus, while the *Euthyphro* certainly fails to produce anything approaching an acceptable definition of piety, it does nonetheless tell us some very important things both about piety and about virtue in general, things of which we were, presumably, not previously aware, or at least not fully so. For instance, when Euthyphro defines piety as the activity of prosecuting an alleged murderer, even if the accused is your father and the murder victim a mere slave (*Euthyphro* 5e), Socrates points out (6b–c) that this merely affirms the consequent without argument, hence provides neither a reason to believe that it is true nor any real insight into the nature of piety. We do indeed want to know whether or not Euthyphro is acting piously in seeking to prosecute his father, but we cannot answer such a question unless and until we come to know piety itself, independent of any examples of it. It turns out, then, that piety is not a specific case of piety. It is, rather, a general kind of thing, something that can be predicated of any number of individual things.[1] This is not a trivial discovery. It is an important part of what makes piety piety. But it also seems to be something that Euthyphro must have known all along. For he comes to accept the truth of this discovery not merely – in fact, not at all – on the authority of Socrates. He does not just take Socrates' word for it. Rather, he himself comes to *recognize* it. When presented to him, he perceives it not as some new datum about the world, a hitherto unknown and unimagined feature of the landscape, like America (to Europeans) before Columbus. To the contrary, he encounters it without surprise, as if to say "Yes, it's natural and necessary that it should be so, and this is something that I should have seen all along."

In effect, Euthyphro already knew piety to be a general kind of thing, something that can be predicated of any number of individual things. But he knew this only implicitly. For whatever reason, it was not a feature of piety that he was either able or disposed to bring to mind on his own. Under the influence of the elenchus, however, it has emerged from the shadows.

---

[1] Nehamas has shown that Euthyphro's answer, like many other answers to Socratic questions, does not necessarily involve supplying a particular where a universal is wanted, as I may have implied. In Nehamas's account, the failure of Euthyphro has to do with the kind of universal answer he has given, or with its level of universality. See Alexander Nehamas, "Confusing Universals and Particulars in Plato's Early Dialogues," *Review of Metaphysics* 29 (1975), pp. 287–306. I think that this is quite correct; but I also think that Nehamas's view is perfectly consistent with the point that I am making here.

Euthyphro now comes to know it explicitly; and such knowledge is a kind of knowledge that may well be helpful in uncovering some of the other things about piety that Euthyphro implicitly knows. Indeed, by the end of a very brief conversation, he has come explicitly to know quite a bit. He has come to know that piety, whatever it is, is a general quality, which, when present, is loved by all of the gods (9e), not just some of the gods, and that is always and necessarily just, although not everything that is just is always and necessarily pious (12c–d).

Of course, when Euthyphro comes to know this explicitly, then so have we, Plato's readers. Like Euthyphro, we have not simply acquired this knowledge as if it were completely new. Rather, in the (indirect) light of Socratic interrogation, we have come to recollect it. We knew it all along, but only through the elenchus have we become aware of it. And if Euthyphro himself had not abruptly broken things off, the inquiry perhaps could have continued until, in principle, our implicit knowledge of it had been rendered fully explicit; and with such explicit knowledge in hand, we might then have grounds for understanding the true nature of Euthyphro's activity in seeking the prosecution of his father, at least with respect to the question of piety.

2. Several features of this general picture deserve special attention:

First, Euthyphro and Socrates are plainly engaged in an ontological discussion. Their goal is to uncover (at least one important aspect of) the essential nature of Euthyphro's prosecutorial activity with respect to its piety; and they conclude, plausibly enough, that they cannot know this unless they know what the nature of piety really is. They seek to understand the meaning of a concept in order to discover the truth about some particular thing in the world.

Now I am inclined to agree with Vlastos that Socrates – or, more precisely, the Socrates of the so-called early dialogues – does not have "a grandiose metaphysical theory of 'separately existing' Forms and of a separable soul which learns by 'recollecting' pieces of its pre-natal fund of knowledge."[2] Such a theory is not to be found until the so-called middle or later dialogues, hence is presumably Platonic rather than Socratic. But from this alone one could hardly conclude that Socrates is not a metaphysician. For even if he lacks a fully worked-out and elaborately

---

[2] Gregory Vlastos, *Socrates: Ironist and Moral Philosopher* (Ithaca, New York: Cornell University Press, 1991), p. 48. Also, C. C. W. Taylor, "Socratic Ethics," in *Socratic Questions: New Essays on the Philosophy of Socrates and its Significance* (New York: Routledge, 1992), pp. 137–39. For an example of the older tradition that attributes to Socrates the full-blown theory of Forms, see A. E. Taylor, *Socrates* (Garden City, New York: Doubleday, 1953), pp. 163–69.

formulated philosophy of being, this would in no way show that his interests are not metaphysical or that his inquiries do not presuppose some kind of implicit ontological theory. It seems to me that Euthyphro and Socrates, in searching after piety, are plainly searching for the truth about Euthyphro's activity in seeking the prosecution of his father, and they understand truth here to involve some characterization of what that activity *really* is, its underlying nature, its essence.

I am also inclined to think that if, as Vlastos goes on to say, the theory of *anamnesis* is not to be found in the early Socratic dialogues, this does not mean that such a theory is inconsistent with Socratic teaching. For the question of how Euthyphro and Socrates are able to talk intelligibly about piety, despite their apparent ignorance of it, is a real one; and Socrates' putative failure to formulate an explicit answer is perfectly consistent with the hypothesis that Plato, reflecting upon his own elenchic experiences, came up with – or recollected – a solution that Socrates himself might have endorsed, had he known it explicitly. Perhaps, that is, the doctrine of *anamnesis* is itself a product of *anamnesis*. Far from being viciously circular, this seems to me exactly the kind of conclusion to which such a doctrine would lead.

It is especially important to observe, moreover, that Euthyphro and Socrates, in pursuing their ontological inquiry, rely fundamentally on a criterion of coherence. Indeed, the search for coherence is the fundamental constitutive feature of the elenchus *per se*. According to the standard account,[3] every Socratic investigation involves an inquiry into the nature of some "F," where "F" is a term from our moral vocabulary denoting one or another virtue such as piety, justice, courage, and the like. The inquiry typically begins when Socrates asks his interlocutor to say what he believes "F" to be. This is followed by a series of subsidiary questions designed to elicit further beliefs, including and especially beliefs that are unlikely to be changed, either because they are very strongly held or because they are not currently at issue. The original belief about "F" is then evaluated in the light of these other beliefs, and if it is shown to be inconsistent with them, it is rejected as incoherent.

Thus, in the instant case, Euthyphro claims at one point that piety is what the gods love (7a). It quickly becomes evident, however, that he also has at least two other sincere beliefs. He believes that sometimes some of the gods love certain things that other gods do not love at all, and also that

---

[3] For a clear statement, see C. D. C. Reeve, *Socrates in the 'Apology'* (Indianapolis: Hackett, 1989), pp. 40–41. See also, Gregory Vlastos, "The Socratic Elenchus," *Oxford Studies in Ancient Philosophy* 1 (1983), pp. 27–58; and Thomas C. Brickhouse and Nicholas D. Smith, *Plato's Socrates* (Oxford: Oxford University Press, 1994), pp. 5–29.

it is impossible for any particular thing both to have and not have a certain feature at the same time. Of these two beliefs, one is religious in nature, the other logical. Each of them could be tested in the same way that Euthyphro's belief about piety is being tested. Each, that is, could be the subject of an elenchic inquiry, and there is, perhaps, no guarantee that either of them would survive. But the fact is that they remain unchallenged in the *Euthyphro*, and this shows that Euthyphro and Socrates are strongly committed to them, so strongly committed that the conversation they are having is not primarily about the gods and their likes nor about the facts of logic – all of which are taken for granted – but about piety. And within the context of such a conversation, it is quite clear that Euthyphro cannot consistently believe that piety is what the gods love while still holding to those other two beliefs. His belief about piety must be rejected, not so much because it has been directly refuted but, rather, because it is inconsistent with his more general view of things.

For Socrates, therefore, and for Plato as well, the truth of our various opinions depends in large part on whether or not the sum total of our beliefs compose a coherent whole. Coherence of this kind is something that Euthyphro, for one, cannot enjoy unless and until he comes up with another, quite different belief about the nature of piety; and it is something that *we* cannot enjoy, at least not fully, unless and until each of our opinions is tested in light of the gamut of our beliefs.

There is, though, another sense of coherence upon which the success of any elenchic inquiry also seems to depend. It is not enough that Euthyphro and Socrates each have an internally consistent set of beliefs. It is necessary, as well, that their respective belief-sets be mutually consistent, the one with the other. To put it (perhaps controversially) in the terms of certain previous discussions, Euthyphro and Socrates may each be said to have something like a comprehensive doctrine, a more-or-less systematic set of claims about how things really are. If it turns out that they share a common belief about the nature of piety, this can only be because their respective comprehensive doctrines are the same, or at least similar enough to accommodate that belief; and as was suggested earlier, any such similarity will necessarily betoken some very fundamental theoretical agreements.

If agreements of this kind do in fact exist, exactly how do they come about? Upon what are they based? Are they merely fortuitous, or do they reflect something substantial about the world itself? Socrates may not have provided an explicit answer to this question (again, as per Vlastos), but Plato surely does. Agreement is possible, according to Plato, for the simple reason that external reality permits it. This is to say that Euthyphro and Socrates are searching not for something arbitrary, conventional or artificial. Whether they know it or not, they are searching for the Form of piety – the unique expression or encapsulation of its reality.

For Plato, piety is quite real. It exists in a world of ideas, as part of a coherent, rational ordering of concepts. Such a world, though independent of space and time, is nonetheless an important part of reality. Its constitutive elements, the Forms, are immutable and necessary. As such, they exist both in themselves and in our minds – in our "immortal souls." These latter function as windows on the world of ideas through which thought and thing are united. It follows from all this that when we come to recollect the idea of piety under the influence of the elenchus, the result will necessarily be the same for each of us, provided that each of us is thinking clearly. To the degree that Euthyphro and Socrates are rational creatures, their underlying belief-sets will reflect accurately the world of Forms; and to the degree that they are able to uncover and recollect those belief-sets, they will arrive at a common conception of piety. Of course, with such a conception in hand, they will be well equipped to arrive at a common understanding of Euthyphro's decision to seek the prosecution of his father. They will jointly discover, that is, whether or not such a decision would in fact be an instantiation of the Form of piety, hence will come to know exactly what the decision really is, at least with respect to piety.

It is at this point, of course, that Plato loses a great many of his readers. The world of Forms seems like so much mysticism – an arbitrary postulation designed to account for facts that could just as easily be accounted for without any such mumbo-jumbo. Plato himself raises deep questions about his own theory, most famously in the *Parmenides*. The point, however, is not to criticize, nor to defend, Platonic metaphysics *per se*. Rather, it is to discover in Plato certain rudimentary features of metaphysical or ontological inquiry broadly conceived, features that are not peculiar to Plato and that can be isolated from the more distinctive and controversial aspects of his work. In particular, my aim has been to show how his philosophy thinks of objective truth in terms of coherence – a move that will prove to be constitutive of ontological theory.

Consider once again our case of the calculus problem. We assumed that two individuals entirely unschooled in calculus and left to their own devices would be unable even to recognize, let alone solve, a difficult calculus problem. Surely this was a plausible claim; but seen in the light of Platonic theory, it may have been hasty. After all, at one point in time Newton and Leibniz were each in circumstances not so completely different from those of our hypothetical case. They were, of course, persons of genius who also happened to be extremely well trained in higher mathematics. In pursuing calculus problems, however, neither of them could consult a textbook in calculus, or seek out a professor of calculus, for the obvious reason that calculus had not yet been discovered. They were forced to work in what might be called a calculus vacuum, to pursue their inquiries by relying on their own respective resources. Of course, they presumably did this quite independently of one another, yet arrived at strikingly similar conclusions. According to the standard (though now perhaps controversial) account, each discovered the general principles of calculus; and with those principles in hand, each was able to solve particular calculus problems correctly, reliably and, for all intents and purposes, identically. To the degree that we do not find this especially astonishing, presumably it is because we believe not only that Newton and Leibniz were persons of genius but also that calculus has some kind of foundation independent of any particular person, that it describes features of the world that we would call "true" such that, at least according to our intuitions, it would actually have been rather peculiar if Newton and Leibniz, or at least two persons like them, had *not*, at some point, come up with the same answers to particular problems; and this suggests, in turn, that calculus was not so much created as revealed.

It seems that calculus is in some sense an extrapolation from, or an extension of, certain less well-developed mathematical ideas. It is, one might say, implicit in – already present in – pre-calculus math. If this is so, then to know such math explicitly is to have in one's possession the materials necessary for doing calculus; it is, in effect, to know calculus implicitly. Little wonder, then, that as soon as calculus is discovered it is very difficult to conceive of mathematics without it. Of course, we can easily imagine circumstances in which mathematicians do not actually do calculus; such was the case with mathematics before Newton and Leibniz, and it could become the case once again if for some reason calculus were to lapse into obscurity. But we know, nonetheless, that mathematics always did, and always will, include calculus; for the solutions to particular calculus problems are the right solutions even before they have actually been arrived at. In this sense, then, the independent discovery of calculus by persons of genius becomes not simply explicable but nearly inevitable. It was not inevitable that those two particular men at that particular point in time would have discovered calculus. But it seems inevitable, or at least very highly probable, that *someone* at *some* time would have discovered it. And it was surely inevitable that calculus, *if* and *whenever* it were discovered, would necessarily be calculus much as Newton and Leibniz found it.

2. Objectivity

My purpose is certainly not to claim that the Platonic doctrine of *anamnesis* is right, or that it is uniquely able to account for this kind of agreement. Rather, my purpose has been to identify *anamnesis* as one example of a particular *kind* of approach, a broad philosophical orientation that has been shared by a great many philosophers, the large majority of whom could hardly be called Platonists; and further, that this general orientation provides perhaps at least one plausible way of addressing a range of questions pertaining to the intelligibility and truth of human thought. Even more importantly, and certainly more radically, I also believe that such an approach is reflected in the ordinary cognitive practices of the most ordinary people, the vast majority of whom would certainly not be called philosophers. There is, I believe, a very real and non-trivial sense in which each of us is, in fact, deeply philosophical, and in which a great many of our intellectual differences reflect not fundamental oppositions of either substance or method but only the degree to which our pursuit of philosophical wisdom is rigorous, disciplined and self-conscious.

The general idea of ontological or metaphysical analysis to which I am attracted has been formulated perhaps most persuasively and expressed with perhaps greatest clarity by Strawson. No one would think of Strawson as a Platonist or as a practitioner of the elenchus; his philosophy owes more to Kant than anyone else. But, as I hope to show, this fact only strengthens the larger claims of convergence that I shall be making.

1. In pursuing the nature of philosophical inquiry, Strawson suggests an analogy with grammar. Philosophy is the study of the rules according to which we use concepts, just as grammar is the study of the rules of a language. But what does it mean, in each case, to "study the rules"? For Strawson, it means nothing other than to make explicit a certain kind of knowledge that we already have implicitly.

All of us can speak at least one natural language. This is to say that we *know* the language, including the grammatical rules that make the language what it is. Who could deny that the average Frenchman "knows" French? And since French is, to an important degree, constituted by its grammar, who could deny that knowing French means knowing its grammar? But it is also true, as Strawson indicates, that "practical mastery of the grammar in no way entails the ability to state systematically what the rules are which we effortlessly observe."[4] The fact that we know how to use nouns and verbs correctly and in such a way as to construct grammatically perfect sentences does not, in and of itself, mean

[4] P. F. Strawson, *Analysis and Metaphysics: An Introduction to Philosophy* (Oxford: Oxford University Press, 1992), p. 7. See also, Peter J. Steinberger, *The Concept of Political Judgment* (Chicago: University of Chicago Press, 1993), pp. 219–20.

that we know how to talk accurately about, say, the accusative case or the past imperfect tense. In order to know *that*, we need to study grammar, to learn the rules explicitly.

In one sense, learning the rules of grammar is not to learn anything new at all, since, as skilled language-users, we already know those rules very well. But in another sense, it is to learn something new indeed, since only after studying grammar can we identify and explain what it really is that we have been doing all along. To study grammar, then, is nothing other than to make our implicit knowledge of grammatical structure explicit, to identify and classify in a systematic way the principles and categories that we have actually been employing throughout our language-using lives. Such explicit knowledge might seem to be perversely redundant, hence largely inconsequential. We already know how to use the language. But in fact, the process of explication can be extremely useful, even indispensable. All competent language-users occasionally run into difficult situations in which the correct choice of a word or a structure is not immediately apparent; and such situations can produce serious problems of miscommunication among people, problems that sometimes turn out to have the most serious practical consequences. One need only think about legal disputes concerning the meaning of a contractual clause, or romantic disputes of the "this-is-what-I-really-meant-to-say" variety. Often, such controversies can be avoided or resolved only through an explicit, self-conscious investigation of grammatical rules.

Strawson wants to say that philosophical inquiry works roughly along these same lines. To think is to use concepts; and the structure of concepts at our disposal at any particular point in time may be said to compose a kind of language – a vocabulary of ideas together with a syntax for their employment. Such a language underwrites our entire intellectual life. It provides the basic tools with which we make intelligible distinctions in the world. As such, it is, of course, constantly in use. Our lives are filled with experiences of things – dogs and snow and anger and red and piety and the like – and we render those experiences immediately intelligible by classifying and distinguishing them in terms of our conceptual apparatus, i.e., by employing concepts of *dog*, *snow*, *anger*, *red*, *piety*, etc. We tend to use such concepts unselfconsciously. We routinely apply them with skill and confidence, and we rarely ponder their exact meanings or their various interrelationships. Usually this presents no problems for us. When we see a dog, we experience it according to our concept of *dog*, and if we think about what it is, or if someone asks us what it is, we immediately and unproblematically say that it is a dog. But sometimes things are not so easy. We may encounter a creature that might or might not be a dog, perhaps a wolf or a coyote or a hyena. It may be important for us to decide whether, or to what extent, it is a dog, but we cannot do this unless we have a clear sense of what a dog really is. Similarly, we may need to know whether or not it is pious to prosecute one's father for the murder of a worker. But we cannot answer this question unless we know what piety is; and we are apt to discover that although we use the concept of piety quite regularly and successfully in normal thought and conversation, we are not immediately able to provide an explicit and acceptable definition of it.

Just as grammar is the activity of uncovering and clarifying rules of language, so is philosophy, for Strawson, the activity of uncovering and clarifying our conceptual apparatus. As such, it is a matter of making explicit that which we already know implicitly. Now to the best of my knowledge, Strawson evinces no special interest in Platonic doctrines pertaining to Forms or to the immortality of the soul, and it seems that any connection between his philosophy and the precise notion of *anamnesis* would be indirect at best. Nonetheless, I believe that the general aim of philosophy as he sees it is not so different from Plato's – again, to make our implicit knowledge explicit – and that the elenchus provides at least one plausible account of how we might go about achieving the kind of thing that Strawson has in mind.

Strawson also shares with Plato the view that philosophy, in pursuing the meaning of our concepts, is a quest for coherence. Once again, the analogy with language is instructive. Every natural language presents itself as a kind of system in which the various grammatical rules comport with one another so as to compose an internally consistent whole. If this were not true, if the rules contradicted one another, then it is hard to see how the language could be a language at all, i.e., a vehicle for successful communication. If, according to the rules, a particular sentence means both X and non-X at the same time, then to utter that sentence is to utter something that defies confident interpretation; and while any natural language can certainly tolerate numerous imperfections along these lines, surely there are limits. A language can accommodate only so many incoherencies before it ceases to be a language at all. It is, for Strawson, much the same with our conceptual apparatus. Such an apparatus presents itself not as a random and unconnected set of ideas but as a "conceptual structure,"[5] the various components of which "are mutually supportive and mutually dependent, interlocking in an intelligible way."[6] It is, indeed, "an elaborate network, a system, of connected items,

---

[5] Strawson, *Analysis and Metaphysics*, p. 7.
[6] P. F. Strawson, *Skepticism and Naturalism: Some Varieties* (New York: Columbia University Press, 1985), p. 23.

concepts, such that the function of each item, each concept, could, from the philosophical point of view, be properly understood only by grasping its connections with the others, its place in the system."[7] As such, it operates according to a principle of coherence that controls, or ought to control, the ways in which we use the individual concepts of which it is composed. Moreover, as we will see, those concepts – and the ways in which we apply them to the world – constitute for us the only available and intelligible account of the nature of things. If, for example, our conceptual apparatus includes the notion that the world is composed of physical bodies whose identities remain relatively stable over time, then I am forced to conclude as an ontological matter that this particular object before me, whatever else it might be, is a physical object, and that if I look away from it briefly and then return to it, it continues to be the same object.

The language/philosophy analogy seems to me a compelling one. It suggests that philosophical analysis (Strawson wonders if "elucidation" might not be a better word), in seeking to make our implicit knowledge explicit, is a never-ending and yet, at the same time, unavoidable struggle to demonstrate how it is possible for us to make sense. If we are to begin with the premise of a conceptual structure, a set of ideas on the basis of which our experience is rendered intelligible, then we can see, first of all, that such a structure must be composed of a virtually infinite number of components. Not only is the conceptual vocabulary of the most ordinary individual self-evidently enormous, it is also limitlessly expandable since, among other things, concepts can be combined with one another to produce ever new concepts ad infinitum. The range of notions to which each of us has access far exceeds the ability of any mortal mind to grasp all of them at any one moment or, for that matter, during any one lifetime. Of course, and despite this, we routinely employ our conceptual apparatus more-or-less effortlessly and as occasions arise; but again, we often encounter circumstances – as with Euthyphro – in which things are not quite so effortless. Such circumstances are perhaps best understood as occasions in which one of the infinite number of concepts at our disposal suddenly becomes problematized. Piety is not a problem until we run into a so-called "hard case" in which our standard practice for using the concept suddenly strikes us as somehow inadequate. Such a hard case is something that we may have avoided for a very long time, but once it arises it may present serious difficulties. If we choose to deal with it, rather than simply ignore it, we cannot hope to do so without attempting to

---

[7] *Ibid.*, p. 19.

provide an explicit account of piety; and what could it mean to provide such an account other than to describe piety in a way that shows how it fits into, and functions effectively as part of, our larger conceptual framework?

The very size and complexity of that framework suggests that this is apt to be a never-ending process. Situations, like Euthyphro's, that force us to think seriously about this or that particular concept arise all the time. Again, we make sense of any one concept only by understanding it in such a way that it comports with, fits into, some larger range of concepts. But we cannot keep anything close to all of our concepts in hand all at once; they are far too numerous and far too complex. Thus, to have solved, say, Euthyphro's problem is no guarantee that we will not immediately be required to deal with any number of analogous problems. If we determine what piety is, i.e., if we discover how piety is to be understood in the light of our other concepts, we might nonetheless encounter Laches at the very next turn, and this might make us realize that, although we now have a pretty good understanding of piety, we are not at all sure about courage. And the successful pursuit of courage does not necessarily give us an acceptable definition of justice or moderation or love or, for that matter, dog or snow or red – each of which could raise serious problems of coherence that would call for a conceptual analysis of some kind. Moreover, at some much later date, long after our discussion with Euthyphro, the problem of piety might arise once again and we might be forced to rediscover the sense in which piety can be formulated as part of a coherent conceptual structure – and so on for all of our concepts.

Understood along these lines, the process is one in which our conceptual apparatus not only controls our philosophical inquiries but is revised by them. One thinks here of a metaphor used by Quine, which he attributes to Neurath: the philosopher's task is like that of "a mariner who must rebuild his ship on the open sea."[8] The necessary repairs "can be effected in a piecemeal fashion, the remaining timbers keeping the ship afloat while one is removed and replaced."[9] With the passage of time the ship could be completely remade. It could be, in effect, an entirely new ship. But the new ship would have emerged out of, hence would be in some sense the natural outgrowth or self-unfolding of, the old one.

---

[8] W. V. O. Quine, *From a Logical Point of View* (New York: Harper & Row, 1963), p. 79. The image appears at least as early as 1616, in the work of John Selden. See Richard Tuck, *Natural Rights Theories: Their Origin and Development* (Cambridge: Cambridge University Press, 1979), pp. 84, 132.

[9] Christopher Hookway, *Quine: Language, Experience and Reality* (Stanford: Stanford University Press, 1988), p. 54.

The ship would have essentially remade *itself*, through the agency of its mariners; and the process could, in principle, be unending.

Indeed, philosophy is a Sisyphean enterprise, both perpetual and inescapable. If our conceptual usage were incoherent, if we were continually to contradict ourselves in applying concepts to things in the world, then we would literally fail to make sense. We would violate, that is, the principle of contradiction upon which all logic and rationality is based, and the consequences of this plainly would be unacceptable. Conceptual incoherence – at least beyond a certain point – would make it virtually impossible for us to communicate with one another, hence impossible to carry on a recognizable social existence; and it would make it difficult for each of us individually to function successfully in the world, to know what to do and how to do it. If Euthyphro's beliefs about piety turn out to contradict a number of his other conceptual beliefs, then whenever he attempts to defend an action on grounds of piety we would be unable to make sense of his argument since, if his beliefs are truly contradictory, they would both support and condemn the action. In such a circumstance, moreover, he himself would be forced to conclude that he both should and should not perform the action, and this would render him at best dysfunctional – literally unable to act – and at worst perverse, since failure to act is itself a kind of action.

2. The foregoing suggests that Strawson also shares with the platonist the view that philosophical analysis necessarily seeks, and should be evaluated in terms of the degree to which it achieves, agreement among individuals. It is not enough that my concepts are consistent with one another. If I am to participate with you in a productive and intelligible social relationship, our conceptual structures must be fundamentally similar; and this implies, in turn, a very close connection between agreement on the one hand and truth on the other.

Perhaps the best way of explaining this idea is to begin by emphasizing that, for Strawson, philosophical or metaphysical analysis, being an analysis of concepts, should be understood primarily as an analysis not of the world but of our thinking about the world: "(b)y talking about our conceptual structure, the structure of our thought about the world, rather than, as it were, directly about the world, we keep a firmer grasp of our own philosophical procedure, a clearer understanding of what we are about."[10] Once again, the philosopher's task is to clarify, to the extent possible, the conceptual apparatus that we use in characterizing and

---

[10] Strawson, *Analysis and Metaphysics*, p. 33.

arranging the various individual things that compose our world. But this means that the goal is to describe not so much what *is* the case as what, according to that apparatus, we *take* to be the case.[11] Insofar as any particular claim is to be considered true, this is less a matter of describing how things really are than a matter of saying something that is consistent with, that makes sense in terms of, our conceptual structure. A claim is to be judged, therefore, in terms of whether or not it is something with which we can all rationally agree.

I think that such a doctrine presupposes a sharp distinction between what might be called, following Putnam, the human's-eye view of things and the God's-eye view of things.[12] This distinction, or distinctions rather like it, have provided during the last two centuries the basis for an extraordinary convergence of philosophical thinking, itself rooted in Kant's critical system. I am referring, in effect, to the so-called Kantian revolution in which "the whole course of philosophy, from the turn of the nineteenth century until the present, can be viewed as a single, complex movement."[13]

Kant was concerned with the connection between thought and thing, word and object; and this is a subject about which a surprising range of seemingly quite different philosophical systems turn out to be at least roughly on the same page, albeit sometimes for very different reasons. Indeed, the enormous gulf between the so-called "analytic" and "continental" dispositions in Western philosophy begins to shrink considerably when considered in the light of the Kantian revolution. Prior to Kant, traditional questions of metaphysics were generally assumed to be questions about how the world really is apart from our perceptions of and thoughts about it – and understandably so.[14] Humans have always entertained a wide variety of theories and conceptions of how things are. What could it mean to decide which of them is correct except to test them against reality? The problem, however, is that the process of evaluating theories and conceptions is itself a matter of formulating theories and conceptions. We cannot assess our thoughts except by thinking about them; and we cannot possibly think about them without using and presupposing the very intellectual tools that we are seeking to assess. Our

---

[11] *Ibid.*, p. 34.

[12] Hilary Putnam, *Reason, Truth, and History* (Cambridge: Cambridge University Press, 1981), pp. 49–54. Also, Hilary Putnam, *Realism with a Human Face* (Cambridge: Harvard University Press, 1990), pp. 7–18.

[13] Robert C. Solomon, *Introducing Philosophy: Problems and Perspectives*, 2nd edn. (New York: Harcourt Brace Jovanovich, 1981), p. 191.

[14] Putnam, *Reason, Truth, and History*, p. 56: "Before Kant it is perhaps impossible to find *any* philosopher who did *not* have a correspondence theory of truth."

conceptual structure is a kind of prison from which there seems to be no possibility of escape. The moment we try to think about that structure, we invoke it, since invoking it is precisely what it means to think. It is true, as will be discussed in chapter 6, that to be in such a prison is also part of what it means to be free; our bondage is at the same time our liberty. But this pertains to the consequences of our intellectual limits, rather than to the fact of them; and it is the fact that presently concerns us now, namely, that our conceptual apparatus provides a distinctively human perspective on the world – a human's-eye point of view that no human can possibly transcend.

To ask, then, about the connection or correspondence between what we take things to be from a human's-eye point of view and how things *really* are independent of that point of view is to ask how things look from, so to speak, the God's-eye point of view. Only by stepping outside of our perspective could we critically evaluate the degree to which that perspective accurately describes reality. None of us, however, is God; none of us can step outside of, or could even concretely imagine what might be involved in stepping outside of, the human's-eye point of view; and this means, again, that we are unavoidably trapped within our own cognitive frame of reference. Thus, says Putnam, "the only access we have to the world is to the world as it is represented in thought and language."[15] Strawson substantially agrees: a metaphysical question "might be an invitation to step outside the entire structure of the conceptual scheme which we actually have – and then to justify it from some extraneous point of vantage. But there is nowhere to step; there is no such extraneous point of vantage."[16] And similarly for Quine: "[T]o talk about the world we must already impose upon the world some conceptual scheme peculiar to our own special language .... We can improve our conceptual scheme, our philosophy, bit by bit while continuing to depend on it for support; but we cannot detach ourselves from it and compare it objectively with an unconceptualized reality."[17]

If, however, our real focus is not directly on how things actually are but on how we take them to be, then what could it mean to talk about particular propositions being true or false? If, in other words, a conceptual prison prevents us from independently assessing our thoughts from the

---

[15] Hilary Putnam, *Words and Life* (Cambridge, Mass.: Harvard University Press, 1994), p. 297. The context is, in fact, a qualification of this theme, long held by Putnam, in light of what he takes to be its misuse by Rorty.

[16] Strawson, *Analysis and Metaphysics*, p. 64.

[17] Quine, *From a Logical Point of View*, pp. 78–79. It is, of course, a matter of some controversy whether or not Quine holds to such views in his later writings.

perspective of the world, how could we know if our thoughts are correct? The point is expressed nicely by McDowell, who worries that internalism leaves us "out of touch with the world . . . . It just gives us a dizzying sense that our grip on what it is that we believe is not as firm as we thought."[18] We are in danger of conceiving human thought as little more than a "frictionless spinning in a void," thereby tacitly licensing us to believe and say anything that we want, unconstrained by reality.[19] It would be wonderful, of course, if we could insist that human thought is, in fact, constantly impinged on all sides by the world and that truth really is a matter of correspondence. But again, the apparent impossibility of escaping our prison in order to test the validity of our propositions means that any such recourse to correspondence – to what McDowell and others have called the "myth of the given"[20] – is unavailable. The result is that we are left to oscillate between an unconstrained coherentism that offers no connection to the real world and an unintelligible empiricism that simply ignores the unavoidable limits of human thought.[21]

Some contemporary philosophers have proposed a way out of this conundrum by appealing, more-or-less explicitly, to the Kantian notion of transcendental argument. A transcendental argument is, roughly, an argument that claims to show what must be true if some particular kind of discourse or experience – for example, empirical/scientific discourse or experience – is possible.[22] Kant says that if we are having experiences of the world, then this absolutely presupposes an elaborate cognitive apparatus involving intuitions of space and time, categories of the understanding, the unity of apperception, and so on. It is, for him, impossible to imagine how it could be any other way. It is, however, equally impossible to imagine or to claim that we are not having experiences of the

[18] John McDowell, *Mind and World* (Cambridge, Mass.: Harvard University Press, 1994), p. 17.

[19] *Ibid.*, p. 66.

[20] *Ibid.*, pp. 5–23. The standard text, of course, is Willfrid Sellars, "Empiricism and the Philosophy of Mind," in Herbert Feigl and Michael Scriven, eds., *Minnesota Studies in the Philosophy of Science*, vol. 1 (Minneapolis: University of Minnesota Press, 1956). See also, Richard Rorty, *Philosophy and the Mirror of Nature* (Princeton: Princeton University Press, 1979).

[21] McDowell, *Mind and World*, p. 46.

[22] See, for example, Barry Stroud, "Transcendental Arguments," *Journal of Philosophy* 65 (May 2, 1968), pp. 241–56; Barry Stroud, "The Significance of Scepticism," in Peter Bieri, Rolf-P. Horstmann and Lorenz Kruger, eds., *Transcendental Arguments and Science: Essays in Epistemology* (Boston: D. Reidel, 1979); and Jonathan Bennett, "Analytic Transcendental Arguments," in Bieri, Horstmann and Kruger. I have previously treated these questions in *Logic and Politics: Hegel's Philosophy of Right* (New Haven: Yale University Press, 1988), pp. 105–11.

world, since the very possibility of having an imagination or of stating and communicating a claim seems to require that such experiences are occurring. If, then, we cannot deny that we are having experiences, and since we can have no experiences unless we have certain cognitive capacities, we are forced to conclude that those capacities exist. In Kant's formulation, their existence is transcendentally proved.

Of course, to prove that having experiences of the world presupposes a certain cognitive apparatus, and to be unable coherently to deny that we are having experiences of the world, is not the same as proving that we actually *are* having such experiences. It is to prove only that we must *think* that we are having them. In thinking that we are experiencing an external world, we might just be wrong; our so-called experiences might all be illusions or dreams, the world itself a phantasm. But possibilities of this kind could be evaluated only if we were to step outside of our cognitive or conceptual prison and take the God's-eye point of view; and since this is something that it seems we cannot do, we can never be sure that we are really having experiences of a world that really exists. Thus, Strawson again: "in order for self-conscious thought and experience to be possible, we must take it, or *believe*, that we have knowledge of external physical objects or other minds." And similarly Searle: "I have not shown [through transcendental argument] that there is a real world but only that you are committed to its existence when you talk to me or to anyone else."[23]

Despite this, however, transcendental arguments provide a foundation for claims that are genuinely objective. Here, "objective" has a special meaning. Since the God's-eye point of view is inaccessible to us, our claims about the world do not necessarily correspond with how things really are. Nonetheless, such claims can be objective in the sense that they cannot coherently be denied or, to put it positively, must be affirmed on pain of contradiction. Thus, when Strawson explicitly argues that the existence of material objects in the world is transcendentally proved, he means that no one can deny the existence of such objects and still make sense.[24] It is not possible for you and I coherently to disagree about this; and if this is so, then belief in material objects is not relative to you or me but is, for both of us, a requirement. Their existence is an objective fact. Objectivity is simply the antithesis of subjectivity. Putnam calls it "objectivity for us," or "objectivity and rationality humanly speaking," and observes that "even if it is not the metaphysical objectivity of the God's Eye view," it is nonetheless "what

[23] John R. Searle, *The Construction of Social Reality* (New York: Free Press, 1995), p. 194.
[24] P. F. Strawson, *Individuals: An Essay in Descriptive Metaphysics* (London: Methuen, 1959), p. 40.

we have" and is "better than nothing."[25] Davidson agrees: "in giving up dependence on the concept of an uninterpreted reality, something outside all schemes and science, we do not relinquish the notion of objective truth."[26] Indeed, if a claim is such that it absolutely *must* be affirmed on pain of contradiction, then what does it matter whether or not it corresponds to what is really out there? Or more accurately, what does it matter *for us*, who presumably can never assume the God's-eye point of view, hence can never know whether or not the claim does so correspond? Objectivity "humanly speaking" is not only the best that we can do; it is all that we would ever need.

There is great controversy about whether or not transcendental arguments actually work.[27] While my intuition is that they do, this is something that I'm hardly prepared to defend. What is remarkable, though, is the extraordinary range of contemporary philosophers who rely explicitly on such arguments – not simply Strawson, Putnam, Searle and, somewhat more ambiguously, McDowell, but also Wittgenstein himself.[28] Many of them are directly influenced by Kant;[29] all of them think of philosophical and metaphysical analysis as focusing not on how the world really is but on how we must take it to be; and all of them, in pursuing such

---

[25] Putnam, *Reason, Truth, and History*, p. 55. See also, Putnam, *Realism with a Human Face*, pp. 21–29, 130–31; and Hilary Putnam, *Meaning and the Moral Sciences* (London: Routledge & Kegan Paul, 1978), p. 105.

[26] Donald Davidson, "On the Very Idea of a Conceptual Scheme," in Donald Davidson, *Inquiries into Truth and Interpretation* (Oxford: Oxford University Press), p. 198. It should be noted that the implicit characterization of Davidson's position that I am offering here is something about which Davidson himself would have serious doubts: "I do not think, as friends and critics have variously suggested, that my argument against empiricism makes me, or ought to make me, a pragmatist, a transcendental idealist, or an 'internal' realist. All these positions are forms of relativism that I find as hard to understand as the empiricisms I attack" (p. xviii).

[27] Stroud, "Transcendental Arguments" and "The Significance of Skepticism." Also, Strawson, *Skepticism and Naturalism*, p. 23: "It is not my present purpose to inquire how successfully arguments of the kind in question... survive these criticisms [i.e., those of Stroud]; to inquire, that is, whether some or any of them are strictly valid. I am inclined to think that at least some are (e.g. self-ascription implies the capacity for other-ascription), though I must admit that few, if any, have commanded universal assent among the critics."

[28] Ludwig Wittgenstein, *Philosophical Investigations* (New York: Macmillan, 1968), sections 269 and 275.

[29] P. F. Strawson, *The Bounds of Sense* (London: Methuen, 1966); James Conant, "Introduction," in Putnam, *Realism with a Human Face*, pp. xvii–xxxiv; Searle, *The Construction of Social Reality*, p. 183. McDowell says that "Kant points the way" to a satisfactory treatment of the mind/world relationship; but he also explicitly criticizes what he calls Kant's "transcendental framework," which he finds "profoundly unsatisfactory" (*Mind and World*, pp. 42–43). Whether he is referring here to the idea of transcendental argument or merely to Kant's insistence on the existence of an utterly non-conceptual noumenal world is not entirely clear to me.

a focus, ultimately rely on a criterion of consistency perhaps best articulated, again, by Putnam, who says that "truth . . . is a sort of ideal coherence of our beliefs with each other and with our experiences *as those
experiences are themselves represented in our belief system* – and not correspondence with mind-independent or discourse-independent 'states
of affairs.'"[30] If we add into the mix a variety of other philosophers who
argue for a range of related views – e.g., Dummett, who claims that
metaphysical questions are largely logical ones – then we can perhaps
begin to appreciate the degree to which seemingly disparate contemporary philosophers have come to embrace a broadly Kantian agenda. In this
respect, I follow Blackburn who argues that the Kantian approach to
problems of reality and knowledge has become, among recent analytic
philosophers, an orthodoxy.[31]

3. The unity of philosophy

Philosophical analysis is, as Strawson and others would have it, a quest for
coherence or connectedness. In attempting to arrive at an understanding
of what something in the world is or, rather, of what we must take it to be,
we need to clarify the meaning of the concepts that we use to characterize
that thing. This, in turn, requires us to examine at least a part of our
overall conceptual apparatus, to uncover and demonstrate its internal
consistency and to discover, therein, criteria on the basis of which problems about particular concepts – inconsistency, vagueness, etc. – can be
intelligently addressed and resolved. It seems to me that transcendental
arguments are philosophical in precisely this sense. They seek to describe
what we must believe about particular things in the world, on pain of self-
contradiction, hence purport to explicate certain aspects of a conceptual
scheme that is already in place and that we use – unavoidably, though
usually inexpressly – whenever we try to make the world intelligible.
Certainly not every philosophical argument is a transcendental argument.
But philosophical arguments, including transcendental ones, are alike in
at least three respects: (1) they appeal to a preexisting structure of concepts in order to distinguish claims that are self-refuting from those that
are not, (2) they purport to arrive at conclusions about particular things
that are objective, in the sense of being required of anyone who claims to
be rational, and (3) they presuppose that an analysis of our conceptual

---

[30] Putnam, *Reason, Truth, and History*, pp. 49–50, 64. Emphasis in original. Also, Putnam, *Realism with a Human Face*, p. 41.
[31] Simon Blackburn, "Enchanting Views," in Peter Clark and Bob Hale, eds., *Reading Putnam* (Oxford: Blackwell, 1994), pp. 12–13.

structure is, at the same time, a metaphysical or ontological analysis of the world, undertaken from the human's-eye point of view, such that when we claim that "this is how things really are" – a claim that will appear, in one form or another, throughout Part III of this book – we should be understood in fact to mean something like "this is how we must take things really to be."

Such a view presupposes a deep connection between what we informally call truth, on the one hand, and agreement, on the other. Truth is simply a matter of what rational individuals will agree to, provided that they are all properly exercising their rationality. Of course, not just any agreement will do. People may reach a certain explicit consensus that turns out to be, upon inspection, irrational and incoherent. The empirical fact of agreement – the fact that we all nod our heads together, or vote the same way, or express the same opinion at the same time – is no guarantee. Agreement and truth coalesce only when the agreement is based on a set of genuinely self-consistent beliefs.[32] But this in no way vitiates the force of the argument. For again, truth is determined not by a correspondence with some external reality accessible only to the God's-eye point of view, but by those cognitive powers that constitute the human's-eye point of view; and the test of whether or not a proposition is true is if individuals exercising those powers faithfully and perspicuously would agree to it.

1. The Socratic method, like Strawson's, is a quest for conceptual coherence. In the elenchus, claims about the meaning of this or that concept are tested for consistency against a wide range of (provisionally) uncontested conceptual claims and are accepted or rejected precisely on that basis. The elenchus activates a process of recollection or *anamnesis*, whereby we make explicit (certain features of) a unified conceptual scheme that describes how the world really is, at least according to our lights. The result is, in principle if not always in fact, a proposition about the world – e.g., about the nature of Euthyphro's decision to seek the prosecution of his father – that is objectively true, in the sense of being a coherent part of our own conceptual apparatus. It is true because it is something to which everyone must agree, on pain of contradiction.

Plato certainly thinks that objective truth must mean something more than this. He is a metaphysical, not an internal, realist, hence fails to acknowledge, and would vigorously deny, any distinction between an analysis of how things really are and how we must take them to be. But

---

[32] *Ibid.*, p. 22. Also, Steinberger, *The Concept of Political Judgment*, pp. 230–32.

it's not clear how much difference this makes in deciding whether or not his particular arguments are actually correct. I am not persuaded, for example, that Plato's analysis of piety is affected in any substantial way by the thought/world problem. For insofar as the elenchus is a quest for coherence, an effort to recollect and make explicit our conceptual scheme, it seems not to matter whether that scheme is thought to correspond with some non-conceptual world "out there" or whether it simply describes that which is "objective humanly speaking." In either case, the results of a successful analysis would be irrefutable; in either case, they would have to be assented to on pain of self-contradiction; in either case, the criterion of correctness or truth could be construed, without any loss whatsoever, as a simple matter of agreement among rational creatures. The fact that Plato did not view things in this way does nothing to prevent us from considering his arguments in post-Kantian terms.

Such an account could be applied even to those Platonic propositions that deal with the question of correspondence itself. It is true, for example, that when Plato explains *anamnesis* in terms of the immortality of the soul, he is saying that objectivity does in fact depend on the external world. But there's nothing (exclusive of exegesis) to prevent us from reinterpreting this as a kind of internal realist argument: the ability of Meno's slave to come up with the Pythagorean theorem means not that the soul is immortal but that we must believe it to be immortal. Obviously, looking at Plato in this way would require some substantial changes. Where Plato says "x is y," we would have to reinterpret him as saying "x must be taken to be y." Having done this, moreover, we might discover that some – perhaps all – of the arguments that he actually makes turn out to be unpersuasive. We might decide, for example, that the ability of Meno's slave to come up with the Pythagorean theorem perhaps *doesn't* necessarily presuppose a belief in the immortality of the soul; other explanations might be equally good, or even preferable, in the specific sense that they might turn out to comport better with our overall conceptual structure. But while such revisions would certainly affect the outward appearance of Plato's arguments, or our ultimate evaluation of them, it would not affect the arguments themselves. Their *content*, in other words, would remain the same.

I believe that similar transformations could be imposed on any number of other philosophical traditions and claims. Aristotle's account of causation, Augustine's view of time, Anselm's ontological proof, Descartes' conception of mind and body, Berkeley's defense of immaterialism – all such arguments could plausibly, perhaps profitably, be recast and evaluated as accounts not of how things are but of how we must take things to be.[33] The fact that Kant himself would have rejected every one of those arguments poses, I think, no problem whatever. For one thing, Kant might have been wrong. But more important, the very nature of his critique – that the views in question, and a great many others besides, are unacceptable because they lead to one or another kind of contradiction – would involve precisely the kind of analysis that I am recommending. Again, coherence is the criterion. Truth is a matter not of correspondence with external reality but of what rational individuals faithfully employing their cognitive powers would agree to. If, say, the ontological argument for the existence of God is to be rejected, this can only be because it does not make rational sense when seen in the light of our own shared conceptual scheme.

2. Contemporary philosophy is famously split along "analytic" and "continental" lines, involving what is often taken to be a near incommensurability of thought. As a rule, so-called analytic philosophers do not read, and have little interest in, the work of so-called continental philosophers; and if the reverse is not true to the same extent, the fact is that continentalists, in studying the writings of their analytic counterparts, often do so with a principled suspicion, sometimes bordering on contempt. This split appears to reflect sharp antipathies not just of argumentative style but of philosophical doctrine as well.

These antipathies begin to soften, however, when considered in the terms of the thought/world problem. Thinkers such as Strawson, Putnam, Searle, McDowell and others – one might also include Carnap, with his distinction between questions internal and external to a "framework," and Quine, whose holism insists that "ontological commitments" are always relative to "conceptual schemes"[34] – may be said to reject two things. On the one hand, they reject the (unreinterpreted) pre-Kantian tradition of dogmatic metaphysics as making claims from a God's-eye point of view that no human can assume. On the other hand, they reject with equal vigor the tradition of logical positivism and

---

[33] Davidson says something similar: "In sharing a language . . . we share a picture of the world that must, in its large features, be true. It follows that in making manifest the large features of our language, we make manifest the large features of reality. One way of pursuing metaphysics is therefore to study the general structure of our language. This is not . . . the sole true method of metaphysics . . . but it is one method, and it has been practised by philosophers as widely separated by time or doctrine as Plato, Aristotle, Hume, Kant, Russell, Frege, Wittgenstein, Carnap, Quine, and Strawson." Donald Davidson, "The Method of Truth in Metaphysics," in Davidson, *Inquiries into Truth and Interpretation*, p. 199.
[34] For the relevance of Quine to the tradition I have in mind, see Susan Haack, *Philosophy of Logics* (Cambridge: Cambridge University Press, 1978), p. 95.

verificationism, on the general grounds that it badly misconceives the nature of human thought by denying that metaphysical claims can have any meaning at all. Emblematic here is Putnam's insistence that " 'objects' do not exist independently of conceptual schemes."[35] Such a claim amounts to a denial of both metaphysical realist claims regarding the world "out there" and positivist claims regarding the transparency and indubitability of sense perceptions. The key implication is that all empirical experiences are rooted in, and transformed by, our conceptual apparatus: "internalism does not deny that there are experiential *inputs* to knowledge; knowledge is not a story with no constraints except *internal* coherence; but it does deny that there are any inputs *which are not themselves to some extent shaped by our concepts*, by the vocabulary we use to report and describe them."[36]

Putnam here presents a version of the kind of broadly anti-empiricist view that I alluded to in the previous chapter (2.3.4). Experience – if it is to be something other than a set of mindless impulses, a "heap or collection of different impressions" – must have a conceptual foundation on the basis of which raw feels are organized so as to become intelligible. Such raw feels, whatever they might be, do presumably impose limits on what we are able to think. But given those limits, whose ultimate nature is opaque to us, the truth of our propositions is to be decided in terms of the degree to which rational individuals find themselves in rational agreement.

Coming from an entirely different tradition – directly from Heidegger and, through him, from Hegel and Husserl – Gadamer says much the same thing, and in a strikingly similar way: "our perception is never a simple mirroring of that which is given to the senses . . . . Even perception that is assumed to be adequate would never be a simple mirroring of that which is. For it would always remain an interpretation [*Auffassen*] of something."[37] Gadamer is referring here to nothing other than the conceptual structure – the structure of "prejudice," as he puts it – under which we operate as thinking beings. Like Putnam, he does not deny that our experiences are influenced and constrained by an external, material world: "in aesthetic phenomena limitations on historical self-understanding become visible as being equivalent to limitations that nature presents as a condition of mental life."[38] But like Putnam, he does deny that we can have

[35] Putnam, *Reason, Truth, and History*, p. 52.
[36] *Ibid.*, p. 54.
[37] Hans-Georg Gadamer, *Wahrheit und Methode: Grundzüge einer philosophischen Hermeneutic* (Tübingen: J .C. B. Mohr, 1972), pp. 85–6.
[38] *Ibid.*, p. 91.

any independent access to this external world: "we are given no standpoint that would allow us to see from the outside such limits and conditions in themselves and to see ourselves as limited and conditioned in this way."[39] He thus explicitly understands knowledge itself to be a matter of *anamnesis*, according to which the observer makes sense of things, and comes to know their essence, by recognizing experience to be embedded in, and to comport with, a preestablished structure of thought and meaning, a structure of metaphysical or ontological truth claims.[40]

Such views echo those of a host of writers in the analytic tradition. Consider Searle's concept of the "Background." For Searle, the Background describes a "set of nonintentional or preintentional capacities that enable intentional states of function."[41] Exactly how these capacities are related to "conceptual schemes" or "horizons" is not immediately clear, and what Searle says is, in one respect, confusing. He indicates that the Background is composed, in part, of features that describe "'how things are'."[42] He explicitly denies, however, that these features are "assumptions," "presumptions" or "beliefs." Assumptions, presumptions or beliefs would be "intentional," while the Background is, to the contrary, "preintentional." It is for this reason that he prefers to identify background features as "capacities" or "practices." But it's hard to see how it makes sense to say that features that do indeed describe "how things are," hence that seem to have propositional/intentional content, are nonetheless mere capacities or practices. One way to solve this problem, I think, is to suggest that, as a *psychological* matter, our background understanding of how things are is implicit or latent. It is not something that we consciously describe to ourselves, hence not something that can be formulated as intentional. But as a *philosophical* matter, it is profoundly propositional. It consists of implicit, unarticulated claims about the world, claims to which we are strongly committed, despite our failure to acknowledge them. Of course, if I am right about this, then presumably such claims could be uncovered, recollected and rationally reconstructed. That which is implicit can be rendered explicit. And indeed, this is precisely what Searle himself does when he describes how the Background accounts for, say, our ability to

---

[39] *Ibid.*
[40] *Ibid.*, for example at pp. 105–15. While it is true that the immediate contexts of these passages concern aesthetic theory, Gadamer also makes clear that its implications are far broader than simply the "question of artistic truth." For Gadamer, "aesthetic experience is not just one kind of experience among others, but rather represents the nature of experience in general" (p. 66).
[41] Searle, *The Construction of Social Reality*, p. 129.
[42] John R. Searle, *Intentionality: An Essay in the Philosophy of Mind* (Cambridge: Cambridge University Press, 1983), p. 144.

interpret speech acts. His own analysis thus concedes the underlying propositional nature of the Background.

It should be no surprise, then, that Searle's approach to the problem of perception sounds remarkably like Gadamer's: "I see this as a chair, this as a table, that as a glass, indeed any normal case of perception will be a case of perceiving as, where the perceiver assimilates the perceived object to some more or less familiar category."[43] We perceive things, in other words, only in terms of a preestablished conceptual structure – composed of "familiar categories" – that makes the perception what it is. Moreover, Searle, like Gadamer, is eager to extend the argument in the broadest possible terms:

All nonpathological forms of consciousness are experienced under the aspect of familiarity. And this is a function of our Background capacities. Because all intentionality is aspectual, all conscious intentionality is aspectual; and the possibility of perceiving, that is, the possibility of experiencing under aspects requires a familiarity with the set of categories under which one experiences those aspects. The ability to apply those categories is a Background ability.

Consciousness presupposes the Background; and to the extent that the Background comprises a set of categories or ideas, together with the capacity and disposition to utilize those categories, our view of the world – our understanding of it, our notion of what is true about it – is, for Searle as for Gadamer, dependent upon a conceptual scheme.

3. Gadamer is, in many respects, a highly representative figure. His approach, or at least something similar, is broadly reflected in a wide variety of continental traditions including hermeneutics, phenomenology and the interpretivist tradition of social inquiry. Without in any way wishing to minimize differences of opinion and argumentative style, I believe that a great many writers associated with these various traditions share with Putnam, Searle, Strawson and the others a certain fundamental approach to the general problem of philosophical method and metaphysical or ontological truth. They agree that:

- The claims that we make about the world are, in one way or another, products of a conceptual apparatus or scheme that is prior to any particular experience we might have. The scheme is prior in the sense of being presupposed in the very possibility of having an experience.
- All thought and judgment about the world is undertaken internal to some such conceptual scheme, and this includes thought and judgment

---

[43] *Ibid.*, p. 133.

about the scheme itself. To the degree that the scheme becomes an object of experience, any criticism of it must therefore be immanent.

• It is certainly true that particular claims about the world might be right or might be wrong. In employing our conceptual scheme, we may make mistakes. But such mistakes could be discovered only through an internal critique, according to which a proposition is ruled out if it fails to comport with the larger structure of propositions and conceptual claims upon which experience is based.

• To make a mistake, then, is to misinterpret an experience. This does indeed suggest that truth is relative to conceptual schemes. But it is also the case that within any particular scheme, the truth or falsity of a proposition is an objective fact. A true proposition, in other words, is something that, from the perspective of a scheme, cannot be denied. If it is the case that each of us operates within such a scheme, and if it is also true that we can find no vantage point external to the scheme from which to judge it – since the activity of judging presupposes the scheme itself – then any proposition that is fully consistent with the scheme is, for all intents and purposes, undeniably, objectively true.

• All of these principles pertain to human knowledge and inquiry of whatever kind, including natural science. The extraordinary successes of the scientific enterprise, and the degree to which scientific inquiry seems to produce a linear increase in human knowledge, is perfectly consistent with the claim that scientific theories – however well confirmed by empirical data – nonetheless reflect premises of a conceptual nature that cannot themselves be directly found in the world "out there." Again, that world is always and unavoidably preinterpreted for us by a structure of ideas, a background. Without such a background, experience itself would be unimaginable.

The convergence of so-called analytic and continental perspectives with respect to these principles is sometimes acknowledged by the practitioners themselves. Habermas, for example, emphasizes the degree to which notions of communicative competence and communicative ethics are informed by the tradition of speech act theory and pragmatics associated with Austin, Searle and Grice. From the other side of things, Putnam occasionally notes the relevance for his work of Gadamer (at one point explicitly linking Gadamer to Quine and Davidson), something that is echoed rather more strongly by McDowell.[44] Perhaps most astonishing of all is the latter's self-described Hegelianism, a fact that seems to have surprised McDowell as much as anyone – as, for example, when he

---

[44] Putnam, *Words and Life*, p. 455; McDowell, *Mind and World*, pp. 115–19.

acknowledges that Hegel plays almost no direct role in "the philosophical tradition I was brought up in."[45]

I have suggested that the basis for this general convergence is essentially Kantian. McDowell agrees. In describing his own philosophical project, he recommends that we "stand on the shoulders of the giant, Kant, and see our way to the supersession of traditional philosophy that he almost managed, though not quite. The philosopher whose achievement that description best fits is someone we take almost no notice of... namely, Hegel." McDowell explicitly links Hegel, especially as interpreted by Pippin, to Kant, especially as interpreted by Strawson; and if we concede that Strawson's Kant is not too different from the Kant that so strongly influenced Putnam, and that is referred to by Searle, then we can begin to see why such theorists might wind up saying things that sound similar to some of the things said by Gadamer, Habermas and Charles Taylor, for whom the influence of Kant and Hegel is manifest and direct. If we add to this another, rather different point of historical connection – namely, the broad philosophical appeal of Wittgenstein's later writings among so-called analytic and continental philosophers alike – then we can perhaps also see why Davidson or Quine or, in quite different ways, Dummett or Gareth Evans might propose things that hermeneuticians or critical theorists or discourse ethicists could themselves propose, albeit in quite different ways. And if, finally, we warrant the kind of historical reinterpretation suggested in 3.3.1 above, wherein authors of the tradition might be usefully treated as though they were internal rather than metaphysical or dogmatic realists, then perhaps we can begin to see the outlines of a philosophical standpoint from which various theories, despite their sharp differences, nonetheless appear to be profoundly commensurable, to the extent that the differences might themselves compose the foundation for intelligible and productive philosophical conversations.[46]

---

[45] McDowell, *Mind and World*, p. 111.

[46] On the role of Heidegger in all this, I would recommend the early pages of Hubert Dreyfus, *Being-in-the-World: A Commentary on Heidegger's Being and Time*, vol. 1 (Cambridge, Mass.: MIT Press, 1991). Dreyfus briefly but suggestively explores (pp. 5–8) connections between Heidegger, on the one hand, and Strawson, Searle and Wittgenstein on the other. He does take pains to distinguish Heidegger's views. Thus, for Heidegger the "Background" should not be conceived as an implicit or tacit structure of knowledge or theory, hence is not something that can be rationally reconstructed (pp. 21–22). I am not entirely persuaded, however. While Heidegger denies, per Dreyfus, the possibility of rational reconstruction, he nonetheless emphasizes (again according to Dreyfus, p. 24) the possibility and importance of something called "consciousness raising." The difference between the two is not at all clear. Dreyfus argues that the kind of hermeneutic inquiry involved in consciousness raising will always be "unfinished and subject to error" (p. 22), but that could be equally true of rational reconstruction; and

4. Among other things, such conversations could well focus on the particular way in which we ought to characterize the conceptual apparatus – the structure, scheme, horizon, Background, etc. – out of which thinking itself emerges. Philosophy is, in some sense, the activity of consulting that apparatus with a view to discovering its coherence and resolving, thereby, certain conceptual puzzles. But exactly what is being consulted? What is the nature of the conceptual apparatus, and how can we best investigate it?

There is a range of possible answers. As we have suggested, for example, Plato locates our conceptual apparatus in an immortal soul, something that we have inherited as a fact of nature, perhaps through a process of transmogrification. The soul, because it "has seen all things both here and in the other world," contains the complete truth about "everything there is." The philosopher's task is essentially to remind us of the contents of the soul, i.e., the Forms; and this task is accomplished through the discipline of the dialectic, wherein particular propositions are evaluated in terms of whether or not they comport with the larger structure of truth to be found therein.

Kant, on the other hand, writes about intuitions, categories and unities of experience that describe not a soul but a set of cognitive capacities and dispositions. We are rational creatures precisely because we are possessed of such capacities and dispositions, and because we use them to impose order and intelligibility upon what might otherwise be an incoherent, structureless universe. As we have seen, important contemporary philosophers such as Strawson and Searle seem committed to some such view.

With Hegel, the idea of a conceptual apparatus becomes both broadened and historicized. Under the name of *Geist* – or "mind" – it is thought to be composed of all true, i.e. coherent, propositions about the world. Each individual person is best understood as a vehicle of *Geist*, a creature through which rationality, otherwise merely latent, comes to be thought and articulated, hence "actualized," in the empirical world. In this sense, *Geist* is both the activity and the content of mind, wherein the one influences the other. The activity of thinking establishes, or discloses, the content of objective truth which, in turn, stimulates and shapes further thinking, leading to broader and deeper truths, thence to yet

when he characterizes the Heideggerian Background as a matter of [preontological] "understanding" based on shared "agreements" and "interpretations" (pp. 19, 21) that allow us to "get clear" (p. 24) about our understanding, the distinction between Heidegger's views and those of Strawson, Searle, Wittgenstein and others becomes problematic indeed. More generally, the mere fact of the comparison, and the terms in which Dreyfus makes it, suggest that the relevant disagreements, whatever else they might be, are essentially family disputes, no less severe and vehement for being internal to a shared tradition of thought, a tradition sharply at odds with, say, Platonic, Aristotelian, Cartesian or classical empiricist approaches.

more thinking, and so on. One important implication is that, for Hegel, the outward appearance or articulation of the conceptual apparatus changes over time; and while this process of change is a single process of self-revelation guided by an internal logic, its particular historical manifestations are likely to differ from one another quite significantly, at least until *Geist* attains – or comes to discover, through us – its final and complete coherence.

With Heidegger and Gadamer, such notions come to be further relativized. Our conceptual apparatus is now understood to reflect neither universal mental capacities nor a single, teleological structure of truth but, rather, the particular presuppositions or prejudices of a culture. Here, objective truth is objective only internal to a "community of interpretation";[47] and it is in the light of this that philosophy (as practiced by a Quine as well as a Gadamer) begins to acquire a new focus, namely, how to explain communication among a diversity of such communities. Indeed, if objectivity is truly relative to distinct communities of interpretation, then we encounter the prospect – as with Davidson – of a mutual incommensurability so radical that various communities could not even recognize one another as communities.[48] Obviously, this poses a serious challenge to the very idea of rationality. But a challenge is not necessarily a refutation; for to the extent that interpretive communities, however disparate, *do* recognize one another, such recognition actually points *away* from relativism and back to a kind of larger and more encompassing "objectivity for us." Indeed, the fact that people holding seemingly disparate and incompatible world-views evidently can communicate meaningfully with one another and make at least some sense of their disagreements suggests, perhaps, that all of us really do share some kind of meta-perspective – a generalized conceptual or transcendental scheme on the basis of which we might actually achieve what Gadamer calls the "fusion of horizons."

4. Human action and ontological commitment

The post-Kantian convergence, though primarily a convergence of philosophical perspectives, also has enormous implications for social theory. Indeed, it informs and underwrites our understanding of the very nature of human and social action. I believe that the linchpin of that understanding, and the source of connection between ontological

---

[47] Stanley Fish, *Is There a Text in this Class?* (Cambridge, Mass.: Harvard University Press, 1980), pp. 322–37.
[48] Davidson, "On the Very Idea of a Conceptual Scheme."

commitment on the one hand and human action on the other, is the theory of judgment. All action, properly conceived, reflects judgment; and all judgment reflects, in turn, a conceptual apparatus that embodies and sustains a structure of metaphysical or ontological presupposition, a structure of truth.

1. I understand judgment to be a species of "intelligent performance" wherein we predicate universals of particulars. When we characterize this individual object as a "dog," or as "snow," or as "red," or as "pious," we are attributing to it some general quality, hence making a judgment. We do not ordinarily doubt our ability to do this and, often, to do it quite well. But our doing it seems to presuppose a particular and identifiable set of intellectual faculties the exact nature of which may not be immediately apparent.[49]

One such faculty is the faculty of insight or intuition – the capacity to perceive certain features of the world immediately, to become acquainted with or knowledgeable about those features without having to rely on any kind of inferential process. Standing in front of a fire engine, I do not ordinarily infer that it is red; I simply see it that way. No step-by-step procedure is involved, at least as far as I can tell – no process of deduction or analysis or calculation. The judgment just occurs.

Exactly how this happens, and why it is that some people seem to have more acute faculties of insight than others, are questions that may or may not have ultimate answers. In one sense, of course, they are of little consequence, for it is obvious that an inability to explain how one perceives things does not ordinarily affect the accuracy or reliability of one's perceptions. Perhaps the science of optics, together with the science of cognition, will some day provide a complete explanation of our ability to see red; but we certainly need not know anything about either science in order to exercise that ability, apparently with great success.

In another sense, though, questions about whether or not we can account for our perceptions are crucial. For judgment is not a species of intelligent performance unless it also presupposes at least the possibility of rationally reconstructing particular claims – or so I have argued.[50] Our idea of judgment involves not simply the faculty of perception but also the capacity to provide a *post festum* accounting, to say after the fact why a particular judgment is justified, to adduce reasons that would demonstrate the rational truth of a claim. Presumably animals can perceive red

---

[49] Much of what follows relies on Steinberger, *The Concept of Political Judgment*, especially chapter 4.
[50] *Ibid.*, pp. 236–40.

every bit as well as we can. But color perception becomes an *intelligent* performance only when it is undertaken by a creature that could, in the proper circumstances, explain after the fact how the characteristics of light and of the human brain might conspire to produce in us the sensation of red. In part, this means recognizing and acknowledging the degree to which our perceptions are shaped and influenced by our perspective, by the conceptual apparatus that inclines us to see and interpret the world in certain ways; and in part, it means formulating arguments or justifications that make sense in terms of that apparatus and that help to compose an internally coherent understanding of things.[51] All of this describes, then, an intellectual process wherein universals are predicated of particulars according to a rational argument of some kind, albeit an argument that is usually made explicit – if it is made explicit – only after the fact.

It should perhaps go without saying that rational reconstruction along these lines is rarely, maybe never, complete. Scientific knowledge is constantly changing – whether cumulatively or not is a different question – and this suggests that few if any of our explanations are ever final and definitive. What counts as a good explanation of color perception in one era may not work very well in another. But to have provided at least some such explanation, however provisional, is a far cry from having provided none at all. For it is precisely with explanation, with the effort to reconstruct and articulate an account, that we enter the realm of intelligibility.

Certainly much of what we humans do is not always intelligent in this way. We share a great deal with animals, and in this sense ordinary color perception may not be a very good example of judgment at all. (One indication of this is that we are rarely inclined to think about what we are doing when we perceive colors. The activity seems so natural and unproblematic as not to require any reflection at all – at least outside of the laboratory.) But we also do many things that animals don't do and that clearly presuppose a capacity to account for our activity. We judge that a sentence is grammatical, an argument logical, a painting beautiful, a policy prudent, an action pious; and in each case, it is understood that we might be expected to provide reasons for believing our judgment to be true, if only after the fact. We expect a grammarian to explain how a rule applies to a particular case, a philosopher to unpack an argument, an art critic to "criticize" an artwork, a politician to justify a policy, a theologian to interpret a doctrine. This is not to say that judgment *follows* analysis. To make such a claim is to commit what Ryle rightly calls an "intellectualistic

---

[51] For a penetrating discussion of how something like rational reconstruction might actually occur, see Larry Wright, "Argument and Deliberation: A Plea for Understanding," *Journal of Philosophy* 92 (November 1995).

fallacy",[52] and again, if anything is clear it is that judgment does not always occur inferentially. But the capacity to provide, in principle, a *post festum* account is nonetheless precisely what makes performance intelligent, hence what distinguishes judgment, properly understood, from mere natural instinct.

Now it seems to me that judgment, so conceived, is connected to metaphysical or ontological inquiry in at least two ways. First, some of the judgments that we make are directly ontological in nature. They are judgments about what some particular thing really, essentially is. Admittedly, it is not always clear how to distinguish these from other kinds of judgment. Presumably it is one thing to say of some X that it is essentially Y, and something quite different to say that Y is merely one characteristic of X. The difference is bound up, presumably, with old and deeply perplexing questions about form and matter, substance and accident, primary and secondary qualities, and the like, questions that are far beyond the scope of the present study. In an important sense, however, they are also beside the point. For our purposes, it is enough to note that when we predicate a universal of a particular we are at least sometimes purporting to say what that particular thing really, essentially is. If I say that this creature is a dog, I am making a claim about the nature of the thing – an ontological claim – and this involves some sense of what it means for a dog to be a dog.

Second, every judgment we make, whether directly metaphysical or not, presupposes a conceptual apparatus that itself implies an understanding of how the world really is. If I say that the thing is a dog, this assumes a complex theory to the effect that the thing has existence, that dogs have existence, and that there can be in the world a kind of substantial connection between particular things and universal things such that it is both sensible and necessary to think of the one in terms of the other. I do not see how I could intelligibly claim that the thing is a dog if I do not believe that it really exists; and if I believe that it really exists but do not believe in the existence of dogs, then again it is hard to see how I could intelligibly call it a dog (other than by engaging in some kind of literary wordplay); and, finally, if I believe that the thing exists and that dogs exist but that there is no possible way to show of any particular thing that it either is or is not a dog, then once more my claim becomes an absurdity. To offer a judgment is to assume that there is in the world *some* fact of the matter such that the judgment can be said to be justified;

[52] Gilbert Ryle, *The Concept of Mind* (New York: Barnes and Noble, 1960), p. 30. See also, Steinberger, *The Concept of Political Judgment*, p. 295.

and this, in turn, presupposes some account both of what it means for the world to be composed of facts and of what at least some of those facts might be.

In describing his concept of the Background, Searle asks us to "[t]hink of what is necessary, what must be the case, in order that I can now form the intention to go to the refrigerator and get a bottle of cold beer to drink. The biological and cultural resources that I must bring to bear on the task, even to form the intention to perform the task, are (considered in a certain light) truly staggering."[53] The task of predicating universals of particulars is no different. My claim that this thing is a dog commits me to an enormous range of propositions regarding not only the object itself and the idea of *dog* but also the very nature of material objects in the world, the physics of space and time, the biology of mammals, the psychology of sense perception, and so on.[54] Indeed, when I claim that the thing is a dog, I also imply that it is not a horse or a chalkboard or a sonata or an ocean or any of the other kinds of things of which the world is composed. These are negative claims, to be sure, but they are claims nonetheless, and not insignificant ones. It is a fact about the little furry object before me that it is not an ocean. I would only rarely give this fact any particular emphasis; it goes without saying. But if it's a trivial fact in one sense, in another it's pretty crucial – virtually as crucial as any other fact about the thing. As such, it is an integral part of my ontology. Since the fact that the creature is not an ocean is something that ordinarily I would not articulate even to myself, it may not be a "belief" insofar as beliefs involve intentional states. But even if it is not a belief in that sense, surely it is some kind of proposition about the world to which I am committed, something easily and immediately reconstructable, such that if someone were to ask me if this particular four-legged creature is an ocean, I would hesitate only in order to decide whether or not the question was facetious.

2. Every judgment that we make thus carries with it an immense and complex structure of ontological commitment, without which the judgment would be unintelligible. I want to argue, next, that judgment of this kind is a ubiquitous feature of human life. Each of us is constantly making judgments, constantly predicating universals of particulars; and the upshot is that each of us is a metaphysician.

---

[53] Searle, *Intentionality*, p. 143.
[54] See Wright, "Argument and Deliberation," p. 568.

Imagine that I have an argument with you about whether or not Billy Williams, the former Chicago Cubs baseball player, belongs in the Baseball Hall of Fame. The argument will undoubtedly rely on an analysis of statistics, a comparison of Mr. Williams's performance with that of others in the Hall of Fame, perhaps some discussion as to whether or not statistics adequately capture the nature of achievement in baseball, and the like. All of this will involve some understanding of the kind of player Billy Williams really was and also of what it means to talk about the Hall of Fame. What is the essence of a Hall of Famer, and to what extent does Billy Williams fit the bill?

In making various claims about this, we necessarily assume that there is a fact of the matter regarding the nature of Hall of Fame players, a truth to be discovered and articulated during the course of our conversation. Of course, one of us might be a radical skeptic who believes, say, that the Hall of Fame is purely political and doesn't reflect the true achievement of players, or that there is no way at all to measure such true achievement, or that the very idea of true achievement in baseball is suspect since so many things could, from one or another perspective, be considered wonderful achievements and so why should someone be rewarded for having hit lots of home runs and someone else not rewarded for having kept a cheerful disposition despite an inability to hit anything, and so on. But all of these skeptical claims would also be metaphysical ones, since they would tie every judgment that we might make to any number of ontological propositions. For example, the proposition that the very idea of true achievement in baseball is somehow invalid is an ontological proposition – it purports to state a fact of the matter about the world – from which it follows either that the Hall of Fame should not exist or else that it should exist as something very different from what it purports to be.

Now it might be objected that I have misunderstood skepticism. A true skeptic does not make metaphysical claims at all but, rather, denies the legitimacy or even intelligibility of any such claim. This may be correct. But the point of tying judgment to metaphysical commitment is simply to show that wherever a judgment is made we find a proposition about how the world really is; and where someone denies that we can say anything about how the world really is, that person is simply denying that it is possible to make an intelligible judgment. Thus, if someone believes that there is no way of measuring the true achievement of baseball players, then it is hard to see how he or she could have any intelligible views about who should be in the Hall of Fame, assuming the Hall of Fame to be an institution that certifies true achievement in baseball.

But in making this argument, haven't I illicitly conflated metaphysical and epistemological questions? Skepticism, after all, says nothing about the world, only about our ability to know it. The general perspective that I have outlined here, however, explicitly denies a sharp distinction between the question of what there is and the question of what we can know. Strawson insists that "the general theory of being (ontology), the general theory of knowledge (epistemology), and the general theory of the proposition, of what is true or false (logic) are but three aspects of one unified enquiry."[55] This, it seems to me, is merely another way of saying that objective truth is always "humanly objective truth," objective for us, hence reflective of and limited to a particular epistemic standpoint, namely, the human's-eye point of view; and as I have argued, such a limitation does not in any way compromise the sense in which objectivity can really be objective. Thus, an account of the nature of Hall of Fame baseball players is, at the same time, an account of what we can know about that topic, hence an account of the kinds of relevant propositions that could be true or false.

Our ordinary lives are filled with conversations of the Billy Williams nature. Each of us is constantly in the business of making decisions, from the most inconsequential (what to wear this morning, what to eat, which section of the newspaper to read first) to the most significant (what career to pursue, whom to marry, what kind of life to live). Each of is inclined to discuss our decisions – if only by engaging in the kind of internal dialogue that is, for Hannah Arendt among others, a characteristic feature of human thought. Hence, each of us is constantly making judgments, constantly engaged in one or another kind of intelligent performance. Of course, in making our various decisions we differ dramatically in the nature and range of options available to us. This morning, the Queen of England will have to choose her wardrobe from an immense array of options, while a Hutu boy desperately fleeing an army of Tutsi invaders may simply have to decide whether or not to wear his only garment; the Queen's decision about what to eat for lunch will be made under few if any external constraints – she can have pretty much whatever she wants – whereas the boy may well be happy to have anything to eat at all; her afternoon will perhaps be preoccupied with judgments about matters of state, family finances, personal recreation, and the like, while his will perhaps be devoted to rudimentary choices that may determine whether or not he survives the day. Ours is a world of the cruelest injustice, fraught with inequalities of condition so extreme and outrageous, and humiliations and degradations so revolting and scandalous, as to be, for the fortunate among us, difficult even to imagine. But this great diversity of

---

[55] Strawson, *Analysis and Metaphysics*, p. 35.

circumstance should not blind us to the fact that each person, even the most humble and downtrodden, forms intentions and pursues them by making choices based on judgments that can be rationally reconstructed after the fact. The Hutu boy who chooses one escape route over another generally does so on the basis of some theory – however inchoate, however incorrect it may be – as to why this path is better than that; and in doing so, he will be engaged in an intelligent performance no less than the Queen who, based on her minister's recommendation, must decide to endorse this or that piece of parliamentary business. It may be, of course, that the boy's theory is based on superstition and irrational prejudice, hence would fail to withstand any kind of genuine critical scrutiny. But this would be equally true of the Queen if she chose to act only after consulting the Royal astrologer; and in either case, the basic point is entirely unaffected, for the fact that action presupposes a metaphysical theory does not mean that it presupposes a *good* one. It may also be the case that the boy's circumstances are so desperate, his fears so intense, his physical condition so deteriorated that he is no longer able to think at all clearly, and then his behavior will perhaps begin to lose some of its intelligence and intelligibility and degenerate into something more purely instinctual. But this would be equally true if the Queen has gone mad, as queens sometimes do.

3. The foregoing suggests, I believe, an approach to action and agency that gives pride of place to metaphysical considerations. Searle's case of getting a beer from the refrigerator is a precise example of an action. It describes an enterprise based on a series of judgments, which in turn reflect a complex understanding of how things really are, a metaphysics, a structure of truth claims. And so too with the Queen's choice of fish over beef, the Hutu boy's decision to follow the river road instead of the mountain road, my friend's determination to start a Billy Williams fan club, and the like. In each case, an agent makes a judgment and then acts in light of that judgment, thereby connecting the action to any number of metaphysical or ontological presuppositions. Of course, merely to judge that this particular thing is a dog is not, in and of itself, to engage in an action. But virtually anything that I actually do with the thing – pet it or feed it, for example – will be informed by such a judgment; hence, the judgment and everything that goes along with it is intimately, indeed inextricably, bound up with the action itself.

The contemporary theory of agency, in its standard formulation, follows very much along these lines. Agency is understood as a kind of gamesmanship in which the individual agent, interacting with others, invokes strategies in order to attain desired results, often through a process of improvisation.

Such strategies reflect, in large part, a system of differentiation and discrimination – a structure of metaphysical presupposition – that describes how things really are and that justifies one course of action over another. To use a term of art, human action reflects the "habitus."

The habitus is "an acquired system of generative schemes objectively adjusted to the particular conditions in which it is constituted."[56] Two points call for emphasis. First, generative schemes are explicitly described as "classificatory" or "practical taxonomies" that distinguish the various things we encounter in the world according to a more-or-less finite set of categories.[57] As such, they unavoidably express some set of metaphysical propositions about how things really are, propositions on the basis of which social interaction is predicated: "(o)ne of the fundamental effects of the orchestration of habitus is the production of a commonsense world endowed with the *objectivity* secured by consensus of meaning (*sens*) of practices and the world, in other words the harmonization of agents' experiences and the continuous reinforcement that each of them receives from the expression, individual or collective (in festivals, for example), improvised or programmed (commonplaces, sayings), of similar or identical experiences."[58] This is to say, in part, that social life presupposes substantial agreement about the kinds of distinctions or categories that are considered appropriate to the world and that describe, in effect, the nature of things. Indeed, it is only through the relative "homogeneity" of the habitus that actions can become "intelligible"[59] – once again understanding intelligibility to be a distinguishing feature of any distinctively human enterprise. The fact that individuals are involved in intelligent performance, hence in meaningful social interaction, absolutely presupposes "a subjective but non-individual system of internalized structures, common schemes of perception, conception and action, which are the precondition of all objectification and apperception."[60] Thus, the habitus is the "unchosen principle of all 'choices.'" Insofar as human action involves making decisions, it invariably reflects an underlying conceptual or classificatory structure; and it is hard to imagine any such structure that does not itself reflect some theory about how things in the world really are.[61]

[56] Pierre Bourdieu, *Outline of a Theory of Practice* (Cambridge: Cambridge University Press, 1977), p. 95.
[57] Pierre Bourdieu, *The Logic of Practice* (Stanford, California: Stanford University Press, 1990), pp. 66–79. Also, Bourdieu, *Outline of a Theory of Practice*, p. 97.
[58] Bourdieu, *Outline of a Theory of Practice*, p. 80.
[59] *Ibid.* Also Bourdieu, *The Logic of Practice*, p. 58.
[60] Bourdieu, *The Logic of Practice*, p. 60. Also, Bourdieu, *Outline of a Theory of Practice*, p. 97.
[61] Bourdieu, *The Logic of Practice*, p. 61.

The second point to be emphasized is that, according to Bourdieu, agents generally invoke this kind of structure unselfconsciously. Arguing, in part, against so-called rational choice theory, he claims that human action and interaction typically occur "without any calculation or conscious reference to a norm" and without "explicit co-ordination."[62] Here we have again, as with so many of the theories that we have already encountered, the idea of a deep structure of metaphysical presupposition that underwrites, however indirectly, most if not all of our judgments and practices. Bourdieu's idea of a generative classificatory scheme is thus strongly suggestive of what is elsewhere called a world of Forms, or *Geist*, or a conceptual structure, or a horizon of prejudice, or a Background, and so on. Despite their manifold differences, each of these notions understands intelligent performance to be informed by and reflective of some underlying and implicit but ultimately reconstructable notion of how things really are. Searle's account of getting a beer from the refrigerator is thus akin to Bourdieu's account of the anthropologist "who recorded 480 elementary units of behavior in 20 minutes' observation of his wife in the kitchen" – a repertoire of improvised, meaningful human activity that could be explained only by presupposing the existence of a habitus or Background in which particular moves "are objectively organized as strategies without being the product of a genuine [i.e., self-conscious] strategic intention."[63]

It is important to emphasize that for Bourdieu, as for the others, the generally unselfconscious operation of the habitus is not to be thought of as a purely mechanical or physical, hence inherently meaningless, process of causation. Indeed, "although practice is accomplished – in Bourdieu's understanding of the social world – without conscious deliberation for the most part, it is not without purpose(s)."[64] The habitus describes an implicit, covert structure of understanding that permeates all of our actions and renders them significant and intelligible, such that to make sense of an activity requires that it be not simply observed but interpreted.[65] As such, the habitus can always be rendered at least partially explicit. Bourdieu notes, for example, that "if witticisms surprise their author no less than their audience, and impress as much by their

---

[62] *Ibid.*, pp. 58–59.
[63] *Ibid.*, p. 62. The connection is explicitly noted by Searle himself: "Pierre Bourdieu's important work on the 'habitus' is about the same sort of phenomena that I call the Background." Searle, *The Construction of Social Reality*, p. 132.
[64] Richard Jenkins, *Pierre Bourdieu* (London: Routledge, 1992), p. 71.
[65] Of course, strictly speaking nothing is simply observed; all observation is an interpretation. But to interpret behavior as merely physical is one thing; to interpret it as itself an interpretation is something quite different.

respective necessity as by their novelty, the reason is that the *trouvaille* appears as the simple unearthing, at once accidental and irresistible, of a buried possibility."[66] Even more strongly, the very activity of the anthropologist – one who might study, say, the marriage practices of Berber peasants in Algeria – is largely a matter of uncovering and rationally reconstructing precisely the conceptual apparatus, the structure of truth, upon which social interaction is based.

Bourdieu's theories are aimed, above all, at overcoming the most basic oppositions of modern social inquiry – objectivism and subjectivism, determinism and freedom, conditioning and creativity, institution and action[67] – by arriving at formulations that do justice to each side of the equation. Bourdieu rejects as one-sided both structural/functional and interactionist/interpretive theories, but then attempts to incorporate both of them in a more comprehensive conception. As such, his work reflects a broad contemporary interest in the convergence of sociological perspectives, an interest that is manifested, variously, in structuration theory, hermeneutical sociology, praxis theory and symbolic interactionism. Such perspectives seek to transcend the apparent opposition between objective determinism and subjective choice. They see human agency as reflecting, at least in part, some underlying set of presuppositions that compose an ontological account of how things are. And they understand themselves as embracing, to one degree or another, larger themes of post-Kantian philosophy. Thus, for example, Bourdieu explicitly invokes Hegel, among others, in describing the intellectual roots of the idea of the habitus.[68] Interpretivist and hermeneutical social scientists rely heavily on Gadamer and/or Wittgenstein.[69] Symbolic interactionists make common cause with writers like Putnam and Quine in emphasizing the centrality of philosophical pragmatism.[70] In all such cases, the premises of contemporary metaphysical or ontological theory – understood as the effort to uncover and explicate shared, underlying presuppositions about the nature of things – are adapted to sociological or anthropological

[66] Bourdieu, *Outline of a Theory of Practice*, p. 79.

[67] Bourdieu, *The Logic of Practice*, p. 55.

[68] Pierre Bourdieu, *In Other Words: Essays Towards a Reflexive Sociology* (Stanford, California: Stanford University Press, 1990), p. 12.

[69] See J. B. Thompson, *Critical Hermeneutics: A Study in the Thought of Paul Ricoeur and Jürgen Habermas* (Cambridge: Cambridge University Press, 1981), pp. 118–20; and W. Outhwaite, "Hans-Georg Gadamer," in Q. Skinner, ed., *The Return of Grand Theory in the Human Sciences* (Cambridge: Cambridge University Press, 1985).

[70] For example, Anselm L. Strauss, *Continual Permutations of Action* (Hawthorne, New York: Aldine de Gruyter, 1993), pp. 11–14.

study so as to provide the basis for an account of human action and agency that recognizes its inherent intelligence and intelligibility.

5. Social institutions and the idea of the state

Such an account of action is closely connected to, and helps to flesh out, the approach to institutions sketched in 1.3.1 above. The word "institution" is commonly used to denote an enduring and structured pattern of social behavior. A set of interactions that recur time and again, and that demonstrate some kind of identifiable and on-going spatial and temporal integrity, is a set of interactions that have become institutionalized; a particular institution is a more-or-less arbitrarily identified domain of such interactions. All of this seems relatively straightforward, though it really doesn't tell us very much about institutions. When we view it in the light of contemporary social theory, however, we can come to see institutions – including the institution of the state – for what they really are: embodiments or expressions of the numberless metaphysical or ontological presuppositions upon which their constituent actions and interactions are based.

1. I believe that every effort to sublate the opposition between structuralism and interactionism necessarily arrives at some such account of institutions. This is perhaps especially clear in Bourdieu's view of things, where institutions are analyzed explicitly in terms of generative schemes of classification. But it is evident, as well, in the extremely influential theory of structuration. Structuration theory aims to refute the "dualism" of standard sociological research by emphasizing the "duality" of social structure. Structure is both the medium and the outcome of conduct. Social action generates social structure and is, at the same time, generated by it: humans "produce society, but they do so as historically located actors, and not under conditions of their own choosing."[71] The view that individual behavior is somehow mechanically produced and reproduced by larger, impersonal social forces is rejected, as is the equally implausible view that such behavior occurs independently of established sociocultural influences.

What is important for our purposes is that structuration theory conceives of social practices and institutions as involving elaborate systems of knowledge and judgment. Giddens insists that "the members of a society

---

[71] Anthony Giddens, *New Rules of Sociological Method: A Positive Critique of Interpretive Sociologies* (New York: Basic Books, 1976), p. 160.

know a great deal about the workings of that society, and must do so if that society is recognizably a 'human society.' "[72] Social action is inevitably informed by such knowledge, and this means that the degree to which structures and institutions are generated by action is the degree to which they are underwritten by meaningful and intelligible truth claims. Moreover, Giddens understands, as do Bourdieu, Searle, and the others, that knowledge of this kind is often, indeed usually, unarticulated: "it is a basic mistake to equate the knowledgeability of human agents with what is known 'consciously,' or 'held in mind' in conscious ways. The knowledgeable character of human conduct is displayed above all in the vast variety of tacit modes of awareness and competence that I call 'practical consciousness' as differentiated from 'discursive consciousness' – but which actors chronically employ in the course of daily life."[73] Clearly, what Giddens calls "practical consciousness" is very much like the habitus or the Background – an implicit conceptual structure that underwrites particular judgments and the actions based on them.

It is also evident that the idea of rational reconstruction, or something rather like it, is a very important feature of structuration theory. According to Giddens, "the rationalization of conduct becomes the discursive offering of reasons when individuals are asked by others why they acted as they did. Such questions are normally posed, of course, only when the activity concerned is in some way puzzling."[74] Our actions are intelligible – they are intelligent performances – insofar as they reflect a structure of metaphysical and ontological presupposition. But that structure generally remains implicit, and only comes to the surface when some problem or puzzle prompts us to think about it systematically. We may go about our lives acting in a manner that we understand to be pious, but that understanding becomes an explicit topic for reflection when a Socrates comes along and raises difficult questions for us or, alternatively, when a Bourdieu or a Giddens comes along and tries to make sense of our social institutions.

The work of Searle, Bourdieu and Giddens, among others, clearly demonstrates the immense influence of the post-Kantian philosophical convergence on contemporary social theory, ultimately manifesting itself

[72] Anthony Giddens, "Agency, Institution, and Time-Space Analysis," in *Advances in Social Theory and Methodology: Toward an Integration of Micro- and Macro-Sociologies*, ed. K. Knorr-Cetina and A. V. Cicourel (Boston: Routledge & Kegan Paul, 1981), p. 163. Also, Anthony Giddens, *The Constitution of Society: Outline of Structuration Theory* (Berkeley: University of California Press, 1984), pp. 281–82.
[73] Giddens, "Agency, Institution, and Time-Space Analysis," p. 163.
[74] Giddens, *The Constitution of Society*, p. 281.

in the notion that social institutions are, as Mary Douglas suggests, structures of intelligibility, embedded in and embodiments of meta-physical or ontological presupposition.[75] Any sensible analysis of social institutions involves an effort to describe or reconstruct their intellectual foundations. Briefly, to understand an institution is to understand the actions that it comprises; to understand an action is to understand the judgments that it embodies; and to understand a judgment is to under-stand the ontological theory upon which it is based.[76]

In saying this, in claiming that the post-Kantian convergence embraces our conception not only of actions and judgments but of institutions as well, I am claiming that these are precisely the terms in which we ought to understand the institutions that compose the political state, including the state itself.

2. I take politics to describe, roughly, the range of human activities that pertain directly or indirectly to the development and distribution of social goods, material and moral alike. Such activities represent efforts – govern-mental or otherwise – to address serious social problems by invoking in a more-or-less comprehensive and authoritative manner the collective resources of a community. Understood in this way, politics is part and parcel of the social world of human activity, not fundamentally different from the vast array of activities described and analyzed by Douglas, Bourdieu, Giddens, and the like. What this means is that political action,

---

[75] For a discussion of the influence of Kantian philosophy on nineteenth- and twentieth-century social thought, see *Rethinking the Subject: An Anthology of Contemporary European Social Thought*, ed. James D. Faubion (Boulder: Westview Press, 1995), especially the editor's introduction, pp. 3–5, 9, 13–15.

[76] I am thus giving a certain priority to what Scott calls the "cognitive pillar" of institutions, as opposed to the "regulative" and "normative" pillars. See W. Richard Scott, *Institutions and Organizations* (Thousand Oaks, California: Sage, 1995), pp. 40–45; also W. Richard Scott, "Institutions and Organizations: Toward a Theoretical Synthesis," in W. Richard Scott and John W. Meyer, *Institutional Environments and Organizations: Structrual Complexity and Individualism* (Thousand Oaks, California: Sage, 1994), pp. 65–68; and W. Richard Scott, "Introduction: Institutional Theory and Organizations," in W. Richard Scott and Søren Christensen, eds., *The Institutional Construction of Organizations* (Thousand Oaks, Califorma: Sage, 1995), pp. xiii–xix. My focus, however, is on what institutions are in essence, rather than how they come about. Scott's discussion of the cognitive approach tends to emphasize (efficient) causal claims involving the "social construction of reality." I neither affirm nor deny claims of this sort; hence, in emphasizing the post-Kantian turn, I am not necessarily endorsing the kind of sociological voluntarism to which much of the "new institutionalism" seems committed.

On the general question of institutions and the nature of social action, see Walter W. Powell and Paul J. DiMaggio, eds., *The New Institutionalism in Organizational Analysis* (Chicago: University of Chicago Press, 1991), especially pp. 22–23 and 25–27 where the editors emphasize, as I have, the importance of both Giddens and Bourdieu.

like any other, is always based on some set of judgments and decisions that themselves reflect, however tacitly, a structure of metaphysical presupposition. When such action occurs according to a relatively enduring, organized pattern, it becomes institutionalized. Political institutions, then, are nothing other than systems of patterned political activity; and to the degree that such activity reflects a structure of metaphysical presupposition, so do the institutions.

Now most political institutions are composed of smaller political institutions and are, at the same time, components of larger ones. But exactly how to distinguish one from another – how to determine where one institution leaves off and the other begins, whether vertically and horizontally – is often unclear. We cannot always draw a hard and fast boundary separating the activities of national governments from those of regional governments, the activities of legislatures from those of executives, the activities of non-governmental lobbying groups from those of the governmental agencies with which they interact, and the like. Thus, for example, the formal distinction between the United States Federal Aviation Administration and the airline industry is clear enough. But the complexities of the policy process, involving all manner of public–private partnership together with the recurrent shuttling of personnel from industry to government and back again, call such clear distinctions into question. Much political science is devoted to an examination of the stresses and accommodations involved when institutional boundaries are permeable and shifting, as they almost always are; and this suggests that institutional distinctions are likely to be, at best, useful approximations. But however elusive it may be, organizational differentiation is hardly inconsequential. This becomes especially clear when we realize that the conceptualization of a particular institution, including an account of its limits or boundaries, is always itself a kind of ontological claim. It represents just one more feature of our conceptual scheme. As such, it constitutes an important part of our understanding of how the world really is, hence is something that can be rationally reconstructed and tested for consistency vis-à-vis the range of other ontological claims to which we are committed.

It is precisely here that we can begin to understand the institutional status of the state. For among the many claims to which we are committed is the proposition that the various political institutions of a society, however distinct and otherwise unrelated they may sometimes seem to be, nonetheless compose a larger, all-encompassing institution. That institution is, and can be nothing other than, the state. The state is, in effect, the political institution that organizes and subsumes all others. It is the source of their mutual connection, the foundation and expression of their unity.

As such, *the state is the ultimate embodiment and manifestation of the structure of metaphysical or ontological presupposition upon which its numerous constituent judgments, actions, and institutions are based.*

I believe that this conclusion follows from everything that I have said thus far. Again, ontological theory is reflected in political judgment, which underwrites political action, which becomes, in turn, organized into institutions, which themselves compose the state *qua* ultimate institution. The entire structure would be incomprehensible without the underlying ontological theory. The state is, thus, a structure of intelligibility that reflects, and that itself expresses, an implicit understanding of how the world really is. But more: to the extent that we conceive of the state as having, in some irreducible sense, the force of law, we must also regard it, finally, as the ultimate certifier of metaphysical truth. In this sense, the state is ontology made authoritative.

It will be argued, of course, that the state must be much more than this. Insofar as it is an institution, it must be characterized not only by ontological principles but also by principles of organization according to which various sub-units – political actors or organizations – are arranged and interrelated; and its identity must also be determined by the more-or-less material substance within which it comes to be embodied, i.e., explicit rules of behavior, structures of hierarchy, and resources of action and influence, including buildings, bullets, buying power and all the rest, without which political action would be impossible. This kind of argument has already been discussed and refuted in 1.3.1 above. In brief, the importance of institutional paraphernalia, however undeniable, in no way undermines the claim that the state is ultimately reducible to an idea or an integrated set of ideas, a structure of truth. For principles of organization – the formal principles of the state *qua* institution – are themselves products of judgment and action, hence express or are underwritten by metaphysical or ontological presuppositions in their own right, presuppositions that compose a view of how things in the world really are. And by the same token, the hardware of the state – like that of a university or a church – is what it is, acquires a meaningful identity and function, only in the light of a conceptual structure, a structure of ontological belief. Institutions are indeed governed by a principle of necessary embodiment, such that occupying and utilizing physical things is an unavoidable part of what it means for an institution to exist. But again, such occupying and utilizing occurs only under the aegis of some set of ideas about how the world really is. The upshot is that the ontological theory embodied in an institution always has a certain ontological priority.

The theory of action sketched in this chapter thus provides an intellectual foundation for the approach to institutions that I have outlined in chapter 1. To attempt to understand any institution, real or imagined, without focusing primarily on the metaphysical or ontological premises that it embodies is to misunderstand it, to overlook just those features of it that make it intelligible, hence very likely to misconstrue seriously the nature of its practical existence, including the nature of the problems, controversies and conflicts with which it may be concerned. Like any other institution, the state is to be understood precisely in this way, as a set of ideas concerning the scope, justification and method of political action.

3. Political activity is of a piece with human activity *per se*. Like all activity, it generally occurs internal to an institution – a political institution. Like all activity, it is informed and underwritten by the particular structure of metaphysical presupposition upon which that institution is based. Like all activity, it is thus implicated in both prudential and philosophical ways of thinking about the world.

Indeed, we are now in a position to understand more clearly than before the precise role that theories of government and policy and the philosophy of the state actually play in political life itself. Prudential theories involve hypothetical claims about options and outcomes. They address the question of what will and will not work in the real world, based on empirical and/or historical experience and analysis. The philosophy of the state, on the other hand, involves categorical claims about the nature of the state itself. It pursues a conceptual analysis that emphasizes the state's foundation in one or another structure of metaphysical or ontological presupposition. Now the first thing to observe is that all political actors, without exception, are directly engaged in prudential theorizing. This is only to say that everyone involved in politics – elected officials, administrators, lobbyists, protesters, ordinary citizens exercising the most rudimentary political rights such as voting – has some sense of how particular goals can best be achieved. Such a sense constitutes, in effect, a kind of pragmatic analysis reflecting, variously, vague feelings or intuitions or educated guesses or informed judgments or detailed historical accounts or rigorous scientific analyses concerning what has happened in the past and what is likely to happen in the future. At the same time, however, everyone is also engaged in an analysis of the state's metaphysical presuppositions. For the relevance of intuitions, judgments and analyses can only be assessed on the basis of some kind of underlying standard. Our intuition that this or that activity will have this or that consequence, and that this or that consequence will have this or that further consequence, cannot but reflect an immense range of shared understandings about how things in the world really are. The political actor – whether a high official or a regular citizen – is much like the John Searle who retrieves a beer from his refrigerator or Bourdieu's paradigmatic housewife working in her kitchen. In each case, the action reflects a structure of truth. Consider, for example, the enormous system of presupposition and implicit knowledge that necessarily underwrites the "simple act of voting." The voter must have at least some sense of what an election is, what government is, what elected officials do and how their doings might relate to the votes they receive, how votes get counted, how counted votes translate into electoral victories and losses, what an electoral district is, how election laws work, what majority rule means, what voter fraud means and why it's bad, and so on ad infinitum. Certainly the act of voting is primarily a prudential act, aimed at maximizing benefits and minimizing costs, hence informed by some set of intuitions, judgments or analyses of what will work and what won't. But to understand the act, we need also to consider what is certainly prior, namely, all those things about which we must agree if voting is to be even possible.

The simple act of voting is thus very much akin to the simple act of being pious, or the simple act of deciding who should be in the Hall of Fame. Most of the time, we perform such actions unproblematically. But sometimes hard cases arise that require us to examine the structure of metaphysical or ontological presupposition upon which those actions are based. Sometimes, in other words, we are required to do metaphysics. We are required to think about what it really means to be pious or to be a Hall of Famer; and by the same token, we are required to think about the real nature of some of the basic features of elections. We want our elections to be decided by qualified voters, but what does that mean? Must a qualified voter be sane, or male, or more than eighteen (or twenty-one) years old, or literate, or propertied? We want our electoral procedures to be fair. But is it fair if the election is not conducted by secret ballot, or if it employs the party strip rather than the Australian ballot, or if various jurisdictions use different kinds of mechanical devices to count votes, or if voting is done by mail or on computers connected to a network in cyberspace? We want our elected officials to represent us. But exactly what do we mean by representation? Must elected officials be similar – socially, psychologically, physically – to their constituents? Must they do exactly what their constituents tell them to do? Ultimately, these are questions about how we understand certain features of the world. All of them have profound prudential or strategic implications. But all of them reflect, at the same time, a structure of metaphysical presupposition that tells us, in the end, just what elections themselves are all about. That structure is embodied in the idea of the state, and this means that all political activity is ultimately hostage to and dependent on the requirements of that idea.

It may be, of course, that our answers to specific metaphysical or ontological questions will change over time, or will vary from society to society. We may discover that our earlier notion of piety was wrong, or that our former account of the Hall of Fame needs to be revised; and by the same token, we may decide that we need to change our view of who is a qualified voter, what is a fair election, how representation should be understood, and the like. To the degree that the idea of the state reflects a structure of metaphysical or ontological presupposition about how things in the world really are, such changes will change our particular idea of the state.

But we need to be clear about exactly what this means; and here we need to advert once again to the distinction, introduced in 1.5.1 above, between the idea of the state itself and particular instantiations of that idea.

4. A state based on the belief that the only qualified voters are white propertied males over the age of twenty-one would be a different state from one based on the belief that non-white propertyless female eighteen-year-olds might also be qualified. Of course, such differences would reflect, in turn, different understandings about the nature of race, gender, age and property. Both of these states, moreover, would also be very different from a state based on the belief that virtually no one is a qualified voter, hence that political leaders should be selected in some other way, e.g., through heredity or armed struggle or the intervention of the gods. Similarly, a state that presupposed, say, a geocentric view of the cosmos and that celebrated the divinity of Zeus would be different, in all kinds of ways, from one that presupposed a heliocentric view of the cosmos and that denied the divinity of anything.

Consider, along these lines, the distinctiveness of the contemporary American state. That state has adopted explicit and detailed policies concerning, among countless other things, the difference between clean air and dirty air, between medical doctors and quacks, between seltzer water and club soda, between prime beef and choice beef; concerning the treatment of charitable institutions, hallucinogens, hazardous materials, motor vehicles of all description; concerning the activities of nurses, airline pilots, ordained ministers, real estate agents, barbers, architects, lawyers, school teachers; concerning the regulation of monopolies, flood plains, weeds, mosquitos, sexual behavior, the education of second-graders; and so on. In each case, particular policy decisions cannot but reflect a particular set of views about what the thing in question really is, some understanding of the true nature of doctors or seltzer water or charitable institutions or monopolies, etc. But such understandings are also apt to be different from, if only in the sense of being absent from, the set of understandings that underwrite public policy in the contemporary Italian state, or the contemporary Iranian state, or the ancient Spartan state, and the like.

The range of possible presuppositions upon which a particular state could be based is obviously enormous, hence the range of possible states is similarly large. It is not entirely clear, moreover, what such variation ultimately means. Perhaps metaphysical and ontological differences represent unavoidable historical and cultural incommensurabilities, hence can never be resolved. Or perhaps such differences reflect mere error and miscommunication, common in practice but corrigible in principle. Perhaps there is, in fact, one true and adequate set of presuppositions to which we all should adhere, if only we could get clear about our own beliefs.

Plainly, this a matter that far transcends the present work. But what we can say is that all states, despite their differences, nonetheless include, in their structure of moral and metaphysical presupposition, some account of what a state itself is. Just as the contemporary American state distinguishes seltzer water from club soda, so does it distinguish, however tacitly and inchoately, the state from entities that are, for one reason or another, not states. In effect, each state has, and must have, an idea of the state, hence an understanding of what it itself is. And in my view, all states, however different they may be, share, though usually only implicitly, a single overarching metaphysical or ontological principle: the idea of the state is that the state is an idea, a structure of intelligibility that embodies and authorizes one or another set of presuppositions about how things in the world really are.

Moreover, as I intend to argue in Part III, this principle itself entails three additional and fundamental claims: every state of whatever kind must be conceived – and must conceive itself – as omnicompetent in scope, absolute in authority, and organic in function. The elaboration and defense of these claims constitutes, in effect, the metaphysical or ontological theory of the state.

Part 3

The Idea of the State

4   The Omnicompetent State: Toleration and Limited Government

Contemporary political discourse is deeply invested in what one writer calls the "art of separation" – the activity of designing, in thought or in practice, walls that figuratively or even literally separate the political sphere from other spheres of human endeavor.[1] Some such notion represents what may be thought of, without too much exaggeration, as a kind of orthodoxy. Political theory today is concerned hardly at all with the question of whether or not to construct and maintain walls of separation. It focuses, rather, on the problem of exactly what should be kept apart from what. Is it, for example, the individual person, understood as a bearer of natural rights and an embodiment of moral personality, who should be protected from the intrusions of the political state; or should we rather afford such protection to communities of persons, each community understood as reflecting a particular structure of values or way of life? Where, moreover, should we draw the line? What kinds of activities should and should not be subject to the exercise of public authority? On what grounds might we make such distinctions, and why should certain spheres of endeavor enjoy privileges that others are denied? How, finally, should we construct our partitions? Which mechanisms can most effectively and expeditiously achieve the desired separations? Liberals and communitarians, individualists and holists, elitists and democrats – all seek in different ways to build walls aimed at limiting or confining the activity of the state.

In the wake of the unprecedented and virtually unspeakable horrors of the twentieth century – nearly all of which were perpetrated in the name of the state – such a preoccupation can hardly be dismissed as peculiar or frivolous. Still, it seems to me deeply problematic. On the one hand, nothing that I have said in previous chapters should be thought to deny certain *distinctions* between the institutions of public authority and those

---

[1] Michael Walzer, "Liberalism and the Art of Separation," *Political Theory* 12 (August 1984), pp. 315–30.

of what today is commonly referred to as "civil society." But a distinction is not a separation; and I intend to argue that the idea of a separation – a wall – between the state and the rest of society cannot be coherently maintained.[2]

In chapter 2, I sought to demonstrate the impossibility of a "political" conception. Any account of the state and its proper scope of action is necessarily underwritten by presuppositions of a metaphysical and moral nature, hence must itself compose, in some relevant sense, an ontological or metaphysical theory. The argument was, in effect, a rejection of "neutrality," understanding neutrality to refer to theories of political right untainted by – neutral toward – the numerous and varied comprehensive doctrines of which modern complex societies are composed. Against neutrality theory, I have claimed that everything the state does necessarily reflects and embodies the larger, non-political commitments of society. But to have shown this is not to have denied the possibility that the purview of the state could nonetheless be limited to certain specified areas of endeavor, that it could thus be separate from and largely uninvolved in an enormous range of social activities, that much of what takes place among the citizens of a state could simply be left alone – unregulated, unpoliticized, inviolate. Yet this is precisely what I do deny.

In the first section of this chapter, I outline and criticize Locke's important and influential defense of toleration, understood as a paradigm of separation theory. In section 2, I consider the larger question of liberal toleration, and attempt to show that standard approaches are often misconceived and unhelpful. Section 3 offers some reflections on the nature of governmental activity *per se*, and seeks to formulate a clearer notion of just what it means for government, as an instrument of the state, to regulate behavior. The fourth section considers some of the implications of all this for our understanding of the separation project and of the nature of political action in general.

To think in terms of walls where none are possible is to commit a fundamental category mistake. It is greatly to misconstrue the relevant subject matter, such as it is, and to risk consequences quite the reverse of those intended. Indeed, the art of separation is apt to exacerbate, rather than resolve, the problem of the state. For the best defense against the abuse of political power is, in fact, to acknowledge that the state – understood

---

[2] While my concerns about the art of separation are certainly philosophical, I cannot deny that walls often inspire in me the inarticulate forebodings of Melville's scrivener, who in the face of Wall Street's endless and implacable partitions – "black by age and everlasting shade" – finds a salvation of sorts in passive resistance. Surely such forebodings can hardly be idiosyncratic to Bartleby and me.

ontologically as a structure of intelligibility, an institution composed of propositions about how things in the world really are – can never be truly separate from, can never be other than an organic, integral and deeply engaged part of the society out of which it itself has emerged.

1. The argument from impossibility

The modern art of separation has its origins in the political struggles of the sixteenth and seventeenth centuries. It invokes what was, arguably, the capital idea of that period, the liberal theory of toleration; and it is in light of this theory that advocates of separation have constructed what amounts to a comprehensive view of political society. To be sure, liberal toleration was originally formulated with the relatively narrow question of church and state in mind. But in seeking to justify the establishment of permanent and inviolable barriers to state action, barriers designed mainly to protect the private rights of religious dissenters, the idea of toleration also embraced and helped legitimize broad principles of government the implications of which far transcended the particular problem of temporal and ecclesiastical power. Specifically, it provided the basis for a general account of public and private and, thereby, grounds for a theory of separation.

Liberal toleration is, if anything, more influential today than ever before. The overriding importance of tolerance, and of the concomitant need to circumscribe the scope of the state in the face of totalitarian peril, have become virtually unquestioned premises of contemporary Western culture. If, as a practical matter, those premises are often observed only in the breach, it is nonetheless the case that, as a theoretical and/or ideological matter, they persist virtually unchallenged. But the problem of defining with precision the nature of toleration itself, and the related problem of identifying clearly the proper limits of public authority, have proven to be vexing in the extreme.

The liberal theory of toleration proposes a relatively simple formula for addressing difficulties of this kind, but history – the history of continuing confusion and conflict about the role of the state – suggests that the formula is inadequate at best. I believe that the reasons for this are, or ought to be, clear. In brief, liberal toleration is based on a mistake. By failing to see that all human action and judgment inevitably involve underlying presuppositions of a metaphysical nature – a background or conceptual structure that informs the entire gamut of social interactions, political and otherwise – both liberal toleration and the more general art of separation seriously misconceive the very nature of the problem of the state. They do so by interpreting distinctions as incompatibilities, by seeking to separate that which is inseparable; and the result is that the analyses they offer and the suggestions they propose cannot but be deeply unsatisfying, both theoretically and practically.

1. In its canonical version, the liberal theory of toleration purports to prove in philosophical terms that the state has no proper authority to prevent individuals from engaging in unpopular religious practices, or to punish them for doing so. In advancing this proposition it seems to proceed along several quite different and perhaps mutually inconsistent lines[3] involving skepticism ("The one only narrow way which leads to Heaven is not better known to the Magistrate than to private Persons, and therefore I cannot safely take him for my Guide, who may probably be as ignorant of the way as my self"[4]), the hyprocisy of would-be oppressors (Locke says that he will cease doubting proponents of intolerance only "when I shall see them prosecute with Fire and Sword the Members of their own Communion that are tainted with enormous vices"[5]), and the teachings of "true religion" (according to which "no Man can be a Christian without Charity, and without that Faith which works, not by Force, but by Love"[6]). In fact, though, Locke's central argument for toleration appears to be none of these but, rather, something quite different, namely, what might be called the Argument from Impossibility.[7] This argument is based on the important empirical premise that government itself is literally unable to change belief, and that when it attempts to do so it is attempting the impossible:

Laws are of no force at all without Penalties, and Penalties in this case are absolutely impertinent; because they are not proper to convince the mind. Neither the Profession of any Articles of Faith, nor the Conformity to any outward

---

[3] Indeed, Vernon suggests that "one could probably distinguish about a dozen different arguments" in the *Letter*. Richard Vernon, *The Career of Toleration: John Locke, Jonas Proast, and After* (Montreal: McGill-Queen's University Press, 1997), p. 21.

[4] John Locke, *A Letter Concerning Toleration* (Indianapolis: Hackett, 1983), p. 37. I am not intending to claim here that liberal toleration begins with Locke. For the standard history of toleration literature in England immediately prior to Locke, see Wilbur K. Jordan, *The Development of Religious Toleration in England: Attainment of the Theory and Accommodations in Thought and Institutions, 1640–1700* (Cambridge: Cambridge University Press, 1940).

[5] Locke, *A Letter Concerning Toleration*, p. 24.

[6] *Ibid.*, p. 23.

[7] For a standard account, see Susan Mendus, *Toleration and the Limits of Liberalism* (Atlantic Highlands, New Jersey: Humanities Press, 1989), pp. 25–26. Also, John Dunn, *The Political Thought of John Locke* (Cambridge: Cambridge University Press, 1969), p. 33 n. For a somewhat different account, see Joshua Mitchell, "John Locke and the Theological Foundation of Liberal Toleration: A Christian Dialectic of History," *Review of Politics* 52 (Winter 1990), pp. 65–67. What I have called the Argument from Impossibility is essentially what Proast, and Vernon following him, call the "argument from belief."

Form of Worship (as has already been said) can be available to the Salvation of Souls, unless the truth of the one, and the acceptableness of the other unto God, be thoroughly believed by those that so profess and practise. But Penalties are no ways capable to produce such Belief. It is only Light and Evidence that can work a change in Mens Opinions; and which Light can in no manner proceed from corporal Sufferings, or any other outward Penalties.[8]

The Argument from Impossibility purports to be a philosophical one. It rests above all on a sharp separation between the physical and the mental. The physical realm is composed of things that can actually be possessed – held and protected – and that when possessed rightfully are items of property. According to Locke, controversies about such items are uniquely the business of the civil authority, the state. For the state is, by definition, that social institution which alone has the legitimate right to use physical force, to impose "corporal Sufferings." This means that it alone has the authority actually – physically – to control the use and enjoyment of physical things including, *inter alia*, one's own body.[9] The state can confiscate property, put people in jail, deprive them of their lives. It can, in short, bring physical matter to bear upon physical matter; and this means that when we authorize the state to act along these lines, we are not asking it to do the impossible. Right or wrongly, we are asking it to do something that is at least intelligible.

Beliefs, on the other hand, being mental or spiritual, are necessarily immune to any such regulation. Locke's argument in this respect surely reflects broader eighteenth-century views of the mind–body problem, of the kind associated with, for example, Berkeley.[10] The physical power of the state cannot reach ideas; as immaterial, they are beyond the realm of mechanical cause and effect. And if this is true, then it makes no sense to authorize the state to use its physical powers to try to regulate our thoughts and feelings. Any such effort would be doomed to fail. Only through persuasion and exhortation can one hope to change someone else's thoughts – and persuasion and exhortation are activities not peculiar to the office of the state.[11]

---

[8] Locke, *A Letter Concerning Toleration*, p. 27. A similar view is held by Thomas Aquinas: "Among unbelievers, there are some who have never received faith, such as the heathens and the Jews, and these are by no means to be compelled to the faith in order that they may believe, because to believe depends on the will" (*Summa Theologiae* II–II, Question 10, Article 8).

[9] According to Mendus, for Locke "the state is defined in terms of the means at its disposal." *Toleration and the Limits of Liberalism*, p. 25.

[10] See *Three Dialogues Between Hylas and Philonous* (Indianapolis: Bobbs-Merrill 1954 [1713]), pp. 48–49.

[11] The argument was already made explicitly by Hobbes in *Leviathan*: "In every commonwealth, they who have no supernatural revelation to the contrary, ought to

To my knowledge, incidentally, Locke offers no principled objection to the state itself engaging in these latter kinds of activities. Even here, though, he seems to have practical doubts. For he certainly believes that persuasion and exhortation are best carried out by institutions that have been explicitly constituted with such activities in mind, i.e., spiritual or ecclesiastic ones. Belief is properly the province of church, not state. One certainly might disagree with this. After all, the inculcation of social and patriotic values – "civics" – has long been an important function of government. But such a disagreement would nonetheless leave the larger point intact: even where the state does insist on involving itself in matters of belief, this can only be an educative rather than regulatory activity. With respect to belief, the state can recommend but cannot coerce, as per impossible.

Now Locke clearly thinks that the immunity of belief from physical coercion means that any pain actually inflicted by the state for the purpose of changing belief will be entirely gratuitous and nonsensical. Individuals will be made to suffer for no good reason, and since no one can think that this could possibly be legitimate, the Argument from Impossibility – i.e., the futility of trying to use the material power of the state to control immaterial belief – prohibits the state from pursuing that goal. Here, then, is the core of Locke's philosophical defense of toleration;[12] and it is in light of this that we may see Locke as pursuing the art of separation by claiming to have discovered *in nature itself* an impenetrable barrier between the government-as-regulator and (at least one element of) the larger

---

obey the laws of their own sovereign, in the external acts and profession of religion. As for the inward thought, and belief of men, which humane governors can take no notice of, (for God only knoweth the heart) they are not voluntary, nor the effect of the laws, but of the unrevealed will, and of the power of God; and consequently fall not under obligation" (*Leviathan, EW*, vol. 3, p. 462).

[12] In his sharp criticism of Waldron, Wootton energetically denies that this is the core of Locke's defense of toleration. (David Wootton, "Introduction," in *Political Writings of John Locke* [New York: Mentor Books, 1993], pp. 99–105). Wootton argues, rather, that Locke's focus is on decision-making theory: to which kind of government would it make sense for individuals to give their consent? The answer is that it would make no sense to give consent to intolerant governments, and this for two main reasons. First, governments have no privileged access to religious truth, so to rely on them for religious guidance would be folly. Second, even if they did have such access, their ability to make people believe the truth would be, at best, suspect. If these reasons are persuasive, then individuals cannot give their consent to any intolerant government, hence governments of this kind cannot be defended. (See also, Vernon, *The Career of Toleration*, pp. 21–22.) It is hard to see, however, that Wootton's arguments really add anything. The first reason for denying consent is essentially based on an argument from skepticism, the second on the Argument from Impossibility. If either of these were persuasive as coherent parts of Locke's entire formulation, then of course it would not be rational for citizens to consent and Wootton would be right. But that plainly begs the question. If, in particular, the Argument from Impossibility does not work, then a basic reason for not consenting simply disappears.

society. Advocates of liberalism do not have to worry about designing and fabricating such a barrier. They need only recognize the fact of its existence – to accept the fundamental premise that physical power cannot coerce non-physical ideas.

Proast doubts the premise, and those doubts have been revived and persuasively reformulated by Waldron.[13] History certainly *seems* to provide many examples of human beings truly changing their minds as a result of physical coercion, e.g., victims of torture whose spirits have been, as we say, "broken" or, less dramatically, subjects (also victims?) of behavior modification whose attitudes have changed as a result of carefully manipulated alterations in external circumstances. More importantly for Waldron, even if the acts of government cannot directly influence belief, they can do so indirectly. Thoughts commonly reflect, and can be changed by, experience. One is more likely to believe in Christianity if one has read the New Testament, and one is less likely to be a heretic if one has never read a heretical text. It would thus be perfectly coherent – not necessarily right, but certainly not irrational – for, say, a Christian state to attempt to influence beliefs by forcing everyone to read orthodox Christian works and by depriving them the opportunity to read heterodox ones.

Waldron is plainly right about this. But what's not so clear is how seriously he has damaged Locke's argument for toleration. While it certainly seems true that most beliefs are influenced, and can even be changed, by exposure to particular kinds of texts and teachings, it is not obvious that all beliefs are like this. The history of religion and of religious literature is replete with stories and theories of belief arising out of other-worldly interventions, the sudden gift of grace, divine revelation, and the like – stories and theories with which Locke was well familiar.[14] Christ himself may or may not have been the son of God, but he was also a man who had certain strong opinions – heretical opinions – long before the texts that enumerated those opinions could have been written; and St. Paul, who wrote some of those texts, likewise cannot be said merely to have "learned" Christianity, for his seemingly instantaneous and inexplicable conversion on the road to Damascus represented a nearly complete reversal of everything that he had stood for hitherto. Beliefs of this kind are not reducible, and might very well be resistant, to any kind of systematic process of indoctrination or education – whether positive,

---

[13] Jeremy Waldron, "Locke, Toleration and the Rationality of Persecution," pp. 61–86 in Susan Mendus, ed., *Justifying Toleration: Conceptual and Historical Perspectives* (Cambridge: Cambridge University Press, 1988).

[14] John Marshall, *John Locke: Resistance, Religion and Responsibility* (Cambridge: Cambridge University Press, 1994), pp. 122ff.

through forced exposure to certain writings and practices, or negative, through censorship. The same may be true, moreover, for any number of ordinary, non-religious beliefs as well. For while it seems to me entirely correct that most of our own ideas are rooted in the particular linguistic and conceptual apparatus that makes it possible for us to think in the first place, the way in which we utilize that apparatus to reconfigure and reformulate our thoughts, to combine old ideas in novel ways and to create, thereby, new ones, may also be, at least to some extent, immune to the influence of intentional external forces. At the very least, many of us share the intuition that some of our cognitive experiences – conceptual innovations, artistic inspiration, sudden insights, dreams – occur independently of, or even in spite of, purposeful efforts to shape our minds.

One may choose to doubt that such ideas – we may call them "influence-resistant ideas" – actually exist, but it is hard to see how those doubts could be proven. More plausibly, one could suggest that the sum total of influence-resistant ideas, even if they do exist, may amount to little more than a drop in the bucket, for surely most of our thinking most of the time is indeed vulnerable to indirect outside influence, as Waldron describes. But what would this tell us about toleration? From a general utilitarian perspective, intolerance and persecution could not be prohibited on Lockian grounds; a state that seeks to control beliefs is doing nothing incoherent if it can be broadly, if only indirectly, successful in controlling them. To this extent, Waldron is absolutely correct. But from what might be called a rights perspective, the case seems not so clear, for if some beliefs cannot be affected by indirect outside influence, and if, as seems likely, the state is unable reliably to distinguish such beliefs from others, then some people may wind up being persecuted gratuitously, i.e., forced to suffer because of a policy that is, in the relevant cases, utterly futile.

This is a line of argumentation that Locke pursues in the responses to Proast. He explicitly focuses in the *Second Letter* on Proast's claim that forceful intolerance can be indirectly useful in encouraging heretics at least to consider or examine their heretical views. He readily concedes the point, hence concedes something close to Waldron's position: "And so, you say, 'Force, indirectly, and at a distance, may do some service.' I grant it; make your best of it."[15] But he insists that this is no argument against toleration. For he points out that some heretics may have already thoroughly examined their heresy – their heretical beliefs are influence-resistant – while many orthodox but lazy believers have never given their

<hr>

[15] John Locke, "A Second Letter Concerning Toleration," in *The Works of John Locke: Volume VI* (Scientia Verlag Aalen: Darmstadt, Germany, [1692] 1963), p. 69.

own beliefs a second thought. To punish the former and not the latter is, says Locke, indefensible: "[I]f the punishment you think so necessary be, as you pretend, to cure the mischief you complain of, you must let it pursue and fall on the guilty, and those only, in what company soever they are; and not, as you here propose, and is the highest injustice, punish the innocent considering dissenter with the guilty; and, on the other side, let the inconsiderate guilty conformist escape with the innocent."[16]

While it is true that the argument in question is different from that of the *Letter* itself, surely it is a recognizable version of it. Not all beliefs are influence-resistant, hence intolerance is not by definition irrational with respect to belief *per se*. But some beliefs *are* influence-resistant, and it would indeed be incoherent to attempt to repress or change them. Given the difficulty of distinguishing the one kind of belief from the other, and given the basic Lockian principle that harm inflicted gratuitously or futilely is harm inflicted unjustly, we have here a serious, principled, philosophical argument for toleration.[17]

Waldron contends that in adopting such a defense, Locke has completely given up his main theory of toleration: "the case in principle against the use of force in religious matters has collapsed into a purely pragmatic argument."[18] But could it not be a matter of principle to insist that force should be avoided where it is possible that at least some otherwise law-abiding citizens will be harmed by a state powerless to change their minds, that the idea of punishing irremediable heretics or unwavering true believers – actual or prospective – is or ought to be anathema, that the very real possibility of futile and unjust persecution in a minority of cases is sufficient to argue against persecution *per se*? Perhaps the answer to these questions is indeed no. But showing that would require a more substantial discussion than that which Waldron provides.

Waldron has correctly raised serious doubts about the central empirical premise of the *Letter*, has shown therefore that intolerance is not self-evidently incoherent, but has not (yet) shown that a Lockian theory of toleration must be wrong. In fact, I believe that such a theory must be wrong indeed. But I think that this can be demonstrated regardless of how we feel about Locke's central premise. For that premise, even if reformulated to take into account Waldron's objections, entails conclusions, amply illustrated in the *Letter* itself, that in fact undermine the very idea of toleration to which Locke himself seems so committed.

---

[16] *Ibid.*, p. 94.
[17] Wootton, "Introduction," p. 104.
[18] Waldron, "Locke, Toleration and the Rationality of Persecution," p. 84

2. We must begin by observing that the Argument from Impossibility is completely and entirely irrelevant to the question of behavior. Behavior is not belief. Locke himself emphasizes the difference by sharply distinguishing "practical" articles of faith from "speculative" ones.[19] The distinction is crucial. For while a (revised) Lockian theory of toleration may or may not entail the protection of speculative articles of faith, practical articles of faith are quite a different matter:

> What if the Magistrate should enjoyn any thing by this Authority that appears unlawful to the Conscience of a private Person? I answer, That if Government be faithfully administered, and the Counsels of the Magistrate be indeed directed to the publick Good, this will seldom happen. But if perhaps it do so fall out; I say, that such a private Person is to abstain from the Action that he judges unlawful; and he is to undergo the Punishment, which it is not unlawful for him to bear. For the private judgment of any Person concerning a Law enacted in Political Matters, for the publick Good, does not take away the Obligation of that Law, nor deserve a Dispensation.[20]

Passages such as this one force us to ask how the idea of toleration could have any meaningful referent at all.[21] Locke had claimed that government is not authorized to (attempt to) coerce belief, as per impossible. Waldron has effectively undermined that claim. But a revised Lockian argument remains: the prohibition on intolerance stems from the possibility that at least some beliefs are influence-resistant, that the state cannot reliably distinguish such beliefs from others, that when it persecutes persons for holding beliefs it may therefore be harming some of them gratuitously, and that from a moral perspective this is an unacceptable outcome. The latter claim is clearly debatable. Perhaps some amount of gratuitous harm is worth it if the result is to promote the common good. But given the nature of beliefs *per se*, a further question arises: how could a state even know about unorthodox ones? How could it identify the actual existence of such non-physical things, whether influence-resistant or not?

In one sense, of course, the answer is obvious: the existence of beliefs is known through their expression. We become aware of what someone believes because of what that person says or does. But from the perspective of toleration and governmental regulation, things change quite dramatically when a belief comes to be articulated. To express is to act. An utterance is a physical thing – it is an action – hence, on Locke's own grounds available for forcible censure. To articulate a belief by actually saying or writing something that another person might hear or read and

---

[19] Locke, *A Letter Concerning Toleration*, p. 46.
[20] *Ibid.*, p. 48.
[21] I raise here what Vernon (*The Career of Toleration*, p. 23) calls the issue of relevance.

that might influence that person's beliefs or actions – clearly this is to invoke a practical rather than speculative article of faith, hence to be eligible for regulation and punishment. The conclusion is inescapable: Locke's Argument from Impossibility, even revised to meet Waldron's objections, in itself implies no protection at all for religious expression and religious practice.[22]

Plainly, this is a conclusion that Locke himself would want strenuously to resist. He emphasizes the liberty of men to "own to the world that they worship God" and insists that "concerning outward Worship ... the Magistrate has no Power to enforce by Law, either in his own Church, or much less in another, the use of any Rites or Ceremonies whatsoever in the worship of God."[23] The question, however, is not what Locke claims – that's pretty clear – but how he justifies his claim. And this is precisely the problem. Locke's philosophical argument for toleration, the Argument from Impossibility, fails to support the assertion that "the Magistrate has no power" to regulate or prohibit rites or ceremonies.

Another way of putting this is that even if we concede that the Argument from Impossibility supports toleration of influence-resistant belief, and even if we concede further that, because of the difficulty in distinguishing such beliefs from others, all beliefs therefore should be tolerated, the fundamental problem remains that toleration of this kind is profoundly uninteresting, uncontroversial, and unrelated to real issues of tolerance. For as long as belief remains mere belief – as long as it fails to manifest itself in word and action – it is perhaps, according to the Lockian premise, beyond the ken but also, as Locke does not so clearly say, beyond the concern of the state. The fact is that mere belief itself raises no political questions whatever. Only actions matter. In the early part of the third century, Perpetua was thrown to the lions not because of her Christian views but because of her explicit refusal to perform a ritual pagan sacrifice, as required by the emperor. The Donatists, in 412 and 414, were deprived of political and ecclesiastical privileges, not because of their heretical beliefs but because of their refusal to partake of sacraments administered by Catholic priests. Prynne was imprisoned and mutilated in 1633 (parts of his ears were cut off and his face branded), not for his heterodox ideas but for his refusal to follow the standard Anglican liturgy.

---

[22] Dunn seems to recognize this, but he fails to identify the kinds of problems that it raises for a Lockian theory of toleration. John Dunn, "The Claim to Freedom of Conscience: Freedom of Speech, Freedom of Thought, Freedom of Worship?", in Ole Peter Grell, Jonathan I. Israel and Nicholas Tyacke, eds., *From Persecution to Toleration: The Glorious Revolution and Religion in England* (Oxford: Oxford University Press, 1991), p. 178.
[23] *A Letter Concerning Toleration*, pp. 38–39.

It is true, of course, that in each case the alleged misbehavior was based on and inspired by dissident belief. The latter presumably caused the former, and it may seem that to punish the practice is indeed to punish the belief, hence to attempt to influence the beliefs of others who have not yet misbehaved. But Locke's own Argument from Impossibility, even in its revised form, belies this. If influence-resistant beliefs cannot be coerced, then they cannot be coerced. Whether or not ideas, values and attitudes must be put into practice is neither here nor there. The crucial point is that the Argument from Impossibility protects, at best, only influence-resistant beliefs which – because influence-resistant – need no protection. It does not protect behavior, including expressive behavior; and this means that either Locke has no consistent theory of toleration or else his theory, if consistent, doesn't amount to very much.

3. Certainly none of this is to defend or justify Septimus Severus's persecution of Christians, St. Augustine's persecution of the Donatists, Laud's persecution of dissenters. These were deeply offensive acts, inimical to ordinary and uncontroversial notions of fairness and humanity. But none of them can be condemned on the basis of the Argument from Impossibility, since all of them were primarily aimed at changing not speculative articles of faith but practical ones. In each case, the main target was not belief but overt behavior; and under Locke's own explicit formulation, such behavior is properly within the purview of the temporal state.

A Lockian might wish to argue, against all of this, that the trouble with the kinds of intolerant acts I have described is precisely that they persecuted *for the purpose of changing belief*; and again, because (influence-resistant) beliefs cannot be changed in that way, such persecution is apt to impose gratuitous, hence unacceptable, harm on at least some people. But this begs the question, for one can well imagine many other reasons for persecuting heterodox behavior: such behavior undermines the fabric and coherence of society, leads to more dramatic kinds of immoral or dangerous behavior, subverts duly constituted authority, and the like – all of which focuses not on the content of belief, nor on efforts to change beliefs, but simply on the effects that actions have on the general good. Indeed, it is almost certain that Perpetua, the Donatists and Prynne were punished, rightly or wrongly, with some notion of the public interest in mind. The crucial point is that according to Locke himself the decision about whether or not to allow behavior to take place is entirely up to the magistrate, i.e., government. Where the magistrate disapproves, and providing that the government is being "faithfully administered," the miscreant is obliged to change his or her behavior; and failure to do so means that the resulting punishment is fully justified.

The real thrust of the Argument from Impossibility is thus to legitimize intolerance as much as the reverse. It is in this sense, moreover, that we can best come to grips with the *Letter*'s famously intolerant view of Catholics and atheists. Such dissidents are to be condemned not because of their beliefs but because of behavior that is likely to undermine the public good. Catholics are loyal primarily to the pope, while atheists are loyal to nothing. In each case, individuals are apt to deny the sovereign authority of the duly constituted civil regime. In each case, disobedience and sedition are held to be legitimate, even where the government has been properly authorized. In each case, then, the public interest is placed in jeopardy.

These claims are widely regarded as embarrassments, ill-conceived exceptions to the theory of toleration that tell us more about Locke's own prejudices and historical circumstances than about his philosophy. But this fails to appreciate the sense in which such claims are entirely consistent with the theoretical framework out of which they arise, as I have described it. While the particular focus of Lockian censure is, admittedly, explicable only in historical terms, the fact of Lockian censoriousness is not. The Argument from Impossibility, presented as a principled, conceptual argument for toleration, in effect allows every outward manifestation of belief – every utterance and every action, in short, everything that could conceivably be the object of intolerance – to be held hostage to the demands and exactions of the public authority.

Not surprisingly, Locke's willingness to be intolerant is hardly limited to Catholics and atheists. He says, for example, that a magistrate who regards the ritual slaughter of cattle as injurious to the public good – perhaps because some disease has threatened the supply of cattle – has every right to prevent such slaughter, even if doing so would make it impossible for certain people to practice their religion.[24] Consider the potential gravity of such a prohibition. Ritual slaughter might be not just another religious duty but a virtual requirement for salvation; and if this were the case, then to debar someone from doing it would be to impose the most onerous kind of sanction imaginable, something cataclysmic in effect and eternal in duration. Well aware of this, Locke nonetheless insists on the superiority of *raison d'état*.[25] The public interest overrules all other considerations. Thus, he argues, for example, that no government has any obligation to tolerate the practices of groups and individuals

---

[24] *Ibid.*, p. 42. The passage is cited and discussed by Waldron, "Locke, Toleration and the Rationality of Persecution," pp. 77–79.
[25] Dunn, "The Claim to Freedom of Conscience," pp. 174, 178, 181, 186.

who "lustfully pollute themselves in promiscuous Uncleanness"[26]; and nothing could be clearer than that he believes the criteria of pollution to be established and applied by the public authority itself. In all cases, the decision about whether or not to tolerate some practice is the state's; and as long as the state is guided by a suitable regard for the public interest, repression is in principle justified.

It will be argued in Locke's defense that this latter provision – the public interest provision – itself constitutes a powerful and important limit on the scope and nature of official intolerance. The state cannot be capriciously intolerant. It must have reasons for its actions, and only certain kinds of reasons will do. Of course, the *Second Treatise* is an account of how a legitimate state should be conceptualized and how such a state may pursue the public interest. But all of this seems to me quite beside the point. For the simple fact is that no one would ever think – or at least purport – to defend a rogue state, one whose actions are plainly gratuitous, or motivated solely or even primarily by the private interests of its leaders.[27] Virtually all states justify virtually all of their activities, including repressive ones, in the name of the common good; and in view of this, the key question concerns not tolerance or intolerance but, rather, the authority of the regime. The *Second Treatise* thus provides, if anything, an account not of tolerance but of how intolerance might be legitimate. There is certainly no peremptory duty to tolerate. If certain religious practices are to be tolerated, it is only and exclusively because the public interest so requires.

None of this is to deny, moreover, Locke's insistence on a person's fundamental right to pursue salvation. Our first duty is to save our souls. But by the same token, the state's first duty is, and always will be, to pursue the common good, as it sees fit. Certainly, these two duties may come into irresolvable and violent conflict, but when that occurs only God can be the judge. The conclusion seems clear: the right to pursue salvation, however absolute and inalienable it may be, provides no right of immunity from the earthly consequences of actually doing so.

Lockian tolerance is, thus, a fundamentally pragmatic doctrine – a matter of prudence and strategy rather than independent moral principle – which actually justifies or at least authorizes intolerance precisely in those cases where the issue of toleration is *most* likely to arise, namely, cases in

[26] Locke, *A Letter Concerning Toleration*, p. 42.
[27] Machiavelli is no exception. For while he is hardly reluctant to advise princes to pursue their own self-interests, it is impossible to interpret him as saying anything other than that the fundamental public goals of peace and security are, in certain circumstances, best achieved by strong, even ruthless rulers.

which the state seeks to disallow certain activities in order to further its view of the public interest.[28]

2. Liberal toleration

The Argument from Impossibility is a paradigmatic case – perhaps *the* paradigmatic case – of the art of separation. To propose a sharp disjunction between the capacities of the state and the nature of religious belief, between the realm of property and that of spirit, is to conceptualize an impenetrable wall constraining the power of the one while protecting the prerogatives of the other. The failure of the Argument from Impossibility is thus, at the same time, a serious problem for the idea of separation. It suggests at the very least that what today is commonly called "civil society," something plainly composed of tangible actions and expressions, possesses no inherent protection against state intervention. There is no natural wall – at least not the one Locke claims to have described, and it is hard to imagine another.

Perhaps the absence of such a barrier, though a serious problem, is not necessarily an insuperable one. If we wish to prevent the state from involving itself inappropriately in the ordinary, "private" lives of its citizens, then maybe we can do so by fashioning on our own account an artificial wall of some kind. That which nature fails to provide we might be able to provide for ourselves.

But here I think that the problem only deepens. For while Locke has (unwittingly) shown that the world does not provide for us a natural wall of

[28] In this sense, the doctrine of the *Letter* merely reflects and perpetuates the character of all of Locke's writings on tolerance, including the early and Hobbesian *Two Tracts on Government* (1660–61) and the very different *Essay on Toleration* of 1667. For a more complete treatment of these issues, see Peter J. Steinberger, "Lockian Intolerance," paper presented at the annual meeting of the Pacific Northwest Political Science Association, Victoria, British Columbia (October 1998). On the Hobbesianism of the *Two Tracts*, see John W. Gough, *John Locke's Political Philosophy* (London: Longman, 1956), pp. 180–81; Maurice Cranston, *John Locke: A Biography* (London: Longman, 1957), pp. 61–63; Peter Laslett, "Introduction," in Locke, *Two Treatises of Government*, pp. 33–41; and Kraynak, "John Locke: From Absolutism to Toleration," *American Political Science Review* 74 (March 1980), pp. 57–59, 66, 68. According to Kraynak (p. 68), "Locke's description of the state of nature and his argument from consent to absolute government are virtually cribbed from Hobbes." On the underlying pragmatism and continuity of Locke's works on toleration, see Philip Abrams, "Introduction," in Locke, *Two Tracts on Government*, pp. 84, 101–2; Dunn, *The Political Thought of John Locke*, pp. 28 n., 30, 33 n., 39; Waldron, "Locke, Toleration and the Rationality of Persecution;" Mitchell, "John Locke and the Theological Foundation of Liberal Toleration," p. 68; and Richard Tuck, "Hobbes and Locke on Toleration," in Mary G. Dietz, ed., *Thomas Hobbes and Political Theory* (Lawrence, Kansas: University of Kansas Press, 1990), pp. 154, 167–70.

separation, the contemporary theory of liberal toleration goes an enormous step further by suggesting (again, in spite of itself) that we are actually prohibited from constructing one on our own. The state, understood ontologically as a structure of intelligibility and distinguished from the instruments of government through which it acts, embraces and subsumes an entire way of life reflecting the gamut of social institutions, actions and relationships; and from this it follows that the state's involvement in the lives of its citizens, though it might take many different forms including passive ones, is and can only be constant and pervasive.[29]

1. The Argument from Impossibility is no longer taken very seriously. Locke may well have won the war – liberal toleration has become a virtually unquestioned premise of contemporary political discourse – but Proast does seem to have won an important battle. Today we recognize what Locke himself denied, namely, that the state, precisely in virtue of its capacity to inflict physical punishment, can indeed influence many of the beliefs of its citizens; and we understand quite well that this may involve practices far less drastic than torture or brainwashing. As we have seen above, Waldron's claim is crucial and undeniable, namely, that even if a people's ideas cannot be controlled *directly* by coercive means, "those who wield political power can put it to work *indirectly* to reinforce belief," for example, by simply preventing citizens from obtaining heretical works.[30] Censorship in particular and the control of information in general can shape minds in powerful ways.

---

[29] I use the phrase "civil society" to refer to a large range of activities undertaken by citizens of the state in an unofficial, non-governmental capacity. It includes what is sometimes referred to as the "private sphere." My usage is thus much broader than that of Jean Cohen and Andrew Arato (see *Civil Society and Political Theory* [Cambridge, Mass.: MIT Press, 1992]) for whom civil society is basically composed of more-or-less formally organized voluntary associations and social movements, hence is to be distinguished not only from the state but also from the sphere of individual activity, including individual economic activity. I have no desire either to deny or aver the importance of such a distinction. My goals are philosophical rather than sociological, and my claim is only that the separation between state and civil society, no matter how broadly or narrowly the latter is conceived, is an impossibility. The question of public and private is somewhat different. The thrust of my argument is to deny a sharp separation between public and private "realms" or "spheres." On the other hand, I do believe, and have argued elsewhere, that public and private are importantly distinct from one another; and I believe that the distinction is best captured if we see public and private as designating not realms or spheres but, rather, different manners of acting that are to be found in all regions of human endeavor. The argument is elaborated in Peter J. Steinberger, "Public and Private," *Political Studies* 47 (June 1999), pp. 292–313.

[30] Waldron, "Locke, Toleration and the Rationality of Persecution," p. 81. Emphasis added.

But if the Argument from Impossibility no longer holds much weight, the appeal of liberal toleration is, if anything, stronger than ever, based now not on claims about the actual power of the state but on a conception of virtue and/or a moral theory involving notions of rights, reciprocity and mutual respect. It is true, as well, that contemporary tolerance theory, having given up the Argument from Impossibility, is for that reason quite free from the specific errors of its predecessor. Rather than strengthening the general case for liberal toleration, however, this serves only to throw its fundamental weakness into sharper relief.

According to a standard formulation, toleration is "the refusal, when one has the power to do so, to prohibit or seriously interfere with conduct that one finds objectionable."[31] It involves, therefore, (at least) four things:

(a) Disapproval. We do not tolerate actions that we genuinely like or otherwise approve of; we embrace them. Nor do we tolerate actions toward which we are truly indifferent; such actions are neither here nor there. If we tolerate X, this means that we find X to be in some sense objectionable.[32]

(b) Power to suppress. In Raphael's words, "one can meaningfully speak of tolerating, i.e., of allowing or permitting, only if one is in a position to disallow. You must have the power to forbid or prevent, if you are to be in a position to permit."[33]

(c) A decision not to exercise that power.

(d) A sharp separation between the decision not to suppress an activity and the disapproval of it. Key to the idea of toleration, as generally understood, is that one permits an activity *in spite of* one's objections to it, and this suggests that the decision to tolerate is not based on, but is taken apart from and independent of, those objections. We have, again, the art of separation. The power to suppress – frequently the power of the public authority – is exercised or eschewed without reference to, i.e., *separate* from, the fact of disapproval or dislike. That fact is important, of course, since it is what makes suppression intolerance and the lack of suppression tolerance. The negative judgment is crucial. But the decision itself overrides that judgment, and does so on entirely independent grounds; and this suggests, among other things, that the public authority, so conceived, is to be neutral toward the various activities of which we might or might not approve

---

[31] John Horton, "Toleration as a Virtue," in *Toleration: An Elusive Virtue*, ed. David Heyd (Princeton: Princeton University Press, 1996), p. 34.

[32] Susan Mendus, "Introduction," in *Justifying Toleration*, ed. Mendus, p. 3.

[33] D. D. Raphael, "The Intolerable," in Susan Mendus, ed., *Justifying Toleration*, p. 139.

and is to suppress them or not suppress them for reasons having nothing to do with its substantive evaluation of them.

Such a view has given rise to at least three difficult controversies:

There is, to begin with, the question of whether or not toleration implies *moral* disapproval of an activity or if, to the contrary, non-moral dislike or distaste is sufficient.[34] If I find my neighbor's religious practices to be morally objectionable but choose not to do anything about them on grounds of religious freedom, surely most people would be inclined to call me tolerant. On the other hand, if I simply find his house to be painted a color that displeases me but again choose not to do anything about it, would that too qualify as toleration? This is an important question – we cannot really know what toleration is unless we at least know its proper range of application – but it is not immediately clear how it should be answered. Evidence from ordinary language seems to cut both ways, and the relevance of other kinds of evidence is far from obvious.

There is, further, the related question of whether tolerance presupposes disapproval simpliciter – either moral or non-moral – or if it requires, rather, justifiable disapproval. Can a virulent and irrational racist who chooses not to act upon his racist impulses truly be thought of as tolerant? At least one author suggests not. He claims that "no account of toleration as a virtue can ignore some assessment of the worth of the objection to the conduct or practice that is tolerated."[35] But this doesn't seem to me self-evidently true. At the least, a self-restraining racist, however objectionable his views, is surely better than a racist who lacks such self-restraint. Why not say, then, that self-restraint of this kind involves a certain degree of tolerance?

Finally, and perhaps most important, is the so-called paradox of toleration itself. In Raphael's formulation,

[t]o disapprove of something is to judge it to be wrong. Such a judgment does not express a purely subjective preference. It claims universality; it claims to be the view of any rational agent. The content of the judgment, that something is wrong, implies that the something may properly be prevented . . . . But if your disapproval is reasonably grounded, why should you go against it at all? Why should you tolerate?[36]

Williams acknowledges the depth of the problem with admirable, if also suitable, candor: if it is true that "toleration . . . is required only for the

---

[34] See Peter Nicholson, "Toleration as a Moral Ideal," in *Aspects of Toleration: Philosophical Studies*, ed. John Horton and Susan Mendus (London: Methuen, 1985), pp. 160–61; and Mary Warnock, "The Limits of Toleration," in *On Toleration* (Oxford: Oxford University Press, 1987), ed. Susan Mendus and David Edwards, p. 125.

[35] Horton, "Toleration as a Virtue," p. 41.

[36] Raphael, "The Intolerable," p. 139.

intolerable," then it seems that the virtue of toleration (though not necessarily its practice) involves a kind of "conceptual impossibility."[37]

I believe that each and every one of these problems largely disappears once
we see that the art of separation itself is incoherent; and we can see this if we
bring to bear on the question of toleration the central insight of contemporary social and philosophical theory, namely, that everything we do, to the
extent that it is intelligent and intelligible, involves implicit and underlying
commitments of a moral or metaphysical nature. If it is true that any political
act cannot but be an embodiment and an expression of truth claims, then
this must be as true for acts that appear to be tolerant as for any other; and if
that is so, then we cannot but conclude that the paradoxical nature of
toleration, standardly conceived, derives from the fact that (d) above – the
idea that the decision to tolerate is to be sharply separated from the negative
judgment of that which is tolerated – expresses an impossibility.

2. Any decision to tolerate necessarily presupposes a judgment that the
thing tolerated is indeed tolerable; and this, in turn, involves the claim
that the thing, however objectionable it may be, in the end must not be so
bad. I can see no way around this. To tolerate is to determine that the
negative features of that which is tolerated are insufficient – either in
number or in degree – to justify its suppression.

In saying this, I am proposing to clarify the way in which we may
coherently use the term itself. Whereas Williams and countless others
insist that "toleration . . . is required only for the intolerable," I find the
paradoxical nature of such a formulation to be, well, intolerable. Instead,
I would suggest a more plausible account: to tolerate an activity means to
permit or allow it to continue despite the fact that there are at least some
good reasons to think that it ought to be prohibited.

Plainly, there are many activities – murder, torture, genocide – that we
might not tolerate under any circumstances. To say that such activities are
intolerable is to say, among other things, that they are worse than all of
those other activities that are also bad but that, in the same circumstances,
we might choose to tolerate. The latter activities are, in a word, less bad
than the former ones, and if they are less bad, then they are *ipso facto* better.

In general, there is no contradiction in saying of something both, nega-
tively, that it is bad and, positively, that it is better. Having severe indigestion
is bad, but certainly much less bad than having a heart attack; and what
could "less bad" mean other than that it is *better* to have the former than the

---

[37] Bernard Williams, "Toleration: An Impossible Virtue?" in Heyd, ed., *Toleration*,
pp. 18–19.

latter? To be sure, a claim of "less bad" or "better" is not the same as a claim of approval. I can disapprove of indigestion without at all denying that it is much better than something else. Indeed, I can positively rejoice in having that bad-but-better thing, not because it is good in itself but because it is very good indeed when compared with the possible alternative.

It seems, then, that to claim in general that something is less bad or better than something else is necessarily to imply a certain kind of comparative approbation, and this speaks directly to the question of toleration. If I tolerate Y but not X, then this can only mean that, much as I hate Y, it is in my judgment preferable to X, so far preferable that I am willing to suppress the one but not the other; and to make such a claim requires determining that the features of Y, taken together, *are preferable to those of X*, and those of anything else that I am willing to suppress. My judgment of them is more positive, and while approbation of this kind may be well be minimal and grudging – it is purely comparative – I believe that it is approbation nonetheless.

The idea of neutrality implicit in the standard account of toleration describes nothing that can exist. Every decision to tolerate is necessarily informed by, and ultimately reflects, a substantive judgment about the relative goodness and badness of the thing tolerated. And this means, in turn, that to tolerate is necessarily to judge favorably, though the judgment is apt to be purely comparative and freighted with all manner of conditions and qualifications.

I take it that there are two standard kinds of cases:

In one kind of case, the decision to tolerate is based on a calculation of costs and benefits, wherein the evils of the activity that would be suppressed are less bad than – hence preferable to – the evils that might be unleashed in the act of suppressing it. Suppression commonly arouses at least some level of resentment, often involves direct and extraordinary expenses (e.g., for police and correctional facilities), sometimes generates harmful and unintended side-effects such as black markets, and the like. It is hardly to be doubted that such consequences *could* be far worse than the behavior that was suppressed in the first place.[38] In such a circumstance, a decision to leave the behavior alone would hardly amount to neutrality. To the contrary, it could only be based on an (ideally hardnosed) assessment of expected utility wherein the behavior's merits and defects would be judged and evaluated. There are reasons to think that an activity should be prohibited. But when all is said and done, the activity

---

[38] Jonathan Harrison, "Utilitarianism and Toleration," *Philosophy* 62 (October 1987), pp. 425–26.

turns out to be less bad, hence better, than the activity of suppressing it. It is, therefore, something to be tolerated.

In the other typical kind of case, the decision to tolerate is epistemic, i.e., while I have concerns about a particular practice, I am not entirely certain that it is bad, hence am loath to use public power to obliterate it.[39] In an important sense, this is merely a different version of the first kind of case. If I don't know for sure how bad a practice is, but am quite sure of the costs involved in suppressing it, then simple prudence may dictate that I leave it alone. But an epistemic limitation along these lines can suggest a more generalized foundation for tolerance: the tangible and demonstrable costs of suppression should not be incurred unless the attendant benefits can be predicted and calculated with some certainty. I believe that most of what we ordinarily call toleration is at least implicitly grounded in some such consideration.

The argument that I have presented, based as it is on costs and benefits, looks to be utilitarian, but in the most relevant sense it is not. It does indeed suggest that the decision to tolerate involves the maximization of expected utility with respect to some value, but it does not in any way presuppose that the value itself is rooted in a utilitarian calculus. It merely follows Aristotle's dictum, that every action aims at some good. Thus, we might decide to tolerate or not tolerate an action simply and solely because of the degree to which it contributes to the goal of treating every person as an end rather than a means, a goal itself that could be understood to express a categorical, rather than a hypothetical, imperative. In such a circumstance, our ethics would be Kantian, not utilitarian, and questions concerning the costs and benefits of toleration would be entirely internal to a deontological framework. Of course, the argument does not *rule out* a utilitarian ethics either. The point, rather, is that the idea of toleration, in and of itself, is indifferent as regards the particular ethical standpoint from which it operates. Any decision to tolerate or not is necessarily based on a claim regarding the inimicality of an action, always considered from within the perspective of a particular moral theory and regardless of what that theory might be.

Understood in this way, toleration plainly does not involve feature (d), as described above. There cannot be a sharp separation between the decision not to suppress an activity and the disapproval of it. If the activity is not to be suppressed, then if it is disapproved of, that disapproval must be of a specific kind, i.e., not strong enough, on whatever moral or practical grounds are thought appropriate, to outweigh the negative

[39] *Ibid.*, p. 434.

implications of intolerance itself. Without this, without a more-or-less explicit consideration of costs and benefits, toleration makes no sense. Stated more generally, the act of toleration, like any other act, emerges out of a complex structure of metaphysical truth on the basis of which we make assessments of good and bad and, thereby, decisions about how to behave.

To reject (d) is, in turn, to raise very serious questions about (a), (b) and (c) as well. As to the first of these – the claim that tolerance presupposes disapproval – I think it easy enough to imagine cases both where tolerance does not involve disapproval and where intolerance involves the opposite. It may be unlikely that I could merely tolerate something that I enthusiastically favor; but surely I can tolerate things of which I neither approve nor disapprove. Many people have provided interesting and plausible reasons for prohibiting doctor-assisted suicide. I, on the other hand, am not sure just how strong I think those reasons are. But my very ambivalence, and my rather sharper awareness of the costs involved in a policy of suppression, incline me precisely to be tolerant. There is nothing remotely odd about tolerating in the face of uncertainty or ambivalence rather than outright disapproval. It is sufficient merely that we know of at least some plausible grounds for thinking that the activity in question ought to be prohibited.

It also seems to be the case that I may seek to suppress an activity of which I honestly approve if I believe that the pursuit of that activity would make it impossible to pursue another, different activity that I like even more. Thus, I may think that freedom of the press is a wonderful thing, but nonetheless refuse to endorse its exercise in each and every circumstance where it might compromise the fairness of criminal trials. The exercise of such freedom in such a circumstance would be literally intolerable to me, not because it is intrinsically bad but because it would rule out the possibility of something even better. One might argue that in this kind of example I would be refusing to tolerate not the activity in question but the situation that enjoyment of the activity brings about. But that would render the whole question of approval and disapproval trivial since ultimately "situations" are always what is at issue. The decision to tolerate necessarily reflects a judgment about a range of costs and benefits with respect to one or another value, and necessarily speaks to a situation that an activity either constitutes in itself or otherwise causes to occur.

In light of this, characteristic (b) – the power to suppress – also seems superfluous; and if *that* is true, then characteristic (c) – the decision not to exercise that power – is obviously irrelevant. I know a lovely, elderly woman who is, most would agree, an uncommonly tolerant individual. She does not get in the least bit upset when the children next door make noise or when their father mows the lawn at odd hours, even though she is aware of at least some reasons why such activity might be prohibited; she's a confirmed Republican, but recognizes on epistemic grounds that she doesn't have all the answers, hence refuses to rule out the possibility that the Democrats might have a point too; and if she is quite convinced that the Messiah appeared about two thousand years ago, she accepts and even values the fact that others disagree, in part because she finds the idea of suppression frightening and abhorrent. A tolerant soul indeed. She's also largely powerless. Her station and resources are such that even if she wanted to change any of these things – and she genuinely does not – she'd surely fail. None of this is to say that she's unprincipled. Far from it. When she encounters something deeply immoral or in some other way odious and offensive, she does not shrink from calling a spade a spade. Her tolerance in fact consists neither in a refusal to judge nor in forbearance, strictly understood as a decision to permit some activity to continue unhindered, since she rarely has any such decision to make. It consists, rather, in the particular nature of her reactions to, and considerations about, the world in which she lives. In the face of something so immoral as to be truly intolerable, she would simply refuse to tolerate it, by which I mean that she would refuse to reconcile herself to its continued existence – deny its right to be – even if there were nothing she could actually do about it. When she does tolerate, then, it is simply because she judges the thing tolerated to be either not self-evidently bad or else not so bad as to justify an act of suppression – an act that almost always would have to be undertaken by someone else.

This woman has the *virtue* of toleration, understood primarily as the exercise of good judgment with respect to the merits and demerits of certain activities and resulting in a decision, real *or* hypothetical, about whether or not those activities should be allowed. Such a virtue presupposes neither outright disapproval nor the power to suppress; and far from involving a kind of disengaged neutrality, it reflects just the reverse, namely, a more-or-less explicit accounting of costs and benefits with respect to some set of established and justifiable principles or values, itself necessarily representing a larger, though typically unstated, metaphysical scheme. As to the *activity* of toleration, what else could it be but the exercise of the virtue? And this, in turn, suggests that to tolerate is either to allow, or to agree with those who would allow, some endeavor to continue unfettered despite an awareness of good reasons for its suppression, and to do so on the grounds that such a policy – considered in light of the costs and benefits of the activity in question when weighed against the costs and benefits of suppressing it – best serves to maximize some set of substantive moral principles. The upshot is that all arguments about toleration are arguments either about the justifiability of such substantive principles or the relative weight of costs and benefits. They are not, and never can be, merely procedural arguments involving a formal, disengaged decision-rule concerning the limits of government or the right to be left alone.

When toleration is understood in these terms, each of the three difficult issues mentioned above turns out to be much less problematic than originally thought. The question of whether or not toleration implies moral disapproval, as opposed to non-moral dislike or distaste, seems clearly to miss the point. On the one hand, since disapproval is not a requirement for toleration, to ask what kind of disapproval must be involved is to ask an inapt question. On the other hand, any judgment about the virtues and defects of an activity is necessarily made with reference to some set of principles; and if we are to raise serious questions about a decision to tolerate or not tolerate, we are inevitably asking about the *justifiability* of those principles. Indeed, it seems to me that to the extent that such questions are not raised, the issue of toleration does not really arise; but when someone asks whether it is right or just or otherwise beneficial that some activity, whether approved or disapproved, be allowed to continue, then this is necessarily to demand precisely the kind of moral judgment that makes toleration what it in fact is.

As to the second question – does toleration imply disapproval that is to some extent rational or well justified? – the answer now cuts both ways. Again, since disapproval is not a requirement for toleration, the question as stated does not apply. But insofar as any decision to interfere or not interfere with some activity necessarily represents a serious theoretical judgment of some kind, and since any such judgment must be based on some set of presumably defensible reasons and a structure of truth claims, it follows that the virtue of toleration, along with the exercise of that virtue, will necessarily be a matter of reasonableness – understanding the reasonable to be bound up with and inseparable from the rational (as in 2.5.2 above). Toleration, as such, is nothing other than a form of judgment itself, hence can never be merely arbitrary or capricious but must embody an argument of some kind. To the extent that a particular decision not to interfere with an activity does in fact reflect merely arbitrary or capricious considerations, it is not, properly speaking, an example of tolerance at all but, rather and at best, unthinking indifference.

Obviously, then, the third question – the question of the paradox of toleration – dissolves into nothingness. To talk about tolerating the intolerable is to talk nonsense, to describe nothing that could possibly exist. If something is to be tolerated despite the fact that it is horrible, then however horrible it may be, its evils must be such as to be outweighed by other evils, actual or prospective – evils that would somehow attend to the activity of suppression itself and that would, in the end, make the original evil seem not so bad after all, at least by comparison.

3. Imagine, then, that we are to decide whether or not to permit, say, a proposed neo-Nazi march in Skokie, Illinois. It seems to me that such a decision could not be made, at·least not responsibly, without arriving at an informed judgment about the costs and benefits of the march and of efforts to prevent it. As to the former, this certainly would require, at a minimum, an evaluation of the march itself and its possible effects, emotional and otherwise, on the citizens of Skokie. That, in turn, would involve an analysis and estimation of its animating ideas, i.e., neo-Nazi doctrine; for no one would ever think to question such an event unless there were something potentially troubling about either its underlying goals or its overt teachings. The march is problematic and raises the specter of suppression mainly because we judge its motivating ideology to be objectionable, dangerous and wrong. As to the costs and benefits of prevention, one would have to consider the feasibility of prohibiting the march, the expense in money and manpower required to do so, the fact that resources devoted to prevention might thereby be unavailable for other projects, and so on. Certainly one would want to think seriously about the risk of violence, but exactly where that would lead might not be immediately clear. Would violence be more likely to erupt if an attempt was made to suppress the march, thereby pitting potential marchers against the police or, to the contrary, if it were allowed to proceed, thereby pitting potential marchers against outraged onlookers? Again, considerations such as these would have to take into account neo-Nazi doctrine, e.g., to what extent would people be enraged, and rightly so, by the expression of neo-Nazi ideas? This would be an important part of an estimation of the overall situation with respect to the public good, and the final decision about whether or not to tolerate the march would follow more or less as a matter of necessity.[40]

It should go without saying that each of these various judgments would necessarily reflect, as do all judgments, the underlying structure of truth and meaning upon which our cognitive activity is based. To believe that

---

[40] The facts of the actual case are these: in 1976, the National Socialist Party, under the leadership of one Frank Collin, held a series of demonstrations in Chicago's Marquette Park. The City of Chicago sought to block the demonstrations and demanded that Collin post a bond of $250,000. Collin filed suit, but in the meantime sought a permit to march in the suburb of Skokie. The City of Skokie went to court and obtained an injunction against the National Socialist Party. Skokie also passed a series of new ordinances banning the dissemination of material promoting or inciting racial or religious hatred, including the public display of markings and clothing symbolizing racist politics and

Jews and blacks are not animals, that racism is irrational and indefensible, that the cult of oppression is inhuman, that angry words often lead to violence, that public celebrations of hatred may increase the level of hatred, that it costs money to provide marchers with police protection – all of this is to presuppose an immense range of truth claims of a moral, psychological, scientific and economic nature, the kinds of claims of which our "Background" or implicit structure of truth is composed. It is to presuppose, for example, a sense of what distinguishes humans from animals and what it means to be a Jew and a black, which presupposes, among many other things, an understanding of race, hence the concept of inheritability, hence genetic theory, hence the science of DNA, hence the most fundamental notions of biochemistry including the notion of a molecule, hence the theory of the atom, hence a basic view of how all of physical reality is constructed; and so on, ad infinitum. One might know all of this only in the sense that Euthyphro and Socrates already know what piety is, or one might know it more explicitly and securely. But one knows it nonetheless.

To consider the Skokie march is to consider the costs and benefits of its suppression; and to consider costs and benefits means placing them more-or-less squarely within an enormous and complex metaphysical theory of how things in the world really are.

Now it might be argued that this way of thinking about Skokie ignores the most crucial and obvious factor. If the march is to be permitted, it should primarily be not because of a cost-benefit analysis but, rather, because of a serious moral commitment to the idea of free speech. Free speech, so the argument goes, is a fundamental human right. As such, it trumps all considerations of cost and benefit; and this means that to tolerate the march on Skokie is to judge neither the march itself nor its effects nor the effort to suppress it. Above all, it is not to judge the ideas it is designed to express. It is, rather, to act on the basis of principle, hence

ideas. After a Cook County circuit court upheld the ordinance, the Nazis filed two suits challenging the city's actions. In *Skokie v. National Socialist Party* (373 N. E. 2d 21 [1978]), the Illinois Supreme Court reversed the lower court, arguing that displaying a swastika was symbolic speech protected by the First Amendment and did not constitute "fighting words." In *Collin v. Smith* (578 F. 2d 1197 [1978]), a federal appeals court, upholding a federal district court ruling, dismissed Skokie's attempt to deny the Nazis a permit to march. The appeals court argued that the ordinance could not be justified since it did not have reasons to fear imminent violence. The court also argued that the "fighting words" doctrine did not apply since there was no direct tendency to "cause violence by persons to whom, individually, the words were addressed." The US Supreme Court denied certiorari in both cases, thus letting the decisions stand. The Nazis obtained a permit for a demonstration in Skokie on 25 June 1978, but they never used it. Two weeks later, they held a demonstration in Marquette Park in Chicago.

to make a decision independent of – separate from – any evaluation of the event in question.

The argument is wrong-headed. For even if one decided on moral grounds to endorse a right to free speech, this would only mean that whenever one faced a decision to tolerate, one would have to approach it in terms of the degree to which such a decision would contribute to the principle of free speech itself. In the instant case, it would require, to begin with, a decision as to whether and to what extent the march on Skokie is the kind of speech that the principle is intended to protect. It should go without saying that the answer would not necessarily be self-evident. As an historical matter, freedom of speech has often been understood to include only political speech; and political speech itself has often been understood to include only expressions of a partisan sort occurring within the parameters of a legitimate political system, broadly conceived, hence to exclude statements thought to be truly radical, subversive, or otherwise "beyond the pale." It may or may not be the case that neo-Nazi doctrine passes the test. But even given a much more generous account of free speech, everyone recognizes that some speech – indeed a great deal of speech including a great deal of political speech – is not and cannot be allowed (see below). The real issue is not whether or not to protect speech but, rather, which speech should be protected and how to draw the line.

To tolerate the Skokie march on free speech grounds thus presupposes two things: a plausible account of what free speech means and an analysis of the march itself so as to determine whether or not it is covered by free speech doctrine. Would such a march be truly "political" as opposed to merely terroristic or nihilistic; would it be the expression of a genuinely partisan political position or would it rather be beyond the pale; would its goals be serious rather than frivolous and would it serve some socially beneficial function? Such questions – conceptual questions – are absolutely crucial; for surely freedom of speech, however defined, would provide grounds for tolerating the Skokie march only to the degree that the march is an example of the kind of speech that merits protection.

We would have to estimate, as well, the impact of tolerance in this case on the general practice of toleration. Perhaps the Skokie march, if permitted, could turn out to be so offensive as to create a climate of opinion hostile to the very idea of toleration, hence harmful in the long run to the principle of free speech. Of course, the opposite conclusion is more likely: however odious the Skokie march would be, to suppress it might be to start down a slippery slope of suppression, helping to establish a habit of inappropriate and unthinking interference and ultimately raising the possibility of gratuitous and wholesale challenges to the very idea of free speech. Much better to err on the side of permissiveness. Indeed, I take this latter to represent a standard civil libertarian approach. But it is important to note that such an approach embraces, as much as any other, the logic of prudence focusing on costs and benefits. A policy of toleration with respect to some particular case should be adopted if and only if it serves a larger moral value.

But indeed, the decision about Skokie certainly would also have to take into account its possible consequences with respect to an entire range of moral values. Again, the principle of free speech, however important it may be, does not necessarily override all other principles, and this means that the march itself would have to be assessed in terms of, say, the "clear and present danger" doctrine, the "fighting words" doctrine, long-standing prohibitions against treason and subversion, libel and slander laws, laws concerning criminal conspiracy and racketeering, and the like. One can thus well imagine an informed, justified and legitimate policy decision to suppress the march *despite* a very strong commitment to the freedom of expression, on the grounds that it poses a threat to the public good in some other, more tangible respect.

It is important to emphasize that all of these questions would necessarily take us into the very heart of the Skokie march, *understood explicitly as an expression of ideas*. They would lead us, that is, into the thickets of neo-Nazi ideology, and force us to evaluate that ideology on substantive grounds. How could one decide about the possible effects of the march, and of suppressing it, without assessing the ideas themselves? How else could one decide if neo-Nazi speech is the kind of speech covered by free speech doctrine? To be sure, disapproval of neo-Nazi ideas would not necessarily imply that the march should be disallowed. But a policy of toleration must mean either that the ideas themselves, however bad, are not so bad; or else that expressing those ideas and the putative consequences of doing so, however troubling, are not troubling enough as to justify the costs and risks involved in saying no. For these reasons, our decision could never be the product of so-called neutrality, understood as a determination not to judge. It could only be the result of a complex account of the thing to be tolerated; and such an account could be nothing other than a more-or-less faithful reflection of our own underlying views about how things in the world really are. Truly to withhold or suspend judgment in such a case is not to tolerate; it is merely to vegetate.

3. The omnicompetent state

The lessons of Skokie, so characterized, are applicable to all manner of social action. Whether or not to suppress an activity or event – either to tolerate it or, alternatively, to declare it illegal, hence eligible for censure and punishment – requires a substantive and prudent evaluation of the activity itself, its merits and defects, its costs and benefits. Every single act of suppression and every single refusal to suppress necessarily presupposes some such evaluation. And since every event or activity is either suppressed or not, it follows that the purview of the public authority is all-encompassing: the state is concerned with virtually everything that we do.

This will seem to some a disturbing conclusion. I believe it to be nonetheless inescapable, for it follows directly from our account of what tolerance and intolerance must mean. Wherever the public authority decides either actively to interfere or not interfere with an endeavor, it thereby determines the endeavor itself to be a matter of public interest, something to be investigated, analyzed and evaluated in terms of its contribution to the common good. I know of no social endeavor that is, or could ever be, exempt from this kind of scrutiny. As a structure of intelligibility reflecting a society's shared understanding of how things in the world really are, the state is thus, at least in principle, a structure of ubiquitous judgment. All of our behavior unavoidably falls within its bailiwick. This is not to suggest that the state actually does judge everything; but it is to suggest that where it fails to judge, such a failure reflects not forbearance or neutrality but simple inattention, itself a product of the natural limits of time and space that make continuous, ubiquitous observation difficult or impossible.

It is important to specify as clearly as possible the fundamental – the ontological – nature of these claims:

The communitarian rejection of strict liberal neutrality, and the consequent insistence that political regimes foster one or another conception of the good, often takes the form of an assertion about what the state should be. Emblematic here is Sandel's claim that Rawls's liberalism would have the effect of "disempower[ing] the deontological self... depriv[ing] us of those qualities of character, reflectiveness, and friendship that depend on the possibility of constitutive projects and attachments."[41] The state must embrace and pursue a substantial theory of the good, because this is the best way to ensure a healthy society and sound politics.

The opposing view generally takes quite the same form. The state should remain neutral, to the degree possible, because this is the best way to acknowledge and defend individual freedom. Such freedom, and not some particular, unified conception of the good, is the foundation of

---

[41] Michael Sandel, *Liberalism and the Limits of Justice* (Cambridge: Cambridge University Press, 1982), pp. 178, 181.

human flourishing; and this means that limitations on freedom can only be justified on the grounds that they in fact allow for more freedom than would otherwise be the case.

Arguments such as these seriously misconstrue the idea of the state, and the ontological premises upon which it is based. Indeed, this brings us quite directly to the crux of the matter. The notion that the state is a structure of intelligibility composed of propositions about how things in the world really are and about how to achieve the good health of society – such a notion entails not a recommendation about what the state should do but rather a description of what is inevitably, unavoidably the case. The neutral state is neither good nor bad; it is impossible. To recognize and understand this fact – a fact about what makes a state a state – is the crucial first step in coming to grips with what is really at issue in the debate about limited government and political liberalism.

But even this is far from the whole story, for we must also note that the judgments of the state and the actions of the state are, like all judgments and actions, merely two sides of the same coin. Where we have the one, we also have the other. This is implicit in, but is not always made explicit by, the literature on toleration, in which the emphasis often shifts imperceptibly from the evaluation of beliefs and behaviors, positive or negative, to the act of suppressing or not suppressing them, and back again. Locke, for example, sometimes talks about the magistrate's estimation of religious doctrines and sometimes talks about the actual suppression of religious behavior, but he often fails clearly to distinguish the one kind of discussion from the other; and so too for much current writing on toleration. This blurriness reflects, in part, the simple fact that it is not possible to act in the absence of judgment, as well as the related fact that while judgment perhaps does not necessarily cause an action to occur, failure to act in accordance with judgment is incoherence. The conclusion is, if anything, more unsettling than before, but equally unavoidable: the state, as a structure of intelligibility, is at the same time an agent of unlimited activity. Insofar as all of our behavior is subject to the scrutiny and evaluation of the public authority, it is also subject to regulation and control by that same authority.

To see this more clearly, we need to think about the nature of regulation and control *per se*, and to consider its implications for the notion of the state in general and the doctrine of limited government in particular.

1. Imagine a farmer who is forced to deal with a difficult technical problem. A wide stream runs across the lower elevations of his property. His largest field, however, is on higher ground. The stream does not reach the field, which, as a consequence, fails to receive adequate irrigation. The farmer's solution is to install an electronically powered irrigation

system in which water is diverted from the stream and pumped through pipes to the upper field.

Imagine another farmer who has a rather different problem. His stream runs along the higher elevations of his farm, while his largest field is on lower ground. Here again the large field does not receive adequate water; but in this case it is because the stream, which would otherwise have fallen naturally to the lower field, has been diverted by some very large tree trunks felled several years earlier by the farm's previous owner, an improvident man. The new owner's solution is to remove these impediments, thereby allowing the stream to resume its natural course downward into the lower field, propelled not by pumps and pipes but by gravity and the lay of the land.

Certainly there is a sense – and not a trivial sense – in which the two solutions are quite the opposite of one another. The first involves the active interference with and disruption of nature. If left alone, the stream would remain on lower ground, and the upper fields would remain infertile. Solving the problem requires the direct substitution of artificial, man-made processes for natural ones, hence the implementation of direct and constant human control. The second case, on the other hand, is a matter of actively *removing* the consequences of human interference, i.e., the felled trees. The farm's previous owner had undermined natural processes – the unfettered flow of the stream – with disastrous results. Once nature is again permitted to take its course, the field can receive the water it needs.

One might say that the second farmer pursues a policy of laissez-faire. Just as he seeks to unleash nature by removing artificial impediments, so does the laissez-faire economist determine that economic goals can be best achieved through the free activity of the market. Just as the farmer determines that his fields would be most effectively irrigated by allowing the stream to follow its natural course, so does the free marketeer seek to unleash the natural power of supply and demand by removing governmental regulations. The first farmer, on the other hand, pursues what might be called a policy of central control. Just as he seeks to substitute his own designs for those of nature, so does the central planner seek to replace the uncontrolled processes of supply and demand with rationally determined and artificially imposed allocations and distributions. Just as this farmer determines that his fields would become productive only by forcibly redirecting the water away from where nature would take it, so does the central planner believe that economic goals can be best achieved by actively controlling the market.

But while these differences are obviously crucial and fundamental, in another sense they are misleading. If, in procedural and mechanical terms, the two farmers are doing radically different things with radically different consequences, at a more basic level they are doing something quite similar. Specifically:

- Each employs reason to analyze a problem and arrive at a solution, relying on a more-or-less explicit understanding of how things in the world really are, a background of presuppositions that, taken together, compose a rich and complex metaphysics.
- In each case, the solution involves a conscious human decision to utilize what the world offers up, with a view toward maximizing the achievement of some humanly chosen goal.
- In each case, the resulting policy is justified by, and is pursued entirely at the sufferance of, some kind of prudential calculation about what will and will not work.
- In each case, then, *the world is being managed and controlled toward some human end.* The specific mechanisms of control in the two cases are obviously and importantly different, but the fact of control – the fact of nature being exploited one way or another by human reason – is fully and equally true of each situation. For in the case of the second farmer, the trees do not *have* to be removed; and once removed, there is (per possible) nothing to prevent their being *replaced*, hence nothing to prevent the stream from being once again diverted from the lower fields. In effect, the second farmer chooses to use gravity and the lay of the land as instrumentalities to achieve a specific goal, just as the first farmer uses a pumping system to do the same.

To see this more clearly, consider that the question of "letting nature takes its course" is almost always a matter of degree and of where one chooses to look. Pumping systems, no matter how elaborately contrived – no matter how "artificial" – necessarily take advantage of what nature has to offer. For example, most pumps utilize gravity as much as they defy it. At some point, water is allowed to fall to the ground "on its own." And so too for a myriad of self-sustaining processes upon which any pump might depend: the "natural" flow of electricity, the tendency of liquid to seek its own level, the physics of compression, and so on. Which, then, is greater, the pump's reliance on or its defiance of nature?

2. In nearly everything we do, we manage nature, sometimes by permitting it to run its course, sometimes by changing its direction. This is as true of economic policy as it is of farms and streams and pumps. Laissez-faire is a system of economic management, just as much as central planning. The mechanisms that it uses, the techniques upon which it relies, the specific activities that it requires – these are distinctive. But it is a mode of social control nonetheless, guided by an understanding of the

goal to be achieved and a theory of how to achieve it. Under laissez-faire, impediments to market activities are identified and removed, results are monitored, new obstacles are discovered, adjustments are proposed, discussed and enacted. If excessive government regulation is shown to interfere with the efficiency of markets, then deregulation may be required. But if deregulation leads to an unhealthy concentration of capital and/or the development of monopolies, then new rules may be required. In laissez-faire, strict limits may be – indeed, almost always are – imposed on market activity and entirely without contradiction, provided only that they are imposed *in the interest* of market activity. Such limits cannot but be evaluated in terms of the degree to which they are effective; and if the definition of what it means for a policy to be effective is not immediately obvious – if, for example, maximization of individual freedom and the protection of property rights are, for whatever reasons, to be seriously considered along with economic efficiency and material prosperity – then this only reinforces the sense in which the political process in general and the state in particular are always and inevitably involved, and deeply so, no matter how unregulated the market seems to be.

And clearly what is true of economic policy must be equally true of the activities of the state in general. Thus, to tolerate certain kinds of expression or action, to allow them to continue unfettered, to leave them "unregulated," is not to refrain from the exercise of control but, rather, to exercise control of a particular kind; and this means that the notion of separation inherent in many forms of liberalism is, at best, misleading. Again, the farmer who decides to let his stream flow unfettered is not refraining from but in fact exercising a very strong kind of judgment and control; the unfettered stream will produce better results, and if this were not so the fetters would quickly be restored. In the same way, a decision not to repress the Skokie march involves not the separation of the state from some non-state realm but, rather and more simply, a particular method for dealing with a situation, a mode of control through what is sometimes called benign neglect. The activity in question cannot but be judged and evaluated by the public authority, and that authority decides, among other things, how the costs and benefits of suppression compare with those of toleration. If, at times, the state appears to be neutral with respect to some such activity, that appearance always necessarily conceals an underlying structure of judgment and evaluation, and a correlative policy. A permissive state permits only that which it deems truly permissible; and this "deeming" cannot itself be anything other than the product of a political process that produces, as does any political process, judgments about the costs and benefits of particular activities, themselves evaluated in the light of the values and metaphysical/moral premises upon which the society in question is based and resulting in one or another management strategy.

To be explicit: the judgmental state, which evaluates everything that comes to its attention, even those things that it chooses to allow and always with a view toward maximizing its own interests, is merely the flipside of the omnicompetent state, wherein even a policy of license and laissez-faire is always itself a mode of social control, an exercise of power and public authority.

Seen in this light, then, the doctrine of limited government merely describes a set of mechanisms or instrumentalities thought to be useful in achieving specific political aims; those aims are themselves thought to be useful in achieving a more generalized array of goals that, in the end, almost always reduce to broad notions of human flourishing; and in all such cases, it is plainly the thinking itself – the metaphysical premises and the various judgments that they authorize – that are fundamental and that truly constitute the state *qua* structure of intelligibility. What this means, among other things, is that liberalism in particular and the art of separation in general do not in themselves describe an idea of the state. Rather, they describe certain methods that the state might employ in order to realize its ends. Of course, if this is true, then it must be equally true for alternatives to liberalism, according to which human flourishing is to be achieved through expansive rather than limited government.

With this in mind, it can hardly be surprising that the so-called liberal–communitarian debate has seemed so intractable. For the debate has been, one might suggest, a debate about incommensurables. Liberalism is, in effect, a theory of government, communitarianism a theory (or part of a theory) of the state. The former holds that the state should limit the ways in which it uses the instrumentalities of government; the latter holds that whatever the state does necessarily reflects a structure of metaphysical and moral presupposition – including a theory of the good life, of *eudaimonia* – that is embedded in society itself. There is, it seems, no point at issue between them, no basis for disagreement; and there is, on such an account, nothing necessarily contradictory in being both a liberal and a communitarian at the same time.

Wittingly or otherwise, all of us embrace a single, overarching notion of the state. The state is, and can be, nothing other than that which determines when and how the instruments of government are to be used. As such, it is the authoritative embodiment of a theory – society's theory – of how things in the world really are; and with this theory society licenses conclusions about the kinds of activity that promote its own good health. The fact that the scope and complexity of any such theory will always be staggering, far beyond what any single human intelligence could grasp and articulate at any one time or during any one lifetime, in no way undermines the basic notion that the state, as a structure of intelligibility, must be understood, and must constantly seek to understand itself, as an elaborate but fundamentally coherent idea.

3. As the embodiment of our understanding of how things in the world really are, and in light of the fact that even tolerance and benign neglect are powerful forms of management and control, the state underwrites whatever means are at its disposal to achieve ends that it has prescribed to itself. There is no state of which this is not true. Always and in every case, the state is an institution of unlimited scope, an institution that in principle knows no external constraints other than those imposed upon it by sheer physical nature.

We seem to deny this all the time. We seek constantly to restrain and limit the activity of the state in all kinds of ways. There is nothing incoherent in attempting to do so, and certainly no contradiction whatsoever with the idea of the unlimited state, provided, however, that we understand exactly what restraint means. For the variety of mechanisms and ideas – rights, constitutions, consent – that seem to limit what governments can do are not, and cannot be, external constraints on state authority. They are simply pragmatic devices that the state itself relies on in order to utilize most effectively the instrument of government. Specifically:

(a) *Rights in general.* We insist that individuals or groups have rights, perhaps even "natural rights," over and against the state, and that such rights limit what the state can legitimately do. Claims of this nature, and the theories upon which they are based, are perfectly comprehensible, and may even be correct. But from the perspective of the state – any state – a rights claim is always provisional. To begin with, no matter how central and no matter how well justified, any proposed and recognized right is subject to suspension and nullification if and when some other, higher consideration is at stake. In the American state, the right of free speech establishes strong limits to governmental activity. But as Skokie shows, the exact nature of these limits is often unclear, and the state itself has determined that free speech is not protected if it is slanderous, violates certain community norms, undermines other enumerated rights such as the right to a fair trial, or threatens the very existence of the state through subversion and treason. The right of free speech is thus conditional in that it exists at the sufferance of the state itself; and so too for all political and civil rights. It is true that political discourse is filled with arguments to the effect that, as a matter of moral theory, a particular right exists even if a particular state fails to recognize it, hence that rights function over and against the state as *external* limitations on state activity. But this cannot be correct. For any rights claim is necessarily rooted in and reflective of the larger structure of truth or metaphysical presupposition upon which society is based and which, in turn, is embodied and activated in the idea of the state itself; and this means that any rights claim can exist only *internal* to, as a part of, the state. Rights claims may well be, and in fact usually are, external to various agencies of *government*, understood as instrumentalities of the state. Rights stand as limitations on, hence are in tension with, governmental action. But this kind of tension can only be addressed and resolved within the authoritative context of the state. It is for this reason that no right becomes, in Hegel's word, *wirklich* until the state itself chooses to recognize its existence; and such recognition would be attendant to the view that the state can best achieve *its* goals by accepting, however provisionally, the force of such a right.

(b) *Rights and the self-limiting state.* Another way of saying this is that wherever rights are in place, they constitute not external limits on state power but self-limits. They represent decisions *by the state* to refrain from certain activities, again presumably because it regards the benefits of such restraint to exceed the costs – benefits and costs here measured in terms of the state's own purposes. When we insist, then, on the existence of a certain, as yet unactualized right, we are making an argument that we hope will convince the state, an argument to the effect that the state can indeed best achieve its ends by accepting the proposed right as an actual one.

Consider, for example, the question of property rights. Obviously, formal rights to private property have been a bedrock of social and political life in the West since at least the thirteenth century. But such rights are accepted and acknowledged by the state only when they suit its interests; and virtually every state, no matter how liberal and limited its government may be, arrogates to itself the prerogative to confiscate the property of individuals who have committed crimes or civil wrongs, to invoke powers of eminent domain when the public interest so requires, to impose "civil forfeiture" when the remedies of the criminal justice system do not avail, and the like. Indeed, the most basic property right – the right to physical life – is itself hostage to the judgment of the state; for even where capital punishment is disallowed, this is a matter of the state deciding, on whatever grounds, to limit the exercise of its own powers.

(c) *Procedural rights.* It is true, to be sure, that in many or most states such forms of interference must themselves be administered according to "due process." Powers of eminent domain are not exercised willy-nilly. Appropriate legal procedures must be followed; and so too for most other forms of state action. But this merely moves the argument back one step, for procedural protections involve rights that are themselves subject to

the judgment of the state, hence exist at its sufferance. No feature of
Anglo-American jurisprudence is more fundamental than the principle of
habeas corpus. But when, during the American Civil War, the state, in the
form of its army, suspended the writ of habeas corpus, it enunciated in no
uncertain terms the provisional nature of due process protections *per se*;
and when, in 1866, that same state, this time in the form of its Supreme
Court, declared the earlier suspensions to have been in error, it was
acknowledging not an external constraint on the state but a judgment
by the state that its own interests would best be served through a policy of
self-limitation; and even here, Mr. Justice Davis, writing for the majority,
plainly recognized the ultimate comprehensive nature of the state by
indicating that "it is essential to the safety of every government [*sic*] that
in a great crisis, like the one we have just passed through, there should be a
power somewhere of suspending the writ of *habeas corpus* .... The government [*sic*], if it should see fit, in the exercise of proper discretion to make
arrests, should not be required to produce the persons arrested in answer
to a writ of *habeas corpus*."[42] The key phrase seems to be "if it should see
fit." The question of limiting the power of the state is for the state itself
to decide.

(d) *Constitutionalism*. But do we not find a genuine and ultimate restraint
on the state in its constitution? Again, the same rejoinder applies. To the
extent that the constitution of a state truly establishes unassailable and
inviolable boundaries to state action, this occurs when the constitution is in
part *constitutive* of the state. Understood in this way, then, the constitution
embodies in a more-or-less formal sense the self-limitations that the state
has adopted, such that to invoke the constitution is, in effect, to exercise,
rather than restrain, state power. As self-limitations, moreover, constitutional restraints are inevitably subject to the state's own discretion; for the
state always has the prerogative to change the constitution, whether
through an orderly process of amendment or a (usually) more complicated
and difficult process of constitutional crisis and replacement.

(e) *Consent*. Fundamental to modern political thought is the notion
that the activities of the state are limited by the consent of the governed.
Unlike rights and constitutions, however, consent is not strictly speaking
a limiting device at all. It is a legitimizing device, and can just as easily be
used to authorize an unlimited as well as a limited exercise of governmental power. Questions of consent, legitimacy, authority and obligation
are, to be sure, fundamental to the idea of the state, and will be examined

---

[42] *Ex Parte Milligan* (4 Wallace 2 [1866]). As should be clear, I believe that the opinion
mistakes "government" for "state."

closely in chapter 5. But they are quite distinct from the question of governmental limitation. Suffice it to say, for now, that the concept of the state as an omnicompetent institution also includes, without any contradiction whatsoever, at least the functional equivalent of what is often called the right to revolution.

Most importantly, we should be clear that there is nothing incoherent, indeed nothing even remotely perplexing or odd, about an (unlimited) state choosing to guarantee for its citizens the broadest liberties of expression and action, and inscribing those guarantees in a formal constitution where they acquire the status of civil rights – provided we understand only this, that the state establishes such guarantees under the presumption that they will conduce to the good health of society and the well-being of the people and that such a presumption is always subject to review and revision by the state itself.

4. The doctrine of limited government is thus completely and entirely consistent with the omnicompetence of the state. Whether defined in terms of rights or otherwise, limited government describes a particular set of mechanisms utilized by a state that has decided it can function most effectively by imposing upon itself certain artificial restraints. The case of Hobbes is, as so often, paradigmatic. Few have understood as clearly the idea that, as a matter of conceptual fact, the power of the state is and can only be unlimited. But he also understood that one could endorse, without contradiction, a policy of "what we should regard today as an extreme state of internal *laisser-faire*."[43] Shapiro is quite correct about the failure of commentators to explain the confluence of omnicompetence and minimalism that one finds in Hobbes's work; and surely he is on the mark in describing Letwin's solution – that Hobbes is a "complicated thinker" – as a non-solution.[44] But Shapiro's own answer, that Hobbes's views must be explained in terms of seventeenth-century English politics and society,[45] is at once undeniably true and largely beside the point. It misses the simple but crucial fact that whereas Hobbes's insistence on unlimited power is a part of his account of the state, his minimalism – like his preference for monarchical government – is merely a pragmatic or

---

[43] Keith Thomas, "The Social Origins of Hobbes' Political Thought," in Keith Brown, ed., *Hobbes Studies* (Cambridge, Mass.: Harvard University Press, 1965), p. 228. See also, Ian Shapiro, *The Evolution of Rights in Liberal Theory* (Cambridge: Cambridge University Press, 1986), p. 31.
[44] Shapiro, *The Evolution of Rights in Liberal Theory*, pp. 34, 65–66.
[45] *Ibid.*, pp. 34–40.

prudential claim about the particular mechanisms that the state might best employ in order to achieve its goals.

In effect, the difference that I have outlined in chapter 2 between the philosophy of the state and prudential theories of politics means that the question of how government should be organized and how it should proceed is a tactical one, pertaining not to the idea of the state but to its apparatus and method of acting – its secondary rather than primary qualities, so to speak – and involving hypothetical rather than categorical claims about what is likely to help the state achieve its ends. Government is an important part of the state, but the two should not be confused. Hobbes thus agrees, to this extent, with Rousseau, for whom government, far from being the state, is rather an agent of the state, a "minister of the sovereign" that serves as an intermediary between sovereign and subjects (*du Contrat Social*, III.1).

In light of all this, we can see that liberalism itself is best thought of as a kind of device. It is, of course, more than that. It is a theory of what the most desirable form of government for the state is likely to be, hence composes a series of arguments on behalf of self-imposed limits. It often supports those arguments by invoking metaphysical views (e.g., atomistic individualism) that are, at best, heuristic and, at worst, dubious; and also with moral views (e.g., the importance of equal respect), some of which may indeed reflect our own understanding of how things in the world really are. But the arguments themselves – like all arguments about forms and actions of government – pertain not to the nature of political society but to those mechanisms that best permit such a society to achieve its ends. They are not ontological or metaphysical arguments about the idea of the state but arguments about what a prudent state should do and how it should do it.

4. Ordinary politics and political philosophy

The art of separation – understood as the project of insulating the "private" lives of citizens from the scrutiny and control of the public authority, of protecting civil society from the state – is an incoherence. The reach and power of the state is always and inevitably unlimited, constrained only by the vicissitudes of time and physical nature. This is not a "normative" or "prescriptive" claim. It describes a conceptual fact, something that we deny only on pain of irrationality.

Certainly nothing that I have said would gainsay either the intelligibility or the importance of deep and enduring controversies between liberals and conservatives, individualists and holists, democrats and elitists, and the like. Such controversies compose the foundations of a great deal of ordinary political conflict, and the argument that I have offered thus far casts not the slightest doubt on their materiality. These are real controversies, and they reflect real theoretical differences. But properly understood, *such differences never involve substantial disagreements about the nature of the state itself*. Rather, they pertain only to the particular ways in which a state chooses to organize itself and to act. They are purely and simply disagreements about policy and government.

In this context, two sets of questions arise. First, what difference does it make whether a disagreement is merely about policy and government rather than the state? Does it in any way affect the substance of political debate? Does it have any implications for the way in which debate is pursued and resolved? Even if my account is correct, have I not merely offered a kind of pedantic clarification about the meanings of words the real-world consequences of which are negligible at best? Second, if my account is indeed descriptive rather prescriptive, if it describes necessary and unavoidable features of the state, then what is its utility for politics itself? If things are as they are and cannot be otherwise, then exactly what problem – other than a lexicographic one – have I addressed? How does the argument help us to determine what is to be done?

1. The debate about Skokie, understood correctly as a debate about government policy, is a matter of assessing costs and benefits. To decide intelligently whether or not the march should be permitted, one would have to specify as comprehensively as possible the range of values that might be affected and determine the consequences for those values of a decision to permit versus a decision to prohibit. The operative question is, by now, a familiar one: does a policy of tolerance – or of laissez-faire, benign neglect, limited government, etc. – produce better results, all things considered, than the reverse?

As we have seen, to answer this question does indeed presuppose an understanding of the underlying nature of political society. Political prudence is controlled and guided by the metaphysical theory of the state. But given such a theory, the political task is, as we have also seen, a matter of identifying concretely the actual impact of the Skokie march itself and of efforts to suppress it. This means attempting to address such questions as: just how dangerous is Nazi ideology, how feasible and how costly would it be to prevent the march, to what extent might the march itself precipitate actual violence, and the like? Each of these involves a certain kind of knowledge, a knowledge of history and of empirical cause and effect, based on a theory of how the world really is and resulting in one or more hypothetical claims of the sort: if X happens, then Y is more-or-less likely to follow. To decide the issue of Skokie is thus to engage in a prudential analysis.

When the issue is cast in quite different terms, when it is formulated as a conceptual question about the nature of the state itself, it is thereby miscast, and the ensuing conversation is likely to be confusing and inapposite. Does the state have a "right" to interfere with a Nazi march in Skokie? But what could this question mean, since the state cannot help but be deeply involved in all such activities that come to its attention, whether or not it chooses to regulate them by overt control or by laissez-faire? Is it legitimate for the state to regulate the expression of personal or political values? But the purpose and scope of the state is, and simply cannot be other than, to pursue the public interest; and since that interest could be affected in important ways by whether or not the march takes place, the state cannot just keep out of it when keeping out of it is tantamount to licensing the march. Is it acceptable for the state to reach beyond its proper bounds? But if the state's role is to pursue the public interest, then it is not clear what the phrase "proper bounds" could refer to. When we focus on such dead-end questions, we lose sight of what is really at stake in Skokie, namely, which policy will best serve the constitutive ends of political society.

To formulate the issues of Skokie as they really are is to attain a kind of clarity without which intelligent discussion and debate is impossible. When we see that disagreement turns not on the proper role of the state – this is something to be discovered and stipulated philosophically – but on the degree to which one policy or another contributes to the good health of society, then and only then can we begin to adjudicate claims and arguments in an orderly and productive manner.

Again, none of this is to deny in any way the appropriateness of invoking, say, a free speech argument, based on some conception of individual or group rights. It is plausible enough to claim that the Nazis have a right to express themselves and that the state ought to recognize and respect that right. But we need once more to be clear about what such a claim could mean. In particular, we must remember that it can never be other than the expression of one value among many. As such, it demands no more and no less than to be weighed as part of the overall calculus of costs and benefits. How important is the value of free speech, to what extent does the Skokie march advance our interest in that value, which other values are served – and, importantly, which are undermined – by a policy that seeks to maximize freedom of speech, and so on? These are the operative and unavoidable questions, and they are all questions of prudence, of pragmatic analysis. Even if we should decide that the right of free speech is a kind of "trump," outweighing or overriding most if not all other considerations – that would be my own predisposition – this too can only be a practical judgment about what the state should do in order to realize the good health of society and the well-being of its citizens. As such, it is always, and can only be, constantly subject to reevaluation by the state, hence retains its status as a trump only and exclusively at the sufferance of the state itself.

2. The concept of the state and its relationship to theories of policy or government are matters of fact. They represent necessary features of our conceptual apparatus, hence describe what we actually do when we think about controversies like Skokie and, indeed, the entire range of social and political issues with which we are regularly and routinely concerned. But if this is so, then what exactly is the purpose of pursuing a philosophy of the state? Is there a political payoff? Is there any reason to believe that the substance of policy itself would be influenced by the kinds of arguments that I have presented?

Such questions bring us back to Socrates and Euthyphro. As we saw in chapter 3, the conversation reported in the *Euthyphro* presupposes that the interlocutors at once know and do not know what piety is. They must know it, since otherwise how could they have a productive discussion about it at all, and how could they hope to recognize it if, in the end, they happen to come upon it? In another sense, though, they do not know it, since they are woefully unable to say what it is. The conclusion seemed clear: Socrates and Euthyphro have an implicit knowledge of piety. The goal of their conversation is to make that implicit knowledge explicit, to uncover and articulate this particular feature of their own conceptual scheme so that they can use it more productively.

As we also saw in chapter 3, the Socratic elenchus reflects a model of intellectual activity that manifests itself as well in the study of grammar, wherein knowledgeable and competent language users become explicitly and self-consciously aware of linguistic rules and principles that they already employ quite successfully without such awareness. In all such circumstances, the payoff is tangible and quite powerful. Socrates and Euthyphro generally know what piety is, but not such that they can deal effectively with hard cases. The clarity that they hope to gain from their conversation would put them in a position to decide not just the obvious situations but the complex ones as well. It seems certain, for example, that profaning a temple for no apparent reason and with a wanton disregard for the practices of Greek religion would have constituted, *ceteris paribus*, a clear case of impiety, and one would not have needed a great deal of discussion to reach such a conclusion. In such a circumstance, moreover, it's doubtful that the question of piety would have arisen between Socrates and Euthyphro. But the case of Euthyphro's father is far different, involving apparently competing notions of filial loyalty, social justice and higher law. Just how piety fits in here is not immediately apparent, and this is something that cannot be addressed unless and until one has a fairly solid and well-articulated account of just what piety is. And so too with many questions of grammar. Each of us uses natural language more-or-less effectively a great deal of the time. This is something that we take for granted, and reasonably so. But we also recurrently encounter hard linguistic cases – cases where our untutored intuitions fail to be of much help – and in dealing intelligently with those cases we would do well to develop an explicit knowledge of grammatical rules, typically by consulting an authority of some kind. These are rules that we already use all the time, hence in some sense "know." But in making our knowledge explicit, our use of language becomes that much more competent, that much more coherent. We make fewer errors and can deal more intelligently with the hard cases.

In politics, the hard cases tend to be the only interesting ones. They are the ones that we talk about and agonize over. To make our own understanding of the state explicit, to be able to articulate that idea and explain its relationship to particular policies and governmental forms, is a necessary condition for dealing with such cases intelligently. We know implicitly what the state is, and thus we know implicitly that our disagreements about Skokie are disagreements not about the scope of the state but about policy or government. But only by making our knowledge explicit can we begin to avoid the kinds of errors and miscalculations that so frequently emerge from the confusions of ordinary political discourse.

In a sense, then, politics is in large part an analysis of the grammar of political society, specifically, an attempt to make explicit our own shared assumptions regarding the nature of the state as a structure of intelligibility, as both an expression and an authoritative embodiment of our understanding of how things in the world really are, hence as the foundation for decisions about how the various mechanisms of government can and should be utilized in order to achieve our social goals. It is a search for coherence and agreement regarding the facts and opportunities of communal existence, and this suggests that political society is both the means and the result of our inquiry. The process itself is not always a pretty one. The search for coherence – the effort to make the implicit explicit – is often, in reality, a callous struggle, impelled by the desire for partisan advantage and fought with the manifold tools of seduction and intimidation, illusion and force. The effort to establish one particular interpretation of reality as the correct, the most coherent, interpretation is often a belligerent, agonistic affair, governed only fitfully by considerations of intellectual honesty. But the ultimate goal is always the same, namely, the achievement of a more-or-less complete consensus concerning how things in the world really are; and to the degree that such a consensus is unfairly imposed, manufactured, and false, it is in principle vulnerable to sustained philosophical criticism, the kind of criticism that exposes contradictions, that seeks the truth, and that virtually anyone can undertake, in one way or another.

The efficient causes of our explicit conceptions are various and complex, but those conceptions are always hostage to our underlying, implicit sense of reality. Just as, say, mathematics is, at one and the same time, a structure of truth claims and an institutionalized practice with which to uncover and explicate such claims, so is the state simultaneously an embodiment of our larger world-view and an on-going meditation on that world-view. The idea of the state is both that the state is an idea of the world and that it is an idea about itself understood as part of that world, an idea of an idea, hence a complex and ever-evolving structure of self-reflection, constantly in search of its own identity as it aims, however imperfectly, to achieve its defining goal: the good health of society and the well-being of its citizens.

3. While the arguments of the present chapter have been various, they have also composed, at least by design, a single, cumulative thread of argumentation. The failure of the Lockian account of toleration is symptomatic of the failure of separation theory in general, understood as a theory about the idea of the state; and so too for the standard contemporary account of toleration. Indeed, the attempt theoretically to limit the legitimate purview of the state – to create some kind of wall between the state and (some of) the other elements of society – ignores the central feature of the metaphysical theory of the state, namely, that the state is essentially a structure of intelligibility that embodies and renders authoritative a society's collective judgment about how things in the world really are. This central feature expresses the degree to which the state is, in every imaginable respect, inseparable from – indeed, is part and parcel of – the larger fabric of social and cultural life. As such, it expresses the degree to which the judgments of the state necessarily reach into every corner of intelligible human existence. To be sure, the form of state involvement is variable in the extreme. The state may choose actively to regulate social behavior, or it may choose to direct such behavior in far more passive ways. But these alternatives – which raise important and contentious issues of limited government, civil liberties, public regulation, and the like – are largely the stuff of policy and prudence. They speak not to external limitations on the state but, rather, to the possibility that the state might choose to adopt more-or-less temporary self-limitations of one kind or another, limitations that could subsist, moreover, only and exclusively at the sufferance of the state itself. These, then, are matters of cost and benefit – informed, to be sure, by considerations of principle, but ultimately to be decided in terms of what works and what doesn't. We badly

misunderstand such issues if we think of them as reflecting competing views of the nature of the state, for there are no such competing views. The state is and must be, at base, a single thing.

It should perhaps go without saying, moreover, that the analysis of this chapter demonstrates once again the complexity of the connection between prudential and philosophical modes of thought. If the state is indeed an authoritative and truly comprehensive embodiment of our understanding of how things in the world really are, and if ordinary political activity focuses largely on establishing and explicating one or another version of that understanding, then what room could there be, and what need would there be, for a distinctive prudential theory? Why wouldn't the particular metaphysical theory of which any particular state is composed answer all practical questions on its own? Now it may well be that some prudential decisions *are* simply and straightforwardly entailed by a shared structure of ontological presupposition. But these cases are apt to be rare, for in most cases – almost certainly the vast majority – our structure of presupposition is in fact equally consistent with a range of possible strategies, or is known only implicitly rather than explicitly, or is silent on questions of prospective empirical causality (is X likely to result in Y or in Z?), or fails to provide definitive answers in a sufficiently timely fashion, and so on. Indeed, such cases reflect the common circumstances of political and social life, and these generally require us to pursue and to rely on pragmatic theories of policy and government that must always be justified in terms of but are also not fully reducible to a prior metaphysical account of things.

5 The Absolute State: Authority and Resistance

The idea of the state is not simply that the state, like any institution, is an idea, but that it is an idea of a certain kind, specifically, one that encompasses in an authoritative manner a society's understanding of how things in the world really are. As such, it is best conceived as the intelligible foundation for all decisions about how the various instruments of government can and should be utilized in order to achieve social goals. I have already dealt at length with much of what is included in this formulation. I have discussed what it means to think systematically about how things in the world really are, and also what it means to talk prudentially about the instrumentality of government as opposed to philosophically about the nature of the state itself. But I have not yet discussed the sense in which the idea of the state is authoritative.

Our intuition is that the state, properly understood, is distinguished from other institutions not only in the scope of its activity – the topic of chapter 4 above – but in the nature of the authority that it exercises over its citizens. This involves, presumably, a variety of related intuitions: the state is sovereign or contains a sovereign element, its rule is morally defensible, its citizens have a responsibility to obey the laws that it promulgates, and so on.[1] I believe that understanding fully the idea of the state requires us to explicate these intuitions, to demonstrate their underlying logic. Specifically, it requires a systematic account of our notion of political obligation, an analysis of the sources of political legitimacy as we understand them, and a clear answer to this most troubling and basic of questions: how can we reconcile the essentially absolutist claims of the state with our own strong intuition that the individual citizen has, at least in certain circumstances, an absolute right to resist?

The first three sections of this chapter seek to defend the idea of political obligation itself against a number of influential contemporary

---

[1] On the connections between political obligation, authority and legitimacy, see A. John Simmons, *Moral Principles and Political Obligations* (Princeton: Princeton University Press, 1979), p. 58.

criticisms. The fourth section offers a general account of the state's authority: its scope and nature. It presents what is, in effect, an absolutist theory – though as the reader will see, this is an absolutism of a particular kind. Sections 5 and 6 deal with subsidiary but crucial questions concerning disobedience and individual rights, and attempt to show that the absolute authority of the state does not, in and of itself, under-mine the individual's right to rebel.

1. The autonomy argument

According to the standard account, political obligations are incurred, when they are incurred, as a result of some specific action that the obligated person has performed.[2] The controlling model is that of a contract. I assume an obligation to the state – to obey its laws – by agreeing to do so in exchange for a benefit of some kind. In effect, I make a promise; and this promise, like all promises, is something I am obliged to keep, provided that the understandings under which I made it actually obtain. Those understandings are, of course, crucial; they define the other side of the contract. I do not consent to the stipulations of the contract unless I have good reason to expect that I will receive, in exchange, the agreed-upon benefits. To the degree that those benefits are not forthcoming, the terms of the contract have been violated, the contract itself has been abrogated, and my obligation has dissolved.

It is important to emphasize here that political obligations, as defined by the contractual model, are rooted in *voluntary* acts. I am obligated only insofar as I have freely done something that entails such an obligation. This is widely thought to be both necessary and sufficient in explaining how it is possible to accept the authority of the law without sacrificing individual liberty. Freedom is not forfeited, at least not in a morally troubling way, if limitations on freedom have themselves been freely accepted.

1. Virtually from the beginning, this general approach has given rise to two central controversies. The first concerns whether or not political obligations, incurred either expressly or tacitly through voluntary acts,

[2] H. L. A. Hart, "Are there any Natural Rights?" *Philosophical Review* 64 (1955), p. 179; H. L. A. Hart, "Legal and Moral Obligation," in *Essays in Moral Philosophy*, ed. A. I. Melden (Seattle: University of Washington Press, 1958); R. B. Brandt, "The Concepts of Obligation and Duty,"*Mind* 73 (1964); John Rawls, *A Theory of Justice* (Cambridge, Mass.: Harvard University Press, 1971), pp. 112–14; Simmons, *Moral Principles and Political Obligations*, p. 14.

can ever be morally justified. One version of the claim that they cannot –
we might call it the autonomy argument – holds that no moral agent can
ever decide to limit his or her own freedom of choice. According to this
view, each individual's moral personality is constituted, in part, by a
faculty of autonomous decision. Autonomy is what makes us moral
agents. But to accept the authority of the state, hence to obey the law
simply because it is the law, constitutes a self-forfeiture of autonomy.
Such a self-forfeiture, since it undermines moral personality, must
involve a kind of contradiction, hence can never be justified on moral
grounds; and from this it follows that the state can never have the
authority it claims to have.[3]

Initially, the argument may seem clear enough, but a little reflection will
show that it is in fact obscure. At times it seems to be saying that political
obligation is impossible because it entails someone else making decisions
for me. When I stop at a stop sign because I independently judge this to be
the moral thing to do, then I am indeed acting as a free, autonomous agent.
If, on the other hand, I stop simply and solely because the state tells me to
stop – if, that is, I stop not because I myself have critically assessed the
morality of stopping itself but rather have uncritically and "blindly" relied
on the state's say-so – then I have ceded my power of decision to something
or someone external to me, hence have forfeited my autonomy.

But if this is the argument, then surely it is not a very compelling one.
When I stop at the stop sign because I judge this to be the right thing to
do, I must, as a responsible moral agent, have some reason for so judging.
I need to know why I believe it's the right thing to do. My reason, moreover, must be at least plausible and sensible. Not just any reason will do.
But we can easily imagine any number of plausible and sensible reasons
for deciding to stop at the stop sign; and certainly *one* such reason might
simply be the belief that the moral thing to do is whatever the state tells me
to do. Of course, nobody should hold such a belief without additional
arguments of some kind. These might pertain to, say, the benefits of
having a state whose authority is widely accepted, the fairness of the
processes by which the state generates laws, the divine, historical or
cultural provenance of the state apparatus, and so on. But it is hard to
see why some such argument would necessarily be any worse than any
other argument for stopping at the stop sign. I might independently

---

[3] Robert Paul Wolff, *In Defense of Anarchism* (New York: Harper, 1970), pp. 16–18. For an
interesting and helpful discussion, see Richard Dagger, *Civic Virtues: Rights, Citizenship,
and Republican Liberalism* (Oxford: Oxford University Press, 1997), pp. 61–68. Dagger's
conclusion is similar to mine, but his argument in support of that conclusion is very
different.

decide to stop because I judge stopping to be the safest thing to do, or out of fear that I would otherwise be found out and ticketed, or to set a proper example for my passengers. In such cases, my action would reflect both a theory of right and wrong and a decision to act in accordance with that theory. But this would be equally true if I decided to stop because of a critical, self-reflective, theoretically sophisticated belief that obeying the law *simpliciter* – because it is the law – is always right. I see no reason why such a belief could not provide the basis for a perfectly intelligible and defensible moral justification of my action. Stopping in a particular circumstance because of a calculation that doing so is the safest course of action is neither more or less principled, nor more or less free, than stopping because of a prior calculation that over the long run the good is maximized by living a life of unquestioning obedience to the law. The upshot is that there seems to be nothing contradictory or even peculiar about saying that a particular act is the moral thing to do *because and solely because* the state says so.

Another way of putting this is both to agree and disagree with Pitkin's claim that political obligation involves the subordination of the individual's judgment to that of others.[4] In obeying the law because it is the law, a person does indeed subordinate his or her power of decision. But if such subordination is itself the product of a free and independent decision to do so – if it is the result of the individual's own best judgment – then exactly how subordinated could that judgment be? Not much, I would say; for in such a circumstance the original judgment would be the controlling one. This is to say that when individuals rationally and reflectively decide to obey the law because it is the law and then actually do so, they are really being true to, hence are being governed by, their own original, autonomous decision. They are doing what someone else tells them to do only because they have self-legislated such obedience, hence in the last analysis are obeying not some external person or force but themselves.[5]

---

[4] Hanna Pitkin, "Obligation and Consent," in *Philosophy, Politics and Society*, 4th ser., ed. Peter Laslett, W. G. Runciman and Quentin Skinner (London: Basil Blackwell, 1972), p. 84. See also, Joseph Raz, "Authority and Justification," *Philosophy and Public Affairs* 14 (1985), p. 13.

[5] The argument applies equally to Raz. In describing the logic of political obligation, Raz claims that "the fact that an authority requires performance of an action is a reason for its performance, which is not to be added to all other relevant reasons when assessing what to do, but should exclude and take the place of some of them" (Raz, "Authority and Justification," p. 13). Certainly so. Again, the individual substitutes the judgment of the state for his or her own judgment. But no individual does this – or, at least, is expected to do this – for no reason at all; and this means that when it occurs, the entire transaction necessarily based on, and is an embodiment of, that reason itself. My criticism may seem similar to, but is in fact quite different from, that of Simmons. Simmons argues, as I do, that Wolff's position would have the implausible consequence of rendering any kind of

2. Maybe, though, the argument is not really about giving the power of decision to someone else but, rather, about consent and time. Perhaps, that is, it is based on a claim that one cannot freely decide at time T to assume an obligation that would limit what one can do at time T^1 without thereby compromising one's moral autonomy at T^1. In the instant case, I cannot today freely give my consent to the authority of the state, hence bind myself to obey tomorrow the laws of that state, including laws as yet unpromulgated; for to do so would be to make it impossible for me to exercise independent moral judgment tomorrow in deciding whether or not to obey one or more of those laws.[6]

Such a view, if taken at all seriously, would seem to rule out as morally objectionable virtually any contract at all, since in a contract one freely agrees in the present to bind oneself to particular actions in the future. Now it might be argued that there is actually a great difference between an ordinary contract and the so-called social contract, and that the latter threatens moral autonomy in a way that the former does not. For in most ordinary contracts, actions to be performed in the future are specified quite clearly in the present. One does not generally buy a pig in a poke; one knows explicitly the nature of one's future commitments. A promise to obey the laws of the state, on the other hand, is a promise to perform unspecified actions. The state may ask you to do things that never would have occurred to you at the time you pledged allegiance, and if you find some of those things morally objectionable, then in being bound by your previous agreement you are, in the present, undermining your own future freedom and agency.

The argument presupposes, however, what I think may fairly be called a grotesque view of the nature of action. Actions are not mere physical motions. Each action that we perform is constituted as much by the specific contexts in which it occurs and the specific intentions with which it is performed as by the motion itself. Thus, if I switch off the lights, this is one action if I am in my bedroom and am about to go to sleep, a different action if I am in a theater and am ready to start the movie, a third if I am signaling someone on the outside that the coast is clear, a fourth if I am attempting to frighten little children, and so on.

---

promise morally unacceptable. But his main claim is that, *contra* Wolff, we do not have a "primary" and overriding obligation to preserve our autonomy at virtually all cost; hence, if we are often forced to sacrifice some of our autonomy, this is not sufficient to render the concept of the legitimate state vacuous. A. John Simmons, "The Anarchist Position: A Reply to Klosko and Senior," *Philosophy and Public Affairs* 16: 3 (Summer 1987), p. 269 n. My view, on the other hand, is to doubt that promises and contracts meaningfully undermine our autonomy at all.

[6] Wolff, *In Defense of Anarchism*, pp. 15–16.

Similarly, if I contract today to pay you a sum of money tomorrow in return for services rendered, this becomes a different action if, in the interim, I become destitute, or if you become mentally incompetent, or if the value of the dollar suddenly plunges dramatically. Clearly, changes of this kind do not, in and of themselves, nullify obligations, for if they did contracts would be relatively inconsequential.[7] But the bottom line is that any contract binds one in the future to perform actions that are, at least to some degree, presently unspecified. And what is true of contracts is true, as well, for any and all promises. Again, when I freely promise today to perform some action tomorrow, I am binding myself to do something that, when the time comes, I might not want to do; but no one – least of all Kant – could think that there is anything morally problematic about that. Indeed, making and keeping promises that turn out to be inconvenient or otherwise difficult to keep might well be, for Kant, a paradigm of moral action.

More generally, to claim that one cannot be bound in the future by decisions made in the present is to make a mockery of the very idea of human choice. For the fact is that all but the most unthinking, impulsive and automatic kinds of behavior involve *some* kind of temporal gap between free decision and actual performance. If I decide to turn out the lights, the actual implementation of this decision might occur a day later, or a minute later, or even only a second later, but in any and every case enough later to allow for the possibility that I might still change my mind. Present performance is *always* bound by past decision. To claim, then, that past decisions cannot be binding, that I must always decide again before performing the action – even *just* before performing it – is, if taken literally, to risk a kind of bizarre infinite regress, a life of constant and unending evaluation and reevaluation prior to action itself according to which, in the extreme case, it would be impossible ever actually to do anything. It is to propose, in effect, a life of permanent paralysis, something worthy of a Borges.[8]

Of course, it may be that signing a particular social contract, or otherwise consenting to the authority of a particular state, would be a mistake. Perhaps the state in question is corrupt, such that its law, if obeyed, would have bad consequences. Perhaps, indeed, all actual states are corrupt, not because they undermine autonomy but because, say, they are based on the oppression of one class by another, or on property-as-theft, or on the

---

[7] Though the obligation might be nullified if the changes are inconsistent with explicit or implicit assumptions upon which the contract was demonstrably based. See 6.4.2, below.

[8] Or of a William James. See *The Principles of Psychology, Volume Two* (New York: Dover, 1950), pp. 524–31.

iron law of oligarchy, or what have you. But any such argument would be essentially empirical and/or sociological in nature, hence would fail to show what the autonomy argument claims to show, namely, that political obligation involves a kind of category error.

2. **Obligation, ought and duty**

The second and rather more significant controversy involving the traditional model of political obligation concerns the kinds of action deemed sufficient to cause an obligation to be incurred. The idea of the social contract is problematic because while comparatively few people – and hardly any who are not naturalized citizens – have ever explicitly and expressly agreed to obey the laws of a state, more than a few people are thought to have political obligations. Such obligations must therefore be rooted not in the act of signing (however metaphorically) a contract but in something quite different, namely, accepting and enjoying the benefits that political society provides. Acceptance and enjoyment are thought to constitute a kind of tacit consent, hence to provide moral grounds for claiming that the individual in question has freely undertaken an obligation to the state.

Since the publication of the *Second Treatise of Government*, some such doctrine has been regarded as indispensable if we are to account for the obligations of all but a relative handful of citizens. The problem, however, is that citizens do not *actively* accept many and perhaps most of the benefits that they receive from the state. Typically, what states provide are "public goods" – safe streets, national defense, clean air, a sound currency, and the like. Goods of this kind cannot easily be given to some citizens and denied to others; what is provided to some is *ipso facto* provided to all. From the perspective of decision theory, the implications of this are substantial. Specifically, many individual citizens will be motivated to enjoy the benefits of government without paying for them and, at the same time, will be unwilling voluntarily to pay for the enjoyment of others. It is unlikely, therefore, that such goods will be produced except through the coercive agency of the state. But the other side of this is that public goods, when produced, are obtained and enjoyed simply in the regular course of things. I get the benefit of clean air just by breathing, the benefit of national defense just by not being annihilated. In each such case, the benefit is passively rather than actively received, and mere passive reception is thought to be insufficient to count as tacit consent. It is precisely here – where the theory of tacit consent as active acceptance encounters the theory of public goods – that we find the source of Rawls's influential claim that "[t]here is ... no political obligation, strictly speaking, for citizens generally."[9]

The argument, as elaborated, reformulated and eventually extended by Simmons and others, rejects what is thought to be a general and unfortunate tendency among philosophers to assume that various kinds of moral judgments are merely different ways of saying the same thing.[10] In this respect, the critique of tacit consent is merely one part of what might be regarded as a tripartite attack on the notion of political obligation *per se*. Specifically, (1) even if it could be established that individuals have political obligations, this would not necessarily be decisive in determining what those individuals should do. What one *ought* to do is not necessarily what one has an *obligation* to do. Moreover, (2) if it turns out that one should indeed obey the law or otherwise do what the state requires, this might well be not an obligation at all but a kind of natural duty, from which it follows that we could dispense with the idea of political obligation without necessarily compromising the idea of political authority. These two claims, together with (3) the critique of tacit consent, have the effect of undermining the traditional conception of an extremely close connection between political obligation on the one hand and the legitimacy of the state on the other. Political obligation is either impossible or, if possible, then far less consequential than was formerly supposed.

1. Simmons says that if Dr. Jones promised to speak at a professional meeting on a certain day, then he has an obligation to do so, but that if a serious medical emergency arose that required his presence and that would conflict with the professional meeting, then he ought to stay and deal with the emergency. According to Simmons, this shows that "obligation" and

---

[9] John Rawls, *A Theory of Justice*, p. 114. For other arguments critical of the standard view of political obligation, see M. B. E. Smith, "Is There a Prima Facie Obligation to Obey the Law?" *Yale Law Journal* 82 (1973); Carole Pateman, *The Problem of Political Obligation* (Berkeley: University of California Press, 1979); Joseph Raz, *The Authority of Law* (Oxford: Oxford University Press, 1979); Leslie Green, *The Authority of the State* (Oxford: Oxford University Press, 1988), ch. 8; and Joel Feinberg, *Freedom and Fulfillment: Philosophical Essays* (Princeton: Princeton University Press, 1992), pp. 152–74. On the question of public goods and its implications for political obligation, see George Klosko, "Political Obligation and the Natural Duties of Justice," *Philosophy and Public Affairs* 23 (Summer 1994), pp. 251–70 and "Fixed Content of Political Obligations," *Political Studies* 46 (1998), pp. 60–64.
[10] Simmons, *Moral Principles and Political Obligations*, pp. 7–8. For similar views, see James K. Mish'alani, "'Duty,' 'Obligation,' and 'Ought'," *Analysis* 30 (December 1969), pp. 38–40; and Harry Beran, "Ought, Obligation and Duty," *Australasian Journal of Philosophy* 50 (December 1972), p. 207. As with Wolff, Dagger's discussion is helpful and informative (*Civic Virtues*, pp. 72–80); but again, Dagger's conclusions, though similar to mine, are based on very different kinds of arguments.

"ought" cannot be merely different ways of expressing the same thing, since "here we have a case in which a man has an obligation which he ought not to discharge."[11] But as far as I can tell, it shows no such thing. Rather, it merely indicates what everyone already knows, that one obligation – or, what is (*pace* Simmons) the same thing, one ought – can outweigh another. In order to see this more clearly, consider exactly what is involved in each of the claims concerning Dr. Jones:

(a) The "obligation" to speak at the meeting involves, first, an empirical fact to the effect that Jones promised to speak and, second, a maxim to the effect that one ought to keep one's promises, along with an "all things considered" (ATC) proviso, implicit in any such claim imaginable, that the maxim, if true, should be followed unless some other, more important consideration overrides it. From these premises one derives a moral judgment to the effect that Jones "ought" to give the speech or, what seems to me another way of saying precisely the same thing, that he has a (moral) "obligation" to give the speech, insofar as the proviso allows. There is absolutely no difference between that which makes it a moral obligation for Jones to give the speech and that which makes it something that he morally ought to do.

(b) That Jones ought to stay and deal with the medical emergency reflects, in an identical manner, an empirical fact to the effect that an emergency exists and that Jones is needed to deal with it and, second, a maxim to the effect that doctors who are needed to deal with medical emergencies ought to do so, again insofar as the ATC proviso allows, from which premises one derives the moral judgment that Jones "ought" to stay and, equally and identically, that he has a (moral) "obligation" to stay. Again, that which constitutes the "ought" conclusion is identical to that which constitutes the "obligation" conclusion.

Obviously the empirical facts in question are quite different from one another, the first involving a voluntary undertaking (the promise), the second an unchosen and unavoidable circumstance (the emergency); and likewise, the relevant moral maxims – promises should be kept and doctors should deal with medical emergencies – are also quite different. But such differences seem to me irrelevant to the question of "obligation" and "ought" since, as the above examples suggest, the features that constitute the "ought" are also the features that constitute, in precisely the same way and for precisely the same reason, the "obligation." Given that Jones cannot physically deliver the lecture and deal with the emergency at the same time, he ought to do the latter and not the former. But this merely

---

[11] Simmons, *Moral Principles and Political Obligations*, p. 8.

shows that one set of considerations (arguably) outweighs the other, that the moral reasons why he "ought" to stay are stronger than the moral reasons why he "ought" to go; and in such a circumstance, nothing could be more natural than to say that Jones's "obligation" to keep his promise is overridden by his "obligation" to deal with the emergency.[12]

Understood in this way, the argument is linguistic and conceptual. An obligation is anything that we are bound or required to do; a moral obligation is anything that we are bound or required to do for moral reasons; and anything that we are bound or required to do for moral reasons – anything that morality imposes on us – is for that reason something that we ought to do. I believe that such a view is amply reflected in ordinary language. Thus, there would be nothing remotely peculiar, discordant or obscure if Dr. Jones were to say: "I did indeed promise to speak at the meeting, but my primary obligation is to stay here and save lives."

But what then of the argument that whereas sometimes you ought not to discharge your obligations, there can never be a situation in which you ought not do that which you ought to do, from which we should conclude that obligations and oughts must be very different? Surely the correct response is still the one derived, *mutatis mutandis*, from Ross. We have prima facie (PF) oughts, and we have all-things-considered (ATC) oughts. The latter override the former, and this means that, contrary to what Simmons suggests, sometimes we ATC ought not to do certain things that we PF ought to do. And if this is true of oughts, then there is no reason to distinguish oughts from obligations, for sometimes one is ATC obligated (ought) not to do that which one is PF obligated (ought) to do. In the instant case, Jones PF ought (and is obligated) to present the speech, but this turns out to be something that ATC he ought not (and is obligated not) to do.

The exact nature of the difference between PF and ATC claims is, in fact, not immediately clear. This issue will be discussed in 6.4.2 below, and the above account will be somewhat modified. For present purposes, however, the basic point holds: what we ought to do PF is not necessarily what we ought to do ATC.

Beran insists that neo-Rossian approaches of this kind necessarily produce peculiar results. It would be odd, he says, to claim that " 'A promised to pay B \$5' entails 'A ought to pay B \$5' but does not entail

---

[12] I have been careful to identify the obligations in this case as moral ones, implicitly acknowledging that many obligations are non-moral. But the fact that there are non-moral obligations should not be thought to imply any general difference between "obligation" and "ought," since "oughts" can also be non-moral, e.g., "you ought to put some more salt in the soup" or "you ought to be careful when crossing the street."

'A has an obligation to pay B $5'." In many situations, this would be odd indeed, but in countless others not. Imagine, for example, that A had made the promise in a casual and off-hand manner, without witnesses, without a written contract, and without B's explicit acknowledgment. It is easy to think of someone saying in such a circumstance that A ought to pay the $5 despite the fact that he has no real obligation to do so. More generally, there is nothing remotely peculiar if we say that " 'A promised to pay B $5' entails 'A ought PF to pay B $5' but does not entail 'A has an obligation ATC to pay B $5'."

Beran insists, further, that "obligation" and "ought" must be different since "if A has an obligation to B to do X then B has a right to A's doing X; but from the fact that A ought, morally speaking, to do X, it does not follow that anyone has a right to A's doing X." But the Jones case is helpful in illustrating a crucial distinction that Beran ignores. When we say *what* we ought to do, hence what we are obliged to do, we are not thereby describing the *reason* we ought to do it, i.e., the relevant moral maxim. Beran seems to confuse the two. The phrase "an obligation to B" describes a matter of fact, namely, that A has somehow incurred a debt – owes something – to B; and this does indeed imply that B has a right to that thing. There can be no doubt, moreover, that these facts, together with the appropriate moral maxim, may well entail that A ought PF to do something, i.e., give B what is owed. A's obligation to B provides a moral reason for A to perform a certain action. But obligation in this sense – *obligation to someone* – is far different from the *obligation to do something*. Whereas the former describes a moral reason for performing an action, the latter describes no such reason but simply the judgment that the act itself is morally required;[13] and whenever such a description is offered, whenever we say that someone has an obligation to do something, this is tantamount to saying that the act in question ought to be performed.[14] Beran fails to differentiate obligations to persons (i.e., debts) from obligations to act. This permits him to say, correctly, that "obligation" and "ought" are not always interchangeable, but it blinds him to the fact that

---

[13] The distinction is to be found, albeit largely between the lines, in Mish'alani, " 'Duty,' 'Obligation,' and 'Ought' " (p. 38), for example, where he differentiates the expression of a "judgment as to what [one] ought to do" from the expression of the "kind of considerations we would be ready to cite" in support of that judgment.

[14] I believe it is also the case that not every obligation to act entails an obligation – a debt owed to – some specific person. There's nothing peculiar in saying "as a Christian, you have a moral obligation to turn the other cheek" or "as an attorney and an officer of the court, you have a moral obligation not to suborn perjury" – neither of which describe a particular debt owed to a particular individual.

when actions are involved, they are. Whenever one is obligated to do something, one ought to do it, and vice versa.

It is certainly true that, for moral reasons, many obligations should not be performed. To that extent, Simmons (*inter alia*) is quite right. But he is just as certainly wrong. If you have a moral obligation ATC, then to say that, on moral grounds, you ought not to perform it is to talk nonsense.

2. The attempt to distinguish ought from obligation would, if successful, have the effect of diminishing, whether rhetorically or logically, the importance of any political obligations that we might have. For in such a circumstance, the claim that someone has an obligation to obey the law would not necessarily be to say that this is what he or she ought to do. If, however, the distinction collapses, as I have argued, then political obligations may well be as weighty as (though not necessarily more weighty than) any other kind of moral claim, hence neither more nor less significant than the entire range of oughts of which our moral life is composed.

Now in differentiating obligations from other kinds of oughts, critics of political obligation want especially to distinguish them from those with which they are most often confused, namely, natural duties. The distinction has been attributed primarily to Hart, and is forcefully embraced by Rawls and Simmons, among many others. Obligations – moral and nonmoral alike – are always incurred, when they are incurred, as the result of some voluntary action, e.g., making a promise or actively accepting a benefit.[15] Natural duties, on the other hand, are "moral requirements which apply to all men irrespective of status or of acts performed," hence are binding simply because they are "natural."[16] The difference is thought to be crucial. For if, as Rawls and Simmons believe, most citizens do not perform the kinds of actions that would obligate them to obey the law, they may nonetheless have a natural duty to do so;[17] and this suggests, in turn, that we can dispense with the idea of political obligation without in any way undermining the authority of the state.

In pressing the obligation/duty distinction, theorists often begin with ordinary language. Simmons notes, for example, that we "obligate ourselves" but do not "duty ourselves," or again, that an obligation can be

---

[15] Hart, "Legal and Moral Obligation," pp. 101–5; Rawls, *A Theory of Justice*, pp. 114ff. See also, Klosko, "Political Obligations and the Natural Duties of Justice," p. 253; Klosko, "Fixed Content of Political Obligations," pp. 54–55.

[16] Simmons, *Moral Principles and Political Obligations*, p. 13.

[17] The actual usefulness of such a duty in explaining why we should obey the law is something that Rawls endorses and Simmons denies.

"disposed of once and for all" while duties remain with us always; and he says that such examples indicate the sense in which obligations do, and duties do not, arise out of actions.[18] But it is hard to see the force of such claims. It is true that I cannot "duty myself," but it is also true that I can "impose a duty on myself." And while I do not ordinarily "dispose of a duty," I can certainly say that "I have done my duty, case closed."[19]

Much more important is the view that claims generated by voluntary actions are, whatever we call them, simply different both in form and substance from those not so generated. Such a view is unpersuasive in both respects. As to form, the fact is that differences between duties and obligations, of the sort that Simmons and others describe, are at best overstated and at worst illusory. As to substance, most critics fail to identify the exact nature of the difference between moral claims that arise out of voluntary actions and those that do not. We can make sense of things only when we come to see that all self-assumed or action-generated moral claims are actually dependent on prior, "natural" ones, hence that the former are (what I shall call) *derivative* while the latter are (correspondingly) *primary*.

Formally, Simmons – again following Hart, Rawls and others – says that a moral obligation is, by definition, something owed by a specific person to a specific person, whereas moral duties "are owed by *all* persons to all others." Thus, anyone has ATC a moral duty to save anyone else from drowning, but my obligation to repay the money I borrowed from you is limited to me and you. Another way of saying this is that moral obligations are analogous to legal rights *in personam*, which are held against a particular person, while moral duties are more similar to rights *in rem*, which are held against all other people.[20] Such a distinction may well be important for the analysis and adjudication of particular legal disputes, but its relevance for moral theory is doubtful. Consider the two cases just mentioned. It's true enough that my moral obligation to repay the money you loaned me is *my* obligation to *you*. But as such, it is merely a particular instance of a general moral claim. *Anyone* who borrows money from *anyone* is obligated to repay the loan – which is to say that

---

[18] Simmons, *Moral Principles and Political Obligations*, p. 14.

[19] Simmons himself acknowledges that the evidence of ordinary language may cut both ways: "It would, of course, be foolish to insist that any of these terms is always used in one way or another." Simmons, *Moral Principles and Political Obligations*, p. 9. See also his footnote "c" to p. 14. Mish'alani (" 'Duty,' 'Obligation,' and 'Ought',") adduces a range of further distinctions in ordinary language between duty and obligation. For example, one cannot be "off obligation" or "called to obligation" or "in the line of obligation," and so on (p. 35).

[20] Simmons, *Moral Principles and Political Obligations*, p. 15.

anyone in the same kind of situation that I happen to be in is morally required to do precisely the same thing that I am required to do. Similarly, while it is true that *anyone* has a duty to save *anyone* from drowning, if I chance upon you while you are drowning then it is surely true that *I* have a duty to save *you* – which again is to say that I am morally required to do what anyone in the same kind of situation would be required to do. In each case, the actual moral requirement arises simply and solely out of the confluence of a general moral principle that applies to all people at all times and a particular circumstance involving only me and you. The cases are structurally identical, at least to that extent; and this helps to explain why we can say that my moral obligation to repay your loan is *ipso facto* my moral duty and, equally, that my moral duty to save you from drowning is something that I am morally obligated to do. We do no violence to ordinary language – to the contrary, we put ourselves in conformity with it – when we acknowledge that our duties are obligations, our obligations duties.[21]

---

[21] Mish'alani ("'Duty,' 'Obligation,' and 'Ought'," p. 33) distinguishes "duties" understood as responsibilities attached to specific offices, callings, roles, etc. from "duty" in the sense that "it is someone's *duty* to do something at a given time." He acknowledges that the latter is "nothing but a special sort of colouring of the word 'ought'."
      Simmons has suggested to me (personal communication, September 1999) that whereas a positive duty such as saving a drowning person becomes a moral requirement only when understood in the light of a particular circumstance, "a negative duty (e.g., to refrain from murder) is not similarly 'activated' relative to particular persons by 'particular circumstances.' That is . . . it is correct to say that right now I have a duty not to murder you, not to murder Smith, not to murder Jones (and so on for all persons), but it is not correct to say that right now I have an obligation to repay you (or Smith or Jones)." I think this is not quite right, for the term "murder" is loaded – it defines an act that is, by definition, wrong in all cases – hence does not represent all, or even most, examples of negative duties. Consider a more representative negative claim: "I have a duty to refrain from killing." Unless one has a moral theory in which killing *per se* is wrong, hence is synonymous with "murder," the claim itself does not describe a moral requirement independent of particular circumstances. After all, I don't have a duty to refrain from killing you, or Smith, or Jones, in cases of self-defense, war, justified euthanasia and the like. Here, then, the correct negative duty must be something like the following: "I have a duty to refrain from killing you unless I am justified in killing you because of circumstances X, Y or Z." This negative claim becomes a moral requirement only if X, Y or Z obtain: "I have a duty to refrain from killing you unless I am justified in killing you because X, Y or Z obtain, a duty to refrain from killing Smith unless I am justified in killing Smith because X, Y or Z obtain, a duty to refrain from killing Jones unless I am justified in killing Jones because X, Y or Z obtain, and so on." To this extent, then, the negative duty is structurally identical to positive obligations such as the following: "I have an obligation to repay anyone to whom I owe a debt," which means that "I have an obligation to repay you only if I owe you a debt, to repay Smith only if I owe Smith a debt, to repay Jones only if I owe Jones a debt, and so on." It is true that some negative duties involve moral requirements regardless of circumstances. But so do some positive obligations. For example, "Having taken my

Now surely Hart, Rawls and the others are right in saying that there is nonetheless a great difference between obligations/duties that are self-assumed, i.e., attendant to voluntary actions, and those that are not. We ought to perform both kinds of obligations/duties, but we ought to do so for different reasons; so much, I think, is uncontroversial. But the exact nature of the difference is rarely well specified in the literature, and the result is a tendency seriously to misconstrue the nature of the claims themselves. In my view, we can make sense of things only when we come to see that while in the case of non-self-assumed obligations/duties (roughly, Rawls's "natural duties") we need to explain only why they are obligatory, i.e., why it is our duty to perform them, in the case of self-assumed obligations/duties (Rawls's "obligations") we in fact need to explain two quite different things: (1) why a particular voluntary action gives rise to an obligation/duty and (2) why that voluntary action ought to be performed, or at least ought to be allowed, in the first place. Unless we can answer both questions, we won't have a sufficient account of what we ought to do.[22]

It will be useful to begin by noting what everyone already knows, that not all promises should be kept. If Walter Huff promises Phyllis Nirdlinger that he will kill her (innocent) husband so that she can collect double indemnity and the two of them can live happily ever after, we know that he should break this promise no matter how solemnly and sincerely it was made.[23] Or again, if two businessmen contract with one another to defraud some third party, we know that each should violate the contract as a matter of moral obligation and duty. But in these kinds of cases, the fact that one ought to break rather than keep a promise is best accounted for by a prior ought, namely, that one ought not to make such promises in the first place. Stated more precisely, one has what may be called a *primary duty* to treat people justly, or to treat them as ends rather

---

vows to become a Catholic priest, I have an obligation to treat people with Christian charity" in itself entails that I have an obligation to treat you, Smith, Jones and so on with Christian charity regardless of the circumstances.

[22] My criticism pertains not just to Rawls's theory of natural duties but to other theories of political duties, such as that of Klosko. See Klosko, "Political Obligation and the Natural Duties of Justice"; and also his book, *The Principle of Fairness and Political Obligation* (Savage, Maryland: Rowman and Littlefield, 1992). More generally, I believe that it applies to at least most versions of the "fair play" account of political obedience. Its thrust is to deny the sharp separation – though not the conceptual distinction – between self-assumed obligations and political duties, including duties arising from considerations of fair play. As the argument unfolds, it should become clear that, in my view, a consent theory of obligation could well presuppose, rather than contradict, a fair play account of some kind.

[23] I refer here to the names of characters in Cain's novel, rather than in the movie version wherein the names have been (for no reason that I can discern) changed.

than means, or to treat them humanely, from which it follows, correlatively, that one has a primary duty not to promise to murder an innocent person or to commit fraud; and from this it follows, in turn, that if and when such a promise has been made, one has what we may call a *derivative duty* to break it.

Cases in which a promise/contract (to commit murder or fraud, etc.) is morally impermissible have their positive counterparts, i.e., cases in which a promise/contract is morally required. If my good wife, who demands so little and gives so much, asks me to promise to be nice to her father, this is a promise that I may well be morally obligated to make. When called into court to testify about a crime that I have witnessed, it is very likely my moral duty to swear an oath to tell the truth, the whole truth, and nothing but the truth. For someone who believes in the literal teachings of the Bible, a promise to do God's work may have the moral status of a commandment. In each such case, my primary duty is to perform a voluntary action – to make a promise of some kind – that itself entails a derivative duty, i.e., keeping the promise by actually being nice to my father-in-law, testifying truthfully, doing God's work; and in each case, the obligatoriness of the latter depends on the obligatoriness of the former. I ought to be nice to my father-in-law not simply because I promised to do so but because it was morally required of me to make that promise in the first place.

3. I believe that all self-assumed duties, i.e., duties entailed by voluntary actions, are derivative duties in that they presuppose and arise out of primary duties pertaining to the performance of those actions. But this can occur in two different ways. Some derivative duties – we may call them *strongly derivative* – are self-assumed duties that one is required to perform because the voluntary actions out of which they arise are themselves morally required. Others – *weakly derivative* – are self-assumed duties arising from voluntary actions that one is morally permitted but not required to perform. Thus, if it is my primary duty D to perform action A, and if A entails derivative duty D^1, then D^1 is strongly derivative. If, on the other hand, A is consistent with but not specifically required by any of my primary duties – if, that is, I do not have a primary duty D not to perform A – and if A entails D^1, then D^1 is weakly derivative.[24]

[24] The distinction should not be confused with Klosko's distinction ("Political Obligation and the Natural Duties of Justice," pp. 260–62) between weak and strong duties, with which it has, I believe, virtually no connection.

My duty to be nice to my father-in-law is strongly derivative because it arises out of a voluntary action – the promise to my wife – that was itself morally required of me; and so too, *mutatis mutandis*, for the negative case of Walter Huff's duty to break his promise to Phyllis Nirdlinger, since this duty arises out of the prior duty not to make such a promise in the first place. The connection between the primary duty and the derivative duty is such that the former underwrites the latter, and this means that the voluntary action – the promise – functions as a kind of intermediary step, a mechanism that signals and facilitates the linkage. (Actually, it is also more than this. Perhaps I have a moral duty to swear an oath to tell the truth in court, hence am behaving immorally if I refuse to do so; but I am guilty of perjury only if I lie after having actually taken the oath. Similarly, it may be morally right for me to consent, however tacitly, to the authority of the state, but strictly speaking I have an obligation to obey the law only if I undertake the kinds of actions that actually constitute consent. In each such case, the violation of the primary duty is a different kind of offense from the violation of the derivative duty. If, then, I refuse to consent to the authority of the state even though I have a primary duty to do so, I may be guilty of sociopathy, or of compromising my own moral personality as a naturally political creature, or of failing to acknowledge and embrace the justice of the regime in question, but it is much less clear that I am guilty of violating an obligation to obey the law. The primary duty and the derivative duty each seems to be a necessary but insufficient condition for establishing the obligation.)

If, on the other hand, I borrow money from you by promising to repay it, my decision to engage in such a transaction, hence to make such a promise, might be something that is morally *allowed* but not morally *required*. Here the connection between my self-assumed duty and any primary duty that I might have is a good deal weaker, since the voluntary action is not merely an intermediary step or mechanism but, rather, the main reason why I ought to repay the loan. But a weaker connection is a connection nonetheless, and in the instant case not an inconsequential one. The fact that the voluntary action of borrowing the money and promising to repay it, though not morally required, was morally permissible is hardly irrelevant; for if it had not been morally permissible, then the question of whether or not I should repay the loan becomes much more problematic. Imagine, say, that I had borrowed the money on terms favorable to the lender, and that I had done so knowing that he himself was a murderous villain who was lending me the money in order to finance some criminal deed. Surely in such a circumstance, and absent very powerful considerations to the contrary, I should not have taken out the loan in the first place; and having done so, surely I would have a moral duty *not* to repay it.[25] In cases, then, where I *do* have a duty to repay a loan, or to keep some other promise that I have made, this generally presupposes that the voluntary action in question was at least consistent with, though not necessarily required by, my primary duties.

There are, to be sure, hard cases. We can well imagine a circumstance in which a promise was wrongly made, but where a generalized duty to keep promises nonetheless outweighs the wrong, with the result that the promise, however objectionable, should still be kept. It is hardly peculiar to say, "You shouldn't have made that promise, but since you made it, you have to keep it." Such cases only show, however, that self-assumed duties, like the duty to keep a promise, are PF oughts that do not become ATC oughts until they have been evaluated in the light of primary duties. Perhaps the self-assumed duty is strong enough to override the primary duty, perhaps not. But in either case, the former is hostage to the latter, insofar as it depends at least in part on the degree to which the voluntary action in question is itself morally acceptable.

All self-assumed duties (Rawlsian "obligations") are derived, weakly or strongly, from primary, non-self-assumed ("natural") duties involving the obligation-generating acts themselves. Any generalized attempt to divorce obligations from natural duties, to find justifications for the former that are entirely independent of the latter, is thus doomed to fail. And the upshot is that the question of "political obligation" – for convenience sake, I shall revert to traditional terminology – is never merely a question of whether or not we have done anything to incur such an obligation. It is always, as well, a question of whether we should have done some such thing, a question of duty. We do indeed need to ask if we have agreed, tacitly or otherwise, to obey the laws of the state. But we also need to ask if it was morally right to have done so.

---

[25] The case, though unusual, speaks to a much wider range of possible cases in which borrowing money is morally problematic. It is easy to imagine, for example, a world in which such transactions are in fact not permitted at all, a culture where, say, money itself was banned on moral grounds because of a belief that the existence and circulation of currency would invariably lead to undeserved accumulations and inequalities, or a culture that simply took to heart the adage "neither a borrower not a lender be." What is morally taken for granted in one world may be morally unacceptable in another; hence, much of what we ordinarily believe to be morally neutral may in fact not be so at all. Consider that the entire global economy of the modern age, affecting directly or indirectly virtually every living human being, is based in large part on a single, common and, at present, morally uncontroversial kind of activity – lending money at interest – that in other times and other settings has been prohibited precisely for moral reasons.

3. **The idea of political obligation**

I have argued, first, that obligations are oughts and oughts obligations, hence that political obligations are, in principle, as weighty as other kinds of moral claims; and second, that obligations are invariably rooted in, hence at least in part justified by, primary natural or moral duties, hence that the sharp separation of obligations and duties is untenable; all of which is to suggest that there is indeed a close connection between political obligation, suitably interpreted, and the idea of political authority. But this only brings us to the most important question: is political obligation possible?

Simmons focuses on, and rejects, the two most influential modern accounts of political obligation: the Lockian theory of tacit consent and the more contemporary theory of benefits accepted under the principle of fair play. Although he deals with these accounts in separate chapters, his criticisms really compose a single, integrated argument involving three basic steps. First, he denies that much of what is typically thought to constitute tacit consent actually does so. His main target is Locke's claim that "every man, that hath any possession, or enjoyment, of any part of the dominions of any government, doth thereby give his tacit consent, and is as far forth obliged to obedience to the laws of that government."[26] Second, he argues that actively accepting the benefits of the state under the general principle of fair play, while not constituting tacit consent as Rawls had thought, might nonetheless provide quite plausible and independent grounds for political obligation. In this respect, he finds Nozick's arguments about fair play and the burdens of benefit to miss the mark. Finally, though, he concludes that while nearly everyone *receives* benefits from the state, very few people can be thought to have accepted them *actively*. Since what the state typically provides are public (or what Simmons calls "open") goods, and since generally such goods are not actively accepted but only passively received, active acceptance cannot explain the political obligations that most citizens are thought to have.

1. The argument is based, in part, on a peculiarly narrow notion of what it means actively to accept a benefit. We cannot but agree that simply breathing clean air, or enjoying safe streets, or having the peace of mind that comes from a strong national defense does not, in and of itself, constitute active acceptance. It is also true that if you sneak into my yard

---

[26] John Locke, *Two Treatises of Government* (Cambridge: Cambridge University Press, 1988 [1690]), Section 119 of the "Second Treatise."

while I am out of town and mow my lawn, to my great advantage but without my knowledge and without ever having been asked, I plainly have received a benefit and just as plainly have not actively accepted it. Acceptance would have occurred only if, for example, you had explicitly asked me if I wanted you to mow my lawn and if I had explicitly said yes.

Consider, though, the following simple case. I walk into the locker room and observe four of my friends playing poker. They invite me to join them. Without saying a word, I sit down at the table, ante up, and begin to play. I do so, at least in part, because I want to play poker for the sake of playing poker, and not solely because, say, I have been threatened with my life if I do not play, or because this is a movie and I am play-acting, or because I am a masochist who wishes to wallow in sin, or because I am part of a police sting operation aimed at catching illegal gamblers. We play all night, and I win a small fortune. When the game ends, I pocket my winnings and leave, maintaining my silence and my poker-face.

Certainly I have benefited from the game, and nothing could be clearer than that I have actively accepted the benefit. But I have done so without ever having made an explicit statement to that effect. What, then, con-stitutes acceptance? Surely the answer is simply that I participated. I freely chose to be part of the process – a rule-governed endeavor involving both skill and luck – and the mere fact that I did so signaled active acceptance of any benefits received. It is important, of course, that the decision to participate, and all subsequent decisions to continue to par-ticipate, was free and sincere, and involved some knowledge of what poker is, what it might mean to win or lose, what the risks of participation might be, and so on. But given assumptions of this kind, my participation was itself sufficient to constitute active acceptance.

Three things need to be said about this case. First, the fact that I actively accepted my benefit despite the fact that I never made an express statement to that effect shows that acceptance can be indicated in a variety of ways. It need not involve explicit speech-acts; other kinds of acts can do just as well. Second, the fact that I sat down and played suggests strongly that I regarded poker as an acceptable activity and that I viewed this particular game as a reasonably fair version of it, hence that I judged my winnings to have been legitimately won. The key, it seems to me, has to do with the idea of poker as an institution – or, more accur-ately, poker as one form of the institution of gambling at cards, itself understood as a structure of intelligibility involving notions (such as probability theory) about how (certain) things in the world really are – and the degree to which this particular game was a faithful instantiation of it. From my action, it would be plausible to surmise that I was, in effect, acknowledging and consenting to the game's legitimacy, hence to the legitimacy of its outcomes. Finally, while such a surmise might in fact turn out to be false – that is, it is possible that I really participated because I was threatened with my life if I did not play, or because I was play-acting or masochistic or part of a sting operation – the burden of proof seems clearly to be on the skeptic. This is to say that my participation in and of itself created a strong presumption of consent, and in the absence of clear evidence to the contrary, the presumption must be taken as fact.

Now this latter claim, which I think Rawls would accept, is something that Simmons at least seems to deny. Using baseball rather than poker as his example,[27] he suggests that merely participating often constitutes not consent but, rather, something very different, namely "implied consent," which in his view is not really consent at all and must be sharply distinguished from that with which it is typically confused, namely, tacit consent. *Tacit consent* involves a deliberate undertaking the specific purpose of which is to indicate consent and the force of which involves, above all, a decision not to dissent. In Simmons's example, a committee chair proposes a policy to the members of the committee and indicates that the policy will be accepted unless there are objections. The committee members remain silent. Provided that their silence is knowing and self-conscious, and not the result of undue coercion, they have thereby "tacitly consented to the chairman's proposal," hence have "undertaken an obligation" to accept it.[28] *Implied consent*, on the other hand, involves no such deliberate consent-indicating action. It does indeed involve actions that lead us to conclude (a) that the actor would have expressly consented "if he or she had been asked to do so," and/or (b) that the actor is "rationally committed" to giving consent, and/or (c) that the actor is "morally bound" to do the same things that he or she would have done if consent had been expressed. But since implied consent does not constitute a deliberate effort to indicate consent, it is not really consent at all, and this means that if it is indeed a source of obligation, that obligation must be grounded not in consent but in something else, i.e., the active acceptance of benefits.[29]

The distinction is a plausible one, but it fails to capture all of the important possibilities. It may well be that to ante-up in the poker game does not count as a deliberate undertaking, the specific purpose of which is to indicate consent. It also seems true that such an act might indeed imply that, if asked, I would expressly offer my consent, that I am rationally committed to giving consent, and that I am morally bound to

[27] Simmons, *Moral Principles and Political Obligations*, p. 89.
[28] *Ibid.*, pp. 80–82. See also, Klosko, "Fixed Content of Political Obligations," p. 58.
[29] Simmons, *Moral Principles and Political Obligations*, pp. 88–89.

do the same things that express consent would bind me to. But whereas the notion of implication typically involves a certain gap between that which implies and that which is implied, a gap that is bridged by a logical argument of some kind, in the instant case there seems to be no such gap, hence no such bridge, between the act of participating and the fact of consent itself. When I plunk my money down on the table, it is – *ceteris paribus* – immediately evident that I am consenting to the rules of the game and its outcomes. No logical argument is required to show this; indeed, none would be appropriate. We are dealing here with something perhaps analogous to illocutionary force. Given the normal social conventions and contexts within which poker is played, the force or meaning of the act itself is, at least in part, that I have consented; which is to say that the act does not merely imply hypothetical consent but in fact constitutes actual consent.[30]

To see this more clearly, consider that once I have started to play the game, it would almost always be superfluous, indeed absurd, to ask me if I was consenting to the rules and the outcomes. Such a question, if asked and answered, would add absolutely nothing new to what everyone in attendance already knows, if only tacitly; and this is very different from standard cases of logical implication in which the conclusion, however straightforward, is enlightening precisely because it does add something new. In the instant case, at least, consent is an integral part of what participation itself means.

It seems, then, that acts relevant to consent can be thought of in terms of four distinct categories: (1) express statements of consent, (2) tacit statements of consent, (3) acts that do not expressly or tacitly state consent but nonetheless constitute it, and (4) acts that imply hypothetical future statements of consent, or that rationally commit the actor to consent, or that morally bind the actor to certain future actions. I am, in fact, not at all certain that (2) and (3) are really different from one another. But I do believe that (3) and (4) identify a clear difference, such that while any example of (3) will also be an example of (4), the reverse is not necessarily true. Cases of free participation in institutionalized activities – whether anteing-up at the poker table or putting on one's mitt and running out to play second base or raising one's hand at the appropriate

---

[30] On the connection between "force"and "meaning," see J. L. Austin, *How to Do Things With Words* (Oxford: Oxford University Press, 1962), p. 100. Also, P. F. Strawson, "Austin and 'Locutionary Meaning,' " in *Essays on J. L. Austin*, ed. Isaiah Berlin et al. (Oxford: Oxford University Press, 1973), pp. 50–51; and John R. Searle, Ferenc Kiefer and Manfred Bierwisch, eds., *Speech Act Theory and Pragmatics* (Boston: D. Reidel, 1980), pp. ix-xi.

time in an auction – would be paradigmatic examples of (3), hence do not simply *imply* consent, as Simmons suggests, but are, like express and tacit consent, directly *constitutive* of it.

It is worth mentioning at this point that Tussman offers a version of the general approach taken by Simmons that is nonetheless different in certain interesting ways. Tussman argues that consent, tacit or otherwise, must be given "knowingly" or else it is not consent at all. This is "a necessary condition which must be satisfied whatever is proposed as a sign of tacit [or express] consent."[31] Such a claim seems plausible enough, but I believe that Tussman seriously misconstrues its implications. We have seen in chapter 3 above that "the members...know a great deal about the workings of [their] society, and must do so if that society is recognizably a 'human society.' "[32] But we have also seen that "it is a basic mistake to equate the knowledgeability of human agents with what is known 'consciously,' or 'held in mind' in conscious ways. The knowledgeable character of human conduct is displayed above all in the vast variety of tacit modes of awareness and competence that I call 'practical consciousness' as differentiated from 'discursive consciousness' – but which actors chronically employ in the course of daily life."[33] Claims such as these seem to me fundamentally correct, and they suggest that the views of Tussman, Simmons and others regarding consent are in fact based on an obsolete and unhelpful conception of human action, one that has been widely rejected by a host of otherwise quite disparate social theorists, from Bourdieu to Giddens, from Gadamer to Searle.

2. The case of poker is typical of the kinds of things that most of us do all the time. We regularly and routinely participate in dozens of institutionalized processes. We go to the hospital, and when we do so we suggest certain beliefs about, among many other things, the legitimacy of medical science, of the medical profession, of medical schools, residency programs, licensing boards, and the like. We deposit our money in the bank and indicate thereby our confidence in the many public and private institutions and procedures of which the banking system is composed. We become active in a religious organization – attending services, joining

---

[31] Joseph Tussman, *Obligation and the Body Politic* (New York: Oxford University Press, 1960), pp. 36–37.

[32] Anthony Giddens, "Agency, Institution, and Time-Space Analysis," in *Advances in Social Theory and Methodology: Toward an Integration of Micro- and Macro-Sociologies*, ed. K. Knorr-Cetina and A. V. Cicourel (Boston: Routledge & Kegan Paul, 1981), p. 163. Also, Anthony Giddens, *The Constitution of Society: Outline of Structuration Theory* (Berkeley: University of California Press, 1984), p. 281–82.

[33] Giddens, "Agency, Institution, and Time-Space Analysis," p. 163.

study groups, contributing money – and in doing so submit ourselves, however provisionally, to its rules and regulations. In all such cases, participation itself is a direct, positive indication that we are consenting to be governed by established procedures and that we acknowledge those procedures to be in some sense authoritative.

Again, such positive indications may turn out to be deceptive. In some cases, participation may turn out not to be a sign of consent at all, for example when it is coerced. Choosing to participate in a game of Russian roulette rather than being summarily and unjustly executed doesn't constitute consent, at least not in the usual sense. But it's hard to see what should follow from this. Express and tacit consent can be coerced too, and just as easily as participation, yet no one – certainly neither Rawls nor Simmons – would deny that, uncoerced, they constitute consent.[34] In this respect, participation is no different. The conclusion seems to me inescapable: the mere fact of participation establishes a strong presumption of consent, a presumption that would be overturned only if it were shown that the consent-indicating act had not been freely performed or that it was in some other way different from what it seemed to be.

To participate in an institutionalized process is to indicate both an active acceptance of benefits received and a belief in the legitimacy of the process itself. While Simmons would disagree with the latter claim, he might agree with the former. He might well admit, for example, that participation in the poker game would indeed constitute active acceptance of the benefits derived therefrom, and that this – though not consent – could be grounds for obligation. But he would go on to insist that even if the argument works for poker or baseball, it cannot work with respect to the state; for again, political benefits are generally provided in the form of public goods, hence their receipt and enjoyment is typically, and often necessarily, passive.

The poker model suggests, however, that even this conclusion is dubious. In poker, obligation is rooted in participation. To participate is to accept the legitimacy of the process, and it is *this* that confers legitimacy on the benefits. The process – the institutionalized, rule-governed pattern of behavior – is what counts. To become an active part of such a process is, by strong implication, to acknowledge its authority, and to acknowledge its authority is to accept the legitimacy of its outcomes.

---

[34] Indeed, Rawls and Simmons think that consent is a problem precisely because so few people ever actually have the occasion, or the desire, formally to express consent.

The model is, *pace* Simmons, perfectly transportable to the political arena, with results that are far different from what he himself suggests. This may well be doubted. After all, political society, unlike the poker game, does not seem to be a voluntary association that one chooses to join. The citizen is sometimes thought to be more like Hume's shipmate, who can hardly be said to have freely consented to the rule of the captain if "he was carried on board while asleep, and must leap in to the ocean, and perish, the moment he leaves her."[35] But the criticism misses the main force of the argument, that free and active participation – rather than formal, voluntary membership – is what counts. Imagine, for example, that the poker game occurs not in a locker room but on a desert island and that the players are survivors of an unfortunate airplane crash. We may suppose that each of them, if they had their druthers, would prefer to be elsewhere; they have not voluntarily chosen the circumstance in which they find themselves. We may even suppose that if the airplane crash had not occurred, none of them would be playing poker. But this seems neither here nor there with respect to the game itself; for insofar as each participates freely in the game, each is effectively consenting to its outcomes, hence acknowledging its legitimacy. Similarly, while rather few of us freely choose to live in the political society in which we find ourselves – and many of us might well prefer to live elsewhere, if only it were possible (I myself think Paris would be nice) – to the degree that we participate in the institutions of our state we effectively consent to its legitimacy.[36]

Anyone who participates in the processes of the state actively accepts, to that extent, the benefits of the state. Voting would be a plausible example. This is widely disputed in the literature, but the principal objections are based explicitly or implicitly on a failure to understand the importance of participation itself as a consent-constituting activity.[37] The fact is that going to the polls and casting a vote in an election is analogous to sitting down at the poker table. It is a kind of engagement that signals PF a belief in the legitimacy of the electoral process and a willingness to accept its outcomes. In this respect, it is important to note

---

[35] David Hume, *Political Essays*, ed. Knud Haakonssen (Cambridge: Cambridge University Press, 1994), p. 193.

[36] It is worth pointing out, further, that Hume's famous example illicitly stacks the deck. For it presupposes a situation – being shanghaied – that plainly involves not some non-moral circumstance but, rather, a deed of the greatest iniquity. Moreover, situations of this kind, often involving what Hobbes calls sovereignty by conquest, raise additional and difficult problems for the idea of the state. See section 5.5.4 below.

[37] Klosko, "Fixed Content of Political Obligations," p. 59. My view accords with the earlier view of Plamenatz, though the argument is dramatically different. See John Plamenatz, *Consent, Freedom, and Political Obligation* (Oxford: Oxford University Press, 1968), p. 170.

that, in elections as well as in poker, such a willingness holds whatever the outcome. My decision to join in the poker game indicates not only active acceptance of winnings, should I win, but also active acceptance of losses, should I lose. My decision to participate implies my belief in the essential fairness of the institution, and while this doesn't mean that I will always be happy with the outcome, it does mean that I will (or should) regard the outcome as legitimate. And so too with political elections. Even if my candidate loses, the fact that I have participated in the electoral process by casting a vote signals a commitment to accept the legitimacy of the result. In such a circumstance, I disagree with the composition, and presumably the policies, of the government, understood as an instrumentality of the state; but I nonetheless acknowledge the authority of the state itself.

I will have more to say about voting and consent shortly. But it is important immediately to observe that active participation in the institutions of the state – again, roughly analogous to joining the poker game – is hardly limited to the electoral, or even "political," process itself. It is true that safe streets constitute a public good the enjoyment of which is generally passive. But if I ever call the police for help, I become an institutional participant, and the benefit that I receive is thereby received actively, not passively. So too if I call the fire department, or the emergency medical team, or the dog catcher. If I choose to send my child to public school, I actively involve myself in state institutions, hence actively accept the services they offer; or if I avail myself of the civil judicial system – if, for example, I choose to sue my neighbor – I am agreeing to the legitimacy of its processes and to the benefits that it confers. I actively accept benefits if I utilize public health services, seek unemployment benefits, live in subsidized housing, apply for and obtain food stamps, participate in a municipal recreation program, enlist in the military, attend community college, patronize the public library, consult my county's gardening hotline or its food preservation hotline or its nutrition education hotline or its crisis intervention hotline, and so on[38] – all of which I am free to eschew, if I so desire,[39] and all of which are possible precisely

---

[38] See Dagger, *Civic Virtues*, p. 74. While my argument here follows Dagger's, I think that he seriously understates his own case.

[39] Some people – survivalists, for example, or members of certain religious cults – do eschew all such activities. They home-school their children, arm themselves for protection rather than rely on the police, abjure social services, and the like; when they do participate in the institutions of the state, they do so not voluntarily but only under duress (when, for example, they are forced to pay their income taxes). Such people in effect deny that the state is a state at all. Rather, they think of themselves as existing in a Hobbesian condition of mere nature and believe that the "state," however powerful it may be, is nonetheless without authority. I think it doubtful that such people have an obligation to obey the law, though it might also be the case that the state would have, at the same time, a perfect right to impose its will on them.

because the state has the authority to impose taxes on its citizens and to use its revenues to provide those services. Simmons seems to me correct in criticizing Locke for attempting to ground political obligation simply in the enjoyment of benefits. Merely living in a state – hence failing to exit, even if it's easy to do so – can hardly be said to constitute consent. Moreover, participating in the institutions of the state under coercion or duress is no more indicative of consent than being forced under the threat of death to play poker. But if we agree that active participation does PF constitute an acknowledgment of the legitimacy of the state, hence provides grounds for obligation, and if we consider that the number of people who actively participate one way or another in the institutions of modern nation states is apt to include all but a very few, then we can see how acceptance of benefits can provide a quite plausible account of political obligation in general.

Now I do believe that participation and active acceptance is always a matter of degree. This suggests, in turn, that the degree to which we can be confident in saying that someone is obligated may itself be variable. For one thing, voluntary participation in civic institutions can be voluntary in very different ways. If, having been drafted into the army, I choose to serve rather than risk jail for draft evasion, this is in an important sense a morally free choice, but also one made under duress. If, on the other hand, there is no draft but I enlist anyway, the choice has quite a different significance. The latter is more clearly a consent-constituting act than the former, hence provides stronger grounds for saying that I am obligated. Similarly, the more intense and sustained the involvement in the institutions of the state, the more certain one can be that the grounds for obligation obtain. If I take you to civil court, this suggests to me a substantial acknowledgment of the legitimacy of the state that underwrites the court's very existence as a court. If, on the other hand, I merely sign a contract, or use a notary public, or get married by a duly authorized clergyman or justice of the peace, these too constitute active involvement in the system of civil law, but to a lesser degree. Still, in each such case, I voluntarily choose to avail myself of a service provided by the state. No one forces me to sign a contract, or to get married officially; and so when I do things of this nature, I actively embrace the attendant benefits. Even if each such activity is itself relatively minor, each nonetheless provides at least some grounds for obligation. As minor involvements multiply, moreover, so do the grounds of obligation; and it seems plain that for a great many people leading ordinary lives in a great many states, involvements quickly accumulate to the point that the grounds of obligation become quite substantial indeed. This is not to say that political obligation itself can be a matter of degree. It seems that, in the end, it must be a question of either/or; one either is or is not obligated. But the reasons for believing that one is obligated can be more-or-less strong, more-or-less convincing; and this is to suggest, then, that claims of political obligation can be asserted and imposed with varying degrees of confidence.

3. In this context, we can reassess profitably the connection between voting and consent. Simmons raises serious doubts about such a connection, but I think that his arguments are unpersuasive.

He essentially makes three claims. First, he presumes that "average voters have very little sense of what they have committed themselves to by voting," and concludes from this that voting cannot be said to be a deliberate undertaking the specific purpose of which is to indicate consent.[40] Simmons himself is unsure about the premise, and in this respect the argument presented above against Tussman would seem to pertain. Voters may understand more than Simmons thinks, even if that understanding is often inexplicit and unexpressed. But more importantly, as I have already argued, consent can be directly constituted by forms of participation that are not themselves deliberate undertakings the specific purpose of which is to indicate consent. Surely voting would be a perfectly plausible example of this, and the upshot is that even if it's true that voters have not specifically intended to indicate consent, this is insufficient to show that voting is not a consent-constituting activity.

Second, Simmons argues that since governments themselves insist that citizens have an obligation to vote, this in effect implies that voting cannot constitute consent; the source of the obligation must be prior.[41] But as we have seen, voting is only one among many possible kinds of consent-constituting activities. It is certainly not at all incoherent to think that a citizen who has freely chosen to use the public schools, the police services, the public library and so on may well have an obligation to vote, and thinking this in no way rules out the possibility that voting itself could be yet another source of obligation. Even more importantly, Simmons's argument also seems to mix apples and oranges. Even if many regimes regard voting as obligatory in some sense, rather few regard it as obligatory in the sense of an obligation to obey the law. Failure to vote is rarely illegal. What can this mean, other than that the so-called "obligation" to vote is really little more than a generalized suggestion, hence quite different from the kind of political obligation with which we are here concerned?

---

[40] A. John Simmons, *On the Edge of Anarchy: Locke, Consent and the Limits of Society* (Princeton: Princeton University Press, 1993), p. 224. My arguments here pertain only to what Simmons calls (p. 221) the "weaker" version of the claim that voting gives consent.
[41] *Ibid.*, p. 224.

Of course, where non-voting is illegal, we can agree that voting, as a coerced activity, is doubtfully constitutive of consent; but such cases are relatively uncontroversial, and certainly not the ones that Simmons has in mind.

Finally, Simmons observes that regimes rarely if ever suggest that "by not voting one would be freed of obligations that voters voluntarily assume."[42] The observation is plainly correct, but it is hard to see why it is germane. As I have shown, voting is almost certainly just one of a wide variety of consent-indicating activities. To say, then, that voting might be a sufficient condition of consent, or that it might contribute positively to a pattern of activities that collectively constitute consent, is not to say that it is a necessary condition for consent. The non-voter may well have obligated him- or herself in numerous other ways. There is, thus, nothing inconsistent in claiming both that voting constitutes consent and that abstention does not necessarily dissolve the obligation to obey. I do believe that failing to vote makes it somewhat less certain that the grounds for obligation obtain – it weakens the presumption of consent – and insofar as states fail to recognize this, they are simply wrong. But this does not in any way affect the claim that free and sincere participation in the electoral process is a consent-constituting activity.

4. Simmons considers an alternative account of political obligation, the so-called Socratic argument according to which our obligation to obey the law is based on gratitude. In a famous passage of the *Crito*, Socrates speaks of children and parents. Just as children should be grateful to their parents for making them who they are, so should we be grateful to the state for all of the benefits that it provides us, and we should acknowledge our gratitude by repaying the state with our allegiance.

Simmons believes that this argument, like the arguments of tacit consent and accepted benefits, will not work. Gratitude always presupposes that the benefit in question be granted not accidentally, nor in the normal course of things, nor again for ulterior or extraneous reasons, but as the result of some special effort or sacrifice on the part of the grantor and with the specific intention of providing just such a benefit. If you do something that benefits me, but do so without any intention of benefiting me, or primarily for the purely selfish reason that benefiting me will really benefit you, or simply because the activity in question is something that you would ordinarily do anyway in the normal course of events and entails no special burden or sacrifice on your part, then we are unlikely to believe

---

[42] *Ibid.*

that I owe you a debt of gratitude. But most of the benefits conferred by the state are precisely of this nature. They are benefits that the state confers not through some special effort or sacrifice but simply because that's what states do; and they usually do it because it serves the interests of the state itself and of those who wield state power.

This criticism of the Socratic argument reflects, in part, a general skepticism about any attempt "to move a principle of gratitude from the realm of interpersonal relations into the realm of benefits provided by institutions."[43] The implication is that gratitude toward institutions, including the state, is impossible, and that gratitude toward individuals must be very different from anything that one might feel toward institutions. But when Simmons actually considers and rejects the possibility of (obligation-generating) gratitude toward the state, he does so by looking primarily at the conditions that must obtain if one is to feel (obligation-generating) gratitude toward another person. He analyzes the logic of gratitude only in interpersonal terms, and thereby ignores the possibility that there is a kind of gratitude owed toward institutions which, though different from the kind of gratitude owed toward individuals, might be gratitude nonetheless.[44]

To say that we owe a debt of gratitude to some other person only if that person benefits us intentionally and through some special effort or sacrifice is to connect gratitude directly to the motives of individuals in performing particular acts. If you save my life because you did X, it matters a great deal whether you intended to do X in order to save my life, or if you intended it for some other reason altogether, or if you did not intend it at all but did it completely involuntarily, through no choice of your own; and it matters a great deal if doing X intentionally in order to save my life was a difficult, dangerous or otherwise extraordinary thing for you to do or if, to the contrary, it was easy and cost-free. Such considerations would pertain to your own moral psychology, and in deciding that I owe you a debt of gratitude I would be, in effect, acknowledging and rewarding you for your virtue. I would be deciding that, at least to some extent, you are a good person, meaning someone who freely chooses to do good things. Naturally, there are degrees here. The more difficult, dangerous or otherwise extraordinary the deed, the more you are to be admired for freely choosing to do it, hence the greater my sense of gratitude and the greater my respect for your character. But whatever

---

[43] Simmons, *Moral Principles and Political Obligations*, p. 187.
[44] Klosko makes the same error ("Fixed Content of Obligations," p. 57).

the degree, the gratitude that I feel reflects a recognition of your capacity for free choice and of your decision to use that capacity for good.

None of this transfers easily to institutions. Institutions are ideas – structures of intelligibility that reflect our understanding of how at least part of the world really is, on the basis of which we produce and/or arrange some of the world's furniture. As such, they do not have moral psychologies. They do not have consciences, are not creatures of good (or bad) will, cannot suffer from *akrasia*, and the like. Of course, it's true that institutions *do* things. Such doings, however, will reflect not some psychological fact – and certainly nothing that could be called the institution's noumenal will – but, rather, the structure of concepts and discourse, the metaphysical presuppositions, out of which the institution itself emerges. It is partly for this reason, for example, that institutions cannot truly be said to have defects of character, to lack (or have) probity or integrity, to be saintly or evil, etc. Of course, institutional *personnel* can be treated or characterized in all these ways, and this is largely what permits us to use phrases that seem to describe institutions in moral terms. Thus, we talk about, say, the venality or excessive greed of this or that corporation. But such talk is inevitably rhetorical. Either it reflects judgments about the moral character of individual human beings who make particular institutional decisions; or else it reflects views about the consequences or implications of institutional practices, in the same way that the rhetoric of morality is sometimes used when we talk about the consequences of natural phenomena (e.g., "The effects of El Niño are evil indeed" or "You were bitten by a very bad dog").

It should not surprise us, then, that the language of personal gratitude does not map very well onto the landscape of the state. When a state provides a benefit, it would be at best strained ever to claim that it has made an extra effort or sacrifice in doing so, or that it has done so out of morally admirable intentions. States are not like that. But one can be grateful for things that are not exemplifications of personal morality. After months of drought, I can be grateful for the rain; or I can be grateful that the pain I had was the result of indigestion rather than heart disease. I can also be grateful for the existence of situations that enable or bring about exemplifications of personal morality; and I can feel an obligation to help ensure that such situations continue to exist.

It seems that feeling grateful does not necessarily imply a *debt* of gratitude, at least not in the usual sense. I may be grateful for the rain, but it would be ludicrous to suggest that I could possibly owe it anything. Surely this is, at least in part, because there is nothing that I can do *for* the rain, no way – absent some kind of religious belief – to express my gratitude in a way that will serve the interests of rain, of which there are none. But despite this, it is also true that my feeling of gratitude might, or even should, have certain attitudinal and/or behavioral implications. Having never previously experienced drought, I might now come to understand better than before just how wonderful rain can be. I might become less inclined to curse the rain when it wipes out my picnic or my golf game, and also more inclined to worry about certain kinds of human activities – industrial activities, for example – that hypothetically have large-scale climatic consequences, including consequences for the amount and location of rainfall. Indeed, we might say that feelings of gratitude could or even should result in the development of a healthy appreciation and respect for rain as rain.

Here, it seems, is a kind of gratitude that is very different from the gratitude that we feel toward someone who has voluntarily done us a good deed. But it is gratitude nonetheless, and it may be roughly the kind of gratitude that we sometimes feel for the state. The state (arguably) benefits us in many ways. It confers benefits not in the way that good Samaritans or other moral agents do. But by being the source of good things, it is something for which we might be grateful. And just as gratitude for certain natural phenomena can, and perhaps should, issue in the development of a healthy appreciation for the phenomena themselves, so might gratitude for the state call for a similar response. This is to suggest that perhaps one best expresses one's gratitude to the state by coming to respect it for what it is.

But what could it mean to respect the state for what it is? Part of the idea of the state is that the state is legitimately in authority, which means that its laws ought to be obeyed simply because they are its laws. This is something about which Durkheim and Weber, whose theories of the state otherwise diverge so dramatically (see 1.3.3 above), are in full agreement; and it has been systematically defended more recently by Pitkin, who argues – *mutatis mutandis* – that obeying the law is simply an integral part of what the concepts of legitimacy and authority mean.[45]

Now Simmons sharply criticizes Pitkin's account, understood as a theory of political obligation.[46] To have shown that obeying the law is part of the idea of the state is not to have explained why we should ever obey the law because it is the law, hence not to have explained the *grounds* of political obligation. The criticism is, at once, correct and beside the point. For it seems plain that Pitkin is merely saying that wherever there is a legitimate state, the laws of that state must be obeyed. Political obligation is

---

[45] Hanna Pitkin, "Obligation and Consent."
[46] Simmons, *Moral Principles and Political Obligations*, pp. 39–45.

analytically part of what we mean when we talk about the state and its authority. In asking after the grounds of obligation, on the other hand, Simmons is wondering if there ever can actually *be* a legitimate state or, what is the same thing, whether a state could ever exist (in Wolff's terms) *de jure* and not merely *de facto*. Simmons is right to say that Pitkin does not answer this question, but he is wrong to deny the importance of Pitkin's account for the broader question of political obligation; for again, *if* a state exists, then it must indeed be obeyed.

To respect the state – a respect generated by gratitude for the benefits provided by the state – is necessarily to accept the existence of the state; and to accept its existence is necessarily to accept the proposition that its laws must be obeyed. It is hard to see, then, why gratitude could not provide, along with notions of tacit consent and the active acceptance of benefits, a coherent and plausible reason for saying that someone has a political obligation.

4. **The absolute state**

In the first three sections of this chapter, I have sought to reconstruct our underlying intuitions about obligation, duty and consent and to rehabiliate, thereby, what is in fact a rather traditional approach to the general question of political legitimacy. I have argued, in particular, that standard claims about tacit consent, the acceptance of benefits under conditions of fair play, and gratitude need not be vulnerable to the kinds of criticisms offered by Simmons and others, hence may indeed provide good reasons for explaining just why citizens might be morally obliged to obey the law as such. So much I have attempted to demonstrate. But can we now go further and suggest a *positive* account of the state's authority such that we can understand not simply how political obligation is possible but when it is required and why? To pursue such an account is, in fact, to address two distinct questions. First, according to the idea of the state, how do we decide whether or not we are morally required to do the kinds of things that entail obligations, i.e., whether or not to participate in, accept benefits from, or feel gratitude toward the institutions of the state? Second, exactly how categorical is the state's authority over its citizens or, what is the same thing, to what extent do we have a right to reject that which the state demands of us? What is our right to resist?

Such issues speak to the very heart of our larger project. For we do not understand fully the idea of the state until we have understood not merely the *scope* of the state's authority – involving, as we have seen, notions of tolerance, laissez-faire, and limited government understood primarily as a kind of self-limitation – but also the *nature* of it. What are the sources of political authority, how extensive are its claims, and what room, if any, does it provide for the individual to disobey?

1. The positive analysis of political obligation is nothing other than an application of the theory of agency outlined in chapter 3 above. According to that theory, human actions invariably reflect deep-seated and widely held judgments regarding the way things in the world really are. They emerge from, are underwritten by, the more-or-less tacit conceptual structure – the universe of metaphysical and moral presupposition – out of which is composed an intelligible way of life. That structure cannot but be pre-scriptive. It indicates what each of us ought to do if we are to live our lives in a coherent and rational manner. From this it follows that the actual obligation to obey the law in any particular circumstance is derived from and deeply embedded in the idea of the state itself. For the latter is nothing other than the authoritative embodiment of a society's understanding of the nature of things. It summarizes the structure of truth upon which all of our judgments, hence all of our actions, are based – and this would naturally include those judgments and actions that are connected with, or that activate, the grounds of political obligation, e.g., deciding to accept benefits from the state. Stated otherwise, if (a) decisions about consent, acceptance and gratitude are matters of judgment and action, (b) judgment and action are governed by an underlying structure of truth, and (c) the state is the effective embodiment of that structure, then (d) it is the state itself that determines when the citizen ought to do the kind of things that generate political obligations.

The word "determines" here should not be misunderstood. It would be wrong to think of the state or its various instrumentalities as independently deciding, over and against the individual, the nature and extent of political obligations. Such obligations are not, strictly speaking, imposed by the state on the citizen. Rather, the idea of the state and the judgment of the citizen both reflect and are jointly constituted by a structure of presupposition and truth that transcends each of them and that creates for them the possibility of an intelligible social existence. As the over-arching embodiment of this structure, the state "determines" the nature and extent of political obligation only in the sense that it organizes, expresses and certifies – it renders in an authoritative and usable form – those truths upon which obligations themselves are based. The state helps to make explicit that which we already implicitly know, namely, the circumstances in which, and the grounds for saying that, we are morally required to obey the law because it is the law.

If, then, consent and/or the active acceptance of benefits provide such grounds, this can only be because of a larger conception of truth that tells us when and where we ought to give our consent and accept our benefits. We have seen above that it is important to know not just whether to keep promises but also whether to make them in the first place. While we may indeed need a theory to explain why promises constitute obligations, we also need one to explain when promising itself is the right thing to do. And so too for any and all activities that generate political obligations. We have to know when it is morally appropriate or morally required actively to accept the benefits that the state offers and, conversely, when not to; we need to understand when we should put ourselves – or maintain ourselves – in circumstances that require us to feel grateful to the state, assuming that we have a choice; and all of this means that we need to understand, to the degree possible, the practical implications of the metaphysical and moral premises out of which all of our thoughts and actions emerge. Those premises constitute the indispensable foundation for everything that we think and do. Thus, if we ask when we should do the kinds of things that generate political obligations, the answer is when it makes sense to do so. We should obey the law, and should obey it because it is the law, when the structure of metaphysical presupposition, the background, the conceptual apparatus that makes us who we are – and that constitutes, among other things, the idea of the state itself – requires it of us.

2. I believe it follows from this that our obligation to the state is absolute; and if our obligation is absolute, then, of course, so too is the authority of the state itself. To talk of a non-absolutist state is to talk nonsense.

The argument is straightforward. Whenever we need to decide what we should do in any area of life, we cannot but consult and be guided by the conceptual apparatus or structure of truth that describes our understanding of how things in the world really are. We have, as far as I can tell, no reasonable alternative. We could perhaps "choose" to ignore the facts of the world and attempt to act in defiance of them. I could ascend to the fifth floor of the building that I am in, leap out of a window, flap my arms, and attempt to fly away – all despite my knowledge that things in the world are such that humans cannot fly unaided. But as I plunge to my death, people will say, with much justification, that what I did was evidence of insanity; and in the absence of strong evidence to the contrary, no one would claim that I made a free choice, foolish or otherwise, since insane people cannot truly be said to have the faculty of decision. Sanity, coherence and intelligibility absolutely require that I act on the basis of how the world really is, as best I understand it; and this is true if we're talking about fifth-floor windows or about the authority of the law.

Of course, my understanding of the world will be limited in all kinds of ways. The truth of things is rarely if ever entirely clear. If, for example,

I wish to know whether or not to prosecute my father for the murder of a man, and assuming that I would do so only if it is a pious thing to do, then I will have to know the truth of piety, and this is, as we are well aware, no easy matter. Indeed, it is sufficiently difficult to know how things really are that in many and probably most cases (and this certainly applies to Euthyphro himself) I may have to act without complete confidence, unsure at least to some degree as to what the truth of the world requires of me. But despite this, the fundamental principle remains: I cannot but act on the basis of the truth *as best I understand it*. Rationality demands, in effect, both that I try to get as clear about things as possible and that I live my life in a timely fashion, and this means that when things are not fully clear, as they rarely are, I often must act on the basis of what might be called the preponderance of evidence. However provisional or definitive the available evidence might be, I have no choice but to let it govern my actions. I am bound by it, absolutely.

It is also true, of course, that our understanding of the world changes, regularly and sometimes with astonishing speed. We are inquisitive, naturally scientific creatures, and as we look at the world in new ways, so we arrive at new understandings of how things are, hence come to see that some of our old understandings were just wrong. Human fallibility is all too obvious; and one result is that our actions sometimes turn out to have consequences far different from what we would have supposed. Thus, the most rational, coherent of individuals will sometimes metaphorically leap out of a fifth-floor window with unfortunate results. Trial and error is an important and extremely useful, if also sometimes perilous, mode of rational inquiry. But again, this in no way undermines the necessary and intimate connection between truth and intelligent action. To leap out of a fifth-floor window in defiance of our best understanding of how things are is radically different from doing so on the basis of the best available theory. The latter is a tragic but intelligible and possibly very helpful mistake, a sensible but failed experiment the results of which can move us closer to the truth. The former is lunacy. For any action to be at all intelligent and comprehensible, it must be based to the degree possible on the actor's best sense of the truth of things, such as it may be.

Since, however, the idea of the state is essentially the effective embodiment of the truth as it is conceived at any point in time – the public instantiation of our structure of metaphysical presupposition – to act on the basis of that structure is nothing other than to act in accordance with, hence to be governed by, the idea of the state itself. Again, I believe that we have no real choice in this. If we are to act intelligently, we must do what the state, as the embodiment of truth, requires of us. The state is, as such, an absolute authority that determines how we are to live our lives.

None of this means that the state must actively dictate all of the details of all of our actions. The truth of the world may be such that each of us has a range of coherent alternatives among which we are "free" to choose, that various kinds of endeavor may be equally consistent with the truth of things as we understand them, and that the idea of the state is thus, at least to some extent, indifferent as to which course of action we select. The state is not necessarily a micro-manager. Here, though, I simply reiterate in different terms the argument of chapter 4 above. The state may choose to limit the control that certain of its instrumentalities – primarily the organs of government – actively exercise over the society as a whole. We need to remember, of course, that any such choice will be made by the state itself, that policies of laissez-faire or benign neglect are types of control, and that the notion of limited government can only be, from the perspective of the idea of the state, a notion of self-limitation. But all of this pertains to the *scope* of the state's authority. It is irrelevant to the question of the present chapter – the *nature* of that authority – hence does not affect in any way our basic conclusion. The authority of the state is absolute. No matter how a particular state chooses to define its scope of activity, the authority that it wields it wields absolutely, and the citizen cannot but recognize and act in terms of that authority, on pain of incoherence.

3. It will be argued that all of this presents a false, even grotesque picture of how societies really operate. People regularly and routinely disobey the law, sometimes in serious ways, sometimes trivially, yet we would not want to say that all those who do so are lunatics. Certainly, some are. But some will at least appear to be perfectly rational, sensible and sane, however criminal their activity; and even many law-abiding people would insist that their behavior reflects not a respect for the law as such but merely a set of prudential calculations designed to maximize self-interest. For such individuals, the ring of Gyges would be a godsend, its magical powers to be exploited eagerly and without compunction. Indeed, for a great many people – arguably, the majority – a society's underlying structure of truth, its foundation of metaphysical presupposition, is so motley, so complex, varied and obscure, so ephemeral and ineffable as to make it very nearly useless as a guide to action. In virtually any society of any substantial magnitude, people disagree, constantly and vociferously, about right and wrong; their presuppositions, their underlying beliefs about truth, are diverse, distinctive and mutually inconsistent; they are frequently at odds with one another both about what the law requires and about what it should be. The notion that all of this could provide a reliable basis of absolute authority seems optimistic at best, far-fetched at worst.

At this point, four important observations are in order. First, the fact that a society is beset by conflict and disagreement does not at all undermine the idea that any society is constituted by an underlying and widely shared structure of presupposed truth. In even the most hermetic and unified of cultures, disagreements occur. But in typical cases, they occur, when they occur, at the margins. This is to say that the kinds of disputes characteristic of most societies most of the time involve matters that are in some sense not fundamental to the continued existence of an on-going, organized way of life; or if they do concern such fundamental matters, they do so only selectively and partially. If this were not the case, if the foundations were entirely and routinely up for grabs, then it is hard to see not only how the society could survive but how the disagreements themselves could be intelligently joined, even articulated. Euthyphro and Socrates may not know explicitly what piety is. But in order to have an intelligible conversation about it, in order for each to make arguments and adduce evidence and arrive at claims or judgments, however tentative, that the other can comprehend, they must share an immense, nearly infinite universe of understanding and knowledge – conceptual, linguistic, historical, empirical. And so too for disagreements about political authority and the law. It would seem impossible, for example, to articulate and make sense of the notion that I will not obey the law simply because it is the law unless I am already at least familiar with, and have some understanding of, the idea that the law is indeed something to be obeyed for its own sake. Without an awareness of the latter, why would the former even occur to me?

Second, the absolute authority of the state doesn't presuppose that everything the state or its agents say or do goes unchallenged. Disagreements at the perimeter are disagreements nonetheless; and if, as a practical matter, society demands a process for adjudicating such disagreements, this in no way implies that the process must be, from the perspective of truth, infallible. In large part, politics may be best understood precisely as an on-going and unavoidable struggle for the margins. It is the activity by which one formulates and seeks to establish a particular interpretation of what a society's underlying structure of truth implies for public policy. The "seeking to establish" may be argumentative or coercive; it may be democratic or autocratic; it may be a matter of rhetoric or of force; it may be thoughtful, scrupulous and motivated by a concern for the common good or it may be capricious, ruthless and self-interested. But in all cases, it will be in the service of a claim to the effect that one particular decision or policy constitutes or comports with the best available interpretation of what the underlying structure requires. Once established along these lines, the interpretation cannot but be authoritative, and absolutely so. This doesn't mean, though, that it is necessarily permanent or something with which everyone must agree. The absolute authority of the state does not presuppose the end of conversation or of politics.

Third, the variability, ineffability and overall messiness of a society's underlying structure of truth necessarily has its limits. As implied in the first point above, when disagreements cease to be merely marginal, or when fundamental disagreements cease to be contained and compartmentalized, the foundations of a society itself necessarily fall into jeopardy. A society of individuals who disagree profoundly about the most basic things cannot long function as a society. We have seen in chapter 2 how the idea of a purely political conception is not viable insofar as any structure of accommodation will unavoidably embody metaphysical presuppositions that inform and underwrite the terms of accommodation; and we have seen in chapter 4 how tolerance of differences is either not tolerance at all or is, at best, sharply limited to those things judged to be tolerable. If agreeable and substantive terms of accommodation cannot be discovered in an underlying structure of truth, if mutually intolerable behavior proves to be pervasive and irresolvable, then society would cease to be society in any meaningful sense. Politics would disappear, to be replaced by a condition of chaos or of war in which political authority – the idea of the state – becomes a mere phantasm.

Finally, the difference between a functioning, orderly society having an authoritative political state and a stateless society of anarchy and war is almost certainly the difference between two points along a continuum. Any political state that has ever existed or that could exist is only more-or-less orderly, more-or-less authoritative; which is to say that the consensus it enjoys is more-or-less widespread, the idea of the world that it represents more-or-less coherent. All states are fragile. The centripetal forces of society, rooted in shared notions of how things really are, invariably operate in perpetual tension with centrifugal forces – ideological differences, conflicts of material interest, and so on – that tend to weaken or unravel the fabric of society.

Of course, where to draw a line on the continuum between societies that successfully resist disintegration and those that do not is an immensely difficult problem. It is not, however, a problem about the idea of the state itself. It concerns, instead, merely the application of that idea to particular cases, hence is a matter of scientific or historical rather than philosophical interest.

5. Resistance

I have distinguished the *scope* of state authority (discussed in chapter 4) from the *nature* of state authority (the subject of the present chapter). But this latter idea itself has two aspects. One pertains to the *grounds* of political obligation; and whereas Simmons and others claim that there are no such grounds, I have argued that this is false. More positively, I have tried to show how a foundation for political obligation may be discovered in the underlying structure of truth that shapes and constitutes, at least in part, a particular way of life. The second aspect of the idea of political authority concerns not the grounds of obligation but its *limits*. I refer here to limits not in the sense of a "limited range of activity" – that would speak to the question of *scope* – but in the sense of a "limited claim of authority," wherein a particular argument for obligation, understood as a moral argument, might be outweighed by some other moral argument. These two senses of limit are conceptually quite distinct; for whatever the proper scope of state activity might be, the question of the absolutism of the state's authority within that scope of activity remains. While I have attempted to show in chapter 4 that the scope of state activity must be unlimited (or, at most, self-limited) in the first sense of the term, I have argued in the present chapter that the authority of the state itself is and must be unlimited in the second sense, hence is and must be absolute; and this because the state embodies and activates our shared sense of how things in the world really are.

Our strong intuition, however, is that individuals or collections of individuals also have unequivocal moral claims independent of the claims of the state, that what is good for the state is not always good for each and every citizen or group, that people, either singly or together, have obligations and immunities over and against the larger community. While notions of this kind are sometimes thought to be peculiarly modern, important traces of them can in fact be found wherever we encounter serious discussions of political life. As such, they typically involve powerfully held and widely shared commitments that would seem directly to undermine the absolutist claims of the state.

Properly conceived, however, they do no such thing. The absolutism of the state is fully consistent with, indeed is intimately connected to, the inviolable and seemingly anti-authoritarian claims of non-political entities. And again in this respect, as in so many others, the case of Hobbes proves to be enormously instructive.

1. Every reader of *Leviathan* must come quickly to the realization that the problem at hand – the problem of absolutism and resistance – manifests itself in that work as an apparent contradiction so central and substantial as to raise serious doubts about the cogency of Hobbesian political thought in general.

On the one hand, Hobbes argues that the sovereign of a commonwealth has complete authority over the commonwealth's citizens. This authority is "absolute" and "unlimited."[47] It is "as great as possibly men can be imagined to make it."[48] Indeed, nothing the sovereign entity does to a subject can "on what pretense soever, be properly called injustice or injury,"[49] and one result of this is that there can be no real distinction between a tyrannical and a legitimate state.[50] On the other hand, Hobbes seems equally unambiguous in saying that each and every subject has a right to resist the sovereign – to disobey – in order to save his or her own life: "if the sovereign command a man, though justly condemned, to kill, wound, or maim himself, or not to resist those that assault him, or to abstain from the use of food, air, medicine, or any other thing without which he cannot live, yet has that man the liberty to disobey."[51] Such a right of disobedience certainly seems to constitute a substantial limitation on the sovereign's allegedly "unlimited" authority. Of course, Hobbes also says that the sovereign has a perfect right to try to overcome any and all resistance; the citizen's limited right to disobey doesn't undermine the sovereign's right to enforce obedience.[52] But Hobbes had claimed that sovereigns are instituted, in the first instance, by a contractual agreement among the citizens in which each party accedes to the following strong stipulation: "I authorize and give up [to the sovereign] my right of governing myself."[53] And if one were to have any doubts about what this means, Hobbes quickly erases them. In the social contract, citizens "confer all their power and strength upon one man, or upon one assembly of men,"[54] and this conferral appears to involve no qualifications or

---

[47] *Leviathan, EW*, vol. 3, pp. 190–91, 211. My argument here is about *Leviathan*. Some of what it says may apply to the *Elements of Law* and, to a much greater extent, *De Cive*; but I make no specific claims in that regard. For a brief treatment of the development of Hobbes's thought on these subjects over time, see Richard Tuck, *Natural Rights Theories: Their Origins and Development* (Cambridge: Cambridge University Press, 1979, pp. 120–32). On the question of a "rhetorical" *Leviathan*, as opposed to an anti-rhetorical *Elements*, see David Johnston, *The Rhetoric of Leviathan: Thomas Hobbes and the Politics of Cultural Transformation* (Princeton: Princeton University Press, 1986) and Quentin Skinner, *Reason and Rhetoric in the Philosophy of Hobbes* (Cambridge: Cambridge University Press, 1996).

[48] *Leviathan, EW*, vol. 3, pp. 194–95.

[49] *Ibid.*, p. 199.

[50] *Ibid.*, pp. 171–72, 188–91.

[51] *Ibid.*, p. 204.

[52] *Ibid.*, pp. 204–5.

[53] *Ibid.*, p. 158.

[54] As Lloyd correctly notes, there is an exception. Citizens have no obligation to obey commands of the sovereign that are repugnant to their duty to God. But as Lloyd also notes, this exception is dealt with in the second half of *Leviathan*, where Hobbes seeks to show how the terms of the social contract are, in fact, entirely consistent with what true religion requires. S. A. Lloyd, *Ideals as Interests in Hobbes's "Leviathan": The Power of Mind over Matter* (Cambridge: Cambridge University Press, 1992), pp. 76–77.

limitations. It seems, then, both that citizens are to transfer all their rights
and that they are to retain the right to self-protection; that the sovereign is
owed absolute obedience and that the sovereign may be disobeyed in
certain cases; that no action of the sovereign can be construed as an injury
to the subjects and that subjects must protect themselves against the
sovereign's injurious deeds.

Numerous commentators have sought to show not so much how
Hobbes can have it both ways – they admit that he can't – but, rather,
what Hobbes must have meant. For some, his insistence that the citizen
has a certain right to disobey and his "refusal to close off completely all
possible paths to resistance"[55] shows that his doctrine is not really as
absolutist as some have thought. This seems to be Goldsmith's position,
for example.[56] On the other hand, Schmitt argues that "[r]esistance as a
'right' is in Hobbes's absolute state … factually and legally nonsensical
and absurd,"[57] while Lloyd agrees that Hobbes "admits of no grounds on
which one could legitimately disobey one's effective government."[58]
Baumgold suggests that Hobbes does propose a right to resist, but that
such a right is entirely "inconsequential," hence doesn't seriously compromise his absolutism.[59] Warrender, of course, argues that "Hobbes
evades the question of whether the discharge of the subject from obedience [in the case of self-defense] is absolute or not,"[60] implying that the
argument of the text is far from satisfactory; and this latter claim is echoed
and emphasized by Hampton.[61] Indeed, it seems to me that Hampton
outlines the problem with unusual clarity.[62] She shows how a so-called
"fallback position" – people retain certain rights to resist a sovereign
whose authority is, as a result, "almost" but not quite absolute[63] – can
indeed be found in Leviathan,[64] but also how that position seems utterly
to contradict the plainly absolutist claims that one finds elsewhere in the
very same text. For Hampton, "a systematic approach to Hobbes's

---

[55] Glenn Burgess, "On Hobbesian Resistance Theory," *Political Studies* 42 (1994), p. 74.
[56] M. M. Goldsmith, *Hobbes's Science of Politics* (New York: Columbia University Press, 1966), pp. 183–84.
[57] Carl Schmitt, *The Leviathan in the State Theory of Thomas Hobbes: Meaning and Failure of a Political Symbol* (Westport, Connecticut: Greenwood Press, 1996), p. 46.
[58] S. A. Lloyd, *Ideals as Interests in Hobbes's "Leviathan,"* p. 298.
[59] Deborah Baumgold, *Hobbes's Political Theory* (Cambridge: Cambridge University Press, 1988), pp. 33–35.
[60] Howard Warrender, *The Political Philosophy of Hobbes: His Theory of Obligation* (Oxford: Oxford University Press, 1957), p. 194.
[61] Jean Hampton, *Hobbes and the Social Contract Tradition* (Cambridge: Cambridge University Press, 1986).
[62] *Ibid.*, pp. 206–7.
[63] *Ibid.*, p. 220.
[64] *Ibid.*, pp. 239–47.

argument reveals a sophisticated attempt at a geometric deduction of absolute sovereignty that ultimately fails. Hobbes's premises do not lead to his conclusions."[65]

In my view, none of these interpretations, plausible and well-established though they may be, takes seriously enough Hobbes's own fundamental dictum that "truth consisteth in the right ordering of names"[66] and that reason is nothing other than "reckoning, that is adding and subtracting, of the consequences of general names."[67] Specifically, they fail to examine closely enough Hobbes's account of that particular idea to which we give the name "state," and from which his theory of obligation is derived. With such an account firmly in hand, I believe it can be shown that citizens have both an absolute obligation to obey the sovereign in every respect and without any exception whatsoever and, at the same time, certain inalienable rights of self-defense; further, that Hobbes can argue this without any contradiction whatsoever; and finally, that the right of self-defense is, in Hobbes's thought, very broad indeed, and forms the basis for a full-scale theory of legitimate revolution, or at least its functional equivalent. In the process, I hope to show that Hobbes's prudential advice to the ruler – namely, to govern well – is not merely incidental or tangential to but, rather, part and parcel of his formal account of sovereignty.

2. We must begin by describing in precise terms the actual goals of the state, for this is an issue that is often misunderstood.

According to Hobbes, the state or commonwealth is best conceived as the product of an agreement, actual or hypothetical, among individuals who would, in virtue of that agreement, become citizens. The *grounds* of obligation are contractual; and insofar as the theory of the social contract fails to explain the obligations of most citizens of most states, Hobbes's formulation is, in this respect, unpersuasive. But on the question of the *limits* of obligation, the situation is quite different.

Many readers of Hobbes have believed that the agreement to constitute political society, as he understood it, is based on each citizen's fear of violent death, hence that the purpose of the contract and of the state that it creates is to preserve life itself. While there is much textual evidence in *Leviathan* to support such a view, there is also important and unambiguous evidence to indicate that it is far from the whole story. Consider, for example, the well-known passage in chapter 13, where Hobbes tells us that "(t)he Passions that incline men to peace, are fear of death; desire of

---

[65] *Ibid.*, p. 247.
[66] *Leviathan, EW*, vol. 3, p. 23.
[67] *Ibid.*, p. 30.

such things as are necessary to commodious living; and a hope by their industry to obtain them."[68] Here, fear of death is but one of three reasons for entering into the compact, hence the appropriate function of the state must go well beyond the securing of mere physical existence. Indeed, if "commodious" means anything in such a context, then surely it means that commonwealths are created, in part, to secure at least some plausible array of creature comforts – and this, presumably, to make it possible for individuals to enjoy something that approximates, one might say, the good life, rather than simply life itself.

In chapter 14, where the discussion considers more directly the right to resist, Hobbes's account is similarly broad. He insists famously that "a man cannot lay down the right of resisting them, that assault him by force, to take away his life; because he cannot be understood to aim thereby, at any good to himself."[69] Again, preservation of life is crucial. But once more, it is not enough, for "the same may be said of wounds, and chains, and imprisonment; both because there is no benefit consequent to such patience; as there is to the patience of suffering another to be wounded, or imprisoned; as also because a man cannot tell, when he seeth men proceed against him by violence, whether they intend death or not." The word "both" here is crucial. It indicates that simply the threat of punishment – the threat of mere imprisonment – may be sufficient, *in and of itself*, to justify resistance, hence to break the bonds of obligation, whatever their foundation might be. One's obligation to the state thus dissolves not simply when one's life is in danger but when one is threatened with jail and/or corporal sanction; hence the purpose of the state is not simply to secure the lives of its citizens but to secure as well their liberty and at least a certain minimal level of physical comfort.

Hobbes (still in chapter 14) elaborates as follows:

[T]he motive, and end for which this renouncing, and transferring of right is introduced, is nothing else but the security of a man's person, in his life, and in the means of so preserving life, *as not to be weary of it*. And there if a man by words, or other signs, seem to despoil himself of the end, for which those signs were intended; he is not to be understood as if he meant it, or that it was his will; but that he was ignorant of how such words and actions were to be interpreted [emphasis added].

Again, we have mere life; but again, we seem to have a good deal more, specifically, a manner of living that is, one must presume, sufficiently comfortable or rewarding or otherwise satisfying such that one does not find it

[68] *Ibid.*, p. 116.
[69] *Ibid.*, p. 120.

unduly tiresome. Indeed, I think it plausible to infer from what Hobbes says that a life of unrelenting pain, of unbroken drudgery and oppression, of stupefying labor devoid of hope and meaning – such a wearying life, even if entirely safe and secure, would not be what individuals have in mind when they agree to the terms of the social contract.

The point is made once more at the beginning of chapter 30. There, Hobbes reiterates his view that the sovereign has been created for one and only one purpose, namely, to procure "the safety of the people." But once again, he is explicit in denying that this is merely a matter of preventing violent death: "by safety here, is not meant a bare preservation, but also all other contentments of life, which every man by lawful industry, without danger, or hurt to the commonwealth, shall acquire to himself."[70] Clearly, then, the aims of the social contract include the protection not just of life itself but of a happy life, hence of all those things – especially material possessions – that make contentment possible. It is for this reason, moreover, that Hobbes insists that certain rights cannot be contracted away, and that these include not only the right to self-defense from violence but also the right to "enjoy air, water, motion, ways to go from place to place" and, indeed, "all things else" that make it possible for humans not simply to live but to "live well."[71]

Now for Hobbes the bonds of the commonwealth dissolve when it fails to achieve the ends for which it was created. Individuals enter into mutual agreement with the understanding that the costs of doing so – the transfer of rights or powers – will be more than compensated by the benefits. If, however, the benefits are not forthcoming, then the terms of the contract have not been satisfied. The agreement has been violated and the contract itself is null and void. It no longer exists.

The point is outlined primarily in chapter 21 of *Leviathan*. There, Hobbes says that "every subject has liberty in all those things the right whereof cannot by covenant be transferred."[72] But what are those things? What rights cannot be transferred? Plainly the answer is to be found, as we have already seen, in chapter 14: one cannot transfer the rights to those things for which one covenanted in the first place. Otherwise, why covenant? If the purpose of the contract is, in part, the preservation of physical life, then it makes no sense to relinquish the right to defend one's physical life when, as a result of the contract, that life comes under threat; and if the purpose of the contract is not simply the preservation of physical life but the achievement of a relatively commodious, free and happy life,

[70] *Ibid.*, p. 322.
[71] *Ibid.*, p. 141.
[72] *Ibid.*, p. 204.

then again the failure of the state to provide such a life – through the imposition of "wounds or chains" or by otherwise "despoiling" the ends of the contract – frees the individual to pursue it independently, even if this means defying the powers that be.

One might be tempted to say that Hobbes has here defined the limits of political obligation. Indeed, this seems to be precisely Hampton's claim in describing the so-called "fallback position," according to which citizens can withdraw their power from the sovereign "whenever an expected-utility calculation tells them it is in their interest to do so."[73] But I think that such a claim cannot be correct, for it ignores the Hobbesian idea of the state itself. When the activity of the state fails to achieve or threatens, directly or indirectly, the ends for which it was created, hence when the costs of living in the state outweigh the benefits, then the terms of the contract are violated. But this means that the contract itself, hence the obligations entailed therein, dissolve. If I formally agree to give up some Y (e.g., a sum of money) for the purpose of receiving, and with the guarantee that I will receive, some X (e.g., a service) in exchange, and if it turns out that giving up Y actually has the opposite effect and destroys my chances of obtaining X, then surely the agreement is (ceteris paribus) null and void and I'm entitled to reacquire Y, if it all possible. And so too for the Hobbesian contract. When the state fails to do what it was designed to do – when it threatens, rather than protects, the interests of the citizens – then the social contract, i.e., the original agreement among the citizens, is annulled.

But what could this mean, other than that the state – whose very existence presupposes the contract – ceases to be a state? It is hard to know how else to make sense of the Hobbesian covenant. The authority of the state qua state is absolute and unlimited, hence the obligation of the citizen is equally absolute. But when the state fails to accomplish the things it was designed to accomplish – when, indeed, it subverts the very ends for which it was created – then the contract that the citizens had entered into with one another has now been abrogated, hence has been rendered null and void, in which case the state is literally no longer. The citizens are no longer citizens but are immediately plunged back into a condition of mere nature, and each individual is obliged only to maximize his or her interests as he or she determines. Individuals who defend their lives, liberty, property or other basic interests, as they are entitled and even obligated to do, are defending them not against a state but against some entity that claims to be but is not a state; for if that entity were a state, it would by definition be protecting rather than threatening those interests, as specified in the social contract

[73] Hampton, *Hobbes and the Social Contract Tradition*, p. 221.

that created the state in the first place; and this is true even if, as Hobbes indicates, the parties to the contract were the citizens themselves, rather than the sovereign.

Hobbes is pretty specific. He says, for example, that "[a] covenant not to defend myself from force, by force, is always void. For . . . no man can transfer, or lay down his right to save himself from death, wounds, and imprisonment, the avoiding wherof is the only end of laying down any right."[74] In other words, a covenant is invalid if it undermines the very purpose – the "only end" – for which it was made in the first place. And while the passage in question emphasizes the purpose or end of avoiding death, pain and incarceration, only a few lines later Hobbes similarly denies that a contractual obligation to testify in court means that one can be contractually obligated to testify against a loved one – or even a benefactor – if the result would bring "misery" to the testifier. In all such cases, the failure of the contract to achieve the ends for which it was made constitues "some new fact or other sign" that has arisen "after the covenant [was] made" and that renders the covenant "void."[75] Paying due attention to names and their consequences, we may say that a contract that turns out to undermine, rather than achieve, the goals for which it was created is a contradiction in terms, hence is no contract at all.

The abrogation of the contract – manifested in a failure to achieve the ends for which the contract was made in the first place – does indeed license the individual to disobey. But such disobedience in no way compromises the absolutism of the state, since the abrogation of the contract means that there is literally no longer a state. The nature of the entity that was the state has changed dramatically, its legitimacy gone. Again, the state's authority had rested entirely on the contract, on the act of sovereign authorization. The dissolution of the contract thus means the dissolution of authority; and a state without authority is, by definition, not a state at all but merely, at best, an entity that claims to be a state.

The close connection between the existence of a state and the fulfillment of its goals – between actualization and functionality – is routinely ignored by commentators. For example, Johnston writes that "Hobbes considers the desire to avoid death to be so reasonable that he regards it as a justifiable excuse for a subject to refuse his sovereign's command."[76] But if the citizen's life (or, indeed, well-being) is threatened, then the terms of the contract have been abrogated, which means that there is

[74] *Leviathan, EW*, vol. 3, p. 127.
[75] *Ibid.*, p. 125.
[76] Johnston, *The Rhetoric of Leviathan*, p. 100.

literally no sovereign; and if there is no sovereign, then the citizen cannot be refusing the sovereign's command. Martinich says that, for Hobbes, the "sovereign's authority is always in potential conflict with the subject's right of self-preservation . . . . Hobbes would abhor this consequence but, given his principles, it is not clear how he can avoid it."[77] If in the relevant circumstances, however, what was a sovereign is no longer a sovereign, then the conflict simply doesn't exist and there is no consequence for Hobbes to avoid. Baumgold tries to demonstrate Hobbes's consistency by arguing that the right to resist is "inconsequential in practice," meaning that the right can be exercised only by individuals in isolation and never by political groupings of individuals.[78] Such a contrivance is unnecessary, however, once we see that there is, in fact, no right to resist a sovereign. Tuck famously argues that Hobbes struggled unsuccessfully to reconcile a theory of natural rights and a theory of natural law, and that as a result his work was "essentially rather confused."[79] But this fails to take seriously the terms of the social contract itself, and the sense in which the contract, and everything that it has created, dissolves when the individual's well-being is put in peril. All of these writers, and the literature in general, have struggled to figure out how it's possible coherently to defend the individual's right to disobey an absolute sovereign. But due attention to the relevant "names" – contract, sovereign, state – and their consequences shows this to be a non-problem, for Hobbes defends no such right.

Absolutism and resistance thus coexist in Hobbes without the slightest contradiction. There are no "fallback" positions, no equivocations or qualifications or compromises, for none are needed. The right to resist is never a right to resist the state. There is no such right. The state's authority is absolute, and this means that the right to resist is and can only be a right against individuals or groups in the condition of nature. It is true that any number of individuals or groups – including some very powerful ones – may *claim* to be the state, hence may insist on an absolute right to be obeyed. But any such claim can be true only insofar as the ends for which a state might be instituted – a secure, commodious, free, non-wearying life – are realized. To the degree that they are not realized, a state does not exist; and in such a circumstance, resistance, far from being a crime, is rather an act of war.

[77] A. P. Martinich, *Thomas Hobbes* (New York: St. Martin's Press, 1997), p. 48.
[78] Baumgold, *Hobbes's Political Theory*, pp. 31–35.
[79] Tuck, *Natural Rights Theories*, pp. 129–32, 175.

3. To summarize: the Hobbesian right to resist – to self-defense – is by definition never a right to resist the state. The very circumstances that make self-defense necessary literally and immediately constitute the abrogation of the contract. And the abrogation of the contract means, literally and immediately, that the threatening entity must be something other than a state.

At first blush, such an account may seem little more than a matter of word-play. To resist a "non-state" – i.e., an entity that claims falsely to be a state – is, in practical terms, perhaps not much different from resisting a state that is corrupt or ineffective or that one simply doesn't like. But much more is involved here. To begin with, Hobbes's argument has the virtue of demonstrating that the very concept of the state itself does not allow for disobedience. What the state characteristically produces is law, and the claims of law *qua* law are by definition absolute, categorical and obligatory. In this sense, laws are sharply different from, say, mere suggestions or admonitions. The speed limit on the highway, the prohibition against murder, tax policies that require a percentage of income to be returned to the government, the First Amendment to the United States Constitution – such positive laws, understood as embodiments of the idea of law itself, are structurally and conceptually distinct from, say, the suggestion that one should be careful when crossing the street, or that one should be neither a borrower nor a lender, or that one should eat a balanced diet or lead a clean life or respect one's mother and father.[80] If an individual were free to decide that the law need not be obeyed according to his or her lights, and if the legitimacy of such a decision were to be enshrined as a general principle of individual action, then as a logical matter the question of whether or not the law will be obeyed would always be up to each and every person, acting more or less independently. In such a circumstance, law would cease to be law. It would become, instead, a kind of recommendation, and its status and character would change dramatically.

---

[80] It is true that a great many recommendations – especially the most plausible and widely held ones – would emerge out of and derive their plausibility from a society's shared structure of moral and metaphysical presupposition, hence would be in some important sense authoritative. But presumably the structure would also define them as what they are, recommendations rather than laws; and this means that they would be authoritatively understood to describe rules of behavior that make sense and should be followed, the violation of which, however, would not be punishable by the state. Of course, it would also be up to the state to decide when and if something that had been defined as a recommendation should indeed be redefined as a law, hence as something that one *must* obey. One society's suggestion might well be another society's requirement.

It may be, of course, that a society of recommendations rather than of laws could, *pace* Hobbes, function perfectly well. Theorists of anarchism have thought so. But such a society would not be state.

Now it seems plain that the actual existence of a particular state, hence of law, could well be a matter of some controversy. Imagine a regime that has lost much its ability to enforce the law. Whether through lack of physical resources or lack of will, it fails effectively to punish, hence to deter, law-breakers. To the extent that potential law-breakers learn that they may be able to violate the rights of others with impunity, they will be inclined to do so. Those whose rights have been violated will learn, in turn, that the state is unable to protect them, hence will be inclined to protect themselves, thereby violating the law in their own right. In Hobbesian terms, the degree to which all this occurs is the degree to which the state ceases to be a state and begins to approximate, instead, a condition of nature in which there is no political authority, no political obligation.

As a practical matter, of course, it is often difficult to know exactly where to draw the line. The difference between a state that is flawed but functioning and one that is utterly dysfunctional may be far from self-evident. But a distinction that is difficult to apply in practice does not thereby cease to be a distinction. Imagine, then, a condition of mere nature – a war of each against all – in which one of the warring parties is able to develop a predominance of physical force. Here there is no authority, no law. One party gets its way simply by coercing the others. In such a circumstance, the average individual who obeys the dominant power does so not out of a sense of political obligation – not because the dominant power has authority, for it has none – but simply because obedience is thought to be the safest choice; and whenever this ceases to be the case, whenever it seems both possible and profitable to disobey, then this is something that the individual is free to do, as he or she determines. But here again, the conceptual distinction between a dominant power on the one hand and an emergent state on the other will often be difficult to apply in practice. For insofar as a dominant power – a war-lord, a junta, a private army, a cabal, a majority faction – begins to provide genuine security and satisfaction, it may start to look more and more like a state, albeit perhaps a "tyrannical" one; and to that degree, whether tyrannical or not, it may be able to claim with increasing plausibility that it deserves, on moral grounds, the respect and allegiance of those it rules.[81]

---

[81] For a relevant historical/empirical discussion, see Charles Tilly, "War Making and State Making as Organized Crime," in *Bringing the State Back In*, ed. Peter B. Evans, Dietrich Rueschemeyer and Theda Skocpol (Cambridge: Cambridge University Press, 1985), pp. 172–83.

At this point, an obvious problem seems to arise, for surely it's possible that a Hobbesian state could threaten me – my physical life and my opportunities for commodious living – but may pose no such threat to you. Perhaps the paradigm case occurs when I am accused, rightly or wrongly, of criminal behavior, as a result of which the state threatens to punish me, while no such accusation, hence no such threat, hangs over your head. Is the state, then, really a state? The problem has long plagued readers of Hobbes, but the logic of his idea of the state in fact provides a straightforward and, I think, highly plausible solution. In the circumstance described, the contract has been abrogated for me whereas for you it has not, my obligations are now dissolved while yours are still in force, and I find myself plunged back into the condition of mere nature while you are still living comfortably in political society. The entity that threatens me is, at best, a dominant power in the state of nature, something to which I have no obligation whatsoever, while the entity that protects you – the very same entity – is a state, something to be obeyed absolutely and unquestioningly. I see nothing to debar such a solution and, indeed, much to recommend it. The social contract is an agreement among the citizens in which each acts as an individual, and there's no reason to doubt that an agreement of this kind might work out for some of the citizens and not for others. The upshot is that the *legitimacy* of a state can never be in dispute. The state must always be obeyed, its authority absolute. But the actual *existence* of a state can be, and often is, a matter of the most intense dispute, since the terms of the contract can be violated for some and not for others. Context and individual circumstance matter a great deal, and it may be that much of political history involves, above all, disagreements as to whether or not one is actually living in a state, properly conceived.[82]

With such an account in mind, we can make sense of any number of passages in Hobbes that would otherwise be troubling. Hampton, for example, cites two well-known passages that seem entirely to contradict one another.[83] According to the first,

---

[82] It is here, moreover, that we can make sense of certain seemingly odd locutions in Hobbes's text. He does talk, for example, of an individual being "compelled to do a fact against the Law" or of otherwise resisting the "state" and "sovereign." How can we account for such formulations in light of the argument that a law that threatens a man's life and well-being is no law, a sovereign that necessitates self-defense no sovereign? Surely the answer is that in many particular circumstances an individual may be threatened by, hence have a right to resist, entities that are, for other, non-threatened individuals, states and sovereigns indeed and that, as a result, can be coherently referred to in that way.

[83] Hampton, *Hobbes and the Social Contract Tradition*, p. 241.

[It] is annexed to the sovereignty, the whole power of prescribing the rules, whereby every man may know, what goods he may enjoy, and what actions he may do . . . . These rules of propriety, or *meum* and *tuum*, and of *good, evil, lawful,* and *unlawful* in the actions of subjects are the civil laws.[84]

The second, on the other hand, says that

By a good law, I mean not a just law: for no law can be unjust. The law is made by the sovereign power, and all that is done by such power, is warranted, and owned by every one of the people; and that which every man will have so, no man can say is unjust . . . . A good law is that, which is *needful*, for the *good of the people*, and withal *perspicuous*.[85]

As Hampton sees it, "[w]hereas in the earlier chapter the sovereign was the sole judge of what was good or bad, in the later chapter Hobbes is admitting that there is a standard for evaluating law independent of the sovereign . . . . And because no sovereign legislator is going to say that some of her laws are bad, the judges of the goodness or badness of the laws must be the subjects."[86] But we can now see that there is, in fact, no contradiction whatsoever. In the earlier chapter, Hobbes merely states the obvious, that anything properly called "law" is, by definition, just and authoritative, that the sovereign, properly so conceived, is the sole source of law, and that the obligation to obey the law is absolute. In the later chapter, Hobbes first restates this – the law is made by the sovereign and is always "warranted" – but then indicates what is also obvious, that some putative laws are not wise or well-crafted, hence fail to achieve the ends for which they were formulated. The laws or "rules of propriety" do indeed determine what is officially deemed to be good or evil action on the part of subjects. But the law can make mistakes about this. What it deems to be a good action may actually turn out to have evil consequences; and if such consequences are, in fact, so evil as to undermine the purposes of the original contract, then again the contract is abrogated, obligation dissolves, and the sovereign is no longer. We can thus see that Hobbes's prudential advice to govern well does not contradict but, in fact, is consistent with and even underwritten by his theory of sovereignty.

Similarly, Schrock finds a sharp contradiction between two passages in chapter 28. According to the first of these,

[i]n the making of a commonwealth, every man giveth away the right of defending another; but not of defending himself. Also he obligeth himself, to assist him that hath the sovereignty, in the punishing of another; but of himself not. But to

---

[84] *Leviathan, EW*, vol. 3, p. 165.
[85] *Ibid.*, p. 335.
[86] Hampton, *Hobbes and the Social Contract Tradition*, p. 241.

covenant to assist the sovereign, in doing hurt to another, unless he that so covenanteth have a right to do it himself, is not to give him a right to punish. It is manifest therefore that the right which the commonwealth, that is, he, or they that represent it, hath to punish, is not grounded on any concession, or gift of the subjects. But I have also showed formerly, that before the institution of common-wealth, everyman had a right to every thing, and to do whatsoever he thought necessary to his own preservation; subduing, hurting, or killing any man in order thereunto. And this is the foundation of that right of punishing, which is exercised in every commonwealth. For the subjects did not give the sovereign that right; but only in laying down theirs, strengthened him to use his own, as he should think fit, for the preservation of them all: so that it was not given, but left to him, and to him only."[87]

But shortly thereafter, Hobbes also says that

the evil inflicted by usurped power, and judges without authority from the sover-eign, is not punishment; but an act of hostility; because the acts of power usurped, have not for author, the person condemned; and therefore are not acts of public authority.[88]

According to Schrock, "[w]ithin the space of four paragraphs... [Hobbes] both says that [the citizen] *cannot*, and yet also assumes that he *can*, authorize his own punishment."[89] But again, we can now see that there is no contradiction. The first passage hinges on the distinction between hurting and punishing. To hurt is to inflict evil; to punish is to inflict evil legally, i.e., through civil law. Individuals in the state of nature do not have the right to punish since law does not yet exist; and lacking such a right, they cannot very well transfer it to the sovereign. They do, however, have a right to hurt other people; and in renouncing this right, they empower the sovereign to do whatever is necessary to keep the peace, including punishment. Thus, the right to punish is not explicitly trans-ferred in the contract, but it is fully authorized by the contract. The second passage simply indicates that the powers of the sovereign, which the sovereign can use to impose punishments if desired, must be rooted in contractual obligations undertaken by all the citizens, each of whom might well become the target of punishment. Again, those obligations authorize the sovereign to keep the peace, and the sovereign must be obeyed until and unless the individual citizen determines that the "acts of power" in question are such as to undermine the goals for which the citizen contracted in the first place, at which point the contract has been

---

[87] *Leviathan*, *EW*, vol. 3, p. 298.

[88] *Ibid.*

[89] Thomas S. Schrock, "The Rights to Punish and Resist Punishment in Hobbes's *Leviathan*," 44 *Western Political Quarterly* (December 1991), p. 861.

abrogated and the sovereign ceases to be the sovereign, at least for that particular citizen.

4. It may be doubted, however, that the distinction I have drawn between an authentic state on the one hand and a dominant power in the condition of mere nature on the other could truly be Hobbesian. Again, Hobbes insists that there is no important difference between a legitimate state and a tyrannical one, that obedience is always rooted in fear, that obligation is fundamentally a matter of pragmatic calculation, and that sovereignty by conquest is no less legitimate than sovereignty by institution. He insists, further, that one of the defining features of the state of nature is the rough equality of power, which is at least part of what makes nature so dangerous. Given all of this, why would a dominant power be any different from a state? Wouldn't the emergence of such a power, hence of inequality, effectively end the condition of nature? How would such a circumstance be different from the case of sovereignty by conquest?

It seems that the state is an entity that either fulfills the terms of the social contract or, in the case of conquest, provides the kinds of benefits for which such a contract might be instituted. Again, it provides opportunities for physical security and for a life sufficiently commodious and comfortable as not to be excessively wearying. Thus, all states are originally established – either through express or tacit consent, either contractually or through conquest – for purely pragmatic reasons, and are sustained, in part, by the power of the sovereign to determine and enforce the law. What this means, I think, is that the citizen is motivated to obey the sovereign by a kind of double fear – fear of being punished for breaking the law and fear of being plunged back into the dangerous condition of mere nature.

But fear is a complicated thing. I myself am not too crazy about heights. The thought of standing on a narrow ledge high above the ground, or of sky-diving, or of bungee-jumping makes me afraid. It fills me with fear; and as a result of this fear, I always make a point of trying to stay as close to terra firma as possible. Sitting here in my ground-floor office, I feel perfectly safe and secure; but this doesn't change the fact that I have, at the very same time, a morbid fear of heights. Surely, though, fear of this kind is very different from the fear that I would have if, say, my loan-shark held me by my ankles and dangled me from a window on the twentieth floor of a skyscraper. In the first case, the fear is hypothetical. *If* I were standing on a narrow ledge high above the ground – which I am not – then I *would be* terrified. In the second case, on the other hand, the fear is immediate. I *am* dangling from the twentieth floor and I *am* terrified.

In the Hobbesian state of nature, fear is immediate. The individual is constantly and perpetually at risk. Violent death or other forms of victimization loom around every corner. A life lived in the state of nature is a life lived on the edge. Once the state has been established, on the other hand, the citizen's fear becomes merely hypothetical. What the citizen seeks is security, and this presumably means enjoying the kind of peace of mind that comes from knowing that one's life, liberty and comfort are not inordinately at risk, that one's fears are largely and merely hypothetical. Such an existence would be very different from one lived in perpetual immediate fear. Any citizen must, of course, be afraid of breaking the law, but he or she also must feel relatively confident that such fear is merely hypothetical, hence that obedience – not breaking the law – will indeed produce safety. In effect, the individual must be afraid to disobey, but not to obey, the law; for if that were not the case – if obedience produced immediate and not merely hypothetical fear – then obedience wouldn't make any sense.

The implications of this are several. First, if fear is to be merely hypothetical rather than immediate, then the citizen needs to have good reason to believe that law-abidingness will be rewarded. He or she must be confident that the decision to accept the authority of the law will provide in a relatively predictable way the kind of benefit that one expects from a state, viz., freedom from immediate fear. This means, among other things, that the law must be reasonably well known and comparatively stable. After all, the citizen cannot obey the law reliably without being pretty certain that his or her actions are indeed in conformity with it and will be interpreted as such by those whose job it is to enforce it – something that is impossible if the law is promulgated and applied in secret, or if it changes without warning or for no discernible reason. And from this it follows, further, that the procedures by which particular positive laws are both produced and enforced must be relatively orderly, systematic, institutionalized and public. They cannot be capricious, ephemeral or irrational; for if they were, one could never be certain about the law, never certain about what it would mean to obey the law, never certain about whether or not one will be punished for obeying what one takes to be the law, hence never free from immediate, as opposed to hypothetical, fear.

These stipulations serve sharply to distinguish a state from a dominant power. The difference manifests itself in the behavior and motivation of private individuals. When the law is established and enforced according to a kind of due process – and whether or not the state exists by institution or conquest – the individual citizen obeys unquestioningly, provided, of course, that the law is generally effective in providing security, liberty and comfort. Such a law is legitimate and carries the state's absolute authority. It may be inconvenient, unwise, unpopular, even painful at times. As such, it may legitimately become the focus of political disagreement, dissent, protest. But insofar as it is produced by a state that generally provides security, comfort, liberty and satisfaction, the inconvenience and pain must in the end be borne with equanimity. In such a circumstance, one is indeed afraid of the sovereign – afraid to disobey – but such fear is merely hypothetical. On the other hand, when the dominant power operates not through consistent, recognizable and rational procedures but capriciously, inconsistently and irrationally, the individual can never feel secure and confident. The fear is immediate. One obeys the dominant power not in the sense of participating in and taking advantage of a stable, institutionalized structure of expectations that provides the kinds of benefits states are supposed to provide. Rather, one lives by one's wits, obeying entirely on a case-by-case basis. There is no predictability, no sense of security or reliability, hence no foundation for obligation or authority. To be sure, the result need not be open war. On this score, Hobbes is clear: "[t]he nature of war, consisteth not in actual fighting; but in the known disposition thereto, during all the time there is no assurance to the contrary."[90] But the absence of fighting suggests only that the individual has evaluated each separate demand that the dominant power has made, and has decided, because of immediate fear, to acquiesce. If it's safer, freer, more comfortable and commodious to obey this time, then I obey; but if not, then I don't. In effect, each demand that the dominant power makes is a kind of recommendation. It is a suggestion that the individual act in a certain way, underwritten by the immediate threat of negative consequences if the suggestion is not followed; and like any suggestion, it is something that the individual follows or doesn't according to his or her lights.

As a practical matter, such an account is best conceptualized in terms of a continuum. For at least some people some of the time, even a good state is more an enemy than a friend; and if one were to deny this, one still cannot deny that the benefits provided by the state always come with costs that need to be monitored and evaluated. Analogously, rare is the dominant power that doesn't provide some rewards to some substantial portion of the populace. It is hardly unusual, moreover, for the activities of such a power to become normalized over time, to acquire some of the regularity and routine that we associate with responsible organization, hence to develop at least the rudiments of what might plausibly be called due process. History shows that just as states can collapse into chaos and disorder, so too can dominant powers evolve into secure and stable instruments of law.

[90] *Leviathan, EW*, vol. 3, p. 113.

For private individuals, the result is a kind of recurrent and episodic existential challenge. The question of the state must be, in the end, a matter of either/or. Each person presumably has to decide whether or not the terms of the social contract are being satisfied. Each, in other words, has to decide if the benefits of obedience outweigh the costs, if the entity that claims to be the state makes the individual sufficiently happy – providing a secure and commodious existence, one that is not oppressively wearying – so as to compensate for the inevitable inconvenience of the law. We cannot have it both ways. Either the putative law of the state is law indeed, in which case it must be obeyed without fail, or else it is merely a set of recommendations, to be followed or not as the individual sees fit, in which case it is no different from the kinds of admonitions, warnings or threats that one might well encounter in a cooperative/anarchist society or, as Hobbes would have it, in a condition of mere nature.[91]

Frequently, we choose to obey the law unquestioningly and simply because it is the law, and we continue to do so without reflection, as a matter of habit and implicit conviction born, in Hobbes's view, of hypothetical fear. But we also reserve the right to revisit that conviction, should circumstances require. If we begin to realize that a practice of unthinking obedience is doing more harm than good, if the security and satisfaction that we expect from political society begins to dissolve, if for whatever reason the state begins to threaten rather than protect life and happiness, then the question arises as to whether the contract has been abrogated, hence whether the state is really a state and the law is really the law. When such questions arise for the single person – whether it be an ordinary criminal or a conscientious objector, a villain or a saint – and presuming those questions are answered in a certain way, we have then the basis for individual resistance. When the same questions arise for large groups of people, and again presuming a certain kind of response, we have the basis for a fully-fledged theory of revolution – a revolution not against the state but against an entity that has ceased to be a state, if in fact it ever was one. While Hobbes doesn't explicitly talk about revolution, I see nothing in his theory to debar it. To the contrary: the contract having been abrogated,

---

[91] The distinction is well established in the popular mind. For example: "As the Russian Army closes in on Chechnya's besieged capital, Grozny, it is using a fresh strategy: promising Chechens that their bedraggled towns will be spared a relentless bombardment if they surrender, and attempting to secure loyalty by restoring services like gas and electricity. But this month's capture of Gudermes, the bleak but strategically important second largest city in Chechnya, shows that it is one thing to scare Chechen civilians into submission, and quite another to win their allegiance" (Michael R. Gordon, "In Occupied Chechnya, Order Without Allegiance," *New York Times*, 22 November 1999, p. 1).

hence voided, it would be perfectly acceptable and entirely natural for individuals to defend themselves by banding together.

It seems clear, to be sure, that Hobbes would counsel his readers to exercise the revolutionary option only with the greatest imaginable caution. The condition of nature is so dehumanizing, the breakdown of authority so cataclysmic, the war of each against all so dangerous and debasing – so immediately frightening – as to provide the strongest possible incentive to accept things as they are, hence to give the benefit of the doubt to whatever entity claims to be a state. And insofar as such an entity has real power to inflict (*inter alia* death, wounds and imprisonment, the individual, who "by nature chooses the lesser evil," is less likely – indeed, highly unlikely – to believe that resistance is less dangerous than non-resistance. But the logic of Hobbes's position absolutely requires that such a strategy has its limits. In order to avoid being plunged into a condition of mere nature, the individual may be forced to accept with equanimity an extraordinary number and variety of inconveniences; this simply comes with the territory. But when the costs of passivity outweigh the benefits, then all bets are off.[92]

5. The theory of resistance and revolution, though formulated in the light of Hobbesian contractarianism, in fact applies regardless of how we understand the foundations of political obligation. To reject the idea of the social contract, as I think we must, is not to reject the basic logic of authority and obedience. If a state exists, then its authority is absolute. If resistance becomes, for whatever reason, morally necessary, then this means that the state itself has ceased to function as – has ceased to be – a state.

---

[92] One may well wonder why Hobbes's language does not more straightforwardly invite the kind of interpretation I have offered. In a sense, this is a historical, biographical or even literary question, hence beyond the scope of the present work. But a couple of observations may be hazarded. To begin with, the contexts in which Hobbes wrote – a time of violent civil upheaval – may well have encouraged him to emphasize certain features of his account (e.g., absolutism) rather than others. One need not subscribe to a strong distinction between esoteric and exoteric texts to believe that some authors take pains to produce works designed to have a salutary influence on the majority of readers. Hobbes may have wanted to encourage obedience and acquiescence, but from this it doesn't follow that his teaching is, at the core, as one-sided or, indeed, simplistic as some have assumed.

But further, it's not entirely clear just how inexplicit Hobbes's formulation is. The standard reading attributes to him an egregious contradiction. It may never have occurred to him that his readers would go in that direction by overlooking the logical implications of the abrogation of the contract. More generally, to reject my account is, it would seem, to presuppose that Hobbes – certainly one of the half-dozen or so greatest political theorists and a philosopher of unusual learning and acuity – could have made the kind of massive and self-apparent mistake that wouldn't be accepted in an ordinary doctoral dissertation, or in a book such as this. That's hardly an appealing proposition.

However construed, the obligation to obey the law is, as we have seen, derived from the underlying conceptual apparatus that tells us what we ought to do, hence whether we ought to accept benefits, feel gratitude, and exhibit other behaviors and attitudes from which the obligation itself is derived. The result may seem to be a kind of paradox. After all, we have described the state as essentially the authoritative embodiment of a society's collective understanding of how things in the world really are. If, on the basis of that understanding, we are to conclude that the state is not a state, then it would seem that the state is telling us authoritatively that it is not a state, hence has no authority – which is tantamount to saying that the state does and does not exist at the same time.

In fact, there is no paradox. At least two possibilities present themselves. On the one hand, some of the citizens of a state might come to believe, in the light of shared metaphysical understandings, that established and entrenched instrumentalities of government no longer function effectively, that these failures are due not primarily to the particular qualities of individuals holding particular offices but are essentially and deeply struc-tural in nature, hence that the instrumentalities in question need to be fundamentally reconfigured or replaced. To the degree that conclusions of this kind are widely shared, the revolution could be bloodless; to the degree that some citizens disagree – i.e., they interpret the society's structure of truth differently, hence derive from it different implications – the result could be, and very often is, internal war. But in either case, the upshot would be a kind of governmental revolution in which the state itself remains essentially intact while its instrumentalities are first destroyed and then rebuilt.

On the other hand, it may be that the underlying structure of truth itself becomes the issue. Every complex society is beset by serious disagreements about how things in the world really are. As we have seen, such disagree-ments may be tolerable insofar as they occur within the context of, hence are leavened by, an even more fundamental structure of consensus. But when the latter itself starts to disintegrate, then the state as such begins to unravel. Each group of individuals begins to consult its own version of how things in the world really are; each comes to decide for itself, therefore, which claims are authoritative and which are not; each arrives at separate conclusions about what the state truly is; hence each develops a unique view of who is politically obligated to whom. The result is, variously, the gradual or sudden disintegration of society into a kind of chaos that produces, in turn, a social – rather than merely governmental – revolution wherein opposing forces battle each other over the very foundations of society.

Distinctions of this kind do not map neatly on to the world of affairs. If the Glorious Revolution or the American Revolution were more like governmental revolutions, if the French Revolution or the Russian Revolution were more like social revolutions, this is hardly to deny that the former reflected powerful and deep-seated social conflicts or that the latter involved substantial continuities from pre- to post-revolutionary periods. Similarly, the difference between a genuine revolution, whether governmental or social, and a serious but non-revolutionary process of reform is, like the difference between red and orange, relatively clear at the core but increasingly blurry at the periphery. If it's easy enough to distinguish, say, the end of British colonialism in the United States from the end of British colonialism in Canada, other cases – the end of British colonialism in India, perhaps – are not so easily categorized. Moreover, it is important to remember that the outcome of any revolutionary process may itself be arguable. Did the French (or Russian) Revolution establish a new state, or did it merely replace a state with a dominant power in the condition of mere nature? Once again, the answer can only be a matter of historical interpretation and will likely reflect, among other things, the essentially Hobbesian insight that one person's legitimate state might be another person's gang of hoodlums.

In all cases, though, the larger theoretical point remains the same. The state is a structure of intelligibility – the embodiment of collective notions of how things in the world really are – that stands as an absolute authority to which all citizens are obligated, but does so only to the degree that it is able to maintain its coherence, its plausibility, and its close connection with what the citizens themselves actually believe. Again, this presents the individual with a rather stark either/or decision. Either a state exists, in which case obedience is obligatory and absolute, or else it does not exist, in which case the idea of political obligation becomes an absurdity.

As we have seen, the reasons leading up to an either/or outcome of this kind are not likely to be simple, unequivocal or obvious. In any particular case, for any particular individual, there may be good reasons both to affirm and deny the obligation to the state. Our job – the job of each citizen – is to weigh those reasons, and to determine on which side lies the preponderance of evidence. Thus, as indicated above, participation in political institutions and acceptance of the resulting benefits is generally a matter of degree. While most of us participate at least to some extent, most of us also distance ourselves from the political process in important ways and certainly receive a great deal of benefit only passively. Most of us thus seek consciously or otherwise to maintain some level of personal and moral independence; and insofar as participation and acceptance are connected to consent, we must say that such consent is implied more or less clearly, hence can be imputed to the individual citizen with more or less justice. Have I participated in the political process to such an extent, and have I actively accepted enough benefits, that it can correctly be said of me that I am morally obligated to the state? Is the gratitude that I should feel sufficient to require me morally to obey the law because it is the law? As a moral matter, the grounds for obligation must always be evaluated in the light of various considerations that may well cut in both directions.

The philosophy of the state, of course, cannot resolve for us the question of whether or not actually to resist. Such a question is a matter of policy or government rather than philosophy, to be decided on prudential grounds and on the basis of historical and other empirical data. As such, it is a recurrent and ever-present, if often only latent, part of the human condition. One cannot read a good newspaper, for example, without becoming aware of the fact that the theoretical continuum having the state at one end and something like the state of nature at the other is teeming with real cases. At any given moment, large numbers of people are forced to confront the most painful ambiguity, uncertain as to whether their regime is truly a state or merely a dominant power, whether the short-term inconveniences that come from obedience should be endured in the hope that long-term benefits will follow, whether their society is evolving into a more stable, more secure political state or, to the contrary, mired in seemingly endless and hopeless patterns of capriciousness, corruption and abuse. But while the idea of the state cannot answer these questions, it remains an absolutely indispensable part of the task. For it is only by considering what a state itself is that one can know what kinds of questions to ask in the first place.

6. The problem of civil disobedience

According to the standard account, civil disobedience is "a public, non-violent, conscientious yet political act contrary to the law usually done with the aim of bringing about a change in the law or policies of the government."[93] It is, as such, sharply different both from ordinary criminal behavior, which is done not for any moral reasons but solely out of self-interest, and from outright resistance or revolution, the purpose of which is not to change a law or policy but to undermine either that which claims to be the state – whose claims the revolutionary denies – or else the structure of government through which the state purports to act. Within the broad category of non-revolutionary disobedience, however, we may also wish to differentiate (1) conscientious evasion, wherein the law-breaker acts

---

[93] Rawls, *A Theory of Justice*, p. 364.

out of moral conviction, but seeks to do so in such a way as to escape detection and punishment, (2) conscientious refusal, in which the motive for breaking the law is moral but the goal is not to change the law, and (3) civil disobedience standardly conceived, which is similar to conscientious refusal except that the goal is precisely to change the law.[94] Obviously, (1), (2) and (3) are alike in that the individual acts primarily on the basis of moral, albeit non-revolutionary, considerations. But there is a further and absolutely crucial distinction to be made. Sometimes, conscientious evasion, refusal or disobedience reflects, as does (some) revolutionary behavior, a denial of the authority of that which claims to be the state – though it reflects as well a decision to eschew, presumably for prudential reasons, open warfare. There is nothing remotely mysterious about such behavior. It is what one would expect from an individual who finds him- or herself in a condition of mere nature but who has no stomach for active revolution. In other cases, though, individuals evade, refuse or disobey while nonetheless claiming to accept the authority of the state. Here we have what is often thought to be civil disobedience in the narrow but, by now, most widely accepted sense;[95] and this is something that certainly seems to be mysterious indeed. Individual civil disobedients recognize the state's legitimacy – i.e., the claims that the state makes for itself – hence acknowledge and accept their own moral obligation to obey the law. But they disobey anyway.

Is it possible to formulate a coherent justification for such behavior? This is an old and uncommonly difficult question, but I believe that it becomes somewhat less difficult if it is viewed explicitly in the light of the idea of the state.

1. The justification of civil disobedience typically involves a kind of Rossian argument. The moral claims of the state are indeed authoritative, for anything that the state demands of us is something that we ought – have an obligation – to do. But any such ought/obligation can only be a prima facie (PF), not an absolute, one. It can in principle be overridden.

---

[94] Here I follow Feinberg, rather than Rawls. See Feinberg, *Freedom and Fulfillment*, pp. 153–57. I generally use the term civil disobedience to refer to what Feinberg calls civil disobedience in "the narrow sense." For Rawls's somewhat different account of conscientious refusal, see *A Theory of Justice*, pp. 368–71.

[95] For Rawls, civil disobedience involves citizens who "recognize and accept" the legitimacy of the constitution (*ibid.*, p. 363) and who maintain, but are at the boundary of, "fidelity to law" (*ibid.*, pp. 366–67). Of course, Rawls's discussion of civil disobedience is limited to the case of a "nearly just society" involving "legitimately established democratic authority" (*ibid.*, p. 363). While this influences certain features of his justification of civil disobedience, his larger argument would seem to be applicable, *mutatis mutandis*, wherever the potential disobedient accepts the authority of the state.

When the civil disobedient disobeys, therefore, this presumably occurs because of some higher or prior claim that outweighs the claims of the state.[96]

Again, the account can be evaluated meaningfully only in light of the distinction between the idea of the state, on the one hand, and the instrumentalities of the state, on the other. In formulating and promulgating the law, the state naturally works through its several agencies. This means that the law properly understood manifests itself in the particular enactments of appropriate government bodies – legislative, administrative, judicial. It is, of course, primarily from these that citizens derive concrete and tangible information as to what the law actually requires. Thus, the practical upshot of the state's authority is that citizens have an obligation to obey what is often called "positive" law, i.e., the explicit instructions, limitations, prohibitions and empowerments that are contained variously in particular ordinances, statutes, regulations and judicial opinions.

Presumably the civil disobedient understands such positive laws to constitute PF oughts/obligations that can be outweighed or overridden by other considerations. There are, however, a number of problems with such a position. To begin with, it is hard to see how it does real justice to the idea that the state is, indeed, in authority. If the civil disobedient truly acknowledges the authority of the state, then this would seem necessarily to involve two things: accepting an obligation to obey the law because it is the law and accepting the state's own account of what it is that makes the law obligatory. Without the latter, the obligation to obey the law would be based, at least in part, on something external to the state – e.g., religious authority, prudential calculation, etc. – the force of which would be actually to deny the state's authority. For in such a circumstance, the individual would be obeying the law not because of the state's authority but because his or her bible or priest or accountant or legal adviser said so. If, then, the civil disobedient really believes in the authority of the state, this means obeying the law because the state says so and according to the state's own form of reasoning; and from the state's point of view, disobedience of any kind – even the most principled – cannot be allowed. Again, the law is not

---

[96] Richard A. Wasserstrom, "The Obligation to Obey the Law," *UCLA Law Review* 10 (1962–63), pp. 780–807. Though primarily concerned to refute absolutist views of political obligation (pp. 782–83), Wasserstrom also purports to raise doubts about the idea that citizens have a prima facie obligation to obey the law. In large part, however, he refutes the absolutist view by relying, often explicitly, on the prima facie view (see pp. 788, 790, 793, 798, 800–2).

I believe that the Rossian approach is implicit in Rawls's attempt to explain how we resolve the "conflict of duties" (*A Theory of Justice*, p. 363) that civil disobedience involves.

conceived of as a set of practical recommendations or moral admonitions to be accepted or rejected by the individual according to his or her lights. It is intended to be obligatory and binding, hence does not allow for individual choice. It must be obeyed.[97] The idea that some higher principle may simply override it is deeply at odds with the most basic and definitive claims of the state itself.

What could it mean, then, to acknowledge the authority of the state without accepting those claims? How can one recognize the legitimacy of the state as the state understands it while at the same time insisting on the right to disobey? The civil disobedient finds him- or herself in a contradiction. On the one hand, to insist that laws are merely PF claims is to deny the kind of authority that the state claims for itself; to acknowledge and accept the authority of the state, on the other hand, is precisely to deny that its laws are merely PF claims.

Historically, one response has been to argue that there really is no contradiction here provided that the civil disobedient willingly accepts his or her punishment.[98] In disobeying, the individual makes an important moral point; in accepting punishment, he or she acknowledges the state's authority. It is doubtful, though, that such an approach can work, since from the perspective of the state an act of disobedience followed by willing acceptance of punishment is only marginally better than ordinary crime. The important point is that punishment itself, whether designed to deter or to exact retribution, cannot erase the fact that the crime occurred, hence rarely if ever can undo the damage that the crime caused. The murder victim cannot be brought back to life, no matter how severely the murderer is punished; the burglary victim's peace of mind can be restored, if at all, only over time and with the greatest effort.

Of course, it is in part for this reason that Rawls and others insist that civil disobedience can be justified only if it is non-violent.[99] But it is hard to see how such a limitation solves the problem. After all, non-violent crimes cause genuine, albeit non-physical, harm, and even the most exacting policy of reparation and recompense is unlikely to eliminate or undo such harm in its entirety and complexity. The victim of, say, fraud may be able to recover his money, but can he recover from the psychological scars, the sense of betrayal, the perhaps unreasonable fears and the questionable,

---

[97] Obviously, this presupposes that the individual has already made those prior choices – e.g., accepting benefits, participating in institutional practices, etc. – from which the fact of political obligation itself derives.

[98] For example, Sidney Hook, *The Paradoxes of Freedom* (Berkeley: University of California Press, 1964), pp. 106–39. Rawls agrees: civil disobedience involves a "willingness to accept the legal consequences of one's conduct" (*A Theory of Justice*, p. 366).

[99] Rawls, *A Theory of Justice*, pp. 366–67.

overly cautious approach to life that he might also have suffered? Fraud, to be sure, is hardly likely to be an act of civil disobedience; but if one kind of non-violent crime can cause serious, even irreversible harm, then why not others? Rawls himself seems to rule out any type of militant action or "obstruction," or anything else that might "interfere with the civil liberties of others."[100] But what, then, would he include? He mentions – though only in passing – breaking traffic ordinances and laws of trespass. Even such laws, however, are designed, correctly or incorrectly, to reduce the chances of harm, and this means that from the perspective of the state their violation cannot in principle be entirely inconsequential. Thus, for example, when hundreds of motorists disrupted traffic in Miami, Florida for several hours to protest the United States government's decision to return a six-year-old refugee to his father in Cuba, we can guess that at least some individuals and businesses suffered a range and variety of negative consequences – emotional, financial, and the like. As a result of the protest, moreover, tempers flared, and several individuals, including at least one police officer, were injured when careless, frustrated drivers sought to circumvent the disruption.[101] More generally, an increase in the mere probability that some harm will occur is itself a consequence, even if in particular cases actual harm is avoided.

Beyond this, the perceived efficacy of the state itself is necessarily weakened to the degree that it fails to forestall, rather than simply respond to, illegal behavior. It is in part for this reason that the law is not typically formulated as a simple quid pro quo. It does not say that criminal behavior is perfectly okay provided that the criminal accepts the punishment. To the contrary, it insists that certain kinds of behavior are simply unacceptable and must be avoided. It does so independent of any contemplated punishment; and punishment itself – whether conceived in terms of deterrence or retribution – is perhaps best understood as a socially necessary response to what can only be thought of as a political failure, i.e., the inability of the state to achieve universal compliance simply on its own account.

It is certainly true that a criminal who breaks the law for moral rather than selfish reasons and who seeks to embrace rather than to evade punishment is different from an ordinary criminal. The difference is largely one of motive, and motive, of course, is hardly unimportant; for insofar as crimes themselves are defined, in part, in terms of aims and intentions, a civil disobedient may be guilty of offenses that are different from, and often less serious than, offenses committed by ordinary

---

[100] *Ibid.*
[101] *New York Times*, 7 January 2000, p. 1.

miscreants. But this in itself does not in any way change the basic fact that crimes committed from the best of motives are crimes nonetheless.

Rawls attempts to deal with the "conflict of duties" in another way, by justifying civil disobedience only when it occurs at the "outer edge" or the "boundary of fidelity to law."[102] Presumably, disobedience not at the outer edge could not be justified. But the distinction is, at best, murky. There can be little doubt that some cases of disobedience are more serious than others; and it is equally certain that the evidence that disobedience has actually occurred is sometimes clear, sometimes not. If, however, civil disobedience truly involves a kind of contradiction, then this will be so whether or not the crime is a serious one; and if it's not always easy to tell whether or not a crime has been committed, hence not always easy to tell whether or not civil disobedience has occurred, this obviously says nothing one way or another about whether or not the idea of civil disobedience itself is coherent.

2. Perhaps, then, the idea of civil disobedience is really different from what we have said. Specifically, it may be that while civil disobedience presumes an obligation to obey the law, it does not do so on the state's own grounds. The fact that the state, through its governmental instrumentalities, has produced a law provides, in and of itself, a good reason for believing that the law ought to be obeyed, all things considered. But the reason need not be the one that the state thinks it is; and this would suggest that the obligation is not absolute. The requirements of the law count as PF obligations, i.e., obligations that have considerable moral weight but that can be overridden by other considerations. Thus, any "conflict of duties" that we might encounter is resolved simply by determining which duty is most urgent or otherwise carries the most weight.

As should already be clear, I believe that such a view does not really involve an acceptance of the state's legitimate authority. It reserves for the individual the right to pick and choose when to obey the law, hence conceives of the law not as law *per se* but as a set of recommendations or admonitions – albeit important ones – to be evaluated by the individual according to his or her lights. Still, might this not be a coherent position? Does it not resolve the apparent contradiction in civil disobedience without entirely sacrificing the moral relevance of the political regime?

I think the answer is no, though the failures of such a view are especially instructive. The operative question is this: given an apparent conflict of duties, how do we decide which duty should take precedence? It seems to

[102] Rawls, *A Theory of Justice*, pp. 366–67.

me that only two answers are possible. Either we have a theory of some kind, based presumably on our larger structure of presupposition, that explains – however provisionally or tentatively – why one duty outweighs the other; or else we have no such theory, hence no such explanation, in which case our choice could not be other than unreasonable, unaccountable and random, essentially a matter of flipping a coin.

In the former case, our theory describes what might be thought of as a meta-duty. If we have a duty A and a conflicting duty B, and if we decide on moral grounds that B takes precedence over A, then this is simply to say that we have come to the conclusion, for more-or-less specifiable reasons, that it is our duty C to do what B demands instead of what A demands. Of course, duty C must reflect, in turn, our best sense of the structure of metaphysical presupposition – the underlying background or conceptual apparatus, the structure of truth – upon which all of our ethical reasoning presumably is based. Again, moral arguments, properly understood, don't come out of thin air. They arise from, and are constrained and ratified by, our sense of how things in the world really are. As we have seen, moreover, the state itself is fundamentally the authoritative embodiment of that sense. It is a shared structure of truth rendered systematic and useful for action. If, then, duty C reflects that structure, and if the state is indeed its embodiment, then C cannot but comport with and indeed be justified in terms of what the state itself prescribes and demands. This is to say that any conflict of duties will be resolved by and through the absolute authority of the state.

Presumably, though, in the most relevant cases duty A would involve obeying the law, whereas duty B would involve breaking it. If, then, the state requires of us duty C, and if C requires that we give precedence to B over A, the state would seem to be requiring us to break the law, and that would appear to be incoherent. In fact, it's not incoherent at all, provided that we bear in mind the fundamental distinction between the state and its various governmental instrumentalities. That distinction suggests that there can be discrepancies between what the state demands of us, on the one hand, and how those demands are interpreted by and translated into particular positive laws, on the other. Now as we have seen, politics can be usefully conceptualized as a series of disputes concerning the nature and meaning of our shared structure of metaphysical presupposition, particularly at the margins. Here, it seems to me, is where such Rawlsian language as the "border" or "outer edge" can make most sense. Most of the time, most of what qualifies as our shared structure of truth is more-or-less clear, more-or-less uncontroversial. This is what allows us to enjoy a relatively coherent and intelligible communal life in which communication and coordinated activity are possible, even easy.

But in any complex society, a certain amount of unclarity, confusion and disagreement at the margins – at the outer edge – is virtually inescapable. The intelligent management of these uncertainties is largely a matter of determining which views are most compatible with the more central, uncontroversial features of the larger background. This is a fundamental, perhaps the fundamental, task of political life. It is a task, however, that is liable to be on-going and perpetual. Every resolution is only provisional, each decision subject to review, criticism and revision. Often, such decisions manifest themselves as positive laws; and the upshot is that any particular law or policy is eligible for being criticized on the grounds that it in fact fails to conform satisfactorily to what the idea of the state, properly conceived, demands.

Such a distinction may be similar in certain ways to an older, Thomistic distinction between natural and positive law. But whereas Thomistic natural law has the status of an unchanging and immutable truth applicable in all times and all places, the demands of a state, as here conceived, may or may not be like that, depending on how we regard the structure of truth upon which it is based; for one can agree that social life presupposes a shared understanding of how things in the world really are without presupposing that that understanding is somehow transcendent and ahistorical. The distinction in question may also be similar to Rousseau's distinction between the General Will, the actions of which are always upright (*toujours droite*), and the deliberations of the people, which are not always successful in serving the public interest. The General Will, though, seems to describe less a set of presuppositions about how things in the world really are than a kind of formal/procedural structure for determining moral right and wrong –something that might well be internal to and justified by, but would not itself constitute, a structure of truth.

It is easy enough to see how positive laws could fail to comport fully with the demands of the state, properly understood. In any complex society, the state will have many governmental instrumentalities. Each of them will attempt to render decisions – make policies, enact laws – that faithfully embody the state's requirements, but will do so on the basis of various kinds of information and various kinds of decision procedures, with the result that mistakes, inconsistencies and misinterpretations are almost certain to occur. The law may vary, therefore, from one jurisdiction to another, or from one point in time to another, with the result that it is not always clear what the law itself requires.

The upshot is that while the law of the state is indeed absolute, any particular positive law may be fruitfully thought of as a kind of PF claim. It is a claim about what the state really requires of us. Insofar as it has been promulgated by a duly empowered instrumentality of the state, it has a very strong presumptive claim on us; we are PF obligated to obey it. But it can be overridden nonetheless by a higher claim, "higher" understood, though, as denoting nothing other than a more faithful interpretation of what the state really demands. Strictly speaking, the kinds of "conflict of duties" that we have been considering involve not conflicts between the authority of the state and some higher principle independent of the state but, rather, conflicts between two different accounts of what the state requires, one embodied in positive law, hence being PF obligatory, the other being perhaps unofficial and non-governmental but nonetheless capable, in certain circumstances, of overriding the first.

3. I believe it is here, and here alone, that we can formulate a coherent doctrine of civil disobedience. Such disobedience can make sense if and only if the disobedient person truly believes that a particular positive law fails to reflect what the state itself requires. The disobedient neither denies nor seeks to override the authority of the state. To the contrary, he or she invokes that authority by questioning the degree to which some particular positive law is in fact consistent with the larger system of metaphysical presupposition upon which the state is based. Of course, such questioning need not involve disobedience. Particular positive laws can be criticized even while they are being obeyed, and one ordinarily seeks to change them not by violating them but by utilizing the regular, established political procedures. But if, as a tactical matter, those procedures seem inefficacious, then civil disobedience may turn out to be a plausible and acceptable alternative, again though understood not as invoking some higher claim over against the state but, rather, invoking the state itself over and against an allegedly erroneous manifestation of it.

The practical consequence of such a view, I believe, is that all coherent examples civil disobedience must be assimilated to what Rawls and Feinberg explicitly distinguish it from, namely, "test cases" in which a positive law of uncertain validity is tested by intentionally violating it.[103] In this sense, Feinberg captures perfectly what is at stake. In civil disobedience as I understand it, "the 'law-breaker' is not intentionally violating a law. He thinks that what he is doing is entirely within his legal rights, an opinion that happens to disagree with that of the local police, the prosecutor and the courts. He wants the appellate courts to settle the disagreement, and 'disobedience' is the only way he can get them to do so."[104] For Feinberg, this is explicitly what civil disobedience is not, since the civil

---

[103] *Ibid.*, p. 365; Feinberg, *Freedom and Fulfillment*, pp. 153–54.
[104] Feinberg, *Freedom and Fulfillment*, p. 154.

disobedient, though acknowledging the authority of the law, nonetheless seeks intentionally to break it. As I have indicated above, however, it is incoherent both to affirm the authority of the state and at the same time to deny it through disobedience. What Feinberg (following Rawls) calls civil disobedience seems to me conceptually impossible. The test case scenario, on the other hand, avoids such problems entirely. It retains the idea of genuine, full-blooded disobedience – positive laws do establish PF obligations – without questioning the authority of the state.

It is true that such a scenario would seem to rule out certain kinds of disobedience (e.g., "indirect" disobedience where the individual protests a particular law by violating not that law but another one); but it would also seem to accommodate what have been historically perhaps the most influential cases (e.g., lunch counter sit-ins during the American civil rights movement aimed at overturning segregation laws). The question as to when such disobedience might be justified could well reflect Rawlsian principles: disobedience must address serious problems in the law, it must not inflict unnecessary harm, it should be understood as a kind of last resort to be utilized only when normal processes fail, and so on.[105] But to these principles must be added a more fundamental and decisive one: civil disobedience can be justified only when the disobedient truly believes that it is in fact sanctioned by, rather than in conflict with, the authority of the state, hence truly believes that the positive law in question is invalid.

Something like this view is argued by Wasserstrom: "One primary claim for the rightness of freedom rides was that they were not instances of disobeying the law.... [M]ost people were confident of the blamelessness of the participants just because it was plain that their actions were not, *in the last analysis*, illegal."[106] Ultimately, though, Wasserstrom rejects such an approach for two reasons. First, he wishes to know why terminological distinctions of the kind that I have introduced above – e.g., the distinction between invalid and valid laws, between positive law and that which the idea of the state itself requires – make things any clearer.[107] Second, he insists that the absolute claims of the state must be based not on "mere assertion" but on some kind of "appreciable substantiation."[108] Both of these demands seem to me reasonable. My goal here has precisely been, at least in part, to address them.

---

[105] Rawls, *A Theory of Justice*, pp. 371–77.
[106] Wasserstrom, "The Obligation to Obey the Law," p. 787.
[107] *Ibid.*, p. 789.
[108] *Ibid.*

4. Three final points bear mention. First, for both Rawls and Feinberg, the test case scenario is understood in explicitly judicial terms. A particular positive law – an ordinance or statute – is to be tested primarily in the courts, with a view toward determining whether or not it is constitutional. This strikes me as plausible, but too narrow. A great deal of coherent civil disobedience, i.e., violating a positive law on the grounds that it does not comport adequately with the idea of the state, is reasonably and appropriately aimed at the political process more widely understood. Wherever questions at the margins arise, wherever serious conversation and political action occurs regarding the outer edges of our understanding of how things in the world really are, there is a place where positive laws can be tested. If the appropriate conditions obtain – in particular, if individuals truly believe that a particular positive law does not validly express that which the state demands – then civil disobedience may be justified with a view toward influencing not just the judicial process but the entire range of instrumentalities that serve the state.

Second, it should be clear, nonetheless, that the theory of civil disobedience presupposes and reinforces the absolutism of the state. The criterion of whether or not disobedience is justified is a criterion embedded in the state itself. Indeed, disobedience reflects not a disagreement with the state about the goodness or badness of a law but, rather, a disagreement with the government about whether or not a particular statute or regulation constitutes an accurate interpretation of the law. Thus, one never disobeys the state; one only disobeys what may be thought of as an invalid or otherwise faulty attempt to express the state's demands. It seems to me that such an account would serve radically to change not only the rhetoric but also the substance of discourse concerning disobedience; and it would reinforce the notion, which seems to me true, that any doubts about the validity of particular laws and the propriety of disobedience can only be decided, in the end, by the state itself.

Finally, though, one can perhaps imagine cases in which the judgment of the state is difficult or impossible to determine, in which the individual faces a conflict of duties but is unable to come up with any plausible account as to which duty should override the other, in which the structure of truth upon which the idea of the state is based itself remains silent or otherwise unhelpful. As indicated above, in such circumstances our ultimate choice could not be other than unreasonable, unaccountable and random, essentially a matter of flipping a coin; and if the coin flip turns out a certain way, the result might be an action that has all the appearance of disobedience. But from this, one cannot derive a doctrine of civil disobedience. For civil disobedience is a moral doctrine, while a coin flip is itself evidence of a dilemma that, though perhaps moral in its origins, does not admit of a moral solution. A true and irresolvable conflict of duties is a circumstance not of politics but of tragedy, in the Aeschylean sense of the term; and if the particular issues involved are serious enough, the result is apt to be not civil disobedience but war.

5. In chapter 4, I argued for the omnicompetence of the state. The purview of the state is, and must be, unlimited in principle. I have now pursued the further claim that the rediscovery and rehabilitation of certain standard intuitions about political obligation, together with an understanding of the state as a structure of intelligibility, entail an absolutist account of the state's authority. We are, I believe, committed to some such view on pain of self-contradiction. Specifically, political obligation – formulated variously in terms of consent or gratitude – is not undermined by but, rather, closely connected to notions of moral duty, whether weakly or strongly "derivative." As such, it is a coherent moral conception that can help explain the civic responsibilities of a great many people. But insofar as the state embodies the gamut of moral and metaphysical presuppositions upon which a society is based, questions about obligation and authority can be addressed and answered only internal to the state itself. There is no external source of appeal; the state is always the final – indeed, the only – arbiter. Of course, none of this would in any way rule out the kind of strenuous and vociferous debate, disagreement and dissent that constitute, in many respects, the heart and soul of a state's political life. Nor would it rule out very sharp efforts to test – through "disobedience" – the relationship between the law on the one hand and particular governmental interpretations of the law on the other. Nor finally would it at all deny the justifiability of forceful resistance and collective action in the face of illegitimate and intrusive instrumentalities of violence and oppression. Indeed, far from contradicting the absolutism of the state, all of these things are directly underwritten by it; and the failure to recognize this conceptual fact – a fact about the essence or nature of the state itself – cannot but give rise to all manner of theoretical confusion and practical error.

6 The Organic State: Democracy and Freedom

During long periods in the history of the West – indeed, for perhaps a millennium or more – discussions of politics and political society presupposed, as though it were a law of nature, the inevitability of monarchy. That this should have been the case is, in a sense, remarkable. For the idea that monarchy is merely one of a wide variety of feasible and potentially desirable political forms is obviously very old, well reflected in the political thought and political practice of antiquity and hardly unknown to thinkers of the Middle Ages. Yet if we consider a vast stretch of history beginning roughly with the era of the Antonines, if not earlier, and extending at least until the end of the thirteenth century, it is not easy to find much in the way of serious political thought that does not presuppose monarchy. In this respect, moreover, political theory and political practice were very much of a piece. Kingly rule may indeed have assumed many different forms and been justified in any number of ways. But the notion that every political society would and should in some sense be monarchical was largely taken for granted.

In our own time, something similar might be said for democracy. It's true that many political regimes of the past hundred years or so – indeed, almost certainly the vast majority – have not been especially democratic. It's true as well that the nature of democracy itself is much in dispute, and that we tend to regard the various forms of democracy (liberal, populist, socialist, communist, revolutionary, and the like) as being much more different than similar. But the fact is that most regimes since the end of the First World War have employed at least the rhetoric of democracy, and one rarely encounters sustained arguments for autocracy or oligarchy, outside of the lunatic fringe. The point was made already at mid-century in a report to UNESCO:

For the first time in the history of the world, no doctrines are advanced as antidemocratic. The accusation of antidemocratic action or attitude is frequently directed against others, but practical politicians and political theorists agree in stressing the democratic element in institutions they defend and theories they advocate. This acceptance of democracy as the highest form of political or social organization is a sign of a basic agreement in the ultimate aims of modern social and political institutions.[1]

Again, this seems to me remarkable. The history of political thought is as thoroughly and intensely studied as it ever was; and yet, throughout that history, strong arguments for democracy have been in a decided minority. A world in which democracy, somehow construed, is a virtual prerequisite for political legitimacy is a world that seems to have dismissed out of hand some of the most important arguments that we find in Plato, Aristotle, St. Augustine and Hobbes, among so many others – writers whose work we otherwise tend to take very seriously indeed.

How to account for this? How to explain the near hegemony of democratic ideas when many of our most important intellectual traditions raise such serious and, as far as I can tell, still plausible questions about democracy? I think the answer is to be found, once again, in a further exploration of the idea of the state. As before, when we focus on the philosophical question of the state itself, as opposed to prudential questions of policy and government, and when we think of the state as an idea that reflects and embodies an underlying structure of metaphysical presupposition, conceptual thickets become untangled and we begin to get at least a glimpse of how we might solve certain long-standing and seemingly intractable theoretical problems.

The first section of this chapter focuses on the question of democratic government, considered in the context of persistent and almost certainly ineradicable social inequalities. Section 2 turns to the very different problem of the democratic state. It suggests that the idea of the state is the idea of an organism, and argues that such an idea is profoundly democratic, though perhaps not in obvious ways. In the third and fourth sections, I address the issue of democratic liberty, and argue that the post-Kantian convergence necessarily conceives of the state as a structure of moral freedom – albeit a freedom at once constituted and constrained by objective, iron-clad rules.

1. Inequality and democratic government

As the case of Rousseau demonstrates, it is possible to be a staunch democrat and, at the same time, a severe critic of democracy. Focusing primarily on the *Social Contract*, one influential commentator plausibly attributes to Rousseau the view that "it is the people as a whole that should exercise the sovereign power, and not a representative body,"

---

[1] Richard McKeon, ed., *Democracy in a World of Tensions* (Paris: UNESCO, 1951), pp. 522–23.

thereby laying the foundation for "the principle of direct and indivisible democracy."[2] And yet Rousseau explicitly claims, in the *Social Contract* itself, that "there is no government so subject to civil wars and intestine agitations as democratic or popular government" and that, in any case, "it is against the natural order for the many to govern and the few to be governed."[3] I have shown in 2.2.2 above how the apparent discrepancy is no discrepancy at all once one sees what is in fact quite clear, that Books 1 and 2 of the *Social Contract* provide a philosophical introduction to the idea of the state while Book 3 examines an entirely different subject, namely, the various forms of government, where government itself is understood to be merely an instrumentality of the state. I have not yet explored, however, exactly what these two different senses of democracy might actually be – either in Rousseau or elsewhere. How are the democratic features of the idea of the state different from the more common conception of democracy understood as a type of government?

1. The very idea of democracy – the power (*kratos*) of the commons (*demos*) – presupposes that deep divisions of class, status, talent and achievement characteristic of any society are or ought to be irrelevant for at least some fundamental political purposes. The problem for the democrat is to show how this can be. How can political equality be justified in the face of undeniable and important differences between ordinary or common folk, on the one hand, and people who are, in terms of wealth, natural ability, acquired skill, and the like, extraordinary or uncommon, on the other?

The problem is exacerbated by at least three facts:

First, many of the personal attributes that we value most and that involve the most salient inequalities – physical strength and beauty, wealth, intelligence, psychological characteristics such as self-esteem – are also among the most difficult to change. We may disagree, of course, about whether such attributes ultimately reflect differences in the natural make-up of particular individuals, differences of circumstance, or both.[4] But either way, it is hardly to be doubted that they will always be, as they have always been, unequally distributed. For even if we insist on a nurture rather than nature theory of differentiation, we must also admit that no

---

[2] J. L. Talmon, *The Rise of Totalitarian Democracy* (Boston: Beacon Press, 1952), p. 46.
[3] *du Contrat Social*, III.IV.
[4] It seems obvious, for example, that physical strength may reflect not just inherent biological features but also socially generated habits of cultivating the body. Similarly, physical beauty is cultural in important ways, such that what is beautiful in one society might not be in another.

amount of social engineering could entirely undo the fact that our individual life experiences will be diverse in all kinds of ways, just as our innate physical and intellectual attributes are diverse; and it seems certain that the range and variety of basic attributes, whether natural or circumstantial, will always produce at least some important differences of ability, opportunity, disposition or social standing. This, at any rate, is the overwhelming testimony of history. Wherever we find serious efforts to eliminate differences and erase inequalities, we invariably see the emergence of new patterns of privilege based on previously unrecognized or previously unimportant structures of difference.

Second, a great many such differences involve profound inequalities of value. Typically, we assess value on the basis of functionality with respect to one or another desirable activity. Something is valuable – an object, a talent, a disposition – to the degree that it helps us do something that we want to do; and since differences among persons almost always have at least some functional consequences, certain individuals will in fact be more valuable than others, depending on the activity. If the activity is basketball, then the tall, athletic person is, *ceteris paribus*, more valuable than the short, unathletic one; if it involves higher level mathematics, then the mathematically gifted is worth more than the less gifted; if it is a matter of buying and selling, then someone who is very rich plays a larger role than someone who is very poor.

Third, it should go without saying that such differences are often immense. Virtually anyone can play basketball, after a fashion. But if, say, the Los Angeles Lakers were to play a basketball game against a team composed of my grandmother's senior-citizen bridge club, the disparity in functional worth would be impossible to exaggerate. Similarly with commerce. Nearly all of us can buy and sell, but our capacity to do so, hence the scope and impact of our economic activity, varies astronomically. Humankind presents itself as a riot of dissimilarity and of unequal value; and this suggests that the task of the democrat – to show how political equality can be justified in the face of diversity – is essentially a matter of identifying some feature of equivalence among persons, common and uncommon alike, that trumps, at least for political purposes, their large functional differences.[5]

Historically, such a feature has been described perhaps most frequently in terms of innate dignity or intrinsic moral worth. While you and I may be of unequal *instrumental* value with respect to basketball or higher

---

[5] For a general discussion of the reference of the word *demos*, see Giovanni Sartori, *The Theory of Democracy Revisited: Part One* (Chatham, New Jersey: Chatham House, 1987), pp. 22–25.

mathematics or commerce or any number of other specific endeavors, we are in ourselves equally valuable – *non-instrumentally* – simply in virtue of being human. This is a view with which no citizen of the modern world can be entirely unfamiliar. But I think it is also an undeniable if unhappy fact that a great many formulations of it – Jefferson's, for example – turn out to be unsatisfying. For while they implicitly reject the kind of functional account of value that I have just described, they often offer, instead, not arguments or explanations but mere assertions of equality based on more or less arbitrary and unsubstantiated claims about the world. They tell us, for example, that we hold certain truths to be self-evident. But whether this is really so – whether we actually hold that set of truths to be self-evident – is plainly an empirical question; and even if turns out that we do hold them to be self-evident, that doesn't mean that we are justified in doing so.

The problem, however, doesn't stop there. For even if we were to develop a compelling account of innate equality, this might not achieve what the democratic theorist wants, since it seems that a functionalist or instrumentalist, rather than non-instrumentalist, approach to value may well be implicit in or required by the very notion of democracy. Democratic arrangements – whether of government or of the state – are essentially tools for realizing extrinsic goals.[6] This, of course, will be disputed. Democracy is thought by many to be valuable and desirable on its own account, independent of what it achieves. But systematic and coherent arguments to this effect are not easy to find. Social contract theorists, for example, will claim to find independent value in the simple fact of consent. But while the social contract may itself represent a kind of fleeting, if hypothetical or fanciful, moment of democracy, there is in fact no necessity – indeed, no tendency – for the contract to produce or imply democratic arrangements, as the medieval roots of contract theory and the otherwise very different cases of Hobbes and Rousseau suggest. Other democratic theorists appeal to the independent value of liberty. But again, democracy's connection to liberty would seem to be hypothetical and instrumental, not categorical. After all, it is certainly conceivable – and has often been argued – that democracy may well undermine liberty (e.g., through the tyranny of the majority) and that liberty sometimes thrives in decidedly non-democratic settings. Many democratic theorists have combined

---

[6] Korsgaard denies that the distinction between instrumental and non-instrumental goods is the same as the distinction between extrinsic and intrinsic goods. Her argument seems to me absolutely correct. But this is certainly not to deny that instrumental goods are usually (though not necessarily) extrinsic, non-instrumental goods usually (though not necessarily) intrinsic. In the instant case, I shall assume that if democracy is instrumentally valuable, then its value is extrinsic to itself. See Christine M. Korsgaard, "Two Distinctions in Goodness," *Philosophical Review* 92 (April 1983), pp. 169–95.

liberty and consent: my liberty can be maintained in the face of political power only if that power is exercised with my consent. But this is plainly an instrumental argument; democratic consent is to be valued only insofar as it maximizes liberty, rather than for its own sake. Still others celebrate the independent virtue of democratic participation. But again, such participation is typically valued because of its putative utility in providing some kind of personal fulfillment – a fulfillment that might, in principle, be achieved in other ways or that, if achieved, might nonetheless compromise some other, equally desirable social goal. And if all of this is correct, i.e., if the value of democracy is essentially instrumental, then the value of particular roles within democracy – the roles of particular individual citizens *qua* citizens – probably needs to be defended in instrumental terms as well.

It is true that certain important egalitarian formulations in fact invoke, rather than reject, the functionalist approach. That is, while many kinds of activity clearly require us to evaluate individuals differently because of different functional capacities, others may have serious egalitarian implications for the very same sort of reasons. Consider, for example, Kantian ethics. On at least one plausible construal, Kant's purpose in the second critique and in the *Foundations of the Metaphysics of Morals* is not so much to identify moral right and wrong as to determine exactly what it means to engage in deliberation about such things. His goal, in other words, is to describe the nature of ethical thinking *per se*, understood as a unique activity of mind quite distinct from the activity of scientific thinking on the one hand and aesthetic or teleological thinking on the other. Ethical thinking is a particular kind of endeavor, a particular type of mental discipline involving a distinctive set of questions, orientations and criteria; and it is precisely from the perspective of such an endeavor that human beings *qua* human are functionally equal in their dignity or worth. For Kant's central claim is that the activity of moral thinking involves a certain process of universalization, embodied in the idea of the categorical imperative, and that this process can be authenticated – can function intelligibly – only if every individual human being, regardless of his or her particular empirical characteristics, is viewed equally as an end rather than a means. Such a view is based, of course, on the fact that each of us has a noumenal will – the existence of which Kant does not merely assert but attempts (transcendentally) to prove. His conclusion is that the activity of implementing the categorical imperative as initially formulated – universalizing the maxim of an action – functionally requires us to implement as well the other formulations of the categorical imperative including, ultimately, the idea of a kingdom of ends in which every human being is understood to be equally capable of free choice.

An argument like this provides, I believe, a useful analogy for demo-cratic theory. In the absence of systematic and compelling claims about the intrinsic, non-instrumental value of democracy, we need some argu-ment for the functional equivalence of people in general if democracy is to be a plausible idea. But again, there are really two very different questions here – the question of democratic government and the question of a democratic state – and these in fact give rise to two quite different issues of functionality. To argue for democratic government is to presuppose that individuals are functionally equivalent with respect to the character-istic activity of government as an instrumentality, specifically, the activity of formulating and implementing public policy. It is to argue, in other words, that all of us – or most of us, or at least a great many of us – are more or less equally good at political decision-making. To argue for a democratic state, on the other hand, is to argue that individual citizens are functionally equivalent with respect to the idea of the state as an institu-tionalized structure of intelligibility and truth that constitutes or under-writes an organized way of life. It is to argue, in other words, that the coherence of the state presupposes that all of us are, in some specifiable way, equally valuable. It seems apparent that functional equivalence in the one sense does not necessarily entail functional equivalence in the other.

2. A democratic government is one in which important decisions are made by the commons. From this it follows, of course, that democratic government is a matter of degree. A regime is more or less democratic in terms of (at least) two factors: the number and significance of decisions that are made by the commons and the scope and variety of individuals of which the commons is composed.[7] The greater the role of the commons and the more inclusive it is, the more democratic the government. Of course, democrats, even the most dedicated among them, may well disagree strongly with one another about just how democratic the govern-ment ought to be. But if democracy describes a wide range of possible arrangements, those arrangements nonetheless constitute a more or less distinct and discernible family, such that all supporters of democracy would agree, for example, that government should be a good deal more democratic than, say, a Platonic regime of philosophers or a Hobbesian monarchy.

---

[7] For a review of standard, social scientific approaches to the definition of democracy, see Mike Alvarez et al., "Classifying Political Regimes," *Studies in Comparative International Development* 31 (Summer 1996), pp. 3–36.

Any argument for democratic government must show that the qualities of intellect, energy, knowledge, judgment, civic mindedness, passion, enthusiasm, experience, or whatever else might be required to operate a government effectively – so that it makes good decisions and fulfills, thereby, the aims of the state – are equally distributed among all of the citizens; or if they are not distributed with perfect equality, then at least (a) they are distributed with sufficient equality to allow us to say that for all practical purposes the citizens are equal indeed and (b) such equality obtains for a quantity and range of individuals sufficiently large to compose what could reasonably be called a commons. Disagreements among democrats are apt to be internal to these criteria.[8] To the best of my knowledge, for example, no government has ever adopted as an operating principle the complete equality of political responsibilities and/or rights. One group or another – aliens, the propertyless, women, slaves, small children, felons, the insane, etc. – is always excluded from much if not all formal decision-making activity. Similarly, rather few if any governments have allowed the *demos*, however defined, to play a direct and dominant role in making *all* decisions. At least some important functions are always reserved for the few. All democratic regimes reflect an underlying conviction that, to one degree or another and in at least some important respects, citizens are broadly equal in their capacity to make a wide array of significant governmental decisions. But they rarely if ever go beyond that.

In light of the immense differences of functional value – whether natural or circumstantial – that distinguish humans from one another, it seems that supporters of democratic government must adopt one or another of three general approaches:

According to the first, the activity of governing is different from many if not most other kinds of activity in that it is comparatively easy. Unlike, say, basketball or higher mathematics, policy-making is suitable for everyone, i.e., something that anyone can do well enough, regardless of innate capacity, social position, training or experience. Such a view is, at the least, curious. Justifying it would require showing that differences among humans are either irrelevant to policy-making or not sufficiently relevant to suggest any kind of serious division of labor; and while I see no a priori reason to believe that a justification of this kind would be impossible, I do believe that some such argument is absolutely required in the face of our strong intuitions about the diversity of abilities and habits, of nature and circumstance. It seems, in other words, that the burden of proof is on the

---

[8] For a useful discussion of some related issues, see Albert Weale, "The Limits of Democracy," in Alan Hamlin and Philip Pettit, eds., *The Good Polity: Normative Analysis of the State* (Oxford: Basil Blackwell, 1988), pp. 35–47.

democrat to show that many of the characteristic activities of government –
understanding, formulating, implementing and assessing complex pieces
of legislation; adjudicating difficult legal disputes involving the immense
tangle of constitutional, statutory and common law principles; participating
effectively in the sometimes delicate, sometimes rough-and-tumble business
of bargaining and negotiation among competing interests; evaluating in an
informed and responsible manner the performance of individuals who have
actually been engaged in such activities – are the kinds of things that anyone,
or nearly anyone, or the vast majority of us would be more or less equally
prepared to do equally well.

The contemporary literature on deliberative democracy illustrates just
how difficult it can be for democratic theorists to sustain such a view.
Gutmann and Thompson assert, for example, that "more participation
is generally desirable,"[9] but one searches in vain for a systematic justification

---

[9] Amy Gutmann and Dennis Thompson, *Democracy and Disagreement* (Cambridge, Mass.:
Harvard University Press, 1996), p. 131. Thompson says that more participation may be
justified for several reasons: it discourages rulers from deliberately violating the interests of
citizens, it makes for better decision-making since only ordinary citizens really feel the
impact of public policies, it makes citizens more knowledgeable about politics, it increases
citizens' sense of satisfaction with both their own role in government and with the system of
government itself, and it promotes "self-realization" (Dennis Thompson, *The Democratic
Citizen: Social Science and Democratic Theory in the Twentieth Century* (Cambridge:
Cambridge University Press, 1970), pp. 55–72). These claims are largely empirical and the
trouble is that, as Thompson himself often recognizes, the evidence in support of them is far
from clear. For example, the claim that greater levels of political participation lead to greater
levels of political knowledge is based on survey data demonstrating an empirical correlation
between knowledge and participation; but surely it seems plausible to suppose that those
traits – psychological or sociological – that incline individuals to become knowledgeable
about politics are precisely the same traits that incline them to participate. The notion that
one independently causes the other is highly unlikely. Moreover, Thompson concedes in
several cases that high levels of democratic participation might well be no more valuable
than low levels (e.g., p. 57); and while he effectively criticizes arguments against higher levels
of participation (pp. 75–79), the failure of those negative arguments certainly does not in
itself constitute an adequate positive case. (In at least one instance – ordinary citizens feel the
impact of public policy more than anyone, hence know best whether or not a particular
policy is good – Thompson denies that the argument is primarily empirical. But this is also a
case where, in Thompson's view, the argument for high levels of participation is especially
weak (p. 57).)
    From the perspective of "liberal equality," Gutmann repeats several of Thompson's
arguments – participation helps prevent tyranny, makes for better public policy, promotes
self-development – but also adds one: "the equal right to participate is an end in itself" that
confers "equal dignity and mutual respect among citizens" (Amy Gutmann, *Liberal Equality*
(Cambridge: Cambridge University Press, 1980), pp. 178–80. The claim is hardly
unreasonable. It refers, however, to the right or opportunity to participate, rather than to
the fact of participation; and it is not at all clear exactly how important such an opportunity is
in conferring equal dignity and respect, especially when compared with other potential
sources of equal dignity and respect. It may in fact turn out to be extremely important, even
crucial, but one would need a quite substantial argument to demonstrate that. Gutmann

of this claim. Cohen agrees that his defense of democratic government presupposes a fairly high level of "judgmental competence" in ordinary citizens, but then admits that such competence "cannot be taken for granted."[10] Cohen, and others like Nino[11] and Estlund,[12] rely on Condorcet's jury theorem in defending majority rule. If most individual voters are even slightly more likely than even-chance to be correct on a yes/no question, then a majority of such voters will be virtually infallible, assuming that the number of voters is relatively large. But as Gaus demonstrates, the theorem in fact tends to support the disenfranchise-ment of a great many voters: "[t]his is clearly so for those who are more likely to be wrong than right, but it also applies to those who are more likely to be right, but who are below the median competency."[13] Perhaps even more importantly, Condorcet's theorem, at its best, works only "when two 'natural' choices confront each other, such as whether the defendant is guilty or not guilty. But in politics we are almost always confronted with a wide variety of choices."[14] In such a circumstance, the claim that a majority may be more reliable than the "average individual"[15] is dubious. Moreover, even if such a claim were true, it would be of questionable consequence; for surely the relevant point of comparison is not the average individual but the individual of very high competence and experience.

The second approach to democratic government, unlike the first, admits that governmental decision-making, like a great many other activ-ities, does indeed demand significant skill, hence requires a certain kind of special excellence. But it insists that such excellence can in fact be acquired by most people. Democratic government should be an "aristoc-racy of everyone" in which the virtues of public spiritedness, good judg-ment and foresight are wedded to formal/governmental principles of

---

says that "*only* by allowing and encouraging equal opportunities for all citizens to participate in a variety of spheres that affect their lives will citizens see themselves and be seen as possessing equal dignity" (p. 181; emphasis added). But I don't find that she defends this assertion, and it doesn't strike me as self-evidently true (though certainly not self-evidently false either).

[10] Joshua Cohen, "An Epistemic Conception of Democracy," *Ethics* 97 (October 1986), p. 35.

[11] Carlos Santiago Nino, *The Constitution of Deliberative Democracy* (New Haven: Yale University Press, 1996), pp. 127–28.

[12] David Estlund, "Beyond Fairness and Deliberation: The Epistemic Dimension of Democratic Authority," in James Bohman and William Rehg, eds., *Deliberative Democracy: Essays on Reason and Politics* (Cambridge, Mass.: MIT Press, 1997), pp. 185–90.

[13] Gerald Gaus, *Justificatory Liberalism: An Essay on Epistemology and Political Theory* (Oxford: Oxford University Press, 1996), p. 243.

[14] *Ibid.*

[15] Estlund, "Beyond Fairness and Deliberation," p. 185.

inclusiveness, representativeness and participation. Some such view seems to have been an important part of the early, Periclean account of democracy. Pericles's Funeral Oration "both expresses the influence of aristocratic values and transposes them into a democratic context."[16] It claims that the "[q]ualities once associated with the individual excellence characteristic of members of the aristocracy – nobility, courage, honor, glory – are now cultivated and expressed in the exercise of political free-dom, which assures to each citizen the liberty to pursue his own aims."[17] And it claims, further, that "the Athenians were able to construe them-selves as an elite ... [in which] all men were capable of pursuing the leisured, genteel activities of warfare, politics and public service."[18] Ideas of this nature recur throughout the history of democratic thought, and remain important today. Barber, for example, contends that there is "no dichotomy between democracy and excellence," and insists that "the true democratic premise encompasses excellence" in which every human being has the "virtues and skills necessary to living freely, living demo-cratically and living well."[19] Cohen similarly calls for the establishment of institutions designed to encourage the "educative effects of political participation."[20]

The account is troubling in several respects, however. To begin with, one would be hard-pressed to provide historical instances of substantial societies, democratic or otherwise, in which political skills, whether natural or learned, were in fact equally distributed. I doubt, moreover, that this can be explained simply by saying (obviously quite correctly) that the vast majority of societies have failed to give their citizens a fair chance to acquire such skills. For it seems virtually certain that in any relatively large society, no matter how open, enlightened and democratically inclined, a great many people will be substantially ignorant of and uninvolved in political matters, not primarily, perhaps not at all, because of any innate incapacity

---

[16] Cynthia Farrar, *The Origins of Democratic Thinking: The Invention of Politics in Classical Athens* (Cambridge: Cambridge University Press, 1988), p. 29.

[17] *Ibid.*, p. 30.

[18] *Ibid.*, p. 28.

[19] Benjamin R. Barber, *An Aristocracy of Everyone: The Politics of Education and the Future of America* (Oxford: Oxford University Press, 1992), p. 13.

[20] Cohen, "An Epistemic Conception of Democracy," p. 36. See also, Gaus, *Justificatory Liberalism*, p. 236. Gaus says that the educative argument for democracy is decisive: voting "encourages ordinary citizens to think in terms of justice and the common good" (p. 236). In a book notable for its critical and intelligent skepticism, it is surprising that this important and central claim is offered without substantiation, and with virtually no supporting argument. I would suggest that the history of democracy provides little evidence to suggest that voting – or, indeed, the opportunity to vote – necessarily improves, or even tends to improve, the quality of public dialogue or strengthens the civic commitments and deliberative capacities of the citizenry.

but for the very good reason that other kinds of activities – time-consuming, labor-intensive and socially productive activities involving work, family, avocation, and the like – are, for them, more important or more interesting. Such people would be ill-prepared in all kinds of ways to participate effectively in many if not most aspects of the decision-making process, itself an extremely time-consuming and labor-intensive endeavor. At the least, the burden of proof falls to the democrat to show that this is not true.[21]

The literature on deliberative democracy – again, a useful exemplar – certainly recognizes the strong distinction between citizens and officials, or between voters and representatives. Democratic deliberation must be informed only by the "most reliable methods of inquiry," and "certainly does not accept as equally valid" any and all reasons.[22] Indeed, making decisions by lot is bad precisely because it fails to distinguish good reasons from bad ones.[23] But surely this points in the direction of "process-independent" standards to which some individuals invariably have greater access than others. Gutmann and Thompson explicitly acknowledge – if, perhaps, understate – the fact that "no doubt there are differences in deliberative ability."[24] They offer as an example a United States senator who, "unlike his constituents, had studied constitutional law and chaired the Senate's Judiciary Committee [and therefore] had good reason to believe that [a] bill to ban abortions in [his state] was unconstitutional and that mounting a test case would be a waste of the state's resources."[25] But while they suggest that deliberation might be useful in helping "to compensate for [such] differences," they fail to say how this might happen or, indeed, what it has to do with democratic government. After all, it is hard to see how deliberation itself could be truly democratic when, as Gutmann and Thompson acknowledge, "the number of people who at the same time can have even a simple conversation, let alone an extended moral argument, is limited."[26]

More generally, democrats would also need to show that socio-historical theories involving or related to the so-called "iron law of oligarchy" are wrong. Here the question concerns not so much the interests or capacities

---

[21] It may be worth noting that Thucydides himself appears unwilling to take up the burden, as when he describes, for example, the utter collapse of democratic virtue in the face of plague and war and its rapid descent into viciousness, brutality and greed.

[22] Gutmann and Thompson, *Democracy and Disagreement*, pp. 15, 17.

[23] Estlund, "Beyond Fairness and Deliberation," pp. 176–77.

[24] Gutmann and Thompson, *Democracy and Deliberation*, p. 132.

[25] *Ibid.*, p. 138.

[26] *Ibid.*, p. 131. Nino admits that ordinary citizens may be less competent with respect to "facts and logic," but claims that this says nothing about competence with respect to "moral" questions. Nino, *The Constitution of Deliberative Democracy*, p. 124; see also Estlund, "Beyond Fairness and Deliberation," p. 183.

of ordinary citizens with respect to the political process but the alleged tendency of any such process to generate systematic and recurrent inequalities of power. I certainly do not presuppose that oligarchy is inevitable. However, the literature itself is, as far as I can tell, equivocal at best; and again, the burden rests with the democrat to show that there is in fact no such iron law.

But even if one could demonstrate that an aristocracy of everyone would be possible and desirable, it's not immediately apparent why it would necessarily be preferable to an aristocracy of the few. If political decisions are made by individuals of genuine excellence – public spirited, perspicuous, knowledgeable, courageous, upright – then what does it matter how many individuals are involved? Since it seems unlikely that the quality of the decisions would depend directly on the quantity of decision-makers, one has to search, again, for some kind of additional – perhaps moral – reason to prefer democratic procedures; and while there is no dearth of argumentation along those lines, the success of such argumentation is, at the very least, open to debate.[27]

A third general approach to democratic government is Churchill's: "democracy is the worst form of government, except for all the rest that have been tried from time to time."[28] The Churchillian does not claim that politics is easy and does not deny that people are unequal in terms of political ability. The argument, rather, is that democratic governments are just less likely to cause serious mischief than others. Intuitively, this seems to me the most promising approach, and at least some historical work – e.g., Sen's argument that societies having democratic governments

---

[27] One kind of approach involves the claim that political activity is essentially ennobling, and that democratic governments provide therefore distinctive opportunities for individuals to improve themselves, morally as well as materially. The first part of the argument – that politics is ennobling – seems to me a moral or ethical claim about individual activity, hence is distinct from any claim that one might make about governmental structure. The second part of the argument – that democratic institutions foster ennobling political participation – seems to me an empirical or historical claim that could be compelling only if it were able to account for an awful lot of evidence that at least appears to suggest otherwise. Democratic institutions do not seem to guarantee democratic participation.

Estlund argues, alternatively, that democratic government is necessary for stability and legitimacy, since "citizens cannot be expected or assumed to surrender their moral judgment, at least on important matters" ("Beyond Fairness and Deliberation," p. 183). Again, this seems to me an extraordinary empirical claim, belied by a mountain of empirical evidence. Thus, for example, the most un-democratic of American political institutions, the Supreme Court, often has the most, rather than the least, perceived legitimacy.

For an extremely interesting defense of democratic government as valuable in its own right – a "foundational political commitment," albeit a subordinate one – see Ian Shapiro, *Democracy's Place* (Ithaca: Cornell University Press, 1996), pp. 109–36.

[28] In a speech before the House of Commons, 11 November 1947.

rarely if ever suffer widespread famine[29] – gives it a measure of credence. Still, the exact reasons for democracy's alleged benignity are not always clear. Perhaps it's because democratic institutions provide citizens with a sense of ownership in government and policy that produces feelings of public spiritedness and political obligation, which in turn conduce to, if not sound decision-making, then at least the kind of order and stability that is essential for a healthy society. While such an account doesn't seem to me obviously wrong, neither do I find it self-evidently correct. It is a prudential or pragmatic argument, as it should be, and like all such arguments it needs to be comparative in nature. Specifically, it needs to ask if democratic government is more conducive to order and stability than other kinds of government. In this sense, I believe that the onus is once more on the democrat – to show, for example, that Snyder's recent empirical/historical claims about the dangers of democratization are false;[30] that Hibbing and Theiss-Morse's account of the ordinary American citizen's lack of interest in democratic participation is misleading or irrelevant;[31] that Zakaria's analysis of the tension between democratic practice and liberal principles is wrong or overstated;[32] or perhaps even more importantly, to show that the good health of society is less likely to be achieved by the mere appearance of democratic government than by democratic government itself.

The range and diversity of approaches to democracy tends in itself to suggest that the feasibility and desirability of democratic government may depend on circumstances – a view articulated famously, though in different ways, by both Aristotle and Rousseau. Democratic procedures might work very well in some situations, in others not. The political theorist needs therefore to pursue the issue of democratic government like any other issue of policy and prudence. Given (a) our empirical knowledge of immediate circumstances, (b) our historical knowledge of similar situations and of past attempts to make the decision-making process more democratic, and (c) our philosophical or conceptual understanding of the fundamental nature and goals of the state, is democratic government – or, more precisely, the increasing democratization of government – likely to be a good bet?

---

[29] To be sure, Sen's argument is more complex than this. Roughly, democratic India has avoided famines, but has suffered from long-term problems of malnutrition. Non-democratic China, on the other hand, has suffered massive famines due to bureaucratic neglect, but has done much better in dealing with long-term malnutrition.

[30] Jack Snyder, *From Voting to Violence: Democratization and Nationalist Conflict* (New York: W. W. Norton, 2000).

[31] John R. Hibbing and Elizabeth Theiss-Morse, *Stealth Democracy: Americans' Beliefs about How Government Should Work* (Cambridge: Cambridge University Press, 2002).

[32] Fareed Zakaria, *The Future of Freedom: Illiberal Democracy at Home and Abroad* (New York: W. W. Norton, 2003).

But even to ask such a question is to suggest that government of this kind does not have a peremptory moral or philosophical claim on us. It is neither self-evident nor conceptually necessary that the democratization of government is always, if ever, either feasible or desirable. Like any other instrumentality, democratic government is to be preferred only if it works better than the alternatives; and in this sense, the contemporary prejudice in favor of democracy, according to which democracy is better than non-democracy and, indeed, more democracy is always better than less, seems to be just that, a prejudice.

3. It will be objected that much of my argument is directed, at least implicitly, against a straw man. After all, most defenders of democratic government do not believe that more democracy is always better than less. Most of them agree that large numbers of people should be excluded from important aspects of the decision-making process, that representative rather than direct democracy is often the best alternative, that the adjudication of constitutional disputes should be left to professional lawyers, that economists have a special role to play in formulating certain economic policies, that military campaigns cannot be run democratically, that well-trained and experienced civil servants are often more know-ledgeable, and should sometimes have greater power, than lay persons, and so on. In short, most democrats are prepared to defend not extreme or pure democracy but moderate or mixed forms of democratic rule, as circumstances require.

Now surely it's true that any effort to moderate or limit the degree of democratization necessarily relies on some number of anti-democratic or inegalitarian presuppositions. I don't see how it can be any other way. To argue for representative as opposed to direct democracy is to say that, for whatever reason, individual citizens are not equally suited to making important policy decisions. To say that complex constitutional disputes should be adjudicated by people who are trained in and knowledgeable about the law is to deny that we are all more or less equally well prepared to interpret the constitution. One cannot reemphasize too strongly, more-over, that such denials need not presuppose that anyone is innately more capable – smarter, wiser, more ethical – than anyone else. Unequal ability may be entirely due to background, training, experience, opportunity, inclination, habit, circumstance, and the like.[33] But however that may be, it seems plain that arguments for mixed, moderate, limited or representative

---

[33] In this connection, it is perhaps worth reminding ourselves that political equality with respect to the decision-making process is not the same as equality of opportunity. One can hold that everyone should have a fair chance to acquire the relevant political skills and

democratic government make no sense unless we agree, again, that the underlying principle of democracy – the power of the commons – has no overriding or peremptory claim with respect to the question of government. It is at best negotiable, at worst entirely hostage to all manner of pragmatic considerations.

If, moreover, the principle of democratic government is problematic in this way, then mixed forms of government must be problematic at least to the degree that they have democratic elements. The difficulties of democracy do not simply dissolve when they are embedded in non-democratic structures. Thus, for example, to concede that individuals are innately or circumstantially unequal in some important respect is to raise at least the possibility that they may be unequal in others. If representative government is to be preferred because only a few people have the knowledge, time or inclination to legislate effectively, then one cannot but wonder if those same few people might not be better suited to perform an entire range of decision-making activities including, for example, voting for representatives. Why should we believe that people who are intellectually, temperamentally or circumstantially ill-equipped to engage in complex legislative activity are nonetheless well-qualified to assess the political skills and accomplishments of legislative candidates, particularly when so much legislation involves elaborate, behind-the-scenes deliberations and negotiations over technical and arcane questions of policy?

Again, such problems are often ignored or left unresolved in the literature on democracy. To look once more at the deliberative approach to democracy: Gutmann and Thompson spend a great deal of time and attention defending the value of deliberation *per se*, but they actually say rather little in defense of *democratic* deliberation. We may agree that hard choices will be more acceptable "if everyone's claims have been considered on their own merits rather than on the basis of wealth," that deliberation can help "clarify the nature of moral conflict," that a deliberative politics "contains the means of its own correction."[34] But none of this says anything about just how democratic the deliberation needs to be, or whether it needs to be democratic at all. For example, it is possible, at least in principle, to consider "everyone's claims" fully and fairly without everyone being an equal and active participant in the conversation. Similarly, we may agree with Gaus that justificatory liberalism requires a decision-making process that is "open" and "widely responsive." But even Gaus admits that a sharply inegalitarian and only marginally

resources while nonetheless insisting that only the most able should rule. Equal opportunity is not peculiar to democratic government, as the case of Plato's *kallipolis* would suggest.

[34] Gutmann and Thompson, *Democracy and Disagreement*, p. 41.

democratic decision-making process might well do the job; and indeed, his own arguments raise questions about the presumptive value of democratic government at all, however constituted.[35]

It bears repeating that nothing I have said here should be construed as a criticism of democratic government. No such criticism is offered and none is implied. What has been criticized, however, is the unargued presumption in favor of democratic government, so widely shared among political theorists today. If democratic government has anything to recommend it, or indeed if it is to be preferred over other possible arrangements, then this has to be demonstrated, not assumed. I certainly do not in any way presuppose that such a demonstration is impossible. But the question nonetheless remains very much an open one; and I do believe that formulating a compelling argument in favor of democratic government – whether on its own account or in comparison with other forms of government – would be a substantial intellectual achievement.

Of course, such an achievement, even if realized, would tell us rather little about the nature of political society *per se*. For again, the question of democratic government is sharply different from and largely irrelevant to the question of the democratic state. It is to this latter question, therefore, that we now turn.

2. The organic state

Following the example of Kantian ethics, a democratic state, as opposed to a democratic government, is one in which all kinds of people – rich and poor, the highly talented and the relatively untalented, the privileged and the deprived – are functionally equal with respect to the fundamental goals and principles of political society. The idea of the state is the idea of an institutionalized structure of intelligibility composed of propositions that describe how things in the world really are and formulated in an authoritative manner so as to reflect and promote the social good. If it is true, or believed to be true, that the well-being of every kind of person, common and uncommon alike, is more or less equally important in constituting the good of society, then the idea of the state, insofar as it embodies that truth, is a democratic one.

---

[35] Gaus, *Justificatory Liberalism*, pp. 228–29, 248. Gaus sees no reason why justificatory liberalism would rule out the kind of scheme proposed by Mill, in which votes might be awarded in terms of education, "with perhaps a 5:1 ratio between the top and the bottom of the scale" (p. 248). But why not a 10:1 ratio? Or 100:1? Or indeed, why should the uneducated have any vote at all? More generally, I believe that Gaus – like the tradition of deliberative democracy in general – tends to elide the question of exactly who gets to participate and how.

Not everyone has thought that people are equal in this way. For Homer, the good of a community would seem to depend disproportionately on the abilities and accomplishments of its uncommon persons – an Achilles or a Patroclos, an Odysseus or a Diomedes, an Aeneas or a Hektor. It is indeed hard to contemplate Homeric epic without concluding that such outsized individuals are functionally far more valuable than any of the undifferentiated human beings who compose the vast, faceless armies of Danaans and Trojans. Similarly, it appears certain that Plato finds guardians more valuable than common citizens with appetitive souls; that Filmer believes kings, directly anointed by God, more valuable than mere subjects; that Nietzsche thinks the heroic artist more valuable than the ordinary bourgeois, and so on. I would also suggest, moreover, that most of us share at least some such intuitions, though we may not want to admit it. If we are honest with ourselves, we are apt to agree that humankind is especially benefited or ennobled by the few great geniuses of science and medicine, of art and spirituality, of courageous and charismatic statesmanship, hence that the good health of society and the state – its orderliness or godliness or vigor – reflects the degree to which its best citizens are able to thrive on their own terms. This is not to say that an elite should rule; that's a pragmatic question of government. But it is to say that public policy, however formulated, should reflect the fact that some people are simply worth more than others and that the interests of such people should therefore enjoy a certain priority.[36]

1. Consider, though, the Aristotelian master and slave. Here is a rather different and, I think, revealing case. Of course, Aristotle's account presupposes the existence of natural slaves, and if anything is clear to us it is that there are simply no such things. But if there were – if we could momentarily suspend our beliefs and ask ourselves how it would be if there were slaves by nature – then several things would follow. To begin with, the master/slave relationship would be, as Aristotle says, a structure of the greatest inequality. The master has the faculty of reason, while the slave – the natural, not conventional slave – "shares in reason to the extent of understanding it but does not have it himself" (*Politics*, 1254b 23–24). Since the faculty of reason is the defining characteristic of humanness, it

---

[36] The notion of differential value is deeply inscribed in popular culture. Recently, a nationally syndicated comic strip entitled "Close to Home" (23 April 2002) depicted a poor schlub named Jerry sitting terrified in shark-infested waters on a leaky, about-to-sink life raft with two fellow passengers. The rescue helicopter announces "We have room for only two of you!" and the caption reads "Jerry's dream yacht cruise with [entertainer] Britney Spears and [American Secretary of State] Colin Powell ends in tragedy."

follows that the slave must be less than human, or not fully human, or only marginally human. The slave is nearly as different from the master as the body from the soul or the animal from the man. The proper task of the human being is to engage in deliberation, to acquire and employ practical wisdom, to participate in the complex and ennobling practice of ruling and being ruled in turn or, in the very best case, to lead a life of contemplation. The slave, on the other hand, is suited only and exclusively to physical labor (*Politics*, 1254b 16–19). From the standpoint of humanness, the master is a complete, the slave a sadly deficient, specimen.

And yet, the relationship of master and slave is, in another sense, one of perfect equality. Clearly the natural slave is utterly dependent on the master. As little more than a tool or instrumentality, he or she simply doesn't know how to act – literally doesn't know what to do next – until told by the master. Bereft of reason, the slave cannot function, and certainly cannot achieve the kind of excellence characteristic of slavery, without explicit instructions. But it seems also to be the case that the master is, at the same time, equally dependent on the slave. For the master cannot do his[37] characteristic work – deliberating, ruling – unless he is free from the kind of manual labor required to secure life's material necessities. Like any other creature, the master needs physical sustenance. But providing such sustenance is an arduous, exhausting, and time-consuming endeavor, incompatible with the activity of deliberation and, importantly, something that most masters would actually be physically too weak to do, even if they were inclined to try (*Politics*, 1254b 27–28). The master's dependence is, thus, every bit as great as the slave's. The existence and excellence of the one equally and entirely presupposes the existence and excellence of the other.

Aristotle explicitly describes it as an *organic* relationship: "a slave is sort of part of his master, a sort of living but separate part of his body" (*Politics*, 1255b 11).[38] Here we have, of course, the germ of an extremely powerful idea. An organism is a complex entity composed of distinct but interrelated elements. The whole is dependent on the parts, the parts on the whole. Absent some particular part, the whole is, to that extent, defective. Absent the whole, the part *qua* part cannot actually be what it is supposed to be. The dependence of whole on part and part on whole means, moreover, that the parts are in some sense dependent on one another. For if the existence or excellence of the whole is threatened by the absence

---

[37] For Aristotle, slaves could be male or female, but masters could only be male.
[38] It is, of course, revealing that Aristotle calls the slave part of the man, and not vice versa. What he should have said, ideally, is that both are part of a larger entity, presumably the *oikos*.

or deficiency of a part, then the existence or excellence of the other parts is, again to that extent, also at risk.

Since the seventeenth century, organisms have been distinguished from machines.[39] The distinction may seem obvious enough: organisms are natural while machines are artificial. But this, in itself, doesn't tell us very much. What exactly does it mean to distinguish the natural from the artificial and why is it important to do so? If the fact of the distinction is most famously attributable to Descartes, the nature of the distinction is addressed most convincingly in the second part of Kant's third critique. According to Kant, the idea of an organism is the idea of an entity that is "self-organizing" in that its various parts, and the whole itself, are said to be "reciprocally cause and effect of each other" (section 65). The organism's existence is, so to speak, internally generated. In an organism composed of Part A and Part B, A and B are simultaneously cause and effect of one another, completely and entirely mutually dependent both for their existence and their form; and this is sharply different from what we find in a machine where the existence of the various parts, and of the whole, is attributable primarily to the activity of an external, intelligent causal agent. From the perspective of the ordinary scientific or empirical understanding, of course, the idea of an organism seems paradoxical or impossible, indeed "unthinkable." Scientific understanding can make sense of causation and organization only in sequential, mechanical and uni-directional terms, i.e., as a matter of "effective" rather than "final" causation. Causes necessarily precede effects in time, hence if Part A is the cause of Part B, then B cannot be the cause of A. For Kant, this doesn't mean that organicist thinking is bankrupt; to the contrary, he regards it as a fundamental feature of mental life. But it does mean that the idea of an organism, in which "the connection of effective causes may come to be judged as an effect through final causes," can only be a "regulative concept for the reflective judgment, to guide our investigation about objects of this kind by a distant analogy with our own causality according to purposes generally and in meditating upon their ultimate ground."[40]

---

[39] Karl Mannheim, *Essays on Sociology and Social Psychology* (London: Routledge and Kegan Paul, 1953), pp. 167–68.

[40] It is here, and here primarily, that Hegel departs from Kant. Hegel accepts Kant's notion of functional or final – teleological – causality. Characteristically, however, he denies that this is merely a regulative idea. Rather, he understands it to be a fundamental and objective principle of philosophical science. It is largely on this basis, moreover, that he conceives of the "Idea" as a kind of organism of organisms, among which the state itself is one important example. For a helpful introduction, see Daniel O. Dahlstrom, "Hegel's

The distinction between organisms and machines has recently come under serious criticism from contemporary theorists of artificial life. Such theorists deny that all "life" is "natural." They insist that artificial, humanly fabricated entities and processes can display all of the characteristics that we associate with living beings – metabolism, for example – and that there is, as a result, no reason to deny that such entities and processes are truly alive. Indeed, they explicitly claim to find in artificial life the very trait that Kant had identified as the defining feature of organisms, namely, the fact of self-organization: "the central concept of A-Life, excepting *life* itself, is *self-organization*. Self-organization involves the emergence (and maintenance) of order, or complexity, out of an origin that is ordered to a lesser degree. That is, it concerns not mere superficial change, but fundamental structural development."[41]

Needless to say, this is a controversial view. But from the perspective of the idea of the state, the controversy is neither here nor there. For it is plain that, whatever their differences, natural organisms and artificial machines are, as Kant himself notes, alike in at least one rudimentary but nonetheless extremely important respect: in each case, the parts "are only possible through their connection to the whole" (section 65). In other words, the whole – whether natural or artificial, whether alive or inanimate – is "itself a purpose, hence is dealt with under a concept or an idea which must determine a priori all that is to be contained in it." From this, it follows that (a) the part simply cannot exist, at least not in a recognizable or intelligible manner, if it is separated or abstracted from its real or hypothetical connection to the larger entity; (b) the part, so connected, is functionally inseparable from the other parts; and (c) the existence of each part is explained by – is "finally" or "teleologically" caused by – its role in the production of the other parts: "every part exists not only through all the other parts, but is thought as existing for the sake of the others and the whole." All of this is as true of machines as it is of natural organisms.

In the history of political thought, the idea that the state – the *body politic* – is organic in this rudimentary way has been perhaps the rule rather than the exception. We find it in theorists modern as well as ancient, secular as well as sectarian. Organicist language is evident in Cicero, Livy and Seneca; and as Gierke has shown, it was a commonplace in the medieval period, of which the work of John of Salisbury is only the

Appropriation of Kant's Account of Teleology in Nature," in Stephen Houlgate, ed., *Hegel and the Philosophy of Nature* (Albany: State University of New York Press, 1998), pp. 168–77.
[41] "Introduction," in *The Philosophy of Artificial Life*, ed. Margaret A. Boden (Oxford: Oxford University Press, 1996), p. 3.

most elaborate example.[42] Organicist theories of the state are perhaps most closely associated with the tradition of Schiller, Hegel and Adam Müller; but we find relevant and suggestive language even in Machiavelli and Rousseau.[43] And while the question of organism *versus* machine is important for modern political thought, it is perhaps notable that the most famous and elaborate organic metaphor of the modern state explicitly denies the importance of this question and invokes, instead, the very language of artificial life: "[f]or seeing life is but a motion of Limbs, the begining whereof is in some principal part within; why may we not say, that all *Automata* (Engines that move themselves by springs and wheels as does a watch) have an artificial life? For what is the *Heart*, but a *Spring*; and the *Nerves*, but so many *strings*; and the *Joints*, but so many *Wheels*, giving motion to the whole Body, such as was intended by the Artificer?"[44] Clearly the Leviathan – the civitas or commonwealth or state – is understood to be organic in the broadest sense outlined above. It is a complete and unified structure in which each part, properly conceived, cannot exist unless it is connected to the whole and is, as such, inseparable from the other parts; so that just as an individual human being is constituted by a soul that functions as the ultimate source of choice and identity, physical organs that allow the body to move, nerves that set those organs in motion, strength that makes the movement consequential, and faculties of memory, reason and will that render it purposive and efficacious, all of which entirely presuppose one another; so is the state constituted by the interdependencies of a sovereign, a government, a capacity to reward and punish, a social and economic infrastructure, an intelligentsia, a system of equity and law. Much is made of the fact, and rightly so, that for Hobbes human beings are natural entities while states are merely artificial. But the relevance of the distinction needs to be put in its proper perspective.

---

[42] Otto von Gierke, *Political Theories of the Middle Age* (Boston: Beacon Press, 1968), pp. 7–8.

[43] For Machiavelli, I am thinking especially of his account of the "humours" that characterize the body politic. For an illuminating discussion, see Anthony J. Parel, *The Machiavellian Cosmos* (New Haven: Yale University Press, 1992), pp. 101–61. For Rousseau, see for example, *du Contrat Social*, Book 3, Chapter 1.

[44] While Skinner finds both organic and mechanical imagery in Leviathan, he insists that the latter – represented in the passage I have just cited – offers "a much clearer indication of how he [Hobbes] believes a commonwealth should be visualized." Quentin Skinner, *Reason and Rhetoric in the Philosophy of Hobbes* (Cambridge: Cambridge University Press, 1996), p. 387. Skinner argues plausibly enough that the image of a machine better captures the Hobbesian notion of the state as something artificial. But he fails to provide a very satisfactory account of the persistence of natural/organic imagery in *Leviathan*. I think this must be, in part, because he ignores the fact that Hobbes does indeed have a notion of "artificial life" in which the difference between an organism and a machine is, for some purposes, not very important.

Hobbesian individuals can indeed exist outside of the state. But they can do so only as savages – without law, without morality, without suitable opportunities to live the kind of existence to which they, as humans, naturally aspire. In this sense, they are deeply dependent on the state, as the state is on them; and what could this mean, other than that for Hobbes, as for Plato and Aristotle, Rousseau and Hegel, the state is essentially constituted by the mutual dependence of whole and part? Whether natural or artificial, the state is an organic structure; and as we shall see, this turns out to have immense consequences for our understanding of democracy.

2. Organicist theories of the state have been of various kinds. For some, the state is *like* an organism; for others, it actually *is* an organism. For some, the relevant organic model is physical; the state is, or is like, a body. For others, it is psychological; the state is, or is like, a mind. For some, the organic state, *qua* artificial, is a product of human volition; for others, it is a "spontaneous" product, self-created, hence metaphysically prior to the elements of which it is composed, including and especially individual human beings. As a historical matter, these distinctions are extremely important.[45] But from the perspective of the idea of the state, they are less important than the widespread commitment to the claim that political society presupposes a strong sense of interdependence between part and whole and among the parts themselves.

We have, of late, lost touch with this commitment. It is, in particular, largely absent from the contemporary literature on liberalism, Rawlsian or otherwise. This can hardly be surprising. It reflects, in part, a failure to see that the interdependence of part and whole is, as both Hobbes and Kant recognized, characteristic of artificial as well as natural organisms. But even more, it reflects a failure to distinguish state from government. Specifically, when state and government are conflated, it becomes easy to think of the state as a mere instrumentality, something that humans may or may not choose to use for their own benefit but with which they have no intrinsic, substantial, organic connection. And when political society is misconceived in this way, it becomes difficult or impossible to reconcile notions of civic virtue, patriotism, loyalty and community, on the one hand, with conceptions of individuality, rights, tolerance and negative freedom, on the other. Such a reconciliation is arguably the most serious problem of contemporary political thought, but the problem largely

---

[45] See F. W. Coker, *Organismic Theories of the State* (New York: Longman, Green, 1910). See also, Sarah Ley Roff, "Group Mind: Psychology and the Construction of the Public Sphere from Romanticism to Psychoanalysis," a dissertation submitted to the Johns Hopkins University (1998).

dissolves when we come to see the state as a complex organism – whether natural or artificial – of which individual citizens are integral parts and in which government itself is understood for what it really is, namely, a convenient, extremely useful and even necessary expedient, but an expedient nonetheless.

The approach that I have outlined in previous chapters suggests, more-over, a particular account of the organic composition of a state, namely, that it cannot but reflect the shared structure of truth – the background or conceptual apparatus – of which society itself is composed. In effect, the mutual dependence of whole and part, and of the parts themselves, is underwritten by the intellectual and cultural fabric of an entire way of life. A society's understanding of how things in the world really are, embodied in language, concepts and propositions, is the glue that holds together the organic state. Thus, even if we regard the state as an intentional, artificial and conventional product of human choice, it still retains a kind of natural and spontaneous connection to the larger social world out of which it has emerged.

Perhaps more clearly than anyone else, Karl Mannheim has seen that the organicist idea of the state is, in itself, deeply and powerfully democratic, and that it provides a plausible account of the ruling principle or power – the *kratos* – of democracy. Citing Kant, he finds that the dependence of the whole on the parts is closely connected to the notion that individual citizens have rights, while the dependence of the parts on one another underwrites the idea of *fraternité* or "community spirit" in which everyone plays a worthy and important role.[46] More generally, organicism embraces what may be thought of as a dual principle of democratic equality and oper-ational differentiation. On the one hand, the various components of the state – individuals or collections of individuals – are each to be valued insofar as the health and integrity of the whole depends on the functionality of the parts. On the other hand, the components, though all valuable, are not identical; for the idea of an organism always involves a sharp division of labor. The various parts are profoundly important, but they are so for very different reasons. They participate in a functionally differentiated whole wherein each performs the more-or-less unique task to which it has been assigned. Just as the character of the slave is very different from that of the master while both are necessary for the well-being of the *oikos*, so too for the various elements of the state: consumers and producers as much as decision-makers, soldiers as much as generals, those who are supposed to

---

[46] Mannheim, *Essays on Sociology and Social Psychology*, pp. 171–72. He also finds the idea of the whole as "an end itself" to be related to the idea of nationalism and the theory of "Volksgeist," which seem to me less clearly democratic.

obey the law as much as those who are supposed to determine it. When all civic tasks are performed well, then the organism thrives; when not, then not.

Plainly, equality of this kind does not necessarily mean that each and every individual person is equally valuable to the health of the organism. With respect to the state, it doesn't deny what seems to us obvious, that a Newton or a Pasteur, a Beethoven or a Kant, a Lincoln or a Churchill makes a greater contribution to the good health of society than the ordinary person of average ability and accomplishment. It does, however, deny that the health of society is simply a reflection of the health of its elites. To the contrary, if ordinary citizens – however categorized and aggregated – do not perform their functions in appropriate ways, if they fail to do the kinds of work and live the kinds of lives for which they are suited, if, in short, they are unable to thrive on their own terms, then the social organism will itself be defective. Individual human beings cannot flourish if their mental powers go haywire; but neither can they flourish if their purely physical organs are destroyed, if their nerve endings cease to function, if they become utterly deprived of physical strength. The health and happiness of such organisms depends as much on basic, simple, homely physical systems as on the most elevated faculties of reason. The stomach is neither more nor less important than the brain; and while each is certainly more important than, say, the little toe, in fact the little toe, taken metaphorically and collectively to include all of the so-called lesser parts of the body, is vitally important in its own right. After all, it can become infected, hence can be a source of debilitating, unendurable pain, the kind of pain that could undermine all other functions, making life miserable, perhaps even not worth living; or it can become gangrenous or cancerous, hence can threaten the very life of the larger body of which it is a part; and if the little toe can be amputated without much consequence while the stomach and the brain cannot, what seems like a difference of kind is in fact only a difference of degree, since it is certainly the case that *parts* of the stomach or even of the brain can be eliminated in the same way and with more-or-less equal safety.

By analogy, the good health of a society's more talented and accomplished individuals is, in principle, no more important to the well-being of the state than the happiness of its other components. If the common people, taken together, are miserable, if they lack the material, spiritual and intellectual resources necessary to thrive, if they are starving or oppressed or severely alienated or uneducated, if they are physically or spiritually or morally bankrupt, then by definition the state is sick. It is not functioning properly; it is failing to fulfill its appointed role. Like a body that is starving or diseased or in pain, it is defective; and to the degree that its defects accumulate, it may cease to be a state at all. The good health of each part of society – the rich and the poor, the rulers and the ruled, the rational, the spirited and the appetitive – is crucial to its existence. If any one part fails to thrive, then that part may find itself thrust into the moral equivalent of a state of nature (see 5.5.3–5 above) wherein law and obligation have dissolved, power is nothing but naked force, and the right of the parts to resist is absolute and limitless.

Insofar as the various parts of society find themselves in such a situation, the state itself is in a condition of crisis verging, in the extreme but all-too-common case, on collapse. In our own time, we have witnessed the dissolution of the state in countless locales – in Beirut and Mogadishu, in Kosovo and Chechnya, in the Congo and Sierra Leone, to name but a few. But it's hardly a phenomenon peculiar to the modern age. Wherever states exist, they are perpetually at risk; the Kosovos and Sierra Leones merely lie at one end of a continuum. The political organism is a fragile creature. It needs constantly to attend to itself, and this means constantly attending to the well-being of its constituent parts. While threats to the good health of society are often external in origin – foreign aggression, natural disaster – they are also at least equally often rooted in internal imbalances and miscalculations, themselves caused by extravagance, negligence, ignorance and prejudice. If the individual human being is gluttonous or ascetic in the extreme, monomaniacally ambitious or hopelessly soporific, careless about illness or obsessively preoccupied with it, the results are apt to be disastrous; and so too for the organism that is the state.

Two possible objections arise. First, if the organic state presupposes that individual persons do not play equal roles in determining the good health of society – if the value of some individuals is greater than that of others – then can this really be democracy? Stated otherwise: how much inequality is one willing to accept and still call a state "democratic"? The answer is far from obvious. But at the very least, one can say that the organic state is analogous to certain forms of parliamentary government based on systems of functional representation, of the kind proposed by Hegel or G. D. H. Cole, among others. Indeed, it is also analogous to the form of democratic government embodied in the United States constitution, where, for example, the specific structure of the legislative branch (and, to a lesser extent, the electoral college) means that a single voter in, say, Delaware carries far more weight – in some sense has a much higher value – than a single voter in California or New York. If these kinds of government can be democratic, then in principle so can the organic state.

Second, one may well ask if the account I have offered means that everyone is, in effect, a theorist of the democrat state, and that the term thus fails to make any meaningful distinctions. Who, after all, would deny the importance of addressing the good health of society, defined in terms of the welfare of its various components? Now insofar as my analysis seeks to uncover an implicit, broad-based understanding of the nature of political society, such a suggestion seems neither implausible nor problematic. An organic – hence democratic – conception of the state reflects, I believe, a range of shared, though typically repressed, presuppositions about how things in the world really are. It's also worth pointing out, though, that a great many important writers at least appear to deny such a conclusion, however perversely, and seem to advocate a sharply undemocratic state. As suggested above, for example, it is doubtful that the ancient tradition of epic poetry evinces much concern for the welfare of the lower classes. Something similar might be said for sophistic tradition, at least in its extreme form as represented by, say, a Thrasymachus or a Callicles. The case of Plato himself is, to be sure, rather more complex. The *kallipolis* of the *Republic* certainly seems to be a kind of proto-organism – which may help account for what one writer refers to as Plato's "democratic entanglements."[47] Yet it's also pretty clear that a philosophic life is, for Plato, far more valuable or worthwhile than an appetitive one. St. Augustine's city of God is, in a sense, strongly democratic, but his city of man is not; and I firmly believe that the author of *The Twilight of the Idols* would find the idea of democratic society virtually as abhorrent as that of democratic government. On the other hand, the fact that many of the canonical writers in political theory do accept, in various ways, an organic/democratic model of the body politic is perhaps itself the best explanation of the contemporary hegemony of democratic sentiments – a hegemony that begins to lose its plausibility precisely when the democratic state is confused with democratic government.

Certainly, the dependence of the whole on the part absolutely requires that the state have some systematic mechanism for monitoring constantly the well-being of each of its elements and for responding effectively to problems as they arise. The true interests of all relevant groups need somehow to make their way into the decision-making process; for if this were not the case, the good health of the whole, dependent as it is on the good health of the part, would always be in jeopardy. Moreover, it may well be that the appropriate mechanism for conveying such information is democratic government, in one form or another. Perhaps the interests of all segments cannot be effectively articulated without free and open elections, representative or direct legislative procedures, institutionalized

---

[47] Sara Monoson, *Plato's Democratic Entanglements: Athenian Politics and the Practice of Philosophy* (Princeton: Princeton University Press, 2000).

political parties, and the like. But as I have suggested in 6.1.2 above, claims of this kind, though now almost unquestioned articles of faith, are not necessarily true. The utility of democratic government is a complex practical and circumstantial issue, and there are reasons to believe that such a government is not always effective in serving the goals of the state. Of course, history also suggests that other methods of decision-making may be equally or even more problematic. The larger point, though, is that none of this pertains directly to the idea of the state itself. As a conceptual matter, the state *qua* organism absolutely requires a government that is sensitive and fully responsive to the real needs of all segments of society. Exactly what kind of government that might be, however, is a prudential or pragmatic question, not a philosophical one.

3. **Universalization**

As children of the modern age, we expect the idea of the state to embrace and sustain the liberty of the individual. Democratic equality, however important, is not enough; democratic freedom must be part of the story as well. But the organic nature of the state, as I have described it, would seem to work against this. For if the individual is best understood as a part of a whole – a part whose behavior is fundamentally determined by the role that it plays in the larger political organism – then one wonders how much real freedom the individual could possibly enjoy. To be merely the effect of some independent cause, perhaps even a functional or "final" cause, is just what it means to be a heteronymous, rather than autonomous, being. And of course, the omnicompetence of the state and the absolutism of its authority seem only to make things worse. They seem, that is, to deepen the unfreedom of the state.

In fact, there is no contradiction between freedom and the state. But we can see this only by exploring in some detail the strong connection between ideas of liberty on the one hand and ethical ideas on the other. That connection is itself reflected in the view, widely shared and deeply held, that the liberty of the individual is fundamentally that which makes morality possible while, at the same time, the faculty of moral action is that which makes us free. From such a view it follows that the problem of freedom and the state is in some sense a question of meta-ethics.

Such a conclusion may appear to be altogether too Rousseauian and Kantian, and to rule out orthodox liberal notions of negative freedom. But even Berlin, in distinguishing positive from negative liberty, says that the difference is largely rhetorical or historical rather than logical. In fact, Berlin actually comes close to conceding that freedom, properly understood, involves the absence not just of external physical constraints but of internal psychological ones as well.[48] In doing so, he acknowledges, if only implicitly, that moral liberty might be a central feature of liberty itself; and this suggests, in turn, that any attempt to find individual freedom in the organic state must be, at the same time, an attempt to show how the functionally determined citizen can be morally free.

I intend to pursue this issue through an examination of the idea of a categorical imperative. Kant's meta-ethics is certainly not the whole of modern meta-ethics. But I believe that his moral problematic, like most things Kantian, has set the terms for nearly all subsequent debate on the subject. Of course, it has been appropriated by Rawls and others as a paradigmatic case of formalist, proceduralist, constructivist ethics, an embodiment of the liberal conception of moral choice, hence an important tool in defending liberalism against the long-standing and largely non-liberal tradition of Western virtue ethics.[49] But this in itself presents us with a special opportunity; for if it can be shown that the Kantian problematic is nonetheless consistent with, perhaps even helps to underwrite, the larger, organicist conception of the state that I have proposed, then I believe we can begin to see seemingly strong oppositions between formalist and virtue-oriented approaches, individualism and holism, liberalism and statism, in a wholly new light.

But showing this requires, as a first step, getting clear about the categorical imperative itself. In particular, it requires a systematic consideration of what might be called the standard view. Such a view seeks to defend Kantian ethics against certain venerable and influential criticisms. In doing so, however, it provides an account that fails to make a persuasive case for the categorical imperative on its own terms and that, as a result, fails to show how Kantian ethics, broadly conceived, can contribute materially to our understanding of freedom and the state.

1. According to the first formulation of the categorical imperative, you should "act only according to that maxim through which you can at the same time will that it become a universal law" (*Grundlegung* 421).[50] The

---

[48] Isaiah Berlin, *Four Essays on Liberty* (Oxford: Oxford University Press, 1991), pp. 131–32. For a discussion, see John Gray, *Isaiah Berlin* (Princeton: Princeton University Press, 1996), pp. 17–18.

[49] For an attempt to reconcile liberalism and virtue ethics, see Stephen Macedo, *Liberal Virtues: Citizenship, Virtue and Community in Liberal Constitutionalism* (Oxford: Oxford University Press, 1990).

[50] In dealing with the "categorical imperative," my focus is entirely on this first formulation, the so-called "formula of universal law," along with its variant, the "formula of the law of nature." Thus, I ignore the later, more "substantive" formulations – the "formula of humanity as an end in itself," "the formula of autonomy" and the "formula of the realm

problem, of course, is to discover exactly when and why you cannot will the universalization of your maxim. Presumably the answer is that you cannot do this just in those cases where trying to do so would lead to a self-contradiction. But the specification and analysis of such cases has proven to be extremely difficult. Indeed, Hegel and Mill, who agree on very little, agree that there are in fact no such cases. According to Hegel, the categorical imperative is "an empty formalism" under which "any wrong or immoral line of conduct may be justified."[51] In principle, anyone can coherently will that any maxim of action should become a universal law. Mill similarly finds that Kant "fails, almost grotesquely, to show that there would be any contradiction, any logical (not to say physical) impossibility, in the adoption by all rational beings of the most outrageously immoral rules of conduct."[52]

It should be emphasized that Kant is being criticized not simply for failing to achieve his evident goal, viz., to show that the formal criteria of rational willing are sufficient to establish for all rational agents a single, universal set of moral laws. Rather, the argument is that Kant's formulation fails to have *any* substantive implications whatsoever. We should understand, moreover, that the issue is not whether one can discover maxims that are ruled out on grounds of self-contradiction. Anybody can formulate a maxim that is nonsensical or paradoxical (e.g., the maxim that I will always perform action A and never perform action A). Rather, the point is that any action that it is possible to perform can be interpreted as being based on a maxim that we can without contradiction will to become a universal law.

Much recent work on Kant's ethics has been concerned precisely to defend his account against the charge of empty formalism. The result is, by now, a standard view of the categorical imperative that is widely accepted on both exegetical and argumentative grounds. This view – attributable, it seems, to Onora O'Neill and Allen Wood – argues, roughly, that the categorical imperative rules out any maxim of action the universalization of which would make impossible the performance of the action itself. Such an account provides a resourceful and initially compelling defense of Kant's basic ethical scheme, one which has the additional virtue of seeming to comport closely with what Kant himself

of ends" – whose relationship to the earlier formulations is a matter of much dispute. For a discussion, see Allen W. Wood, *Kant's Ethical Thought* (Cambridge: Cambridge University Press, 1999).

[51] G. W. F. Hegel, *Grundlinien der Philosophie des Rechts* (Frankfurt: Suhrkamp, 1970 [1821]), § 135; also, G. W. F. Hegel, "Über die wissenschaftlichen Behandlungsarten des Naturrechts," in *Gesammelte Werke: Volume 4*, ed. Hartmut Buchner and Otto Pöggeler (Hamburg: Felix Meiner, 1968 [1802]), pp. 435–38.

[52] John Stuart Mill, *Utilitarianism* (Indianapolis: Bobbs-Merrill, 1976 [1863]), p. 6.

says. In my opinion, however, even the most influential formulations of this standard view turn out to be unsuccessful. Either they fail to show how the categorical imperative can generate substantive moral conclusions or else they fail to fulfill the promise of a truly formalistic ethics. The age-old prejudice against Kantian ethical theory, as articulated by Hegel and Mill, among many others, thus remains unrefuted by the standard view.[53] This does not mean, of course, that the prejudice is irrefutable. But it does suggest that the standard view is far less promising than has generally been thought.

2. The empty formalism charge is attendant to what one author has called the "traditional interpretation of the categorical imperative."[54] According to this interpretation, "the moral value of maxims is determined by reference to their form alone without reference to ends and consequences."[55] Among Kant specialists, such an account is now almost universally rejected precisely because it is thought to leave Kant defenseless against the charge of empty formalism. These commentators have proposed, instead, an alternative kind of interpretation that emphasizes outcomes: you cannot rationally will that a maxim of action should become a universal law if the (hypothetical) result of doing so would be the establishment of a universal law that could not possibly be obeyed.

According to Paton's early and influential version of this argument, Kant insists that we cannot break our promises because "keeping... promises and the mutual confidence thereby aroused are essential factors in the systematic harmony of human purposes."[56] If no individual can rationally choose to destroy the systematic harmony of human purposes, and if that harmony would be destroyed by universalizing the maxim of breaking promises if one so chooses, then one cannot will to universalize that maxim. An action based on such a maxim is thus not morally justified. Of course, the consequence involved here is not the outcome of an individual actually breaking a promise; it is, rather, the (hypothetical) result of universalizing the maxim of the action such that everyone would act

---

[53] See, for example, Philippa Foot, *Virtues and Vices and Other Essays in Moral Philosophy* (Berkeley: University of California Press, 1978), p. 1; Alisdair MacIntyre, *After Virtue: A Study in Moral Theory* (Notre Dame, Indiana: University of Notre Dame Press, 1984), pp. 45–47; and Bernard Williams, *Moral Luck* (Cambridge: Cambridge University Press, 1981), pp. 14, 19.

[54] T. C. Williams, *The Concept of the Categorical Imperative* (Oxford: Oxford University Press, 1968), pp. 37–56.

[55] *Ibid.*, p. 56.

[56] H. J. Paton, *The Categorical Imperative* (London: Hutchinson, 1947), p. 153. See also, Edward Caird, *The Critical Philosophy of Kant: Volume 2* (Glasgow: Maclehose, p. 213).

according to the same maxim. Everyone would be free to break promises, the practice of promising would be gravely compromised, and the result would be to undermine, perhaps fatally, the systematic harmony of human purposes.

The theory so interpreted seems unpersuasive for at least two reasons:

First, it is by no means clear that an analysis of empirical consequences could possibly show that the universalization of the maxim would *necessarily* be self-contradictory. As Harrison has argued, the maxim of breaking promises if one so chooses would, if universalized, undermine the practice of promising, or the systematic harmony of purposes, only under a variety of quite specific contingent circumstances. For example, such a result would occur only if people actually remember past instances of breaking promises. If they did not remember such instances, then "people could quite happily go on obtaining services by making promises they could not keep, and promises would not cease to be made."[57] There would be no self-contradiction. Against this, Kemp has argued that Kant intends the categorical imperative to indicate and rule out self-contradictions that are entirely logical in nature, rather than those that arise from causal processes in the external world.[58] However, Kemp does not describe clearly what such logical self-contradictions might be, and Harrison's point is precisely that the contradictions identified by Kant involve not logical impossibilities but only, at best, causal ones.[59] As such, they are not necessary self-contradictions but are, rather, entirely dependent on circumstances, and this means, for example, that it is not *necessarily* the case that it is wrong to break a promise – a conclusion that Kant presumably could not accept.

Second, it is also unclear why no individual could rationally choose to subvert the systematic harmony of human purposes. Of course, upon analysis it may turn out to be wrong to do so, but that would be the end, not the premise, of a moral argument. Paton provides no such argument. More particularly, he does not demonstrate that undermining the systematic harmony involves a self-contradiction; as a result, he is unable to account for the most central feature of the categorical imperative as a *formal* principle.

---

[57] Jonathan Harrison, "Kant's Examples of the First Formulation of the Categorical Imperative," in *Kant's Foundations of the Metaphysics of Morals: Text and Critical Essays*, ed. Robert Paul Wolff (Indianapolis: Bobbs-Merrill, 1969), p. 217.

[58] J. Kemp, "Kant's Examples of the First Formulation of the Categorical Imperative," in Wolff, ed., *Kant's Foundations of the Metaphysics of Morals*, p. 238.

[59] Jonathan Harrison, "The Categorical Imperative," in Wolff, ed., *Kant's Foundations of the Metaphysics of Morals*, p. 250.

In attempting to circumvent both kinds of objections, Onora O'Neill has proposed a modified account: an action is enjoined if the "normal and predictable" results of universalizing the maxim of the action would lead to a proposed moral law that is *literally* self-contradictory.[60] The emendation purports, I think, to operate at two levels. First, self-contradiction is said to occur not just in any set of contingent circumstances but, rather, in circumstances that are regular and explicable features of the world as we know it. This is presumably designed to address the kinds of objections raised by Harrison, among others. Second, a proposed moral law is self-contradictory if it would justify actions that would be, precisely because of the process of justification, actually and utterly impossible to perform. Specifically, I cannot break a promise if the maxim of my action, once universalized and adopted by everyone, would normally and predictably lead to the end of promising; for in such a circumstance, no one would be able to invoke the maxim of breaking promises if one so chooses since there would be no more promises to break. That is, the consequence would undermine the maxim of breaking promises, since if promising became impossible then it would be impossible to make, hence equally impossible to break, a promise. The result is that one could not without self-contradiction universalize a maxim of breaking promises. Harrison's criticism, that the appeal to consequences depends on contingent circumstances and cannot, therefore, lead necessarily to self-contradictions, is substantially modified: the self-contradictions identified by Kant are necessary self-contradictions given normal and predictable consequences.

I take this to be a much stronger version of the argument from consequences. As such, it has become, in one form or another, the standard view.[61] According to this view, the maxim of action A is said to be ruled out if its universalization would make it impossible subsequently to perform actions similar to A. Evidently, the impossibility may be any one of three kinds. It may involve a *logical* "contradiction in conception," whereby actions similar to A simply cannot be conceived, given the circumstances. Alternatively, it may involve a *practical* "contradiction in conception," in which it would be silly and futile, though not inconceivable, to perform actions similar to A. Finally, it may involve a "contradiction in will,"

---

[60] Onora O'Neill [Nell], *Acting on Principle* (New York: Columbia University Press, 1975), pp. 70–71.

[61] See, for example, Allen Wood, *Hegel's Ethical Thought* (Cambridge: Cambridge University Press, 1990), pp. 614–19; O'Neill [Nell], *Acting on Principle*, pp. 70–71; Brian Aune, *Kant's Theory of Morals* (Princeton: Princeton University Press, 1979), p. 54; Onora O'Neill, *Constructions of Reason: Explorations of Kant's Practical Philosophy* (Cambridge: Cambridge University Press, 1989), pp. 132–33; Barbara Herman, *The Practice of Moral Judgment* (Cambridge, Mass.: Harvard University Press, 1993), p. 137.

wherein circumstances are such that actions similar to A would both serve and undermine the interests of the actor. In all these cases, universalizing one's maxim of action leads to incoherence; and surely the moral law, if it is to be a reliable normative guide to human activity, cannot be incoherent.[62]

The standard view is not only widely accepted; it also has a very strong textual warrant (*Grundlegung* 423). We must, therefore, be surprised to realize that in fact it describes nothing that could even remotely be called a self-contradiction.

If my maxim had said "I will break promises if I so choose *and* I will never undermine the practice of promising," then the universalization of this maxim would indeed be a self-contradiction, assuming that the widespread breaking of promises would undermine the practice of promising. But my maxim doesn't say this. It simply says "I will break promises if I so choose," and from this one can infer absolutely nothing about my views as to whether or to what extent the practice of promising should continue to thrive. Absent such an inference, there is nothing at all self-contradictory about universalizing my maxim. If I were to will its universalization, I would simply be willing the law that it is or can be justifiable for anyone who so chooses to break a promise *if* or *whenever* one has the opportunity to do so.

To see this more clearly, consider that I am already very well aware that the opportunity for making, hence breaking, promises will always necessarily be limited, depending on the circumstances. It is difficult or impossible to make a promise when one is alone, or sleeping, or play-acting, and the like. I recognize, therefore, that any maxim I might propose regarding promising is not something that I could actually put into practice at any time and any place; it is constrained by those circumstances in which promising is unlikely or impossible. But this fact – that my opportunities to make, hence break, promises are necessarily limited – need not in any way affect the content of my maxims about promising. In this sense, then, the demise of promising would be merely another one of those circumstances that limit the opportunity to promise, albeit a very extreme one; and the fact that this circumstance would be the direct result not of extraneous factors but of the universalization of my maxim seems to make no difference whatsoever. The universalization of my maxim is completely consistent with such an outcome. Perhaps promising will end, perhaps not; all that my maxim tells me is to break promises if I so choose, a maxim that I can invoke whenever a promise is possible. To will the universalization of this maxim is simply to propose that anyone may

---

[62] Wood, *Kant's Ethical Thought*, pp. 83–97. Here, Wood generally relies on O'Neill's terminology.

justifiably break promises if one so chooses and whenever it is possible to do so. There is nothing self-contradictory in that. Thus, to universalize the maxim of action A is to say absolutely nothing at all about subsequent opportunities to perform actions similar to A; my maxim, once universalized, speaks only to the justification for performing such an action, should the opportunity arise.

3. The standard view, as formulated by O'Neill and others, fails because it involves a most peculiar understanding of what it means to universalize a maxim of action. Universalization must, I think, mean that a maxim can justifiably be adopted by *all rational agents* who would perform a particular action A; but added to this, O'Neill and others seem to believe that universalization also means that a maxim can be justifiably acted upon *at all times and in all conceivable circumstances*. If it is justifiable to break promises, it must *always* be justifiable to break promises. This means, in particular, that it must be justifiable to break promises that have been made in circumstances where promising is impossible. But of course, it's impossible to break such promises since, because of the circumstance, the promises could not have been made in the first place. The maxim of breaking such promises is therefore an absurdity; hence to say that it is justifiable is an absurdity. Thus, it can *never* be justifiable to break promises; the maxim must be wrong, for its universalization leads to an absurdity.

The argument fails at least in part because it overlooks the fact that actions such as A are constituted in part by the circumstances in which they occur. If the circumstances change, A might no longer be A. If I kill you without provocation and with malice aforethought, I have committed an act of murder; if, on the other hand, I kill you on the field of battle under the rules of war, even with malice aforethought, then I have committed a quite different kind of act. The circumstances are unavoidably part of our understanding of the nature of the action performed, hence of the maxim upon which the action is based, and this obviously can have enormous practical moral consequences: the murderer is punished, the soldier is honored.

Similarly, breaking promises if one so chooses when promising is possible – let's call this action A^1 – is a different kind of action from breaking promises if one so chooses when promising is impossible, A^2. The second of these, A^2 is an absurdity; the first, A^1, is not. If, as an empirical matter, A^1 in fact normally and predictably leads to A^2, we may be unhappy with it. But universalizing the maxim of A^1 – breaking promises if one so chooses when promising is possible – is, in and of itself, a perfectly coherent thing to do. And it is the maxim of *that* action, the action of breaking promises *when promising is possible*, that is being universalized. If such an action is indeed immoral, this cannot be because its maxim, once universalized, is self-contradictory in the way that O'Neill and others have described.

By failing to take this into account, the standard view produces at least two kinds of moral absurdity:

(a) Imagine an action the consequences of which would be the elimination of poverty. According to the standard view, the maxim of such an action, when universalized and implemented successfully, would make it impossible to perform subsequent acts of the same kind. Poverty having been eliminated, one could not coherently will that others should act in the same way to eliminate poverty, since such actions would be impossible. The maxim of the action, when universalized, is self-contradictory and must be ruled out on moral grounds.[63]

Clearly, this cannot be what a Kantian would have in mind. The problem evaporates once we recognize that the action in question is precisely the action of trying to eliminate poverty *when poverty still exists* – the circumstance being an important part of the definition of the action. A Kantian can thus hold that all rational agents who have an *opportunity* to eliminate poverty should do so; and the fact that the elimination of poverty would make it impossible for others subsequently to do so cannot count against the maxim of the action.[64]

Thus, universalizing the maxim of breaking promises if one so chooses means only that *if* or *whenever* it is possible to break a promise it may be justifiable for anyone to do so. You could clear-headedly break a promise and universalize the maxim of that action even knowing full well that the normal and predictable result would be the subsequent end of promising. All that your universal law would say is that anyone who happens to face the same kind of opportunity would be justified in doing the same thing.

It might be objected that the analogy with the elimination of poverty is imperfect, since the impossibility of universalizing the maxim of action in that case would arise only after a long process of cause and effect in the world, i.e., the actual elimination of poverty; the impossibility of universalizing the maxim of breaking promises, on the other hand, would be a nearly immediate consequence of everyone adopting that maxim, thereby making it psychologically impossible that anyone would trust anyone else. I doubt that such a difference seriously undermines the analysis. But even if one accepts the objection, it is easy enough to identify other cases that are

[63] Hegel, "Uber die wissenschaftlichen Behandlungsarten des Naturrechts," p. 439.

[64] Wood implicitly sees this in the case of universalizing actions that are intuitively right: "If my maxim is simply that of trying to abolish poverty as far as possible, then there will be no self-annihilation if everyone follows the maxim and poverty is abolished." Wood, *Hegel's Ethical Thought*, p. 160. The key phrase here is "as far as possible."

immune to it. Imagine, for example, a religious principle that said: "Convert one unbeliever [along with yourself], and you will go to heaven." The (successful) universalization of the maxim of that action according to the standard view would mean that no one would go to heaven.

(b) By misconstruing the nature of what is to be universalized under the idea of the categorical imperative, the standard view is unable to rule out certain important kinds of action that are, from a Kantian perspective, plainly immoral. With respect to promising, the interesting case is precisely the one in which you are tempted to break a promise knowing full well that, even under normal and predictable circumstances, you will be able to get away with it and that the practice of promising will *not* thereby be undermined.[65] Kantian ethics wants to ask if the maxim of *that* action undertaken in *that* circumstance could be coherently universalized: would it be all right for *anyone* to break a promise where the consequences, both for the individual and for society, would *not* be particularly bad?

Imagine that I know that if I break my promise to you, no one else will learn about it; as a result, no damage will be done to the practice of promising. Further, let us assume that by reneging on my obligation, I will profit; and since I have done no damage to the practice of promising, I will be able to continue to make promises in the future. Could I rationally will that anyone else in the *very same circumstance* – i.e., having an opportunity to renege for profit and with utter impunity – may also justifiably break his or her promise? If, as Paton and O'Neill imply, self-contradiction occurs only when the consequences of an action, once universalized in terms of time and circumstance, rule out all subsequent actions of the same kind, then one could legitimately break promises precisely in those universalizable circumstances where one can get away with it. This most surely cannot be what the Kantian has in mind. Rather, he or she must be interested in showing that breaking a promise is intrinsically wrong; and this means showing that universalizing the maxim of breaking promises if one so chooses leads to a self-contradiction regardless of the circumstances or consequences.

It may also be that the standard view confuses self-contradiction with perversity. Breaking a promise knowing full well that the result might be the destruction of promising may seem to presuppose that you are at least somewhat indifferent, or perhaps even hostile, to the practice of promising, and this may be a perverse attitude. It is surely not necessarily perverse, since even if you value promising highly you might also value even more highly other things that would require the end of promising. But even

---

[65] This is simply a particular aspect of the more general problem raised by Adeimantus: *Republic* 365a–366b.

outright indifference or hostility to promising, however perverse, is hardly self-contradictory. Indeed, it might be perfectly coherent for you to break a promise *in order to* undermine (or help undermine) the practice of promising. The standard view would seem to have no argument against that since, among other things, what is an unacceptable consequence for one person might be perfectly acceptable to another. In the present case, the "bad" consequence is that promising would be impossible and this, in turn, would eliminate the possibility of breaking promises in the future. But if you think that promising is a bad practice, then you would find neither its demise nor the resultant impossibility of breaking a promise to be a bad thing.

Perhaps, though, some consequences are necessarily unacceptable. This may be what Paton has in mind when he speaks of the categorical imperative as ruling out maxims that, if adopted by all agents in all circumstances, would tend to destroy the systematic harmony of purposes. Perhaps if we combine this with O'Neill's notion of normal and predictable results, we could get a stronger account of the bad consequences approach: a maxim cannot be universalized if doing so would, under normal and predictable circumstances, tend to destroy the systematic harmony of purposes. But it is difficult to see that this really gets us anywhere. For it may be that someone would want to destroy the systematic harmony of purposes. One cannot argue that it would be immoral to do so since, presumably, the criterion of morality is provided precisely by the categorical imperative, the interpretation of which we are now seeking. To prove that one should not destroy the systematic harmony of purposes would require the application of the idea of the categorical imperative which cannot, therefore, presuppose that one should not destroy the systematic harmony of purposes. If one nonetheless insists that such a systematic harmony has some kind of moral primacy, then the categorical imperative ceases to be categorical and becomes, instead, a hypothetical imperative: if one seeks to sustain the systematic harmony of purposes, then one should do *A* or refrain from doing *B*. Hypothetical imperatives may indeed be important for Kant, but their recommendations are, by definition, not categorical.

4. **Moral freedom and the state**

If, however, I am correct in arguing that the standard view fails to provide a plausible defense of the categorical imperative, then this has in principle far-reaching implications for our understanding of moral obligation in general; and that, in turn, raises serious questions about our concept of freedom. For example, in chapter 5 I sought to show how the notion of tacit consent might help account for the political obligations of citizens. The argument hinges on an analysis of consent-constituting actions. It does not hinge, however, on an analysis of what consent, once established, entails, for that seems to be uncontroversial. Everyone agrees that consent entails a moral obligation to accept, and to act in accordance with, the state of affairs to which one has consented. But why should this be? If I have promised, expressly or tacitly, to obey the law, why am I therefore morally obligated to keep that promise? More generally, then, what kinds of argumentation underlie the moral claims that we make? On what basis do we think those claims justified? How do we get from an empirical fact about the world – e.g., a consent-constituting action – to a statement of ought?

Despite the failings of the standard view as I have described it, Kantian ethics, more broadly conceived, nonetheless offers powerful resources for thinking fruitfully about the character of moral argument. I intend to sketch one way of utilizing those resources that seems to me especially promising and that, in particular, speaks directly to the problem of freedom and the state. The account that I shall provide is plainly not an interpretation of Kant's writings or of the categorical imperative itself. Nor is it intended as an ethical theory in its own right; I have in mind nothing so grandiose. Rather, it purports to describe a general orientation to ethical questions, a way of thinking about moral right and wrong. It reflects, above all, the larger view of philosophical inquiry and social theory that I have utilized throughout this work. It locates the idea of ethical choice, hence of individual moral freedom, directly in the body politic, understood specifically as a structure of intelligibility. As such, it helps describe the idea of liberty itself, understood to be an intrinsic part of, and to be constituted by, the idea of the state.

1. The maxim of breaking promises if one so chooses, when universalized, yields an "objective" principle in the form of an imperative – break your promises if you so choose – from which we can straightforwardly deduce the following moral claim: *It is, or can be, justifiable to break a promise.*[66]

---

[66] Technically, Kant's example is not the maxim of breaking a promise if one so chooses but the maxim of making a lying promise if one so chooses. For our purposes (though perhaps not for others), the difference is irrelevant. Moreover, a proper Kantian maxim presumably should include an end to be achieved.

Kant defines a maxim in a footnote to *Grundlegung* 421: "The maxim is the subjective principle of acting and must be distinguished from the objective principle, namely, the practical law." See Williams, *The Concept of the Categorical Imperative*, pp. 13–21; Rüdiger Bittner, "Maximen," *Akten des 4. Internationalen Kant-Kongresses* (Berlin: Walter de Gruyter, 1974), pp. 485–98; Otfried Höffe, "Kants kategorischer Imperativ als Kriterium des Sittlichen," *Zeitschrift für philosophische Forschung* 31 (1977), p. 360; O'Neill, *Constructions of Reason*, pp. 83–84, 150–53; and Henry E. Allison, *Kant's Theory of Freedom* (Cambridge: Cambridge University Press, 1990), pp. 85–94. I

If this claim is self-contradictory, then so is the principle from which it is deduced; and if that is so, then the maxim of breaking promises cannot coherently be universalized. However, the sentence that expresses the moral claim is a perfectly good one. If it is self-contradictory, then this must be because of its meaning; and of course, that depends in part on the meaning of the words of which it is composed, hence on the concepts that those words denote.[67]

In fact, I believe that the claim in question is indeed self-contradictory. For a promise is, by definition, the assumption of a (moral) obligation. This is just what the concept of a promise, denoted by the word "promise," means. It is what distinguishes a promise from, say, a prediction, a recommendation, a wish, a warning, and the like. To predict, recommend, wish or warn that I will marry you is not to assume an obligation, whereas what makes a promise a promise is precisely that. But if promises involve obligations, then they cannot justifiably be broken, for otherwise they would not be obligatory. After all, what could it mean to say that one has an obligation to which one is not obligated? Thus, the original claim, when elaborated, in fact yields the following sentence: "It is, or can be, justifiable to break something [a promise] that cannot justifiably be broken." But since this is incoherent, we are forced to reject the original claim in favor of its negation: *It is not, and cannot be, justifiable to break a promise* .

Understood in this way, the concept of a promise is part of our conceptual apparatus, hence is embedded in and reflective of a shared structure of truth. Our cultural and social interactions presuppose an understanding of how things in the world really are – dogs, horses, chalkboards, sonatas, oceans, and the like. Among those things are promises. A promise is what it is, and has the moral force that it has, in virtue of our understanding of the nature of the thing – all of which ultimately manifests itself in the meaning of the word "promise."

It might be argued that such an approach must be radically un-Kantian, since it seems to dispense with the very notion of universalization. After all, the maxim in question – "It is, or can be, justifiable to break something [a promise] that cannot justifiably be broken" – is self-contradictory on its own account; its incoherence does not depend on its being universalized. But such an objection would misconstrue (though in a different way than

presuppose, with Bittner, O'Neill, and others, that maxims have a certain generality through which an agent adopts rules or principles on the basis of which he or she conducts a life. They are, thus, to be distinguished from particular precepts that specify the ways in which those principles are to be implemented and that can be assessed primarily in terms of the degree to which they comport with those larger principles.

[67] This is not to argue that the meaning of the sentence is simply reducible to the meaning of its words. It is to argue, however, that we cannot understand a sentence containing the word "promise" unless we know how that word generally functions in English sentences.

before) the Kantian sense of universalization. On the one hand, there seems to be nothing that would, in itself, prohibit an individual – acting in isolation, in his or her pure particularity, as, for example, a merely sensuous creature – from adopting a self-contradictory maxim. There is nothing inherently incoherent in the act of embracing incoherence, nothing to prevent an individual from choosing to be eccentric, illusive, inconsistent or irrational, nothing that would rule out a self-selected life of self-contradiction. But when we seek to universalize the maxim, everything changes. For Kant, universalizing the maxim of action is nothing more nor less than the process by which the maxim acquires the *form of law*. That's what universalization means. But coherence – non-contradiction – is an inherent, essential, defining feature of law. The reasons for this are not hard to adduce. A law is, by definition, an imperative that entails authoritative, interpersonal claims regarding right and wrong, praise and blame, reward and punishment. As such, it demands the obedience of every individual to whom it applies. But obedience is possible – it is a reasonable expectation – only if the law is coherent. For if the law says "do X" and, at the same time, "do non-X," then individuals cannot possibly know what to do. The law becomes an absurdity or, more properly, ceases to be a law at all. It is, thus, impossible for us coherently to will the universalization of a self-contradictory maxim; and it is precisely that which makes such a maxim morally untenable.

Now it seems plainly wrong to say that no promise can ever justifiably be broken. If I promise to return the weapon that I have borrowed from you, am I absolutely required to return it if, in the interim, you have gone mad?[68] Most of us would say no; to the contrary, it is morally wrong to return the weapon. But then how is this to be reconciled with our apparently categorical obligation to keep promises?

Answering such a question requires precisely that we advert once again to the meaning of our claim – *it is not and cannot be justifiable to break a promise* – hence that we focus on what it means to make a promise. A promise is distinct from a prediction, a recommendation, a wish, and the like; it involves the assumption of an obligation. But it clearly involves a number of other things. For example, a promise is not broken if the failure to carry it out is due to some subsequent circumstance that could not have been foreseen and that makes carrying it out unusually difficult or impossible. If, having promised to marry you, I am accidentally killed before the wedding actually takes place, we would not want to say that I have broken

---

[68] Of course, the example is taken from Plato, *Republic* (331e–332b). See also Cicero, *De Officiis* (Book I, Section 10).

my promise unless, perhaps, I should have foreseen my accidental death. Implicit in the concept of a promise, then, is a belief that one will have a reasonable opportunity to keep one's word. Similarly, the concept of a promise also implies that promises are made by individuals who are capable of knowing whether or not it will be possible to carry out their promises. A very small child who "promises," in all sincerity, to give a million dollars to a friend has not really made a promise. We do not believe that the child has any obligation to carry out the deed in question, for the simple reason that a small child is incapable of understanding what it would mean to incur and follow through on such an obligation; and, as we have seen, a non-obligatory "promise" is not a promise at all.

But is it not possible that our obligation to keep promises – real promises – may sometimes conflict with other, equally well established obligations? Surely there are circumstances in which all of the requirements of a promise are met, yet the promise still should not be kept. The case of returning a weapon to a madman seems to be an example, as does the case of Dr. Jones (5.2.1). We may recall that Dr. Jones had an obligation to keep his promise to deliver a speech at a professional meeting; but he also had an obligation to deal with a medical emergency that would necessitate missing the meeting. As I have argued, in such a circumstance Ross's approach still seems useful. Dr. Jones had a prima facie (PF) obligation to deliver the speech that was overridden by his allthings-considered (ATC) obligation to deal with the emergency. But on what basis – in the light of what kind of moral argument – should we decide that "all things" are such that one obligation outweighs the other? In the instant case, why was the medical emergency morally more important than the promise?

Here again, the answer seems to involve the structure of metaphysical presupposition out of which obligations arise. Specifically, a promise is always constituted in large part by the circumstances in which it occurs, circumstances that are and can only be apprehended through a shared understanding of how things in the world really are, a structure of truth. The person who has made a promise, as a rational agent, does so with an implicit awareness of the promise's possible ramifications, at least as far as these can be reasonably discerned. In this sense, a promise is like any other action. It is inevitably informed by an understanding of what it will accomplish and how it will be interpreted.

As we have seen, every promise implies an understanding that the world is constituted so as to make it possible to carry out the promise, and also that the promise has been made by a rational agent who is capable of understanding the relevant circumstances. But the relevant presuppositions are invariably much broader than this. For example, when I promise to return the weapon that I borrowed from you, implicit in the promise is an understanding that you will not in the interim go mad. Such an understanding, however tacit, is a normal feature of promising – an aspect of what we presuppose to be the nature of a promise – hence is part and parcel of the promise itself. It reflects a shared structure of truth that underwrites the way of life out of which the promise itself emerges. Thus, even if I have had some intimation that you might go mad, it is still likely that my promise presupposes that I will return the weapon only if it is safe to do so. If that circumstance changes, then the terms of the promise no longer obtain. I did not promise to return the weapon even if you go mad; and thus, having observed and verified your new insanity, my failure now to return the weapon in no way entails that I have broken a promise. Similarly, if I promise to marry you, I do not expressly qualify this by noting that I am an adult of sound mind, that I will not soon be killed in an accident, that you will not go mad in the interim, and the like. Yet all of these presumptions – rooted in a shared sense of how things in the world really are – are almost certainly implicit in my promise and are, as such, partly determinative of the promise itself. And so too for Dr. Jones. His promise to deliver the speech was obligatory, but implicit in the promise was a wide array of unstated but reconstructable codicils: he would not go mad in the interim, he would not be required to present his speech while standing on his head, he would not be called on to deal with an unexpected medical emergency in his own town, and so on. These are taken for granted, but are no less crucial for being so.

2. Such an account is analogous to, and mirrored in, the common law of contracts. According to the standard work, a contract is a promise that the law will enforce.[69] While not all promises are contracts – the law will not enforce all promises – all contracts are promises; and this means that the basic task of contract law in identifying the terms of a contract is to determine exactly what has been promised. Only then can disputes about a contract be adjudicated intelligently. But it has long been understood that in pursuing this task courts have a responsibility not only to consider what has actually been said but also to discover what are sometimes called implied conditions. Courts, in other words, have to interpret or reconstruct features that are an important part of the contract but that

---

[69] E. Allan Farnsworth, *Contracts* (Boston: Little, Brown, 1990), pp. 3–4. See also, Charles Fried, *Contract as Promise: A Theory of Contractual Obligation* (Cambridge, Mass.: Harvard University Press, 1981). For a critical discussion of this view, see Randy E. Barnett, "Some Problems with Contract as Promise," *Cornell Law Review* 77 (1992), and the related exchange.

have not been expressed by the literal meaning of the contract's words. Such an inquiry will frequently require, among other things, an examination of "all the relevant circumstances surrounding the transaction," and this may include an analysis of "any applicable course of dealing, course of performance, or usage."[70] Thus, under the common law the meaning of a contract often "must be gleaned from its context, including all the circumstances of the transaction," and this may well involve reference to "normal habits in the use of language, habits that would be expected of reasonable persons in the circumstances of the parties."[71] Indeed, it is well established that courts, in determining exactly what was contracted, must often supply terms or conditions that the contracting parties have omitted from their expressed agreements, perhaps through haste or inadvertence: "Even if the agreement does not make an event a condition, the court may supply a term that does so . . . . Such conditions are often referred to as 'implied' conditions, since a court determines whether to supply a term that makes an event a condition and what term to supply by the process of implication."

What is true of legally enforceable promises is true, *mutatis mutandis*, of all promises. In order to understand exactly what it is that a particular promise obliges us to do, we must interpret the promise in the light of circumstances, normal habits of language, implied conditions, and so on. But we can understand those circumstances, habits and conditions only in the light of the shared structure of metaphysical presupposition out of which they themselves emerge. Such a structure provides, in effect, an explication and elaboration of the meaning of the promise. It explains what the promise is, provides standards for determining when the promise has actually been made and what the promise actually means, hence accounts for the fact that some things that look like promises are not really promises and do not, as a result, involve obligations.

Here, then, we have perhaps one plausible way of accounting for the difference between PF and ATC oughts/obligations, as described in 5.2.1 above. PF obligations are exactly what the phrase itself implies: they are prima facie in the sense of being superficial, apparent, phenomenal, unanalyzed. They represent what initially seems to be the case, not necessarily what really is the case. For the actual meanings of obligation-generating actions are always embedded in a complex array of circumstances, themselves understood in the context of a shared structure of truth. An analysis of those circumstances can and frequently does show that the apparent, surface

---

[70] Farnsworth, *Contracts*, p. 511.
[71] *Ibid.*, p. 514. See also, E. Allan Farnsworth, "Meaning in the Law of Contracts," *Yale Law Journal* 76, pp. 939–65.

meaning of an action does not adequately convey its real meaning, its meaning ATC. In the instant case, it's not so much that Dr. Jones's obligation to deal with the medical emergency outweighs his obligation to deliver the speech. Rather, his obligation to deliver the speech itself presupposes, and is in part constituted by, the absence of a medical emergency requiring his attention. It is understood, in other words, that Dr. Jones did not promise to deliver the speech regardless of any and all possible medical emergencies. The actual meaning of the promise, like that of any obligation-generating action, "must be gleaned from its context, including all the circumstances of the transaction."

We can perhaps see this more clearly if we consider another of Kant's moral laws, viz., the prohibition against suicide. At first blush, our formulation seems not to work very well here: the meaning of *it is or can be justifiable to commit suicide if one so chooses* appears to involve no contradiction at all since, in part, the concept of suicide seems not to have the kind of implicit moral content that we have found in the concept of a promise. A promise is inherently obligatory, but suicide is merely taking one's own life.

This is not all that we might say, however. Understanding fully the concept of taking one's own life requires coming to grips with our concept of human life itself and, in particular, of the value that we attach to it; and this means, in turn, referring to the structure of metaphysical presupposition upon which our society is based. It may be that we value human life so highly that nothing else – no combination of other values – could outweigh it. Indeed, human life might be infinitely valuable, and uniquely so. In such a circumstance, the claim that *it is or can be justifiable to commit suicide if one so chooses* would, I believe, be self-contradictory. For if we assume, as I think we must, that justification is necessarily based on a regard for some value or set of values, then our claim in fact reads "it is or can be justifiable to sacrifice, if one so chooses, something so valuable that it overrides any and all other values, in any and all combinations, that might justify such a sacrifice" or, more simply, "it is or can be justifiable to sacrifice something the sacrifice of which cannot be justified." Since this claim is a self-contradiction, suicide would be ruled out. On the other hand, it may be that we do not value life quite so highly. One can well imagine deciding that while human life is extremely valuable, there are other things – freedom, dignity, honor – that might be even more valuable. In such a circumstance, our inquiry might conclude that while thoughtless or negligent or gratuitous or hasty suicide might indeed be self-contradictory, hence immoral, not all suicide is. In some situations – involving, perhaps, the value of the good life as opposed to mere life itself – suicide might well be morally justified. (One thinks, for example, of Seneca's exemplary suicide, as depicted by Tacitus.) We would thus have to revise Kant's blanket rejection of all suicide precisely in the light of an analysis of our own conceptual presuppositions regarding the value of life and the nature of justification.

Our inquiries into the moral law may be best understood as inquiries into the implications of concepts that compose, for us, the basis of culture and that determine, thereby, the kinds of thoughts that it is possible for us coherently to have. To argue about concepts – to argue, for example, about the value of life itself – is simply to try to get clear about the logic of our own underlying beliefs. To the person who insists on the infinite value of life, for example, we would have to point out that such a view would likely entail an absolute prohibition not only against suicide but against capital punishment, war (including defensive war), killing in self-defense, and the like. Arguments such as these would have as their immediate goal not the establishment of the moral law but, rather, the discovery of those fundamental beliefs about the world that characterize a particular form of life. From such a characterization, however, one might indeed derive, for that form of life, a code of ethics.

3. Ought claims are rooted in claims about how things in the world really are, hence are discoverable through an investigation of a shared structure of truth. The tradition of inquiry outlined in Chapter 3 above applies not only to questions about Hall of Famers, horses, chalkboards, sonatas, oceans and the like but to questions about duties and obligations as well. If we want to know what we ought to do, we need to pursue the kind of investigation that Euthyphro and Socrates engage in, or the kind of argumentation that Strawson suggests. It is a quest for coherence or connectedness, and to that extent is very much in the spirit of Kantian ethics. It is an effort to understand how our moral intuitions and our conceptual apparatus – the background or structure of truth that constitutes, in part, our way of life – can be rendered rationally intelligible so that we can avoid contradicting ourselves. Sometimes this will be easy: given the contexts, no one doubts that Dr. Jones should skip the speech and deal with the emergency. At other times, though, it will be extremely difficult. The question of what our obligation-generating actions really mean – i.e., how can we make sense of them given the larger structure of metaphysical presupposition to which we are committed – is often contentious and vexing. It speaks, however, directly to the very nature of our moral life.

But why doesn't such an approach simply revive the question of empty formalism? If, for example, the morality of suicide is to be decided by whether or not a society values life infinitely, then haven't we merely finessed the question of right and wrong by shifting it imperceptibly from the overt realm of decision-making to the shadowy realm of cultural belief? And shouldn't cultural beliefs then become the focus of explicit moral debate? If a culture values life infinitely, then shouldn't we ask if it is right to do so? More generally, if duties are determined largely by the consistent application of a shared structure of metaphysical presupposition, isn't it possible that anything could be justified? In particular, don't we raise the specter of a radical and thoroughgoing cultural relativism? Isn't it possible that our structure of truth could just be *wrong* about what we should do?

Three things need to be said in response:

(1) The kind of analysis that I have described produces at least some results that are and must be universal, though in a rather special sense. The case of promising is typical. As we have seen, the claim that *it is, or can be, justifiable to break a promise if one so chooses* is a self-contradiction in virtue of the meaning of the concepts of which it is composed. This, however, is not a local fact. For the claim is a self-contradiction wherever and whenever it appears, as long as the concepts, including and especially the concept of a promise, continue to mean what they mean. Insofar as promises are promises, they cannot justifiably be broken. It is true, of course, that words themselves do change their meaning. But when we say that the self-contradictoriness of the claim that *it is, or can be, justifiable to break a promise if one so chooses* reflects the meanings of its words, this pre-supposes a relatively stable connection between word and concept. If the meaning of the word "promise" were to change – if it no longer denoted the concept of a promise – then of course our claim would no longer be the same claim; it too would have a different meaning. What counts, plainly, is the concept; and it seems to be quite clear that, in virtue of the meaning of that concept, we always have an obligation to keep our promises (again remembering that the precise content of a promise is often only implicit, that what I appear to have promised may not be what I have actually promised, hence that what seems PF obligatory may not be obligatory ATC). Any sentence in any language that has the same meaning as our claim about breaking promises will always express a self-contradiction. The concept of a promise is what it is. It is eternal, immutable, imperishable. It never changes, and its logical implications – e.g., that it is obligatory – are permanent.

One might object, of course, that concepts do change. Our idea of something at one point in time may be quite different from our idea of it at another. One might suppose, then, that the concept of a promise could so change that it would no longer contain the feature of being obligatory. But if a particular concept can undergo certain kinds of changes – can be understood in different ways – and still retain its essential meaning, obviously there are other kinds of changes that modify a concept to such an extent that it becomes a different concept altogether. Surely this is true for the obligatory nature of promises. If we were to understand promising as involving no obligations, then we would no longer have a concept of something that is distinct – at least not in that way – from predicting, recommending, wishing, warning, and the like. The concept of promising, properly understood, would be lost to us. We would now be using the word "promise" to denote a new and different concept; and if we failed to find a new word to denote the concept that we used to call "promise," then that concept would simply have become moribund.

(2) Even in such a circumstance, however, it would still not be justified to break (what we used to call) a promise. In a widely read and much discussed essay, Korn and Korn purport to describe a culture – in the Tonga Islands of the South Pacific – "where there is no institution of promising."[72] The people of this culture regularly make what might appear to be promises. But Korn and Korn argue that such apparent promises are not in fact promises at all, since "they are not regarded by Tongans as committing the speaker to the performance of the action."[73] Promising simply doesn't occur in Tonga. Indeed, it is "incompatible with the Tongan view of the future and Tongans' conduct of social relationships."[74]

If this description of Tongan culture is accurate – a fairly big if – then we would have to conclude that the concept of promising is not a feature of all conceptual schemes. Promising is, in some sense, culture-specific. And if that is true, then it would seem that the obligation to obey promises is relative to a particular socio-cultural context. The approach to ethical questions that I have described would involve a kind of relativism that, again, bases the moral law in the idiosyncratic features of particular cultures. But in one very important sense, this would be false. For it is always, eternally wrong to break a promise. Wherever a promise has been made – and assuming we understand just what has been promised – it is obligatory. The existence of a culture without promising would in no way change this. In such a culture, of course, no promises would be broken since none would be made; one cannot make a promise unless the concept of promising is somehow available. But this in no way changes the fact that promises are obligatory. A culture that does not have the concept of a triangle is equally a culture that does not know the Pythagorean

---

[72] Fred Korn and Shulamit R. Decktor Korn, "Where People Don't Promise," *Ethics* 93 (1983), pp. 444–51.

[73] *Ibid.*, p. 447.

[74] *Ibid.*, p. 450.

314   The Idea of the State

theorem. From this, however, we would not want to conclude that the Pythagorean theorem is sometimes right, sometimes wrong. It is, in fact, always right; but it is not always recognized, hence not always of practical consequence. And so too with promising.

Does this not leave open the possibility, however, that a society could decide to eschew or adopt a particular concept more or less as it pleases? If so, if it could prescribe to itself any set of concepts that it wishes, then couldn't it in effect legislate any kind of morality whatsoever? Couldn't a culture freely decide, for example, to adopt practices that we would all plainly identify as horrifyingly immoral and – on the account here provided – feel morally justified in doing so?

Such an objection is wrong for the simple reason that cultures do not and cannot choose conceptual materials in this way. Indeed, things are rather the other way around: a culture is itself constituted by a conceptual apparatus, reflecting a shared structure of metaphysical presupposition. An understanding of how things in the world really are is, in large part, what makes a culture what it is. It determines the kinds of thoughts that people can have, the kinds of choices they can make, the kinds of judgments, moral and otherwise, that are available to them. The idea of selecting willy nilly this or that set of concepts is an absurdity; for any such choice could not itself but be informed, guided and constrained by an already established structure of truth.

(3) Cultures do differ, of course, and this means that their moral laws may differ, even quite dramatically. But from this one cannot conclude that the approach to moral judgment that I have described is merely an empty formalism. It has rich moral content in at least two senses. First, it indicates the moral force of concepts such that wherever and whenever a particular concept is known and used – the concept of a promise, for example – its ethical force is precisely and objectively determined. Second, it has the potential to indicate for any particular culture just what its moral laws must be. Perhaps we cannot prescribe to a culture the concept of a promise; but we can say to any culture that employs such a concept that it must acknowledge, on pain of contradiction, the truth of the claim that promises cannot be broken.

In a similar way, the exact content of particular promises can be determined only internal to a particular way of life. Dr. Jones's duties are determined not just by the concept of a promise but by the concept of a medical emergency, the concept of illness, the concept of human flourishing and of its connection to physical health, and the like. It is only in the light of such considerations, rooted in a shared conceptual apparatus, that we can decide whether a particular putative obligation is not merely PF but ATC obligatory.

Moral philosophy is a matter of uncovering ethical principles that are logically implicit in a particular way of life. Perhaps we cannot rule out the possibility of deep and unbridgeable differences among cultures, hence cannot rule out a kind of moral relativism. But the question of whether different societies really do view the world in radically different ways and that such differences are in principle irresolvable is, in the end, an empirical one, something that can be demonstrated only through precisely the kind of analysis that I have described. One culture believes that pederasty, or the ritual sacrifice of young children, or female "circumcision," or euthanasia, or suicide is morally acceptable, even required. In another culture, these things are morally repugnant; one has a duty to avoid them. Do such differences represent contradictions internal to one or the other of the cultures? Is the practice of pederasty in ancient Athens an anomaly, something inconsistent with the larger structure of moral and metaphysical presupposition that underwrites Athenian culture, an inconsistency that could be uncovered through a systematic and thorough philosophical analysis? Or does it reflect, rather, a faithful interpretation of what the larger structure entails, hence a moral claim completely at odds with moral claims based on an equally faithful interpretation of a different culture? The issue cannot be prejudged. But the prospect of deep and abiding incommensurabilities among cultures, though practically troubling in a shrinking world, is itself theoretically unproblematic. For if two cultures are truly different in that way – if their practices faithfully reflect ways of thinking about the world that are deeply different from one another – then conflicts between them would defy any kind of theoretical resolution. Conversation, analysis and moral theory would be useless. Between two such cultures, only two possibilities would be available: mutual avoidance or war.

But many moral conflicts, and perhaps most of the ones with which we are commonly preoccupied, are not of this nature. They reflect, rather, a failure to recognize and act in accordance with a shared structure of truth. Of Germany in the 1930s, Herman writes that "[i]t is not as if individual Nazis were in no position to see (because of impoverishment of culture or upbringing, say) who was and who wasn't a person, or didn't know (because they were moral primitives, perhaps) what kinds of things it was morally permissible to do to persons."[75] Surely this is correct. Individual Germans were raised in a culture according to which Jews were human beings much like anyone else – beings of flesh and blood, of love and hate, of ideas and appetites, beings with whom one could

---

[75] Herman, *The Practice of Moral Judgment*, p. 91.

converse and play and trade – a culture that understood, moreover, that human beings as such should be treated humanely, indeed, a culture that spawned, among so many other things, the idea of the categorical imperative. Even if we accept the claim that German culture was long contaminated by a deep strain of anti-Semitism, this in itself cannot erase the plain fact before the eyes of virtually any German, namely, that the features that distinguish humans from other creatures, hence that make them what they are, were every bit as characteristic of Jews as of non-Jews. From such a perspective, anti-Semitism represents a kind of internal cultural contradiction; and the Holocaust itself is perhaps best viewed as a horrifying episode of persistent mass insanity, evidence of a society radically, pathologically out of touch with itself, engaged in an immense and devastating exercise in incoherence.

In formulating such an example, Herman at once implies and strenuously resists the kind of account that I am offering. She says that moral judgment must be, according to Kant,

> an activity with a customary context of occurrence. Normal moral agents do not question the permissibility of everything they propose to do (having lunch, going to the movies, and so on). We expect moral agents to have acquired knowledge of the sorts of actions that it is generally not permissible to do and of the sorts of actions that, in the normal course of things, have no moral import. And we do not imagine normal moral agents bringing maxims of grossly immoral acts to the CI [categorical imperative] procedure, only to discover (to their surprise?) that these acts are forbidden.[76]

What could this mean, other than that Kantian moral agents necessarily have a tremendous amount of "independent moral knowledge"[77] – they know right from wrong, at least in a great many cases – *prior* to engaging in the kind of deliberation associated with the idea of a categorical imperative? Such moral knowledge is rooted in culture, in the "customary context" that distinguishes grossly immoral acts from morally innocuous ones and that allows agents to "know the features of their proposed actions that raise moral questions *before*" they seek to discover Kantian moral laws.[78]

Now Herman wants to say that moral knowledge of this kind is essentially a matter of knowing "rules of moral salience" whose function is to "guide the moral agent to the perception and description of the morally relevant features of his circumstances of action."[79] This is a crucial function, but also a limited one: knowing the rules of moral salience is

---

[76] *Ibid.*, p. 76.
[77] *Ibid.*, p. 75.
[78] *Ibid.*
[79] *Ibid.*, p. 78.

a necessary condition of, but not the same as, knowing the moral law. It is hard to see, however, why customary moral knowledge should or, indeed, could be limited in this way. According to Herman, the rules of moral salience tell me that a punch in the nose potentially raises morally relevant questions. Surely this is not so, however, if the punch occurs in, say, a boxing match. The rules of moral salience, if they're any good, would indicate as much, since everyone who knows what boxing is knows, in advance, that a punch in boxing is morally unproblematic. But what is involved in such knowledge? What exactly would it mean to say that a punch in boxing is morally unproblematic? Presumably it would mean nothing other than that it is morally acceptable – consistent with the moral law – for one boxer to punch another boxer in the ring; and if rules of moral salience can say this about boxing, then why couldn't they say the same thing about all those situations – self-defense, play acting, accidents – in which punching is morally acceptable? Moreover, when the rules tell us that punching *is* morally salient, how could we possibly interpret this as anything other than an account of precisely those circumstances in which punching is in fact wrong, at least PF? And from such an account surely it is a comparatively short step to uncovering the moral law regarding punches. All of which is to say that the implications of rules of moral salience would seem to go far beyond what Herman allows. To know which actions, and which features of actions, are morally salient and why is in itself to presuppose, if only implicitly, an extensive, substantive knowledge of right and wrong.

4. The analysis of grammar and language provides, as we have seen (3.2.1), a model for philosophical analysis in general, on the basis of which one can come to appreciate the essential unity of philosophical inquiry: ontology, epistemology and logic (3.4.2). To this list we can now add ethics. Just as the analysis of grammatical rules involves the elucidation of materials already implicitly known to native speakers, so does the analysis of a conceptual apparatus – a shared structure of truth – make explicit the moral as well as ontological presuppositions to which the members of a society are committed. To know how things in the world really are, at least according to our lights, is to know what we think is virtuous, what we think is good, what we think is right.[80]

Such an account of moral thinking is profoundly relevant to our understanding of the idea of the state, for it provides special insight into the

[80] I believe that Strawson's own famous essay on freedom and resentment, according to which our way of life forces us to presuppose free choice whether or not determinism is true, is a paradigmatic case in point. P. F Strawson, "Freedom and Resentment," in Gary Watson, ed., *Free Will* (Oxford: Oxford University Press, 1982).

nature and possibility of human freedom. I would emphasize, in this connection, what might be called the two-fold nature of language. On the one hand, language is a social practice involving strict, rigid rules that determine what can and cannot be said. On the other, to engage in such a practice is at the same time to engage in an activity of the greatest freedom imaginable. Language is, and must be, both of these – a structure of limits and a structure of opportunity – coexisting, moreover, in a relationship of complete mutual dependence. The rules presuppose the freedom, the freedom the rules.

If one wanted to tell the story of an imaginary, day-long odyssey through the streets of Dublin, one might begin with a sentence such as "Stately, plump Buck Mulligan came from the stairhead, bearing a bowl of lather on which a mirror and a razor lay crossed." It's a wonderful sentence, beautifully suited to its author's purposes. But surely the story that it introduces might just as easily have began with a different sentence, such as "Plump, stately Buck Mulligan came from the stairhead . . . ." Or a sentence in which Buck Mulligan was "cherubic" rather than "plump," or, indeed, "skinny" rather than "plump." Or a sentence in which Buck came not from the "stairhead" but from the "top of the stairs." Or in which he was "carrying" rather than "bearing" the bowl, and so on. This is not to say that all of these alternatives would have worked equally well. The word "bearing," for example, seems to give the scene a suitably liturgical flavor (along with the crossed implements) that the word "carrying" might lack. The point, rather, is that the author of the very first sentence made a decision, a choice among a wide variety of alternatives, and could well have chosen otherwise. Indeed, the range of highly plausible alternatives is surely staggering. For example, the entire structure of the sentence could have been completely different: "Bearing a bowl of lather on which a mirror and a razor lay crossed, Buck Mulligan – stately, plump – came from the stairhead." Alternatively, the first sentence could just as easily have been the second sentence, the second the first. Indeed, the first sentence could have been eliminated altogether. Moreover, just as the structure of sentences and paragraphs can be configured in all kinds of ways, so can the structure of chapters and of larger narrative forms. The degrees of freedom are seemingly infinite, the flexibility and generosity of language evidently unlimited.

And yet, language is at the same time a structure of iron-clad rules, the violation of which is strictly prohibited. Thus, for example, the author was not free to write "Mulligan the from plump Buck stairhead mirror bowl stately a came crossed lay of razor lather on bearing and which a a." Nor again was he free to write ". . . on which a mirrors and a razors lied crossed." The range of permissible alternatives within the rules is enormous, perhaps infinite, but so too is the range of unacceptable structures and usages. This is not to deny that the rules can be bent or challenged or, in certain cases, deliberately flouted. (Thus, for example, an author who could write about Buck Mulligan, Stephen Daedelus and Leopold Bloom could also write about Humphrey Chimpden Earwicker.) But one cannot flout a rule unless the rule exists; nor can one challenge a particular rule without, at the same time, proposing an alternative rule, thereby affirming the larger structure of rules that makes such a proposal intelligible in the first place.

What is important to emphasize in all this is that freedom in language and the rules of language do not describe two opposed and otherwise unrelated features of linguistic practice. There is between them, rather, a fundamental connection. For without the rules, language is impossible; and without language there is literally – *literally* – nothing to say. The infinite freedom that language permits is completely and entirely dependent on the restrictions and limitations that constitute the language in the first place.

One can perhaps best see this in the conversational use of language. Conversation is an improvisatory art. Typically, when we converse we make things up as we go, responding to one another more-or-less immediately and often saying things that we literally have never said before, at least not in precisely the same way. At any particular moment, the range of possible utterances from which we can choose is immense, incalculable; and it seems virtually impossible to identify any one factor or set of factors external to ourselves that would determine which choices we shall make. We are, in this sense, quite free, indeed radically so. But conversation also presupposes an enormous range of rules – semantic, syntactic, pragmatic. These lend order and direction to what would otherwise be utterly chaotic and random; and again, they make it possible for us to understand one another. Without the rules, speakers wouldn't know what to say or how to say it. They would face what Hegel once called the "freedom of the void," and this is no freedom at all. They would have no basis for making choices; and without such a basis, choice is impossible because unimaginable. Hearers, of course, would be in the same boat. Without rules, utterances would be unintelligible and meaningless except as purely natural emanations, little different from the chirping of birds or the bleating of lambs.

Improvisatory activity within a structure of rules produces some of the most sublime and uplifting instances of human freedom. The miracle of Homeric epic poetry – an oral, improvised art – is the miracle of free decision-making operating within strict parameters of metric, symbolic and narrative formulas. Something quite similar seems to be true of certain medieval traditions of Japanese poetry, wherein groups of bards simultaneously created and performed verse according to established poetic conventions. In our own time, the language of music is exploited by jazz musicians to create improvised compositions of often extraordinary complexity and exquisite invention. In all such cases, the freedom-within-order that we take for granted in ordinary conversation assumes a certain grandeur, reflecting what seems at times to be the very height of human creativity. In a perhaps less elevated but no less influential vein, we see this as well in certain athletic events – for example, in basketball or soccer, properly played – which thrill us in part because we experience in them the coordinated and well-synchronized social activity of free individual athletes. It is, I think, this diversity-in-unity, the seamless order arising out of discrete choices, the spontaneity rooted in fixed rules and roles, that makes such events so appealing for participant and spectator alike.

At its best, a jazz band or soccer team is an organism.[81] It is a complex entity composed of distinct but interrelated elements. In each case, the whole is dependent on the parts, the parts on the whole. The individual jazz musician or soccer player is, when isolated and alone, a greatly diminished figure.[82] Similarly, a jazz band without, say, its bassist makes a hollow sound, and a soccer team without, say, its midfielder is a likely loser. In each case, the roles played by the individual parts are delineated with considerable precision, their functionality determined by the organism's overall structure. But at the same time, the organism is animated by the individual's free and spontaneous embodiment of the role and by the ferment that results from each individual adjusting constantly to the activities of the others. The organism is a pulsating, percolating entity in motion, one that grows and changes direction while maintaining its coherence and integrity, and that provides for its constituent elements both the possibility of freedom and the security of home.

---

[81] The connection is not unknown. The (enormously successful) coach of the women's basketball team at the University of Connecticut put it this way (*New York Times*, 12 November 2000, p. 37): "Because I grew up watching soccer, I've always felt that basketball should be played in the same free-flowing way.... That's the key to soccer. You see things develop 2–3 passes down the road. Everyone is anticipating, playing off each other.... It's like jazz. It can't be chaotic jazz, heroin-induced jazz. There's got to be structure. But there also has to be freedom where players have a chance to improvise." For a related view, see Peter J. Steinberger, "Culture and Freedom in the Fifties: The Case of Jazz," *Virginia Quarterly Review* 74 (Winter 1998), pp. 118–33. The basketball–jazz connection is pursued by Michael Novak, *The Joy of Sports: End Zones, Bases, Baskets, Balls, and the Consecration of the American Spirit* (New York: Hamilton Press, 1988), p. 101. But Novak's treatment is uninformed and crude, to say the least, and is invoked in support of a thesis that might charitably be termed bizarre.

[82] Though there are exceptions. One would be hard-pressed to characterize as "diminished" the solo piano flights of, say, an Art Tatum or an Oscar Peterson.

The organic state, as a structure of moral and metaphysical propositions rendered authoritative and suitable for practice, functions very
much along these lines. As moral agents and citizens of the state, we are
required to make choices about right and wrong, good and bad. The fact
that we have this opportunity is, to be sure, what gives our actions their
"moral" character. It establishes, that is, the foundation of freedom upon
which we can coherently invoke fundamental categories of praise and
blame – categories without which moral discourse becomes unintelligible.
But our moral choices are, at the same time, deeply informed, shaped,
constrained and underwritten by the universe of discourse – the structure
of moral and metaphysical presupposition – within which we operate.
That structure doesn't make our choices for us. But it provides the
materials necessary for us to choose, it establishes the kinds of choices
that are available to us, and it provides grounds – the only comprehensible
grounds – for critically assessing the choices that we have made. Was an
action performed according to the rules? Was an interpretation of right
and wrong in a specific case consistent with recognized and established
standards of right and wrong? Is a particular rule consistent with the range
of other accepted moral rules, or does it need to be amended in the
interest of coherence? We address such questions by consulting, as best
we can, the conceptual apparatus or structure of truth that constitutes the
foundation of our way of life. In this sense, the moral life of the citizen is
an on-going and continuous series of engagements and negotiations with
the often changing and often elusive myriad of facts and circumstances,
intuitions and rules, concepts and presuppositions that populate the
teeming landscape of everyday life – all requiring us to make decisions
of one sort or another and all providing, at once, both the rigid parameters
and the open spaces between those parameters that, together, make it
possible for us to choose. The activity of the moral agent is, thus, an
activity of rule-governed judgment, sometimes premeditated, sometimes
quite improvised; and insofar as it is undertaken in concert with other
agents – as it often is – it is not infrequently an exercise in collective
improvisation, strictly governed by a system of moral and metaphysical
presupposition, animated by the free choices of discrete individual
human beings who are, in spite of their individuality, intimately, essentially and ineluctably connected to one another, and driven by a powerful
if often only dimly felt need to make rational sense, to be coherent.

5. I have argued that the state is and must be unlimited in scope and
absolute in authority. These are metaphysical or ontological claims –
claims about the essential nature of the state – and to them I have now
added a third and final ontological claim, namely, that in its internal

articulation the state is and must be an organism. As children of the modern age, we are strongly committed to the view that political society should embody principles both of democratic equality and of human freedom. But we badly misconstrue these commitments – indeed, we directly subvert them – when we think of democracy primarily as a policy-making apparatus and when we think of freedom primarily as the absence of restriction; for in each case, we find ourselves making dubious or untenable claims that actually undermine the very intuitions they are intended to serve. The idea of the state – understood as a structure of interdependent and mutually coherent propositions about how things in the world really are – is the idea of an organism in which whole and part are deeply bound together in a relationship of utter mutual dependence. Only here – in the idea of the state, rather than government – can we redeem our commitment to democracy; and only here – in the idea of an organically interconnected system of rules that establishes the very possibility of choice – can we actualize our true conception of liberty.

It should be clear that the account of the state that I have provided does not directly address many of the questions commonly raised by contemporary empirical theorists of the state, e.g., questions involving the comparison of particular regimes, processes of state formation, the periodization of state forms, and the like; nor does it address standard varieties of anarchist thought that challenge the very possibility of a legitimate state;[83] nor again does it deal with emergent and influential claims concerning the obsolescence of the state in the face of an increasingly interdependent world. These are important matters. But describing the essence of a thing is, in and of itself, very different from describing all of the particular conditions under which examples of that thing might come into or fall out of existence; and by the same token, to have uncovered and analyzed the nature of a thing is not to have justified its existence in any final or definitive sesne. Certainly the account that I have provided is hardly without implications for empirical theory; after all, one cannot know if the state is obsolete unless one knows first what the state is. Nor is my account devoid of significant moral implications, since it provides, among other things, criteria for distinguishing good states from bad, i.e., better instantiations from worse. But all such implications presuppose a prior commitment to – are in some sense internal to – the state itself. In and of itself, the idea of the state tells us neither whether we will nor whether we should live in a state; and if this is true, then the effort

---

[83] Of course, I have addressed, and have sought to refute, the particular anarchist line of argument pursued by Robert Paul Wolff (see 5.1.1–2 above). That, however, hardly constitutes a refutation of the anarchist project *per se*.

to describe the idea of the state might simply represent another example, however modest, of philosophy painting its gray in gray. That, at any rate, is a possibility that I would not be willing simply to foreclose.

There can be no doubt that the arguments of this book have been presented in, as it were, universalistic terms. But it may well be the case that the idea of the state is in fact embedded in and reflective of merely one world-view among many and is, as such, redolent with partisan or sectarian implications. Surely we cannot peremptorily rule out the possibility that things look very different from very different vantage points, and that, for example, political institutions when seen from the perspective of people who have been colonized might appear very different from the same institutions when seen from the perspective of people who have been colonizers. We cannot reject as simply implausible the claim that certain very basic categories – the idea of a "developed" and an "underdeveloped" world, the notion of East and West, the concept of citizen and nation, of consent and accountability – are reified constructions that lack universal validity and that have become, indeed, illusions of a fetishized discourse. And thus, we cannot simply dismiss the claim that the idea of the state is yet another of these, and that an account such as mine expresses in universal language a notion that is, in fact, only partial and highly contestable.

Claims of this sort pose, in one sense, a very serious challenge; but they also represent a view of things that I have not sought to deny. Indeed, I have insisted that the idea of the state is in fact internal to and reflective of a particular philosophical tradition; and while I have proposed that this is our tradition, I have said little if anything about exactly to whom the word "our" should apply. Obviously, that is a question of the greatest consequence. But it's also a question that – like all questions – can be asked and answered only internal to one or another universe of discourse; and this fact, if it is a fact, suggests both that the problem is staggeringly complex and that our resources for dealing with it are apt to be paltry at best.

It would nonetheless be a serious error to think of the state I have described as just one political, moral, or practical option among many, a picture of political society that we might find attractive or compelling, hence worth choosing over other competing pictures. The idea of the state is not something to be conjured up and recommended, like a policy. To the contrary, the argument of this book has been philosophical. Its aim has been to derive the idea of the state from a set of important and widely held, though often unarticulated, presuppositions about the nature of human thought and action. I have, of course, tried to show that any particular state embodies and is constituted by one or another structure of truth. But I have also tried to show that the theory that underwrites this claim is itself entailed by a particular philosophical perspective. It emerges out of and is deeply embedded in a complex, multi-layered theory of human thought and of our relationship to the world. As such, it reflects, indeed is part and parcel of, what can only be described as a grand intellectual edifice – a powerful conception of things and of thinking about things that has been constructed and elaborated over the course of two centuries by a myriad of otherwise quite diverse authors and that constitutes, in effect, the common ground of the post-Kantian age. I am speaking here of a comprehensive world-view – our world-view – that encompasses a diversity of intellectual habits, dispositions and judgments and that provides a more or less systematic account of the fundamental relationship between thought and object. In providing such an account, moreover, it makes explicit the usually tacit conception that we have of ourselves. It is a structure of self-understanding. It tells us who we are. And among the nearly infinite array of things that it says about our own existence, it offers, as its principal *political* teaching, a claim at once simple in conception and rich in implication. This is the claim that the state is fundamentally an idea; and I believe that the resolute and on-going pursuit of this claim is, or ought to be, the primary task of political philosophy as we confront and try somehow to manage the stubbornly tragic promise of a new millennium.

Index

Index

language, philosophy of:
  and freedom 317–320
  in Hobbes 59–60
  in Strawson 106–110
Laud, William 160
legitimacy: *see* authority; consent;
  obligation
Leibniz, Gottfried Wilhelm 74, 104, 105
Letwin, William 186–187
Levinas, Emmanuel xi
liberalism 72–83
  and the art of separation 149–150,
    163–164, 187–188
  and communitarianism 177–178,
    182–183
  justificatory 75–76, 77, 78, 79–80
  and limited government 150–151,
    182–187
  pure 76, 77–78
  see also toleration
Livy 286
Lloyd, S. A. 235
Locke, John 66, 150
  on consent 200, 212
  on toleration 151–164, 192

Machiavelli, Niccolò 49, 287
Mannheim, Karl 289–290
Martinich, A. P. 241
Marx, Karl 8–9, 13, 22
McDowell, John 114, 116, 120, 124, 125
Mead, G. H. 24
metaphysical theory 3
  coherence and agreement in 102–104,
    108–112
  and the concept of judgment 130–131
  distinguished from prudential theories
    4–8, 13–14, 31–32, 41–55, 73–83,
    143–146, 188–193
  in Hobbes 43–50, 59–67
  and moral argument 311–317
  nature of 29–30, 32–33, 95–105,
    126–127
  in Plato 50–54, 96–104
  and political thought 6–8, 13–14, 31,
    32, 56–58, 95–96
  and post-Kantian thought 112–117
  Rawls' view of 74
  and the state 28–31, 33–34, 141–146
  in Strawson 106–112
  universality of 34–35, 106
Mill, John Stuart 295, 296
monarchy
  Hobbes' preference for 42–46, 47, 48
  in political thought and history 266

moral argument
  in Kant 294–303
  and meaning 304–317
  and metaphysics 311–317
Müller, Adam 287

Neurath, Otto 110
Newman, John Henry 17–19
Newton, Isaac 104, 105
Nietzsche, Friedrich 283, 292
Nino, Carlos Santiago 275
Nozick, Robert 212

Oakeshott, Michael 15
obligation 307–308
  and autonomy 195–200
  distinguished from natural duties
    205–211
  and gratitude 222–225
  political, theory of 195–201, 227–228,
    251–254
  and resistance 233–251
  as tacit consent 212–222
  terminology of 201–205, 205–206
  see also disobedience, civil
O'Neill, Onora 295, 298, 300, 301,
  302, 303
ontological theory, *see* metaphysical theory
organisms
  as democratic 289–293
  and equality 290–293
  Kant's theory of 285–286
  and the master–slave relationship
    283–285
  political theories of 286–288

Paton, H. J. 296, 297, 302, 303
Paul, St. 155
Perpetua, St. 159, 160
Peters, R. S. 65
Pippin, Robert 125
Pitkin, Hanna 197, 225, 226
Plato xi, 14, 28, 41, 49, 55, 56, 57,
  58, 89, 106, 108, 267, 272, 283,
  288, 292
  on coherence 118–119
  Crito 222, 223
  Euthyphro 96–104, 109–110, 174,
    190–191, 231, 311
  on the idea of a conceptual apparatus
    126
  Meno 99–100, 119
  metaphysical and prudential theories in
    50–54, 56, 94, 126
  Republic 50–54

For EU product safety concerns, contact us at Calle de José Abascal, 56–1°,
28003 Madrid, Spain or eugpsr@cambridge.org.

www.ingramcontent.com/pod-product-compliance
Ingram Content Group UK Ltd.
Pitfield, Milton Keynes, MK11 3LW, UK
UKHW042147130625
459647UK00011B/1217